CAMBRIDGE ILLUSTRATED HISTORY OF THE
Roman World

CAMBRIDGE ILLUSTRATED HISTORY OF THE
Roman World

Edited by Greg Woolf

CAMBRIDGE
UNIVERSITY PRESS

PUBLISHED BY THE PRESS SYNDICATE
OF THE UNIVERSITY OF CAMBRIDGE
The Pitt Building, Trumpington Street,
Cambridge CB2 1RP, United Kingdom

CAMBRIDGE UNIVERSITY PRESS
The Edinburgh Building, Cambridge CB2 1RU, UK
40 West 20th Street, New York, NY 10011-4211, USA
10 Stamford Road, Oakleigh, Melbourne 3166, Australia
Ruiz de Alarcón 13, 28014 Madrid, Spain
Dock House, The Waterfront, Cape Town 8001, South Africa

http://www.cambridge.org

First published 2003

This book was conceived, designed and produced by
THE IVY PRESS LTD
The Old Candlemakers
West Street
Lewes
East Sussex
BN7 2NZ

Creative Director: Peter Bridgewater
Publisher: Sophie Collins
Editorial Director: Stephen Luck
Design Manager: Tony Seddon
Designer: Jane Lanaway
Editor: Simon Hall
Picture Researcher: Vanessa Fletcher

Printed in China

ISBN 0 521 82775 2

CONTENTS

PART 1
THE ROMANS AND
their HISTORY

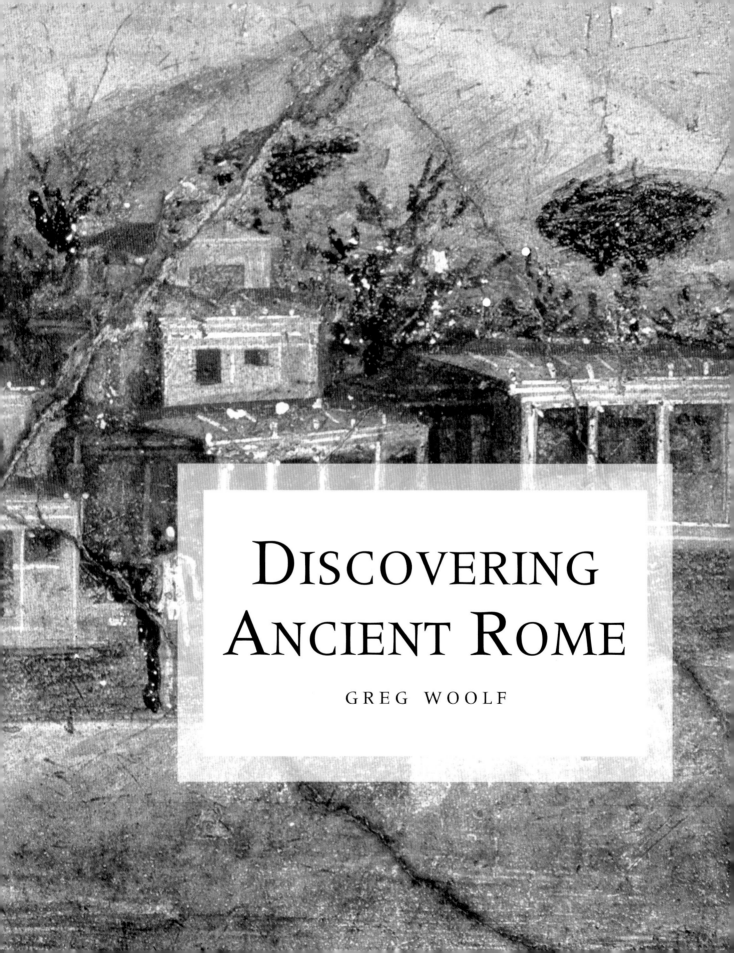

Discovering Ancient Rome

GREG WOOLF

DISCOVERING ANCIENT ROME

How is it that we know about the Roman world, which vanished 1,500 years ago? The answer is that Rome was never entirely lost. Its laws, its late religion and some of its literary works survived, to become part of our own culture. Some of its physical remains have also survived. Roman architecture, converted to new uses or crumbling into ruins, haunted the Dark Ages and the Middle Ages – and inspired the architects of the Renaissance and after. Roman inscriptions were studied from the nineteenth century. From the late nineteenth century, more mundane material remains, from pottery shards to human bones, have yielded stories of life in the Roman world.

The foundation of our knowledge of the Roman world, however, is the historical consciousness that the Romans themselves created. The Romans wondered about the origins of their culture. They worried about how much knowledge of Rome's ancient past had been lost, and about how to fill these gaps in their history. Like us, they found the answer in painstaking research. Writing shortly after the fall of Rome to Alaric's Visigoths in the year AD 410, St Augustine of Hippo wrote that the most learned of all Roman scholars had been the scholar Marcus Terentius Varro, who lived from 116 to 27 BC:

A Roman wall-painting from Pompeii (now in the National Archaeological Museum in Naples) showing a young woman writing. She is shown pausing for thought with the stylus held up to her mouth – a pose that recurs in Roman portraits as a symbolic but intimate indicator of what was clearly a commonplace activity.

Who has investigated those things [Rome's origins and early history] more carefully than Marcus Varro? Who has discovered them more learnedly? Who has considered them more attentively? Who has distinguished them more acutely? Who has written about them more diligently and more fully? Who, though he is less pleasing in his eloquence, is nevertheless so full of instruction and wisdom, that in all the erudition which we call secular... he will teach the student of things as much as Cicero delights the student of words?

Varro wrote over six hundred books on every subject imaginable. Today all that survives is his manual on agriculture and fragments of many other works, including a study of the Latin language. Most precious among all the lost works was a multi-volume encyclopaedia of *Roman Antiquities*, divided into *Things Human* and *Things Divine*. Most of what we know of this work survives in Augustine's *City of God*, because he made *Roman*

Antiquities the basis of his attack on paganism. If even Varro could not make a convincing case for the traditional religion, Augustine's implication was, then Roman religion must itself be false – and the sack of Rome could not be blamed, as the last adherents of the old religion had tried to do, on Augustine's own Christian predecessors.

Poor Varro, to survive only in paraphrases and short quotations made by his critics! But that same fate was shared by most of the works of Greek and Latin literature whose titles we know. The monks of medieval Europe had very different cultural values from those of the ancient authors, and copied only those works that could be reconciled with medieval Christianity. Ancient books were written, by hand, on papyrus rolls. Both the material and the copyists were expensive – papyrus, which grew only in the Nile Delta, had to be imported from Egypt, while the copyists, most of whom were slaves, fetched among the highest prices in the slave markets. As a result, few copies were made of most works of literature. Scholars would travel hundreds of kilometres to consult a book. Rome had no libraries of its own until the generals who led the conquest of the eastern Mediterranean brought back the book collections of Greek kings among their plunder. One of these generals, Marcus Licinius Lucullus, set up a library in his luxurious villa outside Rome. It was here that Varro and Cicero had to come to consult works of Greek literature. (There was very little Latin literature in their day for them to read.)

A medieval edition of the enormously influential *De civitate Dei* (City of God) by St Augustine of Hippo (354–430), one of the greatest Christian writers of Late Antiquity. The illustration shows Augustine, Epicurus, Zeno, Antiochus and Varro. The medieval copyists preserved parts of the works even of some non-Christian classical authors.

Part of the inscription and relief from the tomb of Gaius Statius Celsus, A Roman official described in his epitaph as '*doctissimo*' (most learned). The relief shows Celsus with his wife and son.

Advice from Symmachus

You ask me to place in your hands the ancient memories of the Gauls. Consult the last books of the Paduan writer in which the deeds of Julius Caesar are related, or if Livy is not sufficient for your purposes, use Caesar's brief account from my library, which I send to you for your labour. These works will teach you the origins, places, battles and inform you about the customs and laws of the Gauls. I will try to find for you, if chance aids your request, the Elder Pliny's *German Wars*. Be content with these.

Fourth-century aristocrat Symmachus offering bibliographic help to a would be historian of ancient Gaul.

THE SURVIVAL OF LATIN LITERATURE

Roman education placed great stress on memory, since orators needed to perform long speeches without using notes. But the collective memory was weak. What one generation remembered could be transmitted to the next only with great difficulty. Already by Augustine's day, much had been lost of earlier Latin literature. Correspondence between literary figures of the late Empire, in the fourth and fifth centuries AD, shows how few books were available despite over five hundred years of literary production, and how difficult they were to obtain.

During the centuries from the sack of Rome until the invention of the printing press, ancient literature remained very vulnerable to loss. Papyrus does not last as long as parchment. Only in exceptional conditions have even a few pages of ancient books survived to the present day. Most have been found in the deserts of the Middle East, in Egypt above all, preserved by the aridity of the environment. A few rolls were also preserved in carbonised form in houses incinerated by the eruption of Vesuvius in AD 79, and are painstakingly being deciphered using spectroscopic photography to distinguish ink from carbonised paper. One house, now called the Villa of the Papyri, possessed a private library of philosophical texts including the works of Philodemus, which were virtually unknown until this find. The systematic study of surviving classical literature began with the work of humanist scholars in the Renaissance. Many of the texts that modern Roman historians take for granted – the works of Tacitus are a good example – survived the millennium between the fall of the Western Empire and the Renaissance in only a handful of copies. The humanists gathered, copied and disseminated classical Latin texts, keeping them safe until printing technology could make them widely available. But much had already been lost.

Because the original rolls of papyrus had almost all perished, ancient texts survived only if they had been copied and recopied throughout the Middle Ages. Most of this work was performed by monks, since learning was always closely linked to the medieval church. There were a few other routes through which classical learning survived. Many Greek texts were preserved in the libraries of the Byzantine Empire, and were brought to the West following the capture of Constantinople during the Fourth Crusade in 1204, or in the fifteenth century, brought by the Ottoman Turks as they occupied southeastern Europe. A few works of Greek science, including medicine, survived in Arabic translation, preserved by an intellectual tradition that in many respects dwarfed that of medieval Europe. The three heirs of Rome – Western Christendom, the Byzantine Empire and Islam – only began to share what they had preserved in the thirteenth century. Only in the medieval West had much Latin literature survived.

The monastic copyists who acted as the guardians of classical Latin knew little of ancient Rome. More important, they shared only a few Roman values, and allowed to perish what did not interest them. One enduring interest was Latin rhetoric. Most of Varro was lost along the way, but his contemporary Marcus Tullius Cicero was admired in the Middle Ages as a model of rhetorical style; his works were much copied, and so many survive for us.

One reason Cicero was admired was that he had become a classic within a generation of his death in 43 BC. Along with a handful of other Latin authors – the playwright Publius Terentius Afer (Terence) was one, the epic poet Publius Vergilius Maro (Virgil) another – Cicero became a school text, and so was copied more than almost any other author. It might seem strange that this defender of lost causes who had spent his life fighting to preserve the Roman state from being dominated by great generals should become such a key figure in the culture of empire. The short explanation is that Roman cultural production was never completely under the control of political authorities, and great men often had to find an accommodation with the classics. The prestige literature enjoyed in Rome since its emergence in the third century BC ensured that powerful men always sought to patronise the great poets of their day.

A manuscript illumination, dating from the fifteenth century, showing scholars engaged in a debate. The illustration formed part of a medieval edition of Cicero's *De Senectute* (Old Age), and contrasts the two older scholars with their younger colleagues. Cicero's prestige ensured that many of his works were preserved by copying in the Middle Ages.

A painting by Jean-Joseph Taillasson, of 1787, showing Virgil reading the *Aeneid* to Augustus and his sister Octavia. The painting reconstructs a famous incident in which the poet's added references to the youthful virtues of Marcellus, Octavia's recently deceased son, caused her to faint. The typical Roman combination of literature and patronage is neatly illustrated.

LITERATURE AND POWER

The best example of this relationship between literature and power is that other great classic of the medieval tradition, Virgil. Younger than Cicero, Virgil began his writing career began just after the civil wars that established in Rome the monarchical system often called the Principate (or sometimes simply the Empire – which is perhaps confusing, since the Roman Republic had been an imperial power too). Virgil is best known now for the epic *Aeneid*, in which he recorded the legend of how a Trojan prince, Aeneas, had fled from the Greek sack of Troy, to reach Italy and found the Roman race. There had been other versions of this myth, which fitted somewhat uneasily with the tradition that traced Rome back to Romulus and Remus. But Virgil chose Aeneas as his culture hero, made Augustus one of Aeneas's descendants, and packed the epic with 'flash-forwards' to Virgil's own age. So Virgil has Aeneas visit

Hell to receive a detailed prophecy of the future, he gives him a shield depicting the battle of Actium that had ended the last civil war, and he takes him to the future site of Rome to wander around the locations where Augustus was, in Virgil's day, busy building monuments.

The foreshadowing of Augustan triumph that pervades the *Aeneid* has troubled generations of modern readers. Some have felt that great art should rise above the politics of the moment, others that great poetry is compromised by too cosy a relationship with tyranny. Many modern critics tried to redeem Virgil by seeking anti-Augustan undercurrents in his work, and others imagined an inner tension between the poet's ambition to be a Roman Homer and outdo his Republican predecessors like the poet-philosopher Titus Lucretius Carus (Lucretius) or the epic poet Quintus Ennius, and his consciousness that there was only one patron left, an emperor who burnt the books he did not like. But these concerns are modern ones. It is a recent and romantic notion to demand a great divide between art and politics, and in any age where art is patronised by the powerful, artists have power and prestige of their own.

The *Augustus of Prima Porta*, a monumental statue of the emperor Augustus commissioned in about AD 15 by Augustus's successor Tiberius. Probably a copy of a lost bronze original dating from about 20 BC, the marble statue was found at Prima Porta, about 14 km from Rome, in a villa belonging to Augustus's wife Livia.

Cicero's enduring success under the Principate depended precisely on the prestige his oratory had acquired. All the same, some Romans were aware of the irony that generation after generation of Roman aristocrats and functionaries were educated to serve the emperors by reading texts that condemned autocracy. The speeches with which Cicero condemned Mark Antony after Caesar's death and tried to rally the senate around Caesar's heir Octavian (as Augustus was then) were so critical that when Antony and Octavian joined forces, Antony demanded that Cicero be added to the list of their opponents condemned to death. The old man was killed and his hands and head were cut off and displayed from the *rostra*, the orator's platform in the *forum*, as a warning of the penalties for opposition.

Gaius Suetonius Tranquillus, who wrote a life of Augustus more than a century after these events, tells the story of how the emperor in his old age found one of his grandsons reading a papyrus roll on which was copied one of Cicero's speeches. The boy tried unsuccessfully to hide it, but when the emperor had inspected it he handed it back, praising Cicero as a good man who loved his country. It is a nice story: the tyrant mellowed, the great orator rehabilitated, the prince and his grandfather in harmony across the generations. By Suetonius's time, Cicero had become ancient history, a safe classic. Romans of the second century AD talked – with affected nostalgia – of a period called 'The Republic', but they lived in a different present. The truth about Cicero, however, is different. Augustus had been able to burn his critics' histories because so few copies had been made. Cicero's works, on the other hand, had already been so widely circulated that they could not be censored.

A woodcut by Jost Ammon from an early printed edition of Livy's *Histories*, published in 1568 in Frankfurt. The scene depicted is the death of the Greek mathematician and inventor Archimedes during the Roman sack of Syracuse in 212 BC. Livy recounted that the inventor was so preoccupied with his calculations that he did not even look up when Roman soldiers entered his study.

A LITERARY CANON

The Latin literature we possess, then, is largely a canon of texts made classical at around the beginning of the first century AD. Roman schools, and the medieval clerks who learned their Latin from much the same texts, have preserved this canon, along with a much more random selection of earlier and later writing. There had, of course, been classics before Cicero: Marcus Porcius Cato (Cato the Elder) had been the first orator to circulate his speeches in a polished form, Ennius had written an ultra-Roman epic before Virgil, Gaius Lucilius was the first satirist. But Cicero, Virgil, Horace and the rest successfully represented their predecessors as crude prototypes, and they themselves became the touchstones of Latin style as it was learned all over

An illuminated initial letter from an edition of about 1450 of Livy's *Histories*. The medieval artist has provided a remarkably concise summary of the main action of the book (Books XXI–XXX of Livy's work), which deals with the Second Punic War. Hannibal's feat in marching his army, complete with war elephants, across the Alps is shown in the upper left of the illustration.

the Roman world. Many earlier works survived into the second century AD, from which period we have a few quotations, often in the writings of Roman antiquarians and grammarians interested in archaic forms of Latin – but most of them failed to survive the processes of selection and copying that preserved the canonical works for us. The same fate befell many of the original works written in the late first century AD and later. Virgil's epic had many imitators, but only a few have survived. Much of what we have of later Latin is fragmentary, or else survived in just one or two copies in remote monastic libraries.

As a result, we have parts of the *Annals* of Gaius Cornelius Tacitus, written in the early second century AD, but not his accounts of Caligula's reign or Nero's death, and there are gaps in the reigns of Tiberius and Claudius. His *Histories*, describing the later period, breaks off abruptly at the start of the Jewish War. Of the works of Gaius Sallustius Crispus (Sallust), written just after

Caesar's death, we have two short books: one on the war fought against Jugurtha, the other on Cicero's conflict with Catiline in 63 BC, the year of his consulship. But of Sallust's *Histories*, which once told the story of the collapse of the Republic, we have only a few excerpts, made by a reader more interested in rhetoric than in history. The work of Titus Livius (Livy) also survives only in parts. In his case we also have a summary – one paragraph for each book – that gives us a sense of the original shape of a massive account of Roman history *From the Foundation of the City* until Livy's own age, the age of Augustus 'when we can bear neither our illnesses nor their remedies'. These three authors – Sallust, Livy and Tacitus – are the only major Latin historians of whose work we have any significant part until the fourth century AD. Adding to them minor writers and some later Greek authors, we piece together the history of the Republic and early Empire.

We know the age of Cicero better than any other in Roman history, because so many of his speeches have survived, along with commentaries on some them; because many of his letters – written to many of the great figures of his day – were recovered by the humanist Petrarch; and because Caesar's self-serving accounts of his wars in Gaul and then against Pompey and his supporters during the same period have also survived. The classical status this period acquired later in antiquity attracted other writers, too. One was the Greek philosopher Lucius Maestrius Plutarchus (Plutarch), who included biographies of Lucullus, Pompey, Crassus, Cicero, Caesar and Antony in his *Parallel Lives*, which was designed to construct a moral viewpoint for assessing human action that transcended Greek and Roman cultural norms. So for the 60s and 50s BC we can track the shifting political alliances virtually month by month, and we can also see how men became rich, observe their management of their property and families, watch priests and judges at their work, discover what books men read, enjoy their loves and hates and so on.

Left and centre above: the title page and a text page from a printed edition of the works of Tacitus, translated and published in Spain in 1614.

Above right: An illuminated page from a thirteenth-century French manuscript copy of Cicero's *Rhetorica*. The medieval artist has included a miniature painting of 'A Master (of rhetoric) addressing Six Students and Two Adults'. While Latin remained the official language of the state bureaucracies, Cicero's acknowledged mastery of the language made him essential reading for the aristocracy.

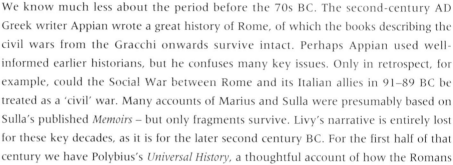

An illuminated initial from a French copy of Livy's *History of Rome*, made in about 1370, showing a monk copying a manuscript.

We know much less about the period before the 70s BC. The second-century AD Greek writer Appian wrote a great history of Rome, of which the books describing the civil wars from the Gracchi onwards survive intact. Perhaps Appian used well-informed earlier historians, but he confuses many key issues. Only in retrospect, for example, could the Social War between Rome and its Italian allies in 91–89 BC be treated as a 'civil' war. Many accounts of Marius and Sulla were presumably based on Sulla's published *Memoirs* – but only fragments survive. Livy's narrative is entirely lost for these key decades, as it is for the later second century BC. For the first half of that century we have Polybius's *Universal History*, a thoughtful account of how the Romans came to dominate the Mediterranean world after the Second Punic War (218–201 BC). But most of Polybius's *History* survives only in fragments, and he was an outsider, a Greek, and one who was more interested in the unification of Mediterranean history by Roman imperialism than in Roman political life or culture.

Livy used Polybius for part of his account of Rome's early second-century wars against the Hellenistic kingdoms. His account of Hannibal's invasion in the late third century BC is fairly full too (though here we are relying on a historian writing two centuries after the events he relates). But although Rome had been in contact with the Greek world from the beginning – traditionally the eighth century BC – Greek writers were not very interested in Rome before it became a world power. The earliest Roman historian, Fabius Pictor, wrote in Greek – but not until the third century BC. Before then, Roman history is lost in darkness.

Roman writers, like us, wanted to know more about their early history. Virgil invented a history of the beginnings of Rome, as others had before him and would do in the future, because he had no other choice. Livy, in his Preface, offered a somewhat disingenuous version of Virgil's justification of this invention:

The traditions of what happened prior to the foundation of the city [by Romulus, that is] or while it was being built are more fitted to ornament the creations of the poet than the authentic records of the historian, and I do not intend to establish either their truth or their falsehood. The ancients are traditionally allowed a certain license to mingle human and divine actions to confer a more august dignity on the origins of states. Now if any nation ought to be able to claim a sacred origin and point back to divine ancestry, that nation is the Roman one. Her reputation for warfare is so great that when she chooses to claim that Mars was her and her founder's father, the peoples of the world accept that claim with the same equanimity that they accept Roman rule. But I have no real interest in whatever opinions and criticisms may be formed on these traditions and others like them.

All the same, Livy could not resist dealing briefly with the traditional story of the Trojan refugees and giving a short account of the kings of Rome before he moved on to the foundation of the Republic.

THE GREEK CONNECTION

We know Aeneas was an extremely attractive founder for Virgil and other Roman writers because he provided the Romans a legitimate connection with the heroic age of Greek myth and with the earliest Greek literature, Homer. Romans wanted a history that predated the Punic Wars for the same sort of reason. Traditions clearly survived into the late Republic about the Gallic sack of Rome, the wars with various neighbours in central Italy, the expulsion of the kings and the foundation of the Republic. There were a number of accounts about a long-lasting struggle between the patricians, who claimed descent from families that had been aristocrats under the kings (and on that basis wanted a monopoly of political office and priesthoods) and the rest, the plebeians. At one point, the plebeians had reputedly abandoned Romulus's city and the area fortified (legend had it) by King Servius, and had threatened to set up their own community on the Aventine Hill.

Modern historians debate fiercely how these traditions were passed on – through 'family memories', encapsulated in drama or ritual retellings, or through competing plebeian and patrician oral histories? We also argue over how much is believable. Perhaps the institution of the monarchy is real, even if the specific names and characters of the individual kings were later inventions? Or maybe the last kings are historical, but the first three were invented founders of civic, cultic and military Rome respectively? Many stories about the kings look suspiciously similar to those told on better authority about Greek tyrants.

Yet it is inconceivable that the complex and sophisticated civic and intellectual society of Rome that we first see clearly in the third century BC had sprung up overnight. Rome in the fifth century must, in general terms, have been like all those Greek cities about which we know so little in recorded history. Yet while Argos, Corinth and Thebes and the rest have numerous walk-on parts in histories oriented on Athens and Sparta, archaic and classical Rome had no near neighbours from whom we potentially might have gained vital historical evidence. Instead, the city of Rome springs into the clear light of history as a dynamic Hellenistic Republic with a population around twice the size of Athens at its peak. How long had it taken to get there?

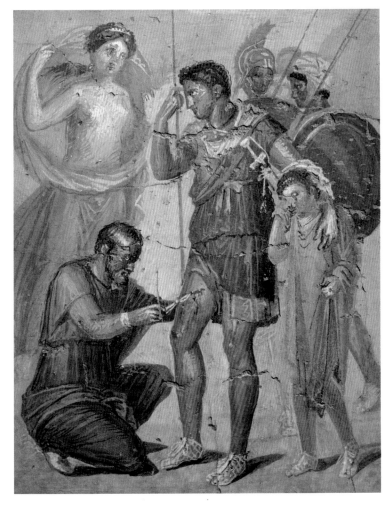

This fresco from Pompeii, now in the National Museum of Archaeology, Naples, depicts Aeneas having an arrow removed from his leg just prior to escaping from Troy. The figure at the top left of the image shows the goddess Aphrodite, who, in Roman mythology was Aeneas' mother.

AN ABSOLUTE CHRONOLOGY

Roman intellectuals of the last generation of the late Republic were also engaged in debates of this kind. One of the questions that Cicero discusses in the *Republic* is whether or not Romulus had ruled over barbarians. At other points, he is keen to stress the antiquity of the central cults of the city, such as the Lupercalia. Varro wondered whether there had once been earlier records that had been lost when the Gauls sacked Rome in the fourth century BC. Histories of early Rome were only possible because Varro and his contemporaries had created a chronology in which the key elements of Roman tradition were fixed relative to key dated events in Greek historical texts. Cicero praised Varro, saying:

'When we strayed and wandered in our own city like strangers, your books, as it were, brought home, so that we might eventually come to know of who we were and where we were. You opened up to us the age of the country, the distribution of seasons, the laws of sacred things, and of the priests; you opened up to us domestic and public discipline; you pointed out to us the proper places for religious ceremonies, and informed us concerning sacred places. You revealed to us the names, kinds, offices, causes of all divine and human things.'

Traditionally Romans had described a date by giving the names of the consuls for that year, but to use these dates it was necessary to have a complete record of all the consuls, and that did not exist until Augustus published official lists, called *fasti*, of consuls and of generals who had celebrated a triumph. Varro was not an isolated researcher. The same generation saw Cicero's friend Atticus compile his *Liber Annalis* and Cornelius Nepos a *Chronica*. All of these (probably, since none survives) were attempts to create an absolute chronology of Roman history. Our standard dates for early Rome up to and including the early third century BC derive from their researches, which must have been based on some shaky conjectures. Problems remain. The seven kings would have to be very long-lived to rule Rome from 753 to 509 BC: an average of thirty-four years' reign each also looks a little like a notional generation. The expulsion of the last king of Rome is suspiciously close to the end of the Peisistratid tyranny in Athens. Roman scholars were systematic, and careful, but their idea of convincing arguments does not always coincide with modern ones.

Livy implies quite plainly that Augustus manipulated early Roman history in order to find an excuse for denying one of his generals the traditional honour of the *spolia opima*. He does not contradict Augustus's claims about the precedent involved, but makes it clear he defers to the emperor, not to his arguments.

Part of a surviving inscription of the Price Edict of Diocletian, from a city in the Greek-speaking east of the Roman Empire. Issued in AD 301 throughout the Empire, the Price Edict represented an attempt by the emperor to control rampant inflation in the late third century. Such inscriptions became common in the Empire, and are a valuable source for historians.

NEW TYPES OF EVIDENCE

Writing the history of the imperial period seems, at first glance, much easier. The chronology poses no major problems, and the sources are much more numerous. Little Latin literature has survived between the mid-second and the mid-fourth centuries, but this is a period from which we have a mass of Greek writing, written by Romans and Jews as well as Greeks. Many speeches survive, unsurprisingly in a society where rhetoric was the basis of education. There are many medical texts, as well as biographies, philosophy, fiction and guides to every science from astrology and dream-interpretation to agriculture, geography and the management of aqueducts.

There are also new types of evidence. Between the late first century and the early third century AD there was a boom in the production of inscriptions on stone and bronze. Inscribing laws and religious material on permanent media was nothing new. Marble copies of the letters of Roman generals had been set up in Greek cities, and a small group of bronze inscriptions from Italy under the Republic record senatorial edicts and laws. There are also a few early funerary inscriptions and dedications. But from the turn of the new millennium, the volume begins to increase significantly. The vast majority are lost: bronze tablets were melted down and stone ones crumbled, were re-used in construction or burnt for lime. Perhaps five per cent have survived.

New inscriptions come to light every year. Scholars have been collecting them for almost as long as they have been hunting Latin manuscripts. But their scientific study, epigraphy, began in the late nineteenth century and, together with the first critical editions of major Latin texts and laws, it created the modern discipline of ancient history. Ancient history is a young discipline, then, compared to mathematics, physics or medicine, and its closest contemporaries are sociology and anthropology. The main institutions that coordinate research on Roman antiquity today, the learned societies with their journals and conferences, and the foreign schools in Spain, Italy, Greece and the Middle East through which much archaeology is organised, are only a century or so old. Their work built on that of the humanists and of Enlightenment scholars, and in a different way on the collecting of Grand Tourists that filled museum collections from the eighteenth century. But scientific studies of epigraphy, papyrology and archaeology have opened new doors onto the Roman world.

Most inscriptions were tombstones or dedications to the gods. Both often included details of the careers of those who set them up. They allow us to reconstruct the career of a soldier as he moved across the Empire, or to see how a great magistrate had risen through junior positions and priesthoods on his way to the top, and from these to generalise about Roman government and institutions. A small number of long inscriptions provide snapshots of great public decisions. Cities advertised their laws on bronze or marble. Some constitutions survive from Spain showing how Roman communities were organised like miniatures of Rome itself. Greek cities often inscribed on marble the text of letters they had received from emperors giving, or confirming, privileges. Some civic inscriptions shed light on their own culture myths. Many record the generosity of great men providing their cities with magnificent baths and gymnasia, with aqueducts and fountains, repairing roads and temples, funding grain funds to alleviate food crises or feasts to mark their birthdays in perpetuity.

A DIFFERENT KIND OF HISTORY

These differences in source material have given the Empire a different kind of history from that of the Republic. It is not simply that the sources are more numerous, or even that they reach more areas of life than Republican literature does. The histories of the Republic and the vivid speeches and letters of Cicero chronicle change and crisis, and the culture, society and politics of Rome collapse into each other. The Empire, on the other hand, lends itself to a much less narrative style of history. Partly this is because much of the source material can easily give the impression that after Augustus, Rome entered some kind of equilibrium in which good and bad emperors alternated, but none of the political essentials were altered. Some modern historians see almost no important changes in the workings of monarchy between Augustus and Constantine. Tacitus insinuated deep connections between monarchy, the end of free speech, the decay of rhetoric and the end of Roman expansion. These allegations are oversimplistic. But much of Roman culture – including the first century literary canon – did seem to remain entrenched for centuries.

Other media contributed to the idea that history had ceased to move on. Tombstones implicitly proclaim their confidence in a posterity that will read them. Votive inscriptions in temples assert that the Roman gods really did answer prayer. Public decrees were inscribed for eternity, announcing benefactions that would never run out. Coins declared that emperors were virtuous and that cities were loyal to them and to their own traditions.

This aspect of early imperial culture – the perception that its history was static while that of the Republic had been dynamic – is part of the wider phenomenon of monumentality that created the fabulous civic centres that tourists still visit today. When archaeologists interpreted their discoveries largely in the light of the narratives provided by ancient writers, these grand ruins seemed to confirm a picture of peace and prosperity, while the ubiquitous portraits of emperors reflected the loyalty of their subjects. Archaeologists now are more inclined to offer independent interpretations. The imperial portraits that filled public spaces and private homes, temples and bathhouses throughout the Empire are now seen as vehicles for image-building, an expression of ideology. Their marked family resemblances are now regarded as exaggerated attempts to claim a greater kinship and unanimity among Rome's rulers than was actually the case.

Recent archaeology suggests that the great cities of the early Empire were surrounded by emptying landscapes, in which peasants and slaves were put to work harder than ever before. Production increased, but at the expense of harder labour. The surplus was consumed by a tiny privileged minority. Excavation of domestic buildings is giving us new insights into the daily lives of ordinary people in the Roman world. Skeletal evidence is beginning to reveal the horrendous levels of endemic disease and malnutrition in which many of the poor lived. Malaria was rife in Rome, leprosy in Egypt, and life expectancy all over the Empire was modest. Archaeological surveys of the territories of Greek cities show the draining of wealth from the countryside, and while the biggest cities grew under Roman rule, smaller towns shrank. Roman society appears more hierarchical, more stratified than the literary

My narrative is quite a different matter from histories of early Rome. The subjects of those works were great wars, cities stormed, kings routed and captured. If they chose to write of domestic affairs they could debate the feuds of consuls and tribunes, struggles over land laws and corn laws, the conflicts of reactionaries and the people. My subject, however, is narrow and without glory. Peace was rarely broken. Rome was plunged into despair, its ruler uninterested in expanding the empire.

Tacitus, Annals, 4.32, lamenting the changed conditions of history writing under the Empire.

sources had suggested, wealth was more unevenly distributed, civic democracies were stifled, slaves were consumed in vast numbers and few enjoyed the comfortable lives of the domestic attendants portrayed in Roman comedies and satires.

Archaeology has also revealed slower, longer-term transformations in the life of ordinary people in Roman Italy and the provinces – changes that were only occasionally remarked on by ancient geographers or historians. In the first and second centuries AD, for example, cities grew up in areas where they had never existed before, from Britain and inland Spain to Anatolia and upper Egypt. Roman styles of consumption – wine-drinking, bathing, rich residences, slave households – became widespread, as local ruling classes signed up to the Roman cultural project. Meanwhile, the use of coinage proliferated, and in at least some areas the demands of taxation and law drew more and more of the mostly illiterate population into systems of control that depended on written records. The army too, from Hadrian's Wall to Tunisia and the Euphrates, produced quantities of writing, as did traders who travelled further in greater number than they had before the Roman peace. More people travelled further and more often, so it is no surprise to see more exchanges of all kinds – pottery styles and new cults, architectural techniques and diseases. Whatever stability there existed at the highest echelons of the Roman state, it rested on shifting foundations. As the number of citizens grew, as Latin literacy spread, as more and more rich provincials found their way into imperial elites, so the very nature of Roman society shifted. Studying the Roman family or Roman religion means one thing in 300 BC, when most Romans lived in or close to the city, and another in AD 300, when there were tens of millions of Romans all over the Empire. The idea that the Roman Empire was stagnant really is a fabrication.

A Roman tombstone found near Isernia, in Molise, Italy. From the tomb of an innkeeper, it includes a relief carving of the innkeeper himself welcoming a mounted traveller in a hooded cloak.

Research into the Roman past is progressing faster today than ever before in the discipline's hundred-year history. Not only are there many more professional historians and archaeologists involved, but new work is being carried out on all fronts simultaneously. Investigations into the intellectual life of the Republic jostle in the learned journals with accounts of the marble trade and publications of new texts; new studies of plague and diet complement investigations into literacy and imperial portraiture. Everything we work with, from the shards of pottery collected by archaeological surface survey to the fragments of Sulla's *Memoirs*, has survived only by chance. Those who study the Roman world always need to be aware of these processes of survival, and of what has been systematically lost or edited out. Our picture of the Roman world is built out of fragments – but then the same could be said of dinosaurs, or dark matter. Varro was not discouraged by the scale of the task, nor by the amount of information that has been lost. Nor should we be.

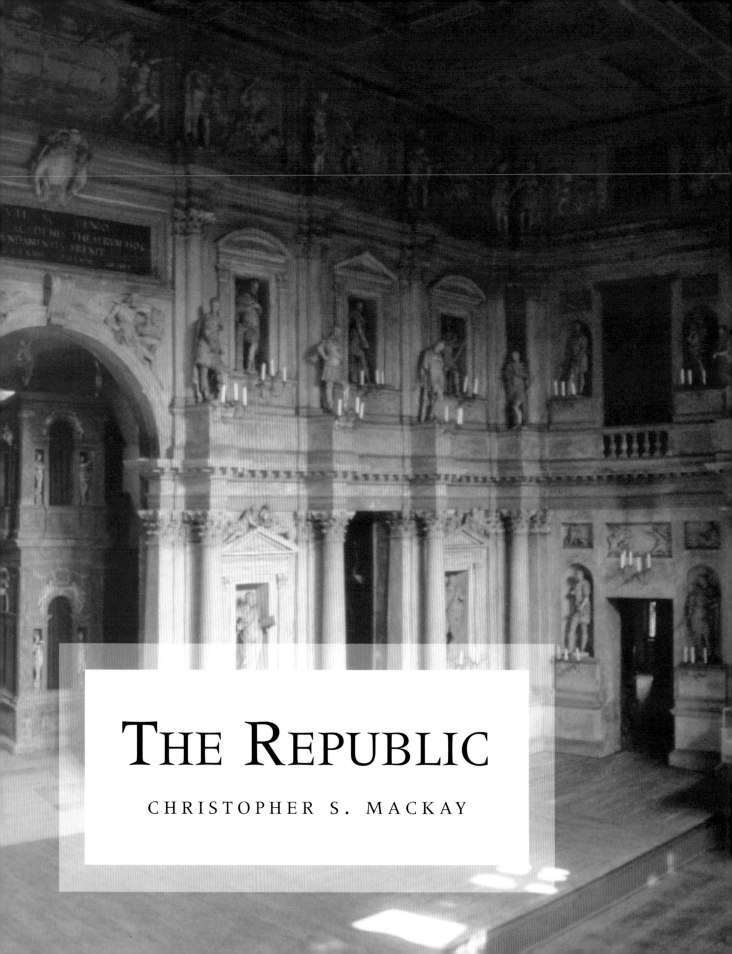

The Republic

CHRISTOPHER S. MACKAY

THE REPUBLIC

The evidence for the history of the Roman Republic is very uneven. The writing of history in Rome began in the third century BC, but the surviving works do not cover all periods evenly, and in any case mainly deal with high politics; they are much less informative about social and economic aspects of Roman society. For the period before the third century, written sources preserve some information, but they are increasingly unreliable the older they are. Archaeology provides some information for the earliest period, but the evidence is hard to interpret and difficult to correlate with the written record. Thus, while our understanding of the written evidence is constantly improving, and new archaeological and inscriptional evidence is steadily coming to light, there remains much uncertainty in our picture of the Roman Republic.

THE EMERGENCE OF THE REPUBLIC

Archaeological evidence shows that like the rest of Italy, the site of Rome was sparsely occupied by individual family groups at the start of the Iron Age, about 900 BC. Over the successive centuries, social and economic life gradually became more complex, and by the late 600s BC large private houses and public structures began to be built. Roman literary tradition maintained that the city was founded by Romulus, who became its first king, around 753 BC: 'The city of Rome was held from the beginning by kings', the Imperial historian Tacitus noted. According to the tradition, Romulus and his six successors ruled the city for 245 years; a good deal of detail about this kingdom is also preserved. Unfortunately, little of this can be regarded as historical evidence. Romulus himself is clearly an invented figure – the city was never officially 'founded', and his name is based on that of the city. The names of the other six kings are not obviously made up, and tradition may indeed have preserved their names accurately – but no reliable evidence is available for the origins of their kingdom. Tradition is probably correct, however, in suggesting that by the end of the kingdom Rome was under the influence of the Etruscans, a more advanced people to the north of the city who spoke an entirely different language.

In the final decade of the 500s BC (the traditional dates are either 509 or 507), the last king was expelled and a republican government established. The term 'republican' is misleading to the modern ear. It derives from the Latin *res publica*, meaning 'commonwealth' or 'state', but the system was not democratic in any modern sense. The Roman Republic is best characterised as an elective oligarchy. In various assemblies dominated by the wealthier members of the community, members of the richest families were elected to annual office. There was no abstract institution that could be called a government. Instead, power was exercised by the various magistrates, and if there were no magistrates, there was no 'government'.

The silhouetted image of a statue of the legendary founders of Rome, Romulus and Remus, who were exposed by their uncle as infants and suckled by a she-wolf. Their names are clearly later derivations from that of the city itself, and there is no evidence that they actually existed. The legend nevertheless retained its power throughout Roman history.

THE MAGISTRATES

Two basic principles governed the office of magistrate in the Roman Republic: annual tenure and collegiality. Magistrates held office for only one year, and were arranged in boards ('colleges') of equals. Magistrates were normally elected every year and direct re-election to a new office was prohibited. Within each college of magistrates, the action of one colleague could also be prohibited by the objection of another. Both these provisions were intended to prevent excessive power falling into the hands of a single individual.

The chief magistrates of the Roman state were the two consuls. They possessed a power known as *imperium*, considered to be the power that the kings had supposedly held. This allowed them to order execution or flogging, but their ability to impose these penalties on Roman citizens became increasingly restricted. *Imperium* also entitled its holder to conscript citizens into armies and to command these armies on campaign – with the restriction that the right of military command existed only outside of the city of Rome itself. The Romans had no separate professional generals, and thus all armies were commanded by magistrates with *imperium*.

In the beginning, the consuls were the sole magistrates, but over the years it became necessary to create additional positions. In 367 BC the office of praetor was

created. The praetor also held *imperium*, though his was considered to be inferior to that of a consul. At first, the praetor looked after affairs in Rome while the consuls were away on campaign, but eventually he came to play a significant role in the development of civil law. In about 244 BC a second praetorship was created, and this office ultimately became responsible for dealing with all legal matters involving citizens and foreigners.

As Rome began to acquire foreign provinces, new praetorships were created, and by the end of the Republic there were eight in all. The Romans were always very reluctant to increase the number, perhaps because each praetor was a potential candidate for the consulship; the number of consuls was always fixed at two. Prorogation, a device that eased the shortage of magistrates with *imperium*, was first instituted in 327 BC. Since it was inconvenient to interrupt the military command of a successful magistrate in mid-campaign, prorogation allowed him to retain his *imperium* until he returned to Rome. Magistrates whose *imperium* was prorogued in this way were known as proconsuls or propraetors.

Ex-magistrates sat in the senate, which was thus the collective body of office-holders. Strictly speaking, it had no legal powers, and the decrees that it passed were merely advisory. In certain administrative matters, however – such as the

A relief showing a Roman magistrate (seated in the centre) reading a testament, from the Colonna palace in Rome. The magistrate's use of the so-called 'curule chair' (*sella curulis*) identifies him as a member of the *ordinarii* – that is, the magistrates who were regularly elected, usually for one year. The *sella curulis* was the official symbol of their status.

disbursement of sums from the state treasury and the determination of which governors would be replaced – the senate gradually acquired real control. While no magistrate was obliged to heed the senate's advice, the overwhelming prestige of the body as the collective voice of the ruling class and the desire of the great majority of magistrates to be accepted by their senatorial colleagues guaranteed that the senate's decrees were seldom ignored. By the third century BC, the senate had acquired the right to authorise the prorogation of magistrates and to control the state treasury.

The 'Roman People' (meaning adult males of military age) had theoretical control of the state. In various assemblies, the Roman People passed all laws, elected magistrates and conducted criminal trials. In practice, voting was skewed in favour of the more affluent. The centuriate assembly that elected all magistrates with *imperium* was originally based on the hundred-man units of the army. Because soldiers had to provide their own armour, military service was restricted to the comparatively well off, and every five years a registration of the citizens' wealth known as the census was taken in order to determine their military obligations. In the census, the citizens possessing sufficient resources to provide their own equipment were assigned to one of five census classes, with progressively higher minimum wealth qualifications. Eventually, the military organisation began to change, but the setup of the centuriate assembly remained fixed. Each class was assigned a number of centuries, and the citizens who met the requirements for that class were divided among these. Since the highest class controlled more than half the total number of centuries, they largely decided the outcome of elections (their share was later reduced to slightly under half). Those citizens who did not meet the minimum qualification for military service were allowed to vote in this assembly, but they formed only one century out of 193. In effect, until the method of recruiting soldiers was changed in the late second century BC, the wealthier citizens who fought in the armies elected the wealthiest as magistrates to serve as commanders. The Roman conquest of the Mediterranean in the third and second centuries ultimately led to the collapse of this system.

PATRICIANS AND PLEBIANS

According to tradition, the early political history of the Republic was dominated by the dispute between the patricians and plebeians known as the Struggle of the Orders. The patricians were the families who sat in the senate, while all the other citizens were plebeians (known collectively as *plebs*). The tradition maintained that the patrician monopoly on power was established with the foundation of the Republic, but examination of the lists of magistrates suggests that their monopoly was made absolute only in about 450 BC. The *plebs* organised themselves during this struggle, and elected representatives called tribunes as their leaders. Eventually, ten tribunes were elected every year, and their right to intervene personally in the activities of magistrates within the city was recognised. The aims of the *plebs* were both political and economic. Once the patrician monopoly on office-holding was established, the wealthy plebeians championed the economic complaints of the poorer plebeians as a way of furthering their own ambitions to be allowed to run for office. The conflict reached a high point in the years before about 367 BC, when a major reform of the political system took place (this was also the year when the praetorship was created). Plebeians were now allowed to run for the consulship, and the wealthiest plebeian families began to enter the senate. The newcomers fused with the old patrician families to form a new ruling class known as the 'nobility' (*nobilitas*). While the system was open to the controlled admission of talented outsiders, the nobility used their wealth and connections to hold the majority of the consulships and to maintain control of the state. This nobility would lead the Romans in their conquest of Italy and the Mediterranean.

In the years after these reforms, the separate institutions of the *plebs* were integrated into the common institutions of the Roman People as a whole, becoming important features of the middle and late Republican political system. The *plebs* met in a special assembly that was based on geographical voting districts known as tribes; each tribe had one vote, which was determined by the voters of that district. The city of Rome never had more than four tribes, but new rural tribes were created as Roman territory expanded, and the twenty rural tribes that existed at the start of the Republic reached a total of thirty-one by 241 BC. This meant that the increasingly large population of the city of Rome was seriously under-represented. (Some sense of the city's comparative size in the first century can be gained from the fact that, while the census of 70 BC enumerated 910,000 individuals in all of Italy, in the mid-40s there were 320,000 recipients of the grain-dole given by the state to the inhabitants of the city of Rome alone. The exact significance of these figures remains unclear, though both totals probably refer to adult male citizens; they suggest that the city contained something like a third of the population of Italy.) The assembly of the *plebs* not only elected the tribunes but passed resolutions that were at first binding only on the *plebs*, but by about 287 BC were recognised as having the force of law. Because of its simpler procedures, the assembly of the *plebs* became the standard place for passing laws. The ten tribunes were also made part of the senatorial system of government after 367 BC. Young plebeian members of the nobility would hold the office and pass laws on behalf of the senate. It was only in the late second century BC that certain tribunes took advantage of the powers of the assembly of the *plebs* to act against the senate.

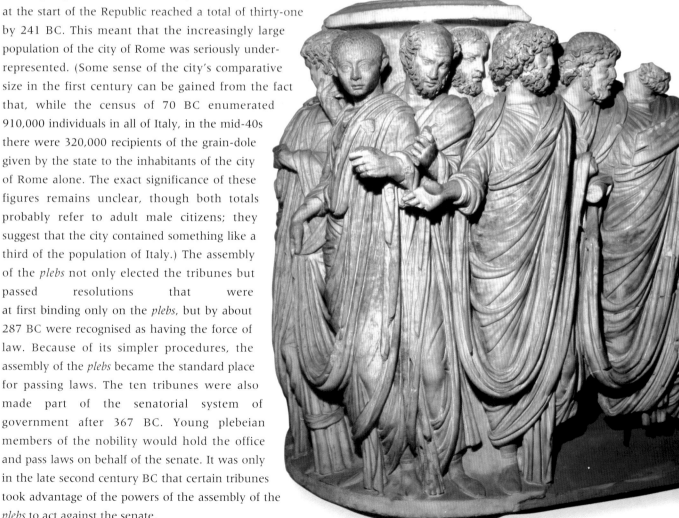

A group of Roman senators from a fragment of a sarcophagus from Ostia, now in the National Museum in Rome. The sarcophagus, decorated in deep relief, dates from about AD 270.

THE CONQUEST OF ITALY

The Romans valued military success, and from the start of the Republic they engaged in a series of wars that conquered first Latium and then all of Italy. This provided a source of manpower that allowed them to destroy the major military powers of the Mediterranean. The literary tradition is probably accurate about the general course of these events, but many details are later inventions.

Latium (modern Lazio) is a broad agricultural plain on the western shore of Italy, and was occupied by a people known as the Latins. They were divided into about thirty communities, the northernmost of which was Rome. From the start of the Republic, the Romans distinguished themselves from the rest of the Latins, who had formed a loose organisation for military cooperation known as the Latin League. The Romans sought to dominate the League, but their plans had to be set aside when Latium was invaded by tribal groups from the Apennine Mountains to the east, and most of the fifth century BC was spent trying to fend off these invaders. By the end of the century the incursions had been halted, though the newcomers occupied lands in the south of Latium.

At the end of the fifth century BC, the Romans began a protracted war with Veii, the Etruscan city immediately north of the city. Veii was finally taken in about 396 BC; the city was destroyed and its territory annexed. Over the next century, the Romans would directly annex large areas of central Italy. This process was interrupted by the capture of Rome by Celts (Gauls) from northern Italy in about 386 BC, but while this debacle made a great impression on the Romans, it proved only a temporary setback in the process of Roman territorial expansion.

In 341 BC the Latins made a final effort to resist Roman domination, but the Romans soon subdued the rebel towns, and in 338 BC they abolished the League. The closest Latin communities were directly annexed to the Roman state, while some distant Latin towns were allowed internal autonomy but no independence in foreign and military affairs. Communities to the south that were less closely related to the Romans were annexed with a sort of second-class citizenship that carried all the military obligations of Roman citizens but gave no political rights. The Latins abandoned their local dialects in favour of the Roman dialect, which became the only surviving form of the Latin language. The wealthy citizens of the newly annexed towns began to hold office in Rome and become part of the Roman nobility, while the Latins became Rome's staunchest allies.

With Latium firmly under control, the Romans embarked on a series of campaigns that ultimately brought all of Italy under their domination. Their major opponents were the Samnites, to the southeast, who were not overcome until the late 290s BC, and even then several further decades were required to consolidate the Roman position. There was some annexation of territory in central Italy, but for the most part the distant communities were bound to Rome with 'unequal treaties', which effectively made them subordinate to Rome though they retained internal autonomy. While this status seems similar to that of the Latins, the Romans treated the Latins with much greater respect. Domination of Italy gave Rome the resources to embark on the conquest of the Mediterranean.

The Roman practice of founding colonies both facilitated expansion into distant areas of Italy and contributed to the romanisation of the entire peninsula. In origin, the term 'colony' (*colonia*) signified an agricultural settlement, and these communities were originally intended as independent towns in foreign territory. The earliest known Roman colonies were established in parts of Latium recaptured from Oscan invaders in the fifth century BC. The settlers were taken both from Rome and from the cities of Latium, and gave up their old citizenship in return for that of the new colonies, which became members of the Latin League. (There were colonies of exclusively Roman citizens, but these were few and insignificant in this period.) The Latin colonies were set up to control strategically important locations far from Rome, where they could both keep watch on potential enemies and hold out until help could arrive from Rome. Although Latin colonies were founded as late as the 180s BC, they became rare from the middle third century. Long after these colonies ceased to serve a military function, they continued to contribute to the spread of Roman language and culture throughout Italy.

Italy in the fourth century BC had a cosmopolitan population. In the north and northeast of the peninsula the Etruscans had been supplanted by Gauls from across the Alps. Some Etruscan territory had also been lost to the Romans, whose main effort at that time was directed against the other Italic tribes of the central region. The non-Italic natives (such as the Apuli) and the Greek and Carthaginian colonists, had yet to encounter the might of Rome.

THE PUNIC AND MACEDONIAN WARS

The rapidity of the Roman conquest of the Mediterranean was a source of wonder in antiquity, and the reasons for it are still a matter of dispute. The Romans themselves believed that all their wars were 'just' (that is, that the Romans were provoked by their enemies and fought on behalf of their allies). This view was long accepted by historians, since the middle-Republic conquests around the Mediterranean provided several examples of Roman reluctance to annex lands that they eventually were forced to rule directly. The imperialism of nineteenth-century Europe, in which states actively sought to annex non-European territories for reasons of prestige and economic expansion, was not the Romans' primary motivation. Nonetheless, a prime motive for conquest was desire of the magistrates of any given time to win prestige through military victory. The control of the consuls over the political process was so great that when they were determined on war, senatorial or popular opposition very seldom prevailed. It is also clear that the sacking of foreign towns and enslavement of their populations made warfare a very profitable activity both for the wealthy classes who provided the officers and for the common soldiers of Rome. The wars of conquest may be viewed as campaigns for plunder, and in the process the Roman state was compelled to take on the task of ruling foreign territories for which it was fundamentally unsuited. In addition, these wars ruined the smallholders who formed the backbone of the Roman army, and the need to maintain an army to defend an empire eventually brought about the replacement of the Republican government by a military autocracy.

Rome's first major opponents in the wider Mediterranean were the Carthaginians, named for their capital in modern Tunisia. A trading people who had settled along the shores of the western Mediterranean from the ninth to the seventh centuries BC, the Carthaginians had become involved in a long struggle with the Greek colonies in Sicily for control the island. In 265 BC, the Romans allied themselves with a Sicilian town, resulting in a protracted war – the First Punic (or Carthaginian) War – between Rome and Carthage. The Romans took the strategic initiative and won several battles, but their inexperience in warfare at sea brought several severe defeats, in which they lost many tens of thousands of men. Despite these disasters, there were no revolts in Italy, and after each defeat the Romans were able to raise a new army. When they launched a renewed campaign in 242 BC, the exhausted Carthaginians came to terms, paying an indemnity and abandoning Sicily. Then, when the Carthaginians' African mercenary troops revolted and effectively placed Carthage itself under siege, the Romans seized the opportunity to occupy Sardinia and Corsica.

The Romans now had territory overseas. Rather than making these new communities subordinate allies as they had done in Italy, the Romans followed local custom by imposing tribute upon them but not making regular use of their military forces. This may indicate that the Romans already felt a sense of kinship with other Italians that they did not feel for the Sardinians and Corsicans. In any case, it soon proved necessary to station a Roman magistrate permanently in the new provinces to ensure that the locals carried out their obligations, and in 227 BC two new praetorships were created to provide governors for Sicily and Sardinia.

Seeking to boost their manpower reserves, the Carthaginians expanded their territory into the interior of Spain, and by the late 220s BC their forces there were under the command of Hannibal, one of the greatest generals of antiquity. He provoked a renewed war (the Second Punic War) with Rome in 218 BC and quickly marched through southern France to Italy, aiming to defeat the Romans there and induce their allies to revolt. In 218 and 217 BC he defeated Romans repeatedly, but was unable to provoke an Italian revolt. In 216 BC, he annihilated a Roman army under Lucius Aemilius Paullus and Gaius Terentius Varro at Cannae. Although some cities in southern Italy and Syracuse in Sicily did rebel, the Latins and communities of central Italy remained loyal to Rome. In time, the manpower resources of Italy allowed Rome to subdue the rebels, contain Hannibal's army and at the same time conquer Spain. In 204 BC the Romans launched an invasion of Africa, and Hannibal was recalled from Italy. There he was defeated at Zama, near Carthage, in 202 BC by a Roman army under Publius Cornelius Scipio 'Africanus'. The Carthaginians had to give up their colonies, and pay the Romans a huge fine.

The ability of individual members of the senatorial oligarchy to influence the course of events is illustrated here by the career of Cato the Elder. Though he was the first member of his family to sit in the senate, his oratorical powers and the force of his personality allowed him to reach the consulship by 195 BC, and his prestige and combative personality meant that he played an important role long afterwards. In the late 150s BC he constantly demanded a final war with Carthage. (He famously ended every opinion he gave in the senate with the declaration, 'Besides which, it is my view that Carthage must be destroyed'.) At the expiry of the fifty-year peace agreed after Zama, the Romans attacked Carthage again in 149 BC, and finally destroyed the city three years later.

The Romans retained their hold on the Iberian peninsula, and in 197 BC two new praetors were created to administer the area. Iberia proved to be the running sore of the middle Republic. The area was divided among many different ethnic and linguistic groups who had no interest in being governed by Rome, and there were repeated wars throughout the second century. Raising Roman troops for wars in the East and against Africa would prove easy since these wars offered the prospect of booty, but service in Spain became increasingly unpopular. The Iberians were formidable and tenacious enemies, and victory offered little reward. The wars became particularly widespread in the 150s and 140s BC, but the back of native resistance was finally broken with the capture of Numantia in 134 BC, though minor revolts would go on for more than a century.

Immediately after the Second Punic War, the senatorial oligarchy undertook a series of wars in the Greek East. In the aftermath of Alexander the Great's death in 332 BC, his empire had been divided among his generals. Three major dynasties had emerged: the Antigonid in Macedonia (which controlled the city-states of Greece proper), the Seleucid in Asia Minor and the Near East and the Ptolemaic in Egypt. The Romans moved first against Philip V of Macedon. At the battle of Cynoscephalae in 197 BC, Philip's Macedonian army was decisively defeated by the superior tactics of a Roman army under Titus Quinctius Flaminius. Rather than occupying Macedonian

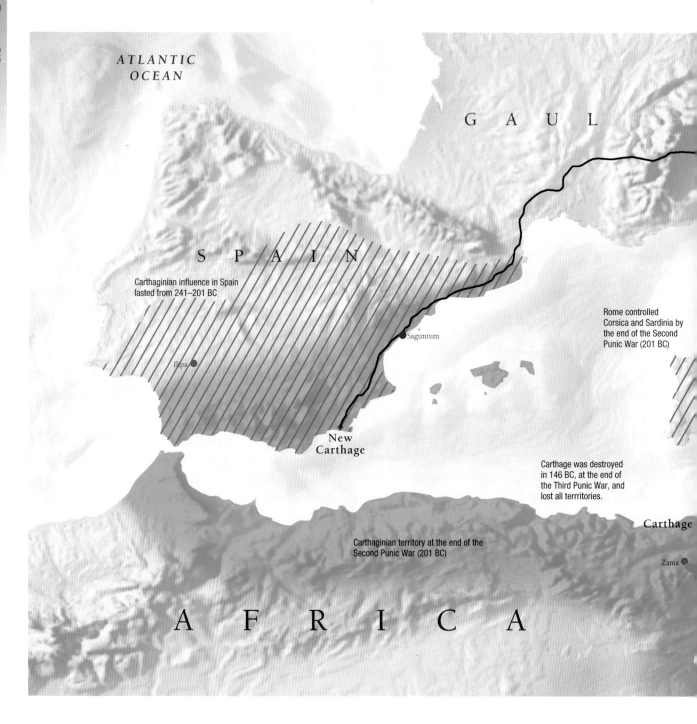

ATLANTIC
OCEAN

GAUL

SPAIN

Carthaginian influence in Spain
lasted from 241–201 BC

Rome controlled
Corsica and Sardinia by
the end of the Second
Punic War (201 BC)

Saguntum

Ilipa

Carthage was destroyed
in 146 BC, at the end of
the Third Punic War, and
lost all terrritories.

New
Carthage

Carthage

Carthaginian territory at the end of the
Second Punic War (201 BC)

Zama

AFRICA

territory, the Romans proclaimed the 'freedom of Greece' – which the Greek city states misinterpreted as an opportunity to assert their independence. Next, the Romans engaged in a war with the Seleucid king Antiochus III, who was attempting to re-establish control over Asia Minor. Roman forces under Lucius Cornelius Scipio decisively defeated a numerically superior Seleucid army at Magnesia (in modern Turkey) in 190 BC, and Antiochus was expelled from Asia Minor. Again the Romans refused to annex the enemy territory.

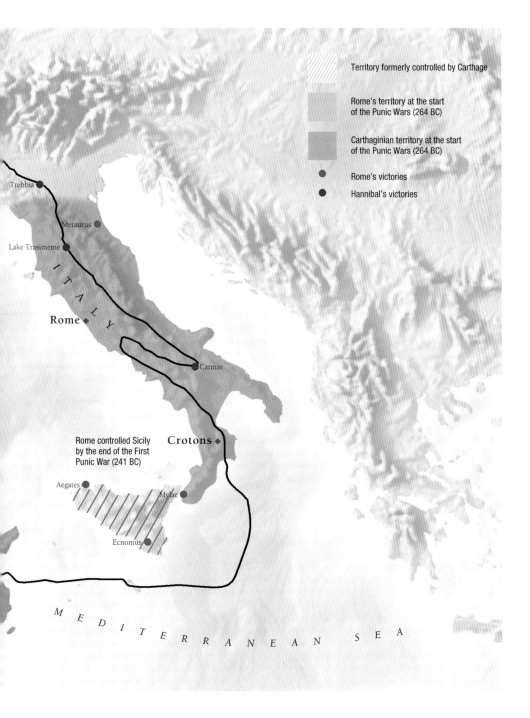

Territory formerly controlled by Carthage

Rome's territory at the start
of the Punic Wars (264 BC)

Carthaginian territory at the start
of the Punic Wars (264 BC)

Rome's victories

Hannibal's victories

Trebbia

Metaurus

Lake Trasimeme

ITALY

Rome

Cannae

Rome controlled Sicily
by the end of the First
Punic War (241 BC)

Crotons

Aegates

Mylae

Ecnomus

MEDITERRANEAN SEA

The Romans now showed their determined hostility to rival powers by going to war again with Macedon in 172 BC; in 168 BC the army of Philip's son Perseus was destroyed at Pydna by Lucius Aemilius Paullus, and the kingdom was abolished. The Romans divided Macedon into four republics, which were expected to ward off the tribes in the interior of the Balkans. In 149 BC a revolt broke out in Macedon and spread to Greece, where there was much resentment of Roman interference. Rome had quelled the insurrection by 146 BC, razing the city of Corinth as a warning to the Greeks.

The map shows the route taken by Hannibal during the course of the Second Punic War, along with the more significant battles and the territories lost and gained by both the Romans and Carthaginians during the First and Second Punic Wars.

ADMINISTRATIVE IMPLICATIONS

In 146 BC, the Romans created two new provinces: Macedonia and Africa (the territory around Carthage). This time, no new praetors were created. From this point on, Rome's conquest of the Mediterranean was accompanied by the creation of new provinces without a corresponding increase in the number of praetors: Asia (western Asia Minor) in 133 BC, southern Gaul (modern France) in the late 120s BC, Cilicia (southeastern Asia Minor) in the late 100s BC. The resulting shortage of praetors was exacerbated by the establishment of a number of new courts in Rome. Trials had traditionally been conducted before assemblies of the People, but this system proved incapable of dealing either with large numbers of cases or with cases involving prominent individuals. The first permanent court was set up in 149 BC to try accusations of provincial corruption, with senators as jurors; its purpose was to curb the increasing abuse of power by Roman governors. As time went on, other courts were set up to deal with various serious charges. Presiding over one of these courts constituted a full-time responsibility for a praetor, and there were never enough of them. The administration of the Roman state and its Empire was beginning to exceed the ability of the senate to manage it.

Two main issues led to a breakdown of the political stability of the second century BC. The first was the failure of the system of military recruitment. The increased demands of military service and competition from slave-worked farms owned by the wealthy combined to undermine the economic viability of smallholdings, leading to a collapse of the smallholder class that provided the backbone of the army. The second issue was the demand of the Italian allies for Roman citizenship. These allies provided half of Rome's armies, but received inferior rewards for equal service; their leaders could neither vote nor hold office in Rome. Furthermore, all the allies were subject to punishment by Roman magistrates, while laws passed in the second century protected Roman citizens against this. The Roman nobility, however, saw no reason to endanger their own political control by expanding citizenship. They thwarted several attempts to enfranchise the allies, and the eventual result was civil war.

A painting by the seventeenth-century French artist Claude Audran, showing the departure of Roman colonists for Carthage, in Roman Africa. A civilian colony was established on the site of the destroyed Carthaginian capital by Julius Caesar, after the failure of an earlier colony established by Gaius Gracchus.

THE RISE OF POLITICAL VIOLENCE

The demise of the Republic can be divided into three periods. The first lasts from the introduction of violence into domestic politics in 133 BC until the civil wars of the 80s BC, when soldiers were used to advance the interest of their commanders. During his tribunate in 133 BC, Tiberius Sempronius Gracchus, who belonged to a prominent noble family, introduced legislation to create a new pool of military recruits by confiscating public land that had been taken over by private individuals and distributing it in small parcels to citizens who would thus become eligible for military service. The proposal met serious opposition from the rich occupiers. To support his plan, Tiberius resorted to measures that seemed to threaten the senate, and when he tried to seek re-election as tribune, a mob of senators attacked and killed him and a number of his supporters. While this *ad hoc* use of violence could in some ways be defended as protecting the constitution, the senate would soon find that violence could be used against it.

Tiberius' brother Gaius served as tribune in 123–2 BC and passed a series of bills intended to halt abuses in the senate. While Gaius managed to secure a second term as tribune without great effort, this second term was a disaster. In order to overcome objections to land redistribution from the Italian allies, he proposed that they should be given citizenship, but his enemies played upon the fears of the existing citizens. He lost an attempt to be elected to a third term, and violence broke out in an assembly that was to repeal one of his laws. To protect themselves, Gaius and his supporters seized one of the hills in Rome, and in response the consul Lucius Opimius had the senate pass a decree enjoining him to defend the state. With this authorisation, Opimius used troops to storm the occupied hill, killing large numbers of citizens (Gaius committed suicide). Now the use of violence in domestic politics was legitimised by official decree. (*See also* pages 123–125)

The last decade of the second century BC saw a major assault on the control of the oligarchy, provoked by a number of military defeats. War against Jugurtha, the king of Numidia (in North Africa), was conducted ineffectively, and there was much anger at the perceived venality and ineptitude of the senatorial oligarchy. Eventually, a competent magistrate undertook the task of subduing Numidia, but this took too long to satisfy the impatient voters. In 107 BC they elected a new man (that is, a *novus homo*, someone who had no senatorial ancestors) to complete the job: Gaius Marius. It proved easy enough to end the war, but in raising reinforcements Marius enlisted the landless into the army, an innovation that would play a major role in the destruction of the Republic. In future, such troops would prove ultimately loyal only to their commanders, who could see to it that they were granted land upon discharge. They could thus be used against the senatorial regime in Rome.

Just as the war in Numidia was ending, a major military threat appeared in the form of the Cimbri and the Teutones, Germanic tribes that had migrated into Gaul. In 105 BC, they inflicted a serious defeat on Roman forces near Arausio (modern Orange). Hostility to the oligarchy was now white-hot in Rome, and Marius was illegally elected as consul for 104 BC, holding the office every year until 100 BC. He wiped out the Cimbri and Teutones, but his career came to a temporary eclipse when in 100 BC he allowed the killing of a tribune who had formerly been one of his allies.

In 91 BC, the tribune Marcus Livius Drusus was also assassinated. One of his proposed reforms had been to grant citizenship to the Italian allies, who now despaired of gaining it through legal means. Many went into open revolt, and the subsequent Social War (from *socius*, the Latin word for 'ally') saw several major Roman defeats. By 89 BC the Romans had largely suppressed the revolt, but they were compelled to grant citizenship to all of Italy south of the River Po.

A dispute over the method by which the allies were to be enrolled as citizens led to a Roman civil war. The tribune Publius Sulpicius Rufus wished to implement an equitable distribution of the new citizens among the voting tribes and sought the help of Marius, who wanted command of a war that had broken out in the East. There, Mithridates, king of Pontus in eastern Asia Minor, had been provoked into war by a border dispute with the Romans and had overwhelmed the poorly garrisoned Roman territories. Command of this war had been given to the consul Lucius Cornelius Sulla, who had served Marius in Numidia but had fallen out with his former commander. When Rufus passed a law to transfer this command to Marius, Sulla took a step that doomed the Republic. He used his troops to seize Rome, killing the tribune and driving out Marius. After settling affairs in Rome to his satisfaction, Sulla left for Greece in early 87 BC – at which point Marius and his followers retook the city. By 86 BC, Sulla had defeated Mithridates' forces and was willing to negotiate with the consul Cornelius Cinna, the dominant politician in Rome (Marius had died in 86). Meanwhile, Sulla secured the loyalty of his troops by allowing them to extort money from the disloyal communities of Asia. The death of Cinna in 84 BC led Sulla to invade Italy the following year. After much bloody fighting, he gained control of Italy by late 81 BC and had himself elected dictator (a traditional office reserved for military emergencies). Sulla posed as the defender of the nobility against the Marian faction, and engaged in a violent purge of his enemies – but there was no revoking the precedent he had set of using troops to secure political domination. Sulla died in 78 BC.

Lucius Cornelius Sulla, statue of the first century BC now in the Louvre, Paris. The ruthless Sulla rose to the office of dictator of Rome, setting a precedent for the use of military force for domestic political ends that strongly influenced the young Julius Caesar.

THE RESTORATION OF SENATORIAL GOVERNMENT

The second period of the demise of the Republic lasts from Sulla's restoration of senatorial government in 78 BC until the outbreak of renewed civil war in 49 BC. During this period, military threats to the empire made it necessary to grant unprecedented powers to certain generals, who used their wealth and troops to interfere in politics in Rome. The first major warlord was Gnaeus Pompeius ('Pompey'), who as a young man had raised an army for Sulla. After suppressing an insurrection against Sulla's settlement in Italy in 78–7 BC, Pompey used his troops to extort from the senate a command in Spain against the remnants of Marius' supporters. In the meantime, a slave rebellion broke out in Italy in 74 BC. Captives being trained as gladiators in Campania broke out of their barracks under the leadership of Spartacus and freed agricultural slaves in southern Italy. Eventually, tens of thousands of slaves took up arms and defeated several hurriedly conscripted and inexperienced Roman armies. In 72 BC, the ex-praetor Marcus Licinius Crassus took up the command against them and broke the back of the rebellion. Pompey and Crassus were together returned as consuls for 70 BC, but while Crassus was legally

A statue of Pompey the Great, sculpted in 1540 by Giulio Mazzoni, in Rome. Pompey followed his former patron Sulla in using troops to overawe the senate in pursuit of his own political ends. He maintained a semblance of legitimacy for his hold on power by ensuring that a succession of spurious military commands were conferred on him.

entitled to hold the office, Pompey was not only below the legal minimum age for the highest magistracy but had never held any of the mandatory lower offices. He soon found a way of securing his position. In the course of the second century, Rome had destroyed the naval powers that had kept order in the Mediterranean, and piracy became widespread. The Roman system of divided provincial command could not cope with this threat, and in 67 BC Pompey was voted a command that encompassed the entire Mediterranean and gave him huge resources to tackle the pirates. His forces swept the seas within forty days. The next year, Pompey was given command in the east, where a renewed war with Mithridates had broken out in 73 BC. Lucius Licinius Lucullus, Pompey's predecessor, had expanded the war into the kingdom of Armenia, but he was unable to bring it to an end, and after a setback in 67 BC his troops refused to campaign any further. Pompey not only ended the war, but he established the eastern

Roman frontier by settling affairs in Asia Minor and annexing the Seleucid kingdom in Syria. In late 62 BC Pompey came back to Rome an extremely wealthy man.

Politics in Rome were chaotic at this point. The orator Marcus Tullius Cicero had held the consulship in 63 BC and suppressed a plot to overthrow the state. (Many of Cicero's writings survive, and the last two decades of the Republic are the best-recorded period of Greco-Roman history. *See also* pages 177–178) It was widely feared that Pompey would attempt to seize power – in imitation of Sulla – but he dismissed his troops. Nonetheless, he had made many enemies and the senate refused to grant him either ratification of his arrangements in the East or land for his veteran troops. At the same time, the senate also blocked the attempts of Crassus to reorganise the collection of taxes in Asia. Crassus agreed to cooperate with Pompey in securing the election of Gaius Julius Caesar as consul for 59 BC, in return for Caesar's promise to overrule the senate's attempts to obstruct the ambitions of his two supporters. Caesar was elected, and used intimidation to force through the necessary legislation. The three men formed an uneasy alliance known to history as the 'First Triumvirate'.

During his consulship, Caesar was voted a five-year command in Gaul (later extended for a further five years). He proved to be a highly effective general and in a series of aggressive wars from 58 to 52 BC extended Roman rule far to the north, to incorporate all the area west of the Rhine (modern central and northern France plus the Low Countries). In the process, he acquired a devoted veteran army that would follow him anywhere.

Meanwhile, the electoral system in Rome broke down in violence and bribery. Pompey and Crassus served as consuls in 55 BC, voting themselves commands in Spain and Syria respectively and extending Caesar's command in Gaul. Pompey remained in Rome, but Crassus, seeking military prestige to match that of his allies, invaded the Parthian kingdom beyond the Syrian border. In 53 BC, he was killed in a disastrous defeat at Carrhae (in modern Turkey). Political power in Rome was now polarised between Pompey and Caesar.

By the late 50s BC, Caesar's command in Gaul was approaching its end and he needed to be re-elected consul to avoid prosecution for his misdeeds in 59 BC. By 50 BC, however, Pompey had been accepted by Caesar's opponents in the senate as their leader, and he was ready to use force against his former ally. Outmanoevred in the senate, Caesar marched his army into Italy, provoking civil war. The majority of senators took Pompey's side, but Caesar proved by far the more effective general, defeating his opponents in a series of campaigns that lasted until 45 BC. He consciously rejected the bloody example of Sulla and pardoned his enemies, so that many of those who had fought for the Republic went over to his side, while the leaders of the opposition (including Pompey) died during the war. His supporters old and new expected the victorious Caesar to restore the Republic, but it became clear that he had no such intention. He had elections held to fill the traditional offices years in advance, adopted the trappings of royalty and accepted honours associated with the kings of the Greek East, and had himself appointed dictator for life in early 44 BC. On 15 March of the same year, the senators took matters into their own hands: sixty of them collaborated to assassinate him.

THE END OF THE ROMAN REPUBLIC

The period after the death of Caesar represents the final phase in the demise of the Republic, when the electoral process in Rome counted for nothing and all power lay in the hands of warlords. The assassins expected that the Republic would be revived by the death of the tyrant, but they were mistaken. The surviving consul, Marcus Antonius (Mark Antony), tried to rally Caesar's supporters under his own leadership while coming to an accommodation with the assassins, but he did not count on the influence of Caesar's heir. Having no surviving children, the dictator had adopted as his heir the nineteen-year-old grandson of his sister, who is generally known as Octavian. While Caesar had not been able to reconcile one-man military rule with traditional senatorial values, his ruthless heir would emerge victorious from a decade and a half of civil war to found the Imperial government, all the while ostensibly restoring the Republic.

The years following the dictator's death saw a whirlwind of changing alliances. Octavian first attempted to use his influence with Caesar's veterans to seize power. When this failed, he entered into an alliance with the senate against Antony. In late 44 BC Antony attempted to seize northern Italy, and Octavian campaigned against him, forcing him to withdraw into Gaul. Octavian then changed sides and formed an alliance with Antony and another Caesarian general, Marcus Aemilius Lepidus. Together they seized Rome and had themselves appointed triumvirs. A purge of their enemies brought the death of Cicero, who had spoken repeatedly against Antony.

Meanwhile, Gaius Cassius Longinus and Marcus Junius Brutus, the leading assassins, had seized the eastern provinces, realising that it would be impossible for them to cooperate with the heir of their victim. In 42 BC, Antony and Octavian defeated them at Philippi in Greece, and now the Roman world was effectively theirs. While Lepidus was relegated to Africa, Antony was allotted the Roman East as his sphere, and Octavian received Italy. Octavian quickly forced Lepidus into dishonourable retirement. Antony beat back a Parthian invasion of the eastern provinces, but his counter-invasion was defeated.

Though he was married to Octavian's sister, Antony became involved with Cleopatra, the last Ptolemaic ruler of Egypt, and granted Roman territory to her and her children. Octavian responded by requiring the Roman cities under his control to swear an oath of personal loyalty, and prepared for war. In 32 BC, his forces met Antony's in western Greece. Antony was outmanoevred and attempted to flee to Egypt by sea; his fleet was routed at Actium in 31 BC. Octavian was now the undisputed leader of the Roman world.

The last century of the Republic had brought a remarkable spread of Roman citizens throughout Italy and the Mediterranean. Gaius Gracchus had resumed the practice of establishing colonies, but on a rather different basis from the earlier Latin examples. The new colonies were intended to provide land to landless Roman citizens. While most of Gaius' settlements were in Italy, he also began the practice of placing them elsewhere (such as the former site of Carthage). This policy was generally associated with politicians opposed to the senatorial oligarchy, which rejected foreign colonies (and land redistribution) as a matter of principle. From the

time of Marius, the major purpose of colonies was to give land to veterans of successful wars; he founded colonies both in Italy and overseas. Sulla established colonies in Italy on land taken from cities that had opposed him in the civil war. Caesar established colonies for veterans both in Italy and overseas after his victories in the early 40s BC, as did Octavian after Philippi and Actium. All these colonies helped in the romanisation of much of western Europe, North Africa and the Balkans.

The Republic fell for three reasons. First, it provided no effective means of overseeing provincial governors, which allowed the unscrupulous among them to exploit their provinces and misuse the troops they commanded for their own political benefit. Though there were attempts in the last century of the Republic to supervise governors through legislation, there was no administrative structure to coordinate such provision and ensure compliance. Second, the strategic demands of empire necessitated the establishment of a large and permanent military force, and this led to the recruitment of landless soldiers, who had no allegiance to the old electoral system in Rome. Finally, the political system lost legitimacy as the assemblies came to be dominated by violence. The small assemblies in Rome were no longer representative of the Roman People as a whole, which after the Social War consisted of the entire population of Italy. It would be the genius of Octavian to provide the autocratic framework needed to control the military while at the same time accommodating senatorial sentiments by seemingly restoring the Republic.

The assassination of Julius Caesar, as depicted by the nineteenth-century French painter Jean-Léon Gérôme. The senators, led by Brutus and Cassius, took the drastic step of stabbing Caesar to death on the floor of the Curia, the senatorial debating chamber.

THE EMPERORS

DAVID POTTER

THE EMPERORS

In September AD 14 the man we now know as the emperor Tiberius made a fool of himself in the senate. The body of his adoptive father, whom we know as the emperor Augustus, had just been incinerated at the climax of an extraordinary public funeral; the consuls, at that moment the chief executive officers of the state, had prepared the text of a law that would confer upon Tiberius diverse powers that had once been held by Augustus.

THE DEVELOPMENT OF IMPERIAL RULE

Tiberius, who already held the two most important of Augustus's powers – *imperium maius*, defined as 'power greater than that of the man who should govern any province that he should enter,' and the *tribunicia potestas*, which enabled him to bring measures to a vote by the people, to bring public business to a halt and to protect any Roman from the action of a magistrate – seems to have suggested that he would prefer not to have the additional powers. These powers probably included some authority to administer the city of Rome, the power to run meetings of the senate, the power to make peace or war and, in all likelihood, a provision that would free Tiberius from the constraint of the laws. Along with those Tiberius already held, these powers would constitute what was referred to as the *paterna statio*, or ancestral station, the position that Augustus had occupied in the state prior to his death. No one seems to have used the word *princeps*, which was coming only gradually into common usage, and would become the usual Roman word for the person we call the emperor. Indeed, it would only be after an assembly of the people voted on the motion proposed by the consuls and passed by the senate after Tiberius stopped speaking obscurely, that there would be a definition of what it meant to be a Roman emperor. The position that Augustus had occupied was an extraordinary collection of powers that had accrued to him after Mark Antony's suicide at Alexandria in 30 BC. In the course of the next forty-four years, he had arranged for various relatives to exercise some of these powers, but no one, until AD 14, had held them all.

It is unfortunate that we do not know the day upon which the Roman people voted in favour of the consuls' proposal, though it is quite likely that it was not until a month later that they assembled to do so – it was tradition that three *nundinae*, periods of nine days, should pass between the time a law was proposed and the time it was actually voted on. It was at this point, however, with the passage of this *lex de imperio* (law concerning power) that there was a coherent definition of the role of the *princeps* within the state. The traditions governing this procedure were more than a century old, and had been used in the course of the previous century to create a variety of extraordinary positions. What makes the law for Tiberius so different from these earlier laws is that, while they tended to be associated with some specific emergency, this law was required because there was general sentiment that what the state needed was a monarch. This sentiment had grown during the lifetime of

Augustus, who harped endlessly upon the restoration of peace and order to Rome, Italy and the provinces while he occupied his *statio*.

The passage of a law defining the powers of a *princeps* at the start of Tiberius's reign was the beginning, not the end, of the development of imperial government. If we move some three hundred years into the future and to a flat plain outside the modern Turkish city of Izmit, ancient Nicomedia, we may see a very different version of the way that the imperial power was defined. On 1 May AD 305, the emperor Diocletian summoned representatives of the legions to witness a ceremony at the platform where, twenty-one years earlier, he had assumed the rank of Augustus – the name of the first emperor having long since become a title – and had cut down in front of the assembled army the man who had hoped to be proclaimed in his stead. There had been no meeting of the senate that day, and there had been few members of the senate among the marshals who had selected Diocletian as their leader. This time there would be no meeting of the senate either – and no meeting of the senate at Milan, where Diocletian's long-serving junior Augustus, Maximian, would be conducting a similar ceremony. On this day Diocletian and Maximian would abdicate, the only Roman emperors ever to do so voluntarily. Here at Nicomedia, Diocletian would take off the purple cloak that was his symbol of office and drape it around the shoulders of Maximinus Daia, elevating him to the rank of deputy emperor (Caesar). Maximinus was replacing Diocletian's son-in-law, Maximianus Galerius, who now became Augustus. Maximian would perform the same action with his son-in-law, the other Caesar Constantius, and a man named Severus.

A college of rulers since 293, the four emperors claimed to have restored the Empire from chaos, to have salvaged its ailing economy, restored justice and purified the Roman state. Their authority derived not from a law passed by the people, but from the acclamation of their soldiers and the favour of the gods.

Part of a large public dedication to the emperors Diocletian and Maximian (AD 285–305) on a fragment of papyrus from Oxyrhynchus in Egypt. The dedication was made by a detachment of the Fifth (Macedonian) Legion. The papyrus may have been a draft used by a stonemason when cutting the inscription – or it may have formed the notice itself.

An onyx cameo known as the *Gemma Augustea* dating from about AD 10. It shows (above) Tiberius and Augustus with the personified goddess Roma, and (below) soldiers of Tiberius with symbols of victory, including a bearded captive.

THE EMPEROR'S PATRIMONIUM

How do we get from Tiberius to Diocletian? Perhaps the best way to begin is with what Tiberius did before he made his clumsy speech to the senate. Before he did so, he accepted his designation as primary heir to Augustus's estate, meaning that he had to pay the legacies that Augustus had written into the will and to take possession of the largest estate in the Mediterranean world, his *patrimonium*.

The private wealth of the emperor was as important as any legal formula in establishing his position. Even in the lifetime of Augustus, the emperor's territory required an administrative staff that may have exceeded the (admittedly attenuated) bureaucracy that was charged with provincial administration and tax collection on behalf of the Roman state. Augustus's staff in the provinces was largely made up of the slaves or freed slaves who ran his estates, reporting to officials called procurators at the provincial level (most of them also freed slaves). His personal entourage consisted of 'friends', fellow aristocrats who assisted him with important functions. He also had a staff of secretaries, slave and freed, who could take dictation, and a staff of readers whose tasks ranged from entertainment to letting him know what was in the letters he received. Even then, it is unlikely that Augustus heard every letter that was written to him; his personal staff would sort the mail, and even answer some letters in his name. This nascent secretarial and financial bureaucracy was supplemented by equestrian officials who oversaw the administration of important tasks mandated to him by the senate, tasks such as the government of the province of Egypt and the care of the grain supply for the city of Rome. The guard that the senate had decided that he should have was commanded by two more equestrian officials, to whom the officers commanding the 10,000 men who made up this force reported.

The crucial issue in subsequent Roman administrative history would be defining the role of the emperor as property owner and magistrate. The reason why this is so was that the staff who looked after his property had better access to the emperor than did most senators, and with access came influence. As a consequence, in the course of the first century AD, aristocrats came to replace the freed slaves who had earlier dominated much of the business of the *patrimonium*. During the second century, a rough equilibrium developed between the aristocrats who made their way through service in the *patrimonium* and those who sought influence by holding traditional magistracies. In the third century, for reasons ranging from some very difficult personalities to the inability of what often seems to have been a staggeringly unimaginative governing class to meet new challenges, the balance of power shifted to generals and court officers. By the end of the third century, the emperor ruled as the master of the army and the patrimonial staff.

The crucial moment in the administration of the *patrimonium* came in AD 68, when the emperor Nero was driven from the throne and committed suicide. At that moment, since Nero had not made a valid will, the *patrimonium* had no legal owner. We do not know by what technicality Nero's property became Galba's when the people voted him the legal powers that constituted the imperial office some months after Nero died. All we know for certain is that Galba moved into an imperial palace and took over control of the staff. It may be that he received it as *bona vacantia*, an estate with no legal heir, which by law became the property of the emperor. What we also know is that, by the third century, the emperor's power to dispose of his property was less than absolute: the third-century jurist Ulpian noted that there were parts of the *patrimonium* that the emperor could no more dispose of than the state could relinquish the forum Romanum. In AD 193, when Pertinax took the throne after the murder of Commodus (who had ruled from 180 to 192), he made an issue of the way that Commodus had squandered the *patrimonium*, as if it were a matter of public business. Behind these statements lies a sense of the distinction between the man and the property attached to the position of emperor. This is not quite the same as saying that the emperor had two bodies, as was said of kings in medieval Europe – that is to say, the individual who was king on the one hand, and the royal authority that defined the state on the other. The emperor would never be identified with the empire: he had supreme power within the *res publica* (the Roman state), which is a very different thing from saying that his power was the *res publica*.

THE EMPEROR AND HIS OFFICIALS

In the second century AD, Cornelius Tacitus, the great Roman historian, wrote that a historian of the emperors was concerned with small matters that often, in unpredictable ways, swayed greater things. Cassius Dio, who wrote a century after Tacitus and was no mean historian himself, noted that it was often very hard to know what was happening in imperial circles since the emperor controlled access to information. Despite these limitations, both men described the exercise of imperial power with remarkable ability, and from perspectives reflecting the fact that one man wrote at the beginning of the age of equilibrium between the palace and the traditional aristocracy, while the other wrote at the end of that age. The second century AD is, in many ways, a deceptive period, a period of stability in a political system that was inherently unstable.

Augustus saw himself in the tradition of the dominant political leaders of the previous generation – and this is how he is portrayed not only in the inscription that he had placed on bronze tablets in front of his mausoleum, but also by Velleius Paterculus, who composed a short history of Rome in AD 30. The odd ceremony in which Tiberius took up power is a reflection of this as well, justifying Velleius's view. For a Caesar, a Pompey or a Sulla, political power arose from military success. So it was that the lifetime of Augustus was marked by the most extensive conquests of any period of Roman history. Although he was himself a rather poor general, given to bouts of physical illness before some of the decisive battles of the civil wars, Augustus devised a system by which he could claim success for the triumphs of others, and surrounded himself with an aura of military genius. By taking the *imperium maius* in 28 BC, first for limited terms and later for life, he could claim that his generals fought under his auspices, meaning that his relationship with the gods guaranteed their success. Since Augustus was able to appoint the men who would command the legions in the provinces that made up the gigantic *provincia* that he was granted in 28 BC, encompassing almost all of the regions where armies were stationed, he could ensure the personal loyalty of his generals.

The triumphs Augustus could claim were not inconsiderable. In the 20s BC he brought those portions of Spain that were not yet under Roman control into the provincial system. At the end of that decade and the beginning of the next he secured peace with Persia on terms favourable to Rome. After that his armies conquered the Balkans and Germany as far north as the Elbe. Although the German province was lost in AD 9, the empire he left at his death, bounded by the Rhine and Danube in the north and by the line of the Euphrates in the Middle East, would remain roughly the same size for nearly two hundred years. Only two later emperors engaged in large-scale annexations of territory. One was Claudius, who added Britain and some territories that had previously been client kingdoms in North Africa, thus completing Roman domination of the Mediterranean rim; the other was Trajan, who conquered Dacia, the region north of the Danube that forms much of modern Romania. Both these men took power under dubious circumstances: Claudius after the murder of his nephew Caligula in 41, Trajan as the result of his adoption by Nerva in 97, an adoption that followed upon a riot by the Praetorian Guard. In both cases, the

---

Augustus's account of his settlement

In my sixth and seventh consulships, after I had extinguished the civil wars and, by the agreement of all people, held all power, I transferred the republic from my control to that of the senate and people of Rome. For this reason I was named 'Augustus' by decree of the senate.

*Augustus Res Gestae 34.1
(trans. David Potter)*

A detail from a plaster cast of the spiral frieze of Trajan's Column, erected in AD 113 to commemorate the campaigns against the Dacians in 101–2 and 105–6. Here the emperor himself makes a ritual offering beside the great Danube bridge built by his soldiers at Turnu Severin.

conquests were accompanied by massive building projects at Rome that were intended to secure popular favour. At the end of his life, Trajan also contemplated adding that portion of the Parthian kingdom that occupied what is now Iraq, but decided, just before his death, that Rome lacked the power to hold it. He decided instead to be content with a superficial 'regime change'.

This relative stability of the imperial frontiers appears to have suited both the emperors and members of the aristocracy. Men who rose to senior commands and desired military glory were content with the job of protecting Roman territory – it garnered credit to themselves without arousing the jealousy of the emperor. Many of these emperors were little inclined to take the field themselves. Claudius, who was an older man when he assumed power and in indifferent health, was poorly suited to the rigours of command, while his successor, Nero, lacked military training of any sort. Vespasian, who ultimately succeeded Nero, was a soldier of considerable ability, but he too was an older man by the time he became emperor and he trusted only Trajan's father with a wide-ranging command. His son Domitian desired military glory, but his personal failings meant that his wars were defensive in nature. Hadrian, who succeeded Trajan, eschewed conquest and his own successor, Antoninus Pius, was another elderly man who had no interest in warfare. It was only in the reign of Marcus Aurelius (AD 161–180) that an emperor was compelled to take the field for the bulk of his reign, and this was in a series of defensive wars against first the Persians and then against the tribes north of the Danube.

ROMAN TAXATION

The revenues of the Roman state derived from a variety of taxes. These fall into three basic categories: the land tax, the tax on persons and direct imposts on a wide variety of economic activities. Liability for the land tax and the head tax was established by censuses that were conducted in each province on a regular cycle that was set for each province. This same census cycle established liability for the head tax.

Responsibility for collection of the tax assessment rested with local authorities. Other monetary taxes, such as export and import taxes, were farmed out to corporations of tax collectors, the *publicani*. In each census period corporations bid for the right to collect certain of these taxes. The corporation was responsible for payment of the tax to the state from its own resources; it expected to make up these resources from collection of the tax. If the corporation collected more than it bid, it kept the surplus. If it collected less than its bid, it swallowed the loss unless it could negotiate relief for itself from the state. *Publicani* also tended to collect transport taxes, known as *portoria*, which were assessed on goods moving across provincial barriers. In addition to these taxes, which fell most heavily on non-Romans and on Romans living in the provinces, there were monetary taxes assessed upon Roman citizens (and also farmed out on five-year contracts). These were chiefly a five per cent tax on inheritances, which was established by Augustus to fund the treasury set aside to pay retirement benefits to retiring soldiers, a five per cent tax on the manumission of slaves and a one per cent tax on goods sold at auction. A four per cent tax on the sale of slaves, introduced by Nero, may also have survived his reign, though the evidence for it is highly circumstantial.

The principle behind both the land tax and the head tax was that the state should be able to know in advance how much revenue it could expect to receive in each year. Given that the land tax was reassessed on a

relatively long cycle and that contracts to tax farmers were for a five-year period, the system was remarkably inelastic. There was little scope for raising new revenues in case of a sudden emergency, and it appears that emperors would respond to local requests for money by relieving them of taxes, except when food crises threatened, in which case food collected as part of the land-tax could be diverted to the area where food was short.

The inadequacy of the tax system was recognised as early as the reign of Augustus, who paid enormous sums from his personal fortune into the state treasury. The vast estates of the emperor provided him with the discretionary revenues that were needed to meet exceptional expenses, and there were avenues open to the emperor that were not open to the *Res publica* to maximize his income in time of need. Two of these were the right of succession to estates to which there was no heir, and the right to claim vacant land. Another – and this was a serious issue in aristocratic society – was to seize the estates of persons convicted of serious crimes. Emperors would often swear an oath to the senate that they would sentence no senator to death, which was one way of saying that the emperor would not regard their estates as a potential source of revenue. But even emperors who had sworn this oath would not necessarily keep it, and there was a long history of confiscation as a method of raising ready cash. A needy emperor, in the words of the fourth-century AD historian Ammianus Marcellinus, would 'fall upon the rich like a torrent'.

Above: a relief image of a sack of money belonging to a *viator ad aerarium*, an official of the Roman state treasury.

Left: a detail of a tomb relief of the second or third century AD from Trier. Even at the edge of the Empire, Roman coins were used in many financial transactions.

A DEFENSIVE STRATEGY

Tiberius is in many ways the key figure in Roman imperial history, transforming the late Republican aggression that was characteristic of the Augustan age into the defensive strategy that was to typify the next two centuries. This was not, however, the result of some particular intuition on his part, but rather of the peculiarity of his character. When Tiberius took the throne, the spirit of Augustan aggression was still alive and well, represented by his adopted son Germanicus, who commanded a large army on the Rhine. Germanicus had been appointed to command by Augustus so that he could avenge the disaster of Publius Quinctilius Varus in AD 9. The destruction of three legions under Varus in the Teutoberger forest in Germany had ended the image of Roman invincibility that had enabled the control of the frontier with a relatively small army. After two years, with trouble threatening in the East, Tiberius ordered

Agrippina landing at Brundisium with the ashes of Germanicus, painted by Sir Benjamin West in 1768. Germanicus, adopted by his uncle, Tiberius, was one of the Rome's greatest soldiers. He died in Syria, possibly poisoned on Tiberius's orders because his power threatened the emperor's position. His children with Agrippina included the emperor Caligula.

Germanicus back to Rome and off to Syria, where he died in AD 19, after having arranged a peaceful settlement with Persia. Four years later, Tiberius's natural son Drusus, who had spent much of his father's reign with the armies in the Balkans, was murdered by his wife. Tiberius only learned of the circumstances of the murder eight years later. In the intervening years he fell under the influence of his praetorian prefect, Aelius Sejanus, who took over the day-to-day management of affairs, while Tiberius withdrew to live on the island of Capri, from which he never returned, in AD 27. Sejanus used his power to persecute men who achieved prominence outside his own circle of supporters, and had no interest in any sort of military adventure. When Tiberius discovered that Sejanus was planning to use his position to replace him as emperor, he had Sejanus murdered and executed a large number of his supporters, many of them members of the senate.

The execution of senior aristocrats, and the demonstration that the power of the emperor at Rome lay in the loyalty of the guard to the house of Augustus, made many wary of trying to achieve great prominence. The need to regulate the emperor's contact with the senate emerged as an important issue. It became something of an imperative after the reign of Caligula, who was plainly unbalanced. Under Claudius and Nero, the day-to-day management of the state fell into the hands of other imperial favourites – freedmen in the case of Claudius, members of the equestrian order under Nero – who reached a modus vivendi with the senate by helping to formalise terms of command and expectations of promotion. In return for accepting diminished opportunity to win wealth and glory, members of the senate were given a greater sense of security. If an emperor broke this implied contract, he did so at his peril. The widespread conspiracy that resulted in the eviction of Nero from the throne in AD 68 stemmed from a change in the leadership at the court, and the use of access to the emperor to attack rivals in the aristocracy. The conspiracy, in the court this time, that resulted in the murder of Domitian in AD 96 stemmed from similar causes: Domitian was felt to be unpredictable, leading to a number of conspiracies before the one that finally succeeded. At no point, with the exception of some brief muttering in the senate after the murder of Caligula, was there a suggestion that there should not be an emperor. The office was important as a guarantee of security. And not just for the senate – people who made their careers in the emperor's personal service had just as much interest in making sure that relations were pacific as did the senate. After the reign of Claudius, whose dependence upon freedmen was deeply resented, the chief officials of the imperial service tended to be drawn from the equestrian order. Equestrians were aristocrats too, and they do not appear to have perceived a great deal of difference between their interests and those of senators.

The good emperor was a man who could negotiate with the various interest groups that surrounded him, and build consensus. The senate arrogated to itself the ability to remind the emperor of his role by voting upon his record after he died as a way of reminding a new emperor of what he should do. An emperor who had succeeded in keeping order was deified; an emperor who was murdered was held up to future generations as a disaster, a man who had failed to do his part and a reminder to future emperors of what could happen.

THE CHANGING ARISTOCRACY

What is perhaps most interesting about the imperial senate is that, unlike the senate of the Republic – which was dominated, generation after generation, by a relatively few families, all based in central Italy – its membership was constantly changing. Although the Julio-Claudian line was itself deeply implicated in the dynastic politics of the later Republic, uniting a minor patrician house, the Julii, with one of the grandest, the Claudii, their years in power brought devastation to old families. Galba was the last member of a family that had been prominent in the Republic to be emperor. Families from municipal Italy and from provinces with a long history of Italian settlement – most obviously Spain – began now to rise to the fore. They were joined some of the wealthiest families of the Greek East. By the middle of the second century AD only about half the members of the senate came from Italy, though by law senators from the provinces had to have Italian estates.

Although we cannot trace changes in the equestrian order as easily as we can those in the senate, it is clear that its membership was becoming ever more cosmopolitan even more rapidly. Distinguished provincial families that were awarded the Roman citizenship were almost by definition of equestrian standing. Even a small town like Oenoanda in southeastern Turkey could boast an equestrian family in the early second century. Thanks to the growth of the equestrian bureaucracy, the government of the Empire was rapidly coming to mirror the population of the Empire as a whole. Some important regions, like Syria, which produced few senators, seem nonetheless to have produced large numbers of equestrians, perhaps because the expansion of the citizenship in those areas began somewhat later, at a time when the advantages of a senatorial career over an equestrian were less obvious.

The openness of the imperial aristocracy to outsiders sets the Roman Empire apart from other empires. Leading provincial families gained a stake in preserving the imperial order – and it was even possible for a provincial to become emperor. Septimius Severus, for instance, was of Punic stock from North Africa, and spoke Latin with a Punic accent. He was married to a woman from the Syrian city from Emesa, and every member of the dynasty that he founded was the product of marriages in the Semitic part of the Empire. From the accession of Claudius II in 268 AD to the accession of Theodosius I, who was from Spain, in 379 almost every emperor had family roots in the Balkans rather than Italy. A consequence of this openness is that there were very few 'national' revolts against Roman rule – there were only two, both involving the Jewish population of the Middle East, which for economic and cultural reasons was loath to assimilate to Greco-Roman cultural norms, in the course of the second century. In the third century, when the prestige of the imperial government was seriously challenged as a result of military failure there were more revolts, but these are less 'national' revolts than they are acts of protest against imperial incompetence. The two uprisings that would, at first sight, appear to challenge this view – that of Palmyra, the great trading city in the Syrian desert, in the 270s and of Amandus in Gaul in the 280s – are on closer inspection linked to quarrels over standing within the imperial bureaucracy. Internal threats to the authority of the emperors arose, for the most part, within the imperial system itself.

SOURCES OF INSTABILITY

The balance between emperor and the aristocracy that came into existence during the first century AD failed at the beginning of the third. To understand why this happened, it is important to understand that the governing aristocracy was responsible for the implied contract with the emperor. Members of the aristocracy were willing to sublimate their ambitions for the good of the system as long as the emperor did his part. When he did not, another member of the aristocracy might try to make it work by making himself emperor.

In AD 68, Servius Sulpicius Galba became emperor not so much because he was the leader of the conspiracy that unseated Nero, but because the governor of Upper Germany, Lucius Verginius Rufus, who had a much larger army, was willing to allow him to march on Rome. We do not know why Rufus was willing to do this, but in all likelihood it had to do with the fact that Galba was old and had no children, making it easier for him to build a coalition. The expectation was that Galba would do this by adopting some other member of the aristocracy as his heir. But Galba failed, largely because he alienated supporters at Rome by failing to give them what they regarded as their just rewards; he alienated the Praetorian Guard, whose desertion had driven Nero from the throne, by failing to pay its members the enormous gift (donative) they felt they had earned; and he failed to reward the soldiers of the Rhine legions who felt that they too deserved special treatment because they had broken their oath to Nero. The guard, which backed Marcus Salvius Otho, best known hitherto as the cuckolded husband of Nero's second wife and the man who had taught Nero the pleasures of perfuming his feet, murdered Galba in January of AD 69. Otho's record, undistinguished as it may seem, marked him as a man who knew the ins and outs of palace politics, which included the guard. If the guard had not killed Galba, it is unlikely that he would have lasted much longer anyway. The governor of Lower Germany, Aulus Vitellius, had already risen in rebellion.

Vitellius defeated Otho, at Cremona in northern Italy in April 69, because he had a better army, but in doing so he alienated the legions in the Balkans, which had sided with his rival. He did not have time to repair that relationship because Titus Flavius Vespasianus (Vespasian), who commanded an army that had been assigned the task of suppressing the Jewish revolt that had broken out in Palestine under Nero, wanted the throne and had had himself declared emperor in Caesarea in July. The Balkan legions rallied to Vespasian's cause and Vitellius was defeated in October, again at Cremona. Vespasian's Balkan allies occupied Rome in December, and Vespasian himself arrived in the city early in 70.

The historian Tacitus noted that Vespasian's success revealed the secret that an emperor could be made outside Rome, provided that he had the necessary military support. He may well, as he wrote this, have been thinking of events closer to his own time than the revolt of Vespasian, for he would have known that Trajan was adopted as a successor by Nerva in AD 97 precisely because he was a successful soldier, and because he commanded a very large army at the time: Nerva plainly thought (and he was right) that the guard would be less likely to interfere in the succession if it was threatened by a powerful provincial army.

Tacitus on the secret of political power

The end of Nero, after the initial surge of joy, aroused various responses not only in the city amongst members of the senate, the population as a whole and the garrison, but also amongst all the legions and generals. The hidden secret of empire was out: it was possible for an emperor to be made somewhere other than Rome.

Tacitus Histories 1.4
(trans. David Potter)

THE EMPEROR AND THE ARMY

One point that the events of AD 69 and 97 underscore is that it is wrong to think in terms of a single, unified Roman army. In truth the Roman army was becoming, in the course of the first and second centuries, a group of regional forces. While officers rotated rapidly from unit to unit, soldiers remained with the units into which they were first enlisted for very long periods of time. Their terms of service were set at sixteen years. If they survived, they were liable to be recalled to the ranks in cases of emergency. Quite often they would remain in the areas where they had served. These soldiers did not always share the interests of their officers, and they almost never shared the interests of the civilian population in the areas in which they were stationed. Each unit had its own traditions, and was jealous of others. Moreover, by the end of the second century AD, there had been no significant change in the basic tactics of the legions for three hundred years – a sign that the army was no longer a tool of imperial expansion, but rather of domestic repression.

By the end of the second century AD there were signs that the army was losing its ability to dominate the frontiers. It took Marcus Aurelius more than a decade to restore order on the Danubian frontier, and the task was not completed at the time of his death. The long years of warfare began to introduce stresses in the governing classes, as some men – often men who had risen to prominence from outside the upper echelons of the aristocracy – served very long terms as commanders of large army groups. One praetorian prefect threatened to kill a senior senator who appeared before Marcus on a legal matter, and Marcus himself had to intervene to protect one of his best generals, the son of a freed slave, from conspiracies on the part of other generals. It plainly demanded all his political skill to hold the diverse factions together, and after his death the government fell into disarray. His son, Commodus, was very young when Marcus died, and he handed the day-to-day management of affairs over to a series of favourites, none of them members of the traditional governing class. When Commodus's conduct became so erratic that his court could tolerate him no longer, he was assassinated.

The murder of Commodus was followed by chaos as different groups within the imperial system sought power for themselves. The Praetorian Guard murdered Commodus's successor, Helvius Pertinax, because he seemed insufficiently solicitous of their welfare. When the Guard proclaimed as emperor Didius Julianus, the rich senator who had offered the Guard the most money in an open auction, three provincial armies supported their own generals as emperors in Julianus' place. Septimius Severus, who was able to unite the Balkan armies under his control, was able to take advantage of his central position to secure power for himself in a series of civil wars that lasted from 193 to 197. After the murder of his son, Caracalla, in 217, another civil war broke out, pitting one faction of the court against another. This was rapidly resolved in favour of the faction supporting a distant relative of Severus, Marcus Aurelius Antoninus, against the faction that supported Marcus Opellius Macrinus, who had been proclaimed by the army after Caracalla's assassination.

EMPERORS IN BATTLE

In these years the army emerged as the pre-eminent political force, requiring significant changes in the way that emperors ruled. While, as we have seen, very few emperors took the field in person in the first two centuries AD, it became absolutely necessary for the emperor to assume personal command of the army on major expeditions during the third century. Emperors are now found taking an active role in the fighting; the record of emperors like Decius who was killed in battle, or Gallienus who was wounded, suggests that their involvement in military life was more than mere image-building. Senatorial status ceased to be a requirement for the position, and senators are rarely found occupying important positions in government.

This development strengthened the hand of the palace bureaucracy, as well as of the army, leading to the situation that we have seen on 1 May 305. A further corollary of this development was that Rome itself ceased to be the centre of government. While the old capital would always retain an important ideological and symbolic site, government was now effectively run from wherever it was that the emperor decided to base himself. New imperial capitals were established in various cities closer to the frontiers, at places like Trier, Milan, Nicomedia and, finally, Constantinople.

Bust of the emperor Gallienus (reigned AD 253–268), son of the unfortunate Valerian. Like most, although not all, of the 3rd-century 'soldier emperors' he did not flinch from leading his troops in person. At a time when the legions decided who was to occupy the imperial throne – the trend had been established by Severus in the AD 190s – an emperor could not afford to be too distant from his soldiers.

Detail of a 2nd-century AD carved stone relief depicting the emperor Marcus Aurelius (standing at centre) receiving the adoration of the Roman people. The people are represented by a shaven-headed child, an elderly man and, standing between them, a semi-nude figure who personifies the 'genius' – the ethnically defining spirit – of the Roman people.

THE EMPEROR AND THE EMPIRE

When members of the Pharisee sect wanted to embarrass the Jewish religious teacher Jesus of Nazareth, they asked him to declare whether they should pay taxes to Rome (an unpopular thing in first-century Galilee). He responded by asking them whose face was on the coins they used every day. When they replied that it was the face of Caesar, he told them that they ought to render unto Caesar what was Caesar's. Although his teachings would change the intellectual fabric of the ancient world, Jesus himself never saw an emperor, and, prior to his crucifixion, seems to have had almost no dealings with the imperial government other than those imposed by the tax system. To most of his subjects, the emperor was as distant a figure as he was to Jesus. Yet they would all have some idea what he looked like because his face was stamped on the coins that they used. When they undertook some financial transaction, they would date it by his years of rule. When they took a road that had been constructed by Roman soldiers, they would pass a stone every mile that told them the distance from the starting point of the road, and what emperor was responsible for its construction. In these minor, but significant ways, the emperor was omnipresent.

What people saw when they looked at the emperor was often a highly stylised picture. The images on coins in all likelihood did not look much like the emperor: Augustus never ages on his coin portraits; Tiberius, who was bald, is shown with a good head of hair; Septimius Severus looks very much like Marcus Aurelius (into whose family he adopted himself). The emperor's titles reflect claims to victories over foreign peoples that, until the third century, were won by his generals and were often the result of defensive rather than offensive actions. Yet the emperor was more than a face on a coin, or a collection of titles: he was the symbol of the unity of the state; he was, in theory, a source of protection against the oppression of his own officials; and he could change the landscape in which a person lived. The crucial roles that the emperors played in the lives of their subjects were defined, in many ways, by the desires of those subjects. (*See also* pages 270–273)

One of the most important myths of imperial government was that the emperor was accessible to everyone. There is a story that when a woman approached the emperor Hadrian as he entered a city with a petition, he told her to go away. She shouted after him, 'then stop being king'. He halted and allowed her to tell him what was on her mind. While, strictly speaking, this story may not be true – it is told of a number of other rulers throughout antiquity – it nonetheless sums up the importance of the ruler as a source of protection. The emperor did indeed receive an enormous number of petitions from people of all sorts, and he was expected to put on a show of listening to them. Even if the bulk of these petitions were handled by secretaries, and may never have been read by him, the responses that came back from the palace did so in his name. In some cases we can even see him acting to help those who were oppressed. A number of petitions to the emperor have survived on inscriptions from rural regions in which groups of villagers are granted redress from violent acts by imperial officials. The form of these petitions are so similar that it looks as if people had access to documents that provided models for the form that petitions should take.

Extending from the individual to the community, the system of petition and response created a scale upon which cities could compete with their neighbours, and gave the emperor a way to shape the lives of his subjects. Cities would write to the emperor to congratulate him on important anniversaries; every year ambassadors would be sent to Rome, and there they would see all the magnificence that surrounded the master of the world. They would see his games; they would see him listening to the assembled people in the amphitheatre or the circus – where, as one imperial adviser put it, the crowd ruled. They would see spectacles on a scale unimaginable anywhere else, and they would desire to imitate them in their own ways at home. The emperor's interest in certain kinds of entertainment would spark interest elsewhere. The form of performance known as pantomime, a form of ballet on mythological scenes performed by a single actor to the accompaniment of singers and percussion may have had its origin in the Greek world, but it achieved new prominence as a result of the affection of Roman emperors. Gladiatorial combat spread around the Empire, a celebration of the virtues that had made the Empire great, as was made clear by its association with annual celebrations of the emperor in the provinces, the so-called imperial cult.

Cassius Dio on the duties of office

He [Marcus Aurelius] was industrious, and applied himself with diligence to all the duties of his office; he never said, wrote or did anything as if it were of secondary importance, but he would sometimes devote whole days to minor issues, thinking that it was not right for the emperor to do anything in haste.

Cassius Dio History 71.6 (trans. David Potter)

THE IMPERIAL CULT

The term 'imperial cult' is a modern one, used to describe the innumerable local festivals modelled on earlier celebrations of Hellenistic monarchs and – later – Roman magistrates, that arose to celebrate Augustus. These local festivals were transformed in the Augustan age into a two-fold system of communication. Every province had an assembly that would celebrate the emperor in an annual festival, while individual cities would compete to have their own festivals recognised by the emperor as a sign of their importance, for emperors could reward cities or individuals by allowing them to celebrate him in special ways. At these celebrations people would listen to speeches honouring the emperor, giving them some insight into who he was and what he was doing. These celebrations were closely controlled exercises in propaganda, but they contributed to the image of the emperor as a beneficent ruler.

In determining who should celebrate him, and how, the emperor could impose his own taste. Hadrian, for instance, was known to look favourably upon requests to celebrate him with Greek-style cultural events. Thus a man named Demosthenes from Oenoanda was able to found a festival to celebrate himself by petitioning Hadrian to allow him to do so with a festival of this sort. When Hadrian completed the temple of Olympian Zeus, begun centuries earlier by the tyrant Pisistratus, he allowed the Greeks to found a 'league of the Hellenes' that would meet every year to celebrate the cult of the god: admission to the league was determined by a city's ability to create a suitable Greek pedigree for itself. By so doing, Hadrian promoted not only his own values, but also those of the governing classes of Asia Minor, who desired recognition of their heritage. When his favourite, Antinous, died in Egypt, cities competed to celebrate the boy as a sign that their loyalty to the regime was recognised.

In a world whose cultural life was dominated by cities, the emperor shaped the urban landscape by granting civic status to villages that had grown; he promoted cities to higher status by grants of new privileges, or demoted places that had displeased him in a similar way. These grants varied over time, as old forms lost their meaning or acquired new significance – but the process of petition and response remained the same. Emperors were often aware that there was little that they could effect by central dictate; if they were to be effective as rulers, they needed their subjects to invest in the system of rule. By and large their subjects did so because they were left to determine the way in which they would participate, allowing them to align their own needs with the desires of government.

The imperial system worked as long as the central government could guarantee peace and security. There were always be divergent opinions, there were countless sources of stress, instability at the centre could lead to crisis in the periphery, and such a system of administration was inherently conservative. That said, it was a Roman emperor, responding to petitions, who would ensure the most significant intellectual transition in the first four centuries. This emperor was Constantine, and it was due to him that Christianity moved from the fringes of Roman society, where it had developed largely by offering an alternative to the value system of the classical city, to become the central religion of the Mediterranean world, and, paradoxically, an institution that would preserve the heritage of classical antiquity

Fragment of a Roman wall painting from Herculaneum, dating from the first century AD. The scene depicted is that of actors in a Greek drama, and is believed to be a copy of a fourth-century BC Greek original. Theatre, and the use of theatrical scenes for household decoration, is just one of the many unbroken strands connecting Greek and Roman culture.

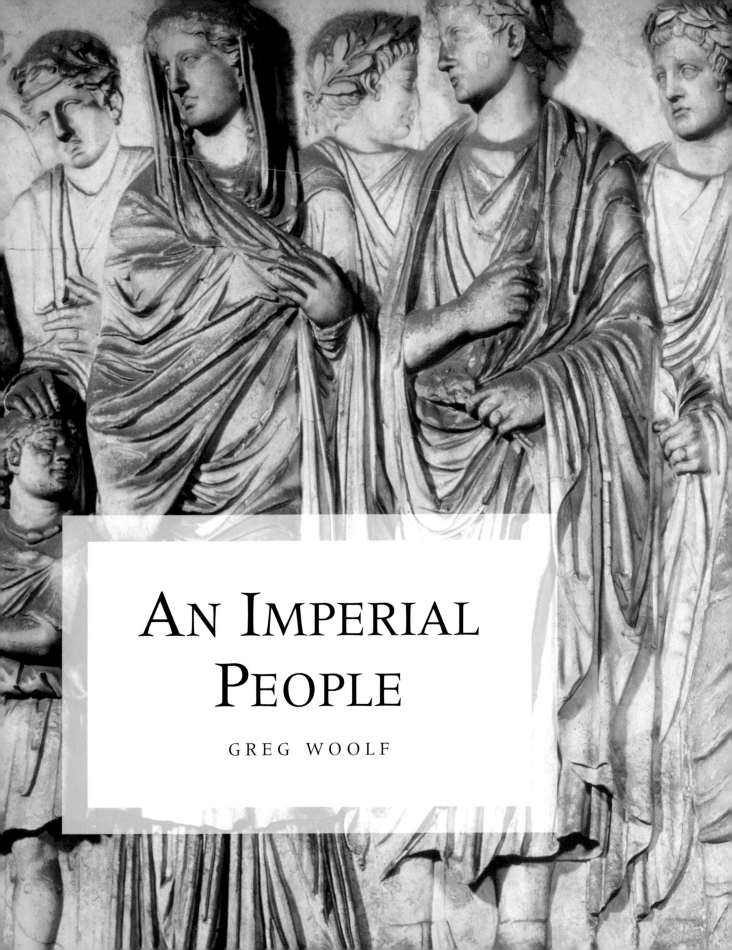

An Imperial People

GREG WOOLF

AN IMPERIAL PEOPLE

Historians have wondered since antiquity what it was that raised up this one city-state, Rome, among the hundreds in the Mediterranean world, to become an imperial power. Virgil and Pliny the Elder suggest that the Romans enjoyed a divine mandate, and some Romans regarded themselves as a chosen people. Livy and Caesar attribute victories to the virtues of individual Romans, just as Sallust and Augustus blamed catastrophes on the spread of vice. Polybius argued that Rome's political and social institutions, and the ideas and behaviour they promoted, provided the best explanation of its comparative advantage over other Hellenistic empires. For many modern historians, this is probably the most compelling explanation.

THE IMPORTANCE OF ROMAN INSTITUTIONS

Modern writers sometimes invoke the geographical centrality of Italy within the Mediterranean world, and sometimes claim that the Romans were exceptionally enthusiastic about warfare. Yet Rome was not the only power based in the central Mediterranean. Carthage and Macedon, let alone the other city-states of the Italian peninsula, would qualify in terms of geopolitics. Likewise many – perhaps most – city-states were militaristic in that they employed citizen-armies, surrounded war with ritual and expected their political leaders to be good generals. It is hardly surprising that the Roman Republic, when it emerges into history in the third century BC, exhibits a militaristic ideology. By that stage, it would be more surprising if it did not.

Of all the kinds of explanation on offer, those that look at Roman institutions seem the most plausible. What was it about Roman society that provided it with the means to convert military victories into lasting dominance, and to enjoy and use the profits of expansion while recycling some of them into continued expansion and stability? Some modern analogies are helpful here. British imperialism was made possible and strengthened by institutions that had evolved at home for quite different purposes. Commercial operations like the East India Company, out of which the British Raj in India grew, were created from existing legal and financial instruments. Equally, the class-based nature of British society provided a basis for controlling other societies by strengthening their indigenous gradations of status and dignity. Institutions can also help account for the weaknesses in empires. The emergence of nationalism in Europe over the nineteenth century would eventually weaken the European empires, by providing subject peoples with models for self-rule and self-determination. Equally, the emphasis Hellenistic empires put on Greek identity set limits on how far non-Greek subjects might ever become fully integrated into them. Even in Roman antiquity, one writer compared Athenian and Roman imperialism and argued that Rome's generosity with citizenship compared to Athenian exclusivity explained the superior strength, extent and durability of Rome's empire.

Historians have seen the importance of Roman institutions since antiquity; Polybius saw it clearly at the time. Another influential explanation for Rome's expansion in Italy stresses the way the Romans institutionalised their dominance over their allies. Defeated enemies tended to be compelled to enter into unequal alliances with Rome, alliances that did not impose tribute but required them to send troops to assist Roman armies. Campaigning thus became the main way that Rome could continue to enjoy the fruits of previous victories, and also a vital way of reasserting Roman leadership. Past victories become an incentive to future wars of conquest, and so on.

This chapter is not intended to offer a comprehensive explanation of Roman success in these terms. Political systems, military organisation, Roman law, slavery and much else would need to be covered. Instead, the focus here is on a cluster of domestic institutions that together played a new role in Roman imperialism. Military institutions are dealt with in Chapter 13, and much of Chapter 6 is relevant to this discussion. This chapter is designed to be read alongside both.

A section from Trajan's Column in Rome. This particular section depicts Roman soldiers escorting recently captured prisoners. Prisoners became a valuable asset as slaves.

By the time of Boudicca's revolt in AD 61, southern Britain had already been divided into nine civitates, each administered from a regional 'capital' town. The underlying tribal nature of these Roman administrative regions is evidenced by the full names of most of the towns. Leicester, for example, was Ratae Coritanorum (Ratae of the Coritani), Cirencester was Corinium Dobunnorum (Corinium of the Dobunni), and Winchester was Venta Belgarum (Venta of the Belgae).

MINIATURE ROMES

Let us begin on a hillside in Andalucia, southern Spain, around twenty years ago, when a remarkable set of bronze tablets was discovered by metal detector enthusiasts. On these six tablets was inscribed just over half of the constitution of a previously unknown Roman city, *Municipium Flavium Irnitanum*, 'Irni' for short. The tablets could be dated to the very end of the first century AD, as they included a letter from Domitian appended to the original constitution. Fragments of inscriptions of this kind had been found elsewhere in Spain, each referring to a different city, but this copy is by far the most complete yet. By combining this *Lex Irnitana* (Law of the Irni) with some of the other fragments, it has been possible to reconstruct around two-thirds of the common constitutional template on which each law was based. Individual copies varied only in details, such as in the name of the city and perhaps the precise fees for holding office, the numbers of councillors (*decuriones*) in the senate (the *curia*) and the names of the chief deities worshipped in the annual festivities laid down in the statute. The origin of all these laws seems to be the grant that Pliny the Elder tells us Vespasian made to the Spanish communities, allowing them to establish themselves as Latin municipalities. For whatever reasons, it had taken the Irnitani a while to get their own copy, but they were evidently pleased to have it. The scale of the bronze tablets implies they were displayed on some public monument, perhaps a temple. No visitor or citizen could be in any doubt that Irni had arrived.

Imperial Rome ruled its provinces, and Italy too, through a network of city-states. Each province was divided up into territories, each with a single urban centre. To begin with this had been a pragmatic device. Many regions controlled by Republican Rome were already in effect mosaics of city-states – Sicily, Greece and Punic Africa, for example. Other regions were controlled through kings, some formally recognised as 'friends and allies of the Roman people'. These client kingdoms persisted in some areas as late as the mid-first century AD, and the Romans never gave up trying to influence the governments of neighbouring peoples by subsidising their candidates and keeping hostages. But kingdoms were inherently unstable. Occasionally – as the late Republican wars against Jugurtha of Numidia and Mithridates of Pontus had shown – Rome's friends would become enemies.

After defeating Mithridates, Pompey dismantled the kingdom of Pontus and replaced it with city-states based on existing settlements. Julius Caesar's decision as *dictator* that the cities of Asia could collect their own taxes had a different origin. Rome had gathered the taxes of Asia by developing the same institutions used to carry out public works, provision the army and generally relieve the state of the administrative burdens: Republican Rome, that is, put out tax farming to contractors, who had to be rich, Roman citizens and not senators. Polybius had already remarked on how many people in Rome – he meant rich people – were involved in public contracts. But the system, which had worked for repaving the Appian Way, had disastrous consequences when used to collect tax. The contractors were corrupt, sought short-term advantage over long-term sustainability and provoked a series of damaging revolts. Caesar's solution, to allow the cities themselves to collect what they owed, became the model for Augustus's organisation of Rome's western and northern provinces. Tribes were treated as states and given the same broad responsibilities as cities in the East. Soon, within each tribal territory, a small Roman-style city emerged.

Convergence on the civic model took various routes. In Pontus, territories were added to cities, but in Gaul cities were added to territories. Meanwhile, the old Egyptian administrative districts known as *nomes* and the temple-cities of Asia Minor and Syria were also transformed into city-states. Whatever the route followed, this cellular structure of city-plus-territory was reproduced all over the Empire. It was more fundamental to the Empire's structure than the provinces.

Those city-states, whatever their traditions or origins, were ruled by councils selected from the landowning classes. Democracies and chiefdoms alike withered. There was no conspiracy and little administrative or fiscal coordination even under Augustus, but soon the government of the Roman Empire resembled a federation of propertied civic elites. Soon the richest members of local elites began to acquire land in the territory of other cities, married the daughters of the richest members of neighbouring cities, sought Roman citizenship, then equestrian and in some cases senatorial status. An imperial aristocracy began to emerge, rooted in provincial elites drawn from the richest families of each city-state. Social mobility was always a dream to many more than would ever achieve it, but it was part of the glue that held the Empire together. Only the wildest zones were left under direct military rule – and in most cases this was only temporary. Centurions on detachment acted as midwives for

The geographer Strabo writing at the time of Tiberius

The Allobroges used to wage war with many thousands of men, now however they farm plains and valleys of the Alps, some of them living in villages but the most important of them live in Vienne, a city which they have made into the capital of their people, although it was once a village.

Strabo is describing the transformation of a Gallic tribe into a city-state, now Savoy.

the emergence of tribal assemblies, forts were eventually replaced by towns in Britain and the Rhineland, and all over the West communities of various kinds – some ancient and urbanised, many not – were transformed into Latin *municipia* like Irni. Cities, ruled by the wealthy, aped Rome, the City, in the provinces.

A SOCIETY GRADED BY WEALTH

Perhaps it is unsurprising that Romans made use of familiar institutions to consolidate their power: most empires do. Late Republican Rome was organised on explicitly hierarchical principles, and that hierarchy was based on wealth. Every five years, two *censors* were elected whose jobs included awarding state contracts to any non-senators wealthy enough to undertake them, and conducting a review of the whole citizen body. How much property you owned determined the 'century' in which you fought and voted, in the complex manner described in Chapter 2. The most senior status group were the *equites* (often awkwardly translated as knights). The magistracies that gave access to the senate were only open to *equites*, and the loss of wealth was as sure a route to expulsion by the censors as was moral inadequacy. Cicero used the term *boni* to mean both those who were good and those who possessed goods. This was not just a political tactic. In his philosophical works, especially *On Duties* and *The Laws*, Cicero presents a reasoned case. Who but the wealthy could resist bribes, or afford the moral and educational formation that made them reliable and competent leaders? His elitism has a logical foundation, even if it strikes us as odd and unattractive.

For similar reasons, the major priesthoods of Republican Rome were monopolised by senators. Like magistrates, the priests were mostly organised in colleges, of pontiffs, of augurs, of *decemviri* and so on. Perhaps one intention was to prevent individuals abusing their power. The rationale of much of Roman constitutional law often seems to have been to limit fighting between aristocratic lineages as much as to ensure their collective power over poorer Romans. But these priesthoods were mostly for life, and the colleges themselves coopted new members to replace those who died. Age, experience and interest dominated the priesthoods just as it did the senate from which priests were drawn. Patricians still had the right to a few priesthoods, but there were few patrician families left; by the second century BC (if not even earlier) most of the Roman aristocracy rated wealth over descent. Plutocracy, not democracy, was the legacy of the Struggle of the Orders.

The constitution was, naturally, a battlefield. At the end of the second century BC the same politicians who promoted tribune power and tried to use the popular assemblies and the *equites* against the senate and its magistrates managed to introduce election to the priesthoods. Caesar became chief pontiff through spectacular bribery in 63 BC. But none of these changes – which sought only to give the people more say in which of the wealthy won political prizes, not to open the competitions up more widely – survived the Republic. Augustus enhanced the dignity of the senate, separating the senatorial class off as a privileged order with special costume and special seats at the theatre. There was also a new, higher property qualification for senators, so differentials of wealth and status were enhanced. Senators were no longer subject to trial before equestrian juries. When Roman aristocrats were given jobs in the provinces, as governors, as commanders of legions and fleets, and as supervisors of taxation and imperial property, senators received the most prestigious posts and *equites* the second-rank provinces and responsibilities. Augustus conducted the same reviews of the upper classes as censors had once done of the whole citizen body. He and his successors distributed most magistracies and priesthoods. Elections were transferred to the senate under Tiberius. Rome's plutocratic hierarchy was entrenched in the principate, until there were grades of equestrian officials whose titles referred to their salary levels. Half-hearted attempts to make these orders hereditary failed rapidly when emperors realised they would have to subsidise indigent would-be senators. It was, in any case, more important to provide opportunities for the richest landowners from Italy and the provinces.

A detail from a panel of the Ara Pacis (Altar of Peace), erected on the Campus Martius to commemorate the victories of Augustus in Gaul and Spain. The sculpted reliefs on three sides of the structure show the emperor and his family processing together with magistrates, lictors, priests and victims for sacrifice. The imagery places the imperial house at the centre of Roman religion, and recruits for Augustus the power and prestige of traditional cult.

A HIERARCHY OF CITIES

Irni was hardly a plutocracy. Its territory was perhaps only a few hundred square kilometres in extent. But the template constitution had been designed to apply to cities of all sizes. It was probably developed from models drawn up in the Augustan age that themselves grew out of a tradition extending back to the Roman and Latin colonies of the middle Republic. As a result, the *Lex Irnitana* describes a city that is a miniature of Rome. Magistrates were elected annually and in colleges, but two *duoviri* and two *aediles* were enough. Every five years there would be a census conducted by special magistrates. Ex-magistrates formed a council, called a *curia* rather than a senate, with extensive powers. There were property qualifications, rules for Roman-style juries and limits on the amount the community could borrow. There was an annual cycle of *ludi* (games on the traditional Roman model over which magistrates presided), in which the emperors and the *Penates*, the collective household gods, were featured prominently. The section on priesthoods is missing, but the functions of the *duoviri* include an oversight of civic religion. Rules for elections were provided, regulations about building, against food speculation and so on. The rudiments of civil law are provided for, but a telling paragraph informs citizens that where the civil code is deficient, things should be decided as if the Irnitani were subject to Roman civil law. As if, that is, they were real Roman citizens.

Historians have not yet reached agreement on the precise ramifications of the civic status of the ordinary Irnitani. But one central point is clear. Holding a magistracy entitled an Irnitanan to Roman citizenship, and this status was shared with his immediate kin. 'Latin' communities like Irni, then, operated as machines that disseminated Roman citizenship among the propertied classes of the western provinces. Along with service in the auxiliary detachments of the army and certain kinds of manumission, political service must have accounted for the majority of enfranchisements before Caracalla extended a somewhat debased kind of citizenship to virtually the entire free population of the Empire in the so-called Antonine Constitution of 212. 'Latin' in this context, then, is a new usage to describe a halfway house between being a Roman citizen and being a foreigner, a 'peregrine'.

Latin communities of one kind or another spread through Rome's western provinces. There were also other kinds of cities. Peregrine cities had the same responsibilities for tax collection and law and order, but without the same rewards for their elites. A few, like Athens, had privileges, giving them some autonomy in their law codes. Colonies, fewer in number and comprised entirely of Roman citizens, were subject to Roman laws. The same was true of all the Italian communities following Julius Caesar's completion of the mass enfranchisement of the Italians which started after the Social War.

Much of our understanding of how these communities differed in practice is obtained from accounts of promotions. Many peregrine cities wished to become Latin *municipia* or *civitates liberae* (Free Cities), while many Latin cities sought colonial status. Where we have evidence that individual communities changed status, political loyalty usually figures as one recommendation, but a sense that these areas now enjoyed civilised lifestyles (as judged by Roman standards, that is) was also important. Just as for individuals, a promotion of civic status was a powerful inducement to loyalty; just as for individuals, the emperors kept close control of the promotion of urban communities.

A view of the Acropolis of Athens, built in the fifth century BC, with in the foreground the Odeon built by the second century AD Athenian millionaire Herodes in memory of his Roman wife Regilla. Athens was a 'free city' within the empire, meaning it enjoyed its own constitution and notional autonomy in many areas, but successive emperors – Hadrian above all – intervened in civic politics, and bestowed on the city privileges and monuments in recognition of its role as a centre of the Greek culture.

THE PROCESS OF URBANISATION

The process by which communities came to converge on Roman norms can also be traced archaeologically. Roman urbanisation is discussed in detail in Chapter 9, but it is worth pointing out here some of the key features. First, the creation of new cities on Roman lines hardly begins before the 40s BC and in most areas is a phenomenon of the Augustan period. Second, the sequence was broadly the same in all areas. Public monuments were the first structures to be built. Even the street grid often came later, leaving some temples and *fora* slightly oddly located in their cities. Urban populations began to expand from the beginning, but most early Roman cities began as clusters of traditional housing around new-style temples. Only later did Roman-style houses emerge. Third, the process of town building took several generations, not least because early forum complexes and temples were often replaced on a grand scale in the second century. Fourth, the process was fabulously expensive, involving imported architects and craftsmen as well as materials in many areas. Architectural style allows us to map the way Italian architects moved out into neighbouring provinces at the beginning of the principate to design the first generation of provincial Roman cities. The process can also be traced in the opening up of new quarries, in the setting up of kilns to make tiles and in the spread of new materials like brick and concrete and new techniques such as vaulting and underfloor heating. Many people must have grown rich from this building boom.

This 'typical' sequence was not always followed, even in the West. A few cities were spectacular failures, a cluster of public monuments surrounded by hectares and hectares of vacant lots. Others developed in a quite unexpected way – London is a good example – because their location on communications routes made them wealthy. Egyptian *nome* capitals gradually built classical-style temples, and town planning on Roman lines emerged slowly. The most ancient Greek cities – Athens and Ephesus for instance – already had their great monumental centres, but new quarters developed with buildings constructed on a grander scale than had ever before been possible. Some ancient cities were remodelled on Roman lines: Corinth and Carthage, both destroyed in 146 BC, became the sites of spectacular new colonies in the late first century BC, but retained a few traces of their pre-destruction organisation.

Cities were not the only sites at which these building processes took place. All Roman cities had public cults, and often these took place at sanctuaries on the edge of cities or quite distant from them. Eleusis, a regional Attic sanctuary, developed as a world-famous shrine. More humbly, many British and Gallic sanctuaries were located on ancient places of cult remote from the new civic centre. In all these centres too we can often observe the same sequences of building. Neither the archaeological chronology nor that of the constitutional development of each community is usually well enough known to show for certain whether civic promotion was followed by periods of building, or whether some communities could build themselves into the sort of places emperors promoted. But Greek and Roman writers made the association between civic building and a mature political culture, and saw urban monuments as some proof of the civilised nature of their builders. Those associations were old ones in classical culture; they can be found in Homer's *Iliad* as easily as in Tacitus's *Agricola*.

The great building campaigns that created the monumental remains through which we often imagine the Roman world are another reflection of plutocracy. As the rich grew richer they used this style of benefaction to display their civic feeling, to advertise their adherence to Roman values and to demonstrate how much richer they were than their fellow *decuriones*. Western aristocrats who sponsored such building programmes were showing how well they had learned the lessons of Roman education, and followed the hints of governors like Agricola. Easterners simply displayed wealth. Technical advances are part of the explanation of why Romano-Greek cities were so much more splendid than their classical predecessors. Greater distances could be spanned, better stone was often available. But the key factor was the concentration of wealth in the hands of a smaller and smaller proportion of the population. Classical Athens had maybe 600 families rich enough to take on burdens like paying for a chorus or a warship. By Hadrian's day, the Athenian millionaire Herodes was able to build half a dozen monuments that dwarfed the Parthenon, a monument that had been funded by the resources of the entire Athenian Empire. In all the great cities of the east, the story was the same. The great cities grew, the small ones withered and the super-rich won the friendship of emperors.

The emperors fostered the spread of city-states and the urbanisation of their capitals for a variety of reasons, some practical and some sentimental. The reproduction of Rome in the provinces was reassuring. When the new elites behaved like those of Republican Rome, and in accordance with civilised values, it was easy to believe in their loyalty to the Empire. Cities also provided the essential infrastructure needed to govern the Empire – or rather, not to have to govern it. One of the striking revelations from Lex Irnitana is the almost complete absence of mentions of Roman officials – the governors, procurators, quaestors and judicial officials, imperial freedmen and legates who represented Rome in the provinces. Irni was clearly designed to be as self-sufficient as possible. Governors exercised a hands-off supervision of such communities.

The emperors governed a population of between 50 and 100 million people through a few hundred aristocratic amateur officials, a few thousand imperial slaves and freedmen and whatever soldiers could be spared from an army of around one-quarter of a million based mostly on the frontiers. Cities were essential because their landowning aristocracies carried most of the responsibility for ensuring peace in the provinces and the delivery of taxes. In return, Rome rarely meddled in the internal affairs of the city-states. The growing wealth of many of these local elites strongly suggests the bargain was made at the expense of the free, semi-free and servile populations of the Empire, and that the price they paid was sometimes a very high one. Systematic impoverishment and, as new research shows, widespread malnutrition seem to have been quite common. Certainly the land-registers that survive from late antiquity sometimes show terrifying inequalities in wealth. In fourth-century Hermopolis in Egypt, the eight richest landowners together owned more than a third of the land, and another third was divided among just thirty-eight others. Even within the decurial class, in other words, vast disparities of wealth built up under Roman rule.

'My lord, the Prusans have a public bath: it is old and decrepit. They are very keen to rebuild it and in my view you could reasonably grant their petition. The money is available, partly from the money I have already begun to claim back from individuals in debt to the town, and partly since the citizens are willing to divert to this project money normally earmarked for free olive oil. Most importantly, this scheme will adorn the town and contribute to the splendour of your reign.'

A provincial governor passes on the request of a city in Bithynia to be allowed to undertake new public building.

ROMAN FAMILIES

The Lex Irnitana shows a special concern that the new constitution would not disturb the existing rights of the Irnitani, rights such those enjoyed by a father over his children, a patron over his clients or a master over his slaves. Being elected *duovir* might win you Roman citizenship, but would not diminish your father's authority over you. This is not surprising. Cicero was not alone in considering property rights to be fundamental to a civilised society, and the rights of the head of a household, the *paterfamilias*, were largely property rights. The family was a central concern of the Roman civil law on which that of Irni was based. It was also featured prominently in the school texts through which the children of western aristocracies learned Latin, and in many of the rhetorical exercises they practised as adolescents. Myths about the family made up a great part of the traditions of early Rome. The semi-legendary fifth-century BC heroine Verginia was slain by her father to preserve her chastity, while the equally celebrated fourth-century BC military hero Manlius Torquatus executed his son for fighting a duel against orders; and there was also the fratricide of Rome's legendary founder, Romulus.

Another sign of the centrality of the family in Roman thought was that the language of family relations was widely used to express other relationships. Deities old and new were often worshipped as Mother or Father. Imported Cybele was the 'Great Mother of the Gods'. There were older cults of Mater Matuta and Liber Pater, and Jupiter was often 'Father Jupiter'. On earth, senators were formally addressed as *patres conscripti*, Conscript Fathers, as if the state were merely an association of heads of households. One of the greatest honours for men was to be hailed as *pater patriae*, Father of the Fatherland. Cicero and Caesar won this honour, and the emperors added it to their titles. The empress Agrippina was known formally as *mater castrorum*, Mother of the Camps. Dedications to deities in the third century often begin, 'In Honour of the Divine Family...', meaning the imperial house.

Law defined the family, but family members were also drawn together by common economic interests and common cult. Aristocratic families could provide the basis for political faction, and connections between the families of the wealthy might have political significance as well as financial consequences. The most famous examples are the marriage alliances between Caesar and Pompey and Octavian and Antony that underwrote the first and second triumvirates respectively. Families were often politically divided, of course. The chief enemies of the Gracchi included as many close relatives as did their supporters. And families then as now were often riven with rivalry. In the period when we can best see Roman families under pressure, through the court speeches of Cicero, we see the same struggles over inheritances and contests between children of different marriages that characterise all aristocratic societies. Strong emotional bonds are also sometimes visible, especially between parents and children, but also sometimes between spouses and apparently also between ex-slaves and their former masters. Cicero's correspondence offers a rare window onto the emotional dynamics of Roman families. Often, they seem quite like our own. Roman family history often feels like an exercise in deciding how far all families are alike, and how much is peculiar to those of any given time, place or culture.

Let us begin with the peculiar. The Roman term *familia* denoted, in its most formal sense, a group of adults and children all subject in a legal and social sense to one man, the *paterfamilias*. This man usually had no living father or grandfather, and most or all of his descendants were under his *potestas*, his legal power or authority. Up to a point, archaic Roman law had dealt with relations between heads of household, leaving them to control their own family members. So all the slaves of the household were also part of the *familia*, and nearly all those who had once been its slaves but were now free. One result was that by the early Empire, some *familiae* included hundreds of people. The *familia Caesaris*, the emperor's *familia*, numbered thousands. Formally, the *paterfamilias* owned all the property in the family, and his power over them extended to legal jurisdiction: even under the early Empire it was possible for a father to convene a family court and try one of his children.

There were only a few ways to leave the *potestas* of one's *paterfamilias*, and all required his consent. Some forms of marriage transferred the woman to her husband's *familia*, but the form that became increasingly common from the late Republic on did not. A father might consent to one of his sons being adopted into another *familia*, usually as an adult in order to provide an heir for the adopter and cement a political bond. Scipio Aemilianus was the means by which the two great warrior dynasties of the Cornelii Scipiones and the Aemilii Paulli were allied. Vestal virgins were transferred to the *potestas* of the chief Pontiff. Disinheritance was possible, but rare. Roman courts had a strong presumption in favour of the rights of natural children. Only the death of a *paterfamilias* changed everything. Each of his children, daughters as well as sons, received a roughly equal share of the property, and each son became a *paterfamilias* in his own right. Daughters and widows had some financial independence. After Augustus, those who had given birth to enough children could in effect head their own households.

So much for theory – or rather, for myth. The large family rotating around a stern, domineering *paterfamilias* is a powerful image of patriarchal power, but it is not historically plausible. To begin with, it was impractical for adult children to depend absolutely on their father financially. Roman law admitted the idea of a *peculium*, a portion of property a

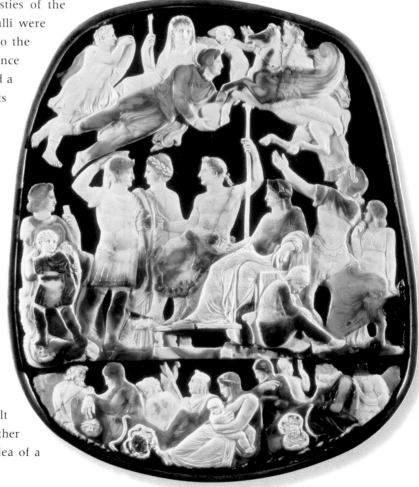

Augustus and his wife Livia, shown in a sardonyx cameo made in about AD 40. The imperial couple are shown surrounded by members of their family and (bottom right) representatives of the nations defeated by Rome during Augustus's reign. The close relationship between the emperor's family and the Roman state was a common theme in Roman art.

ROMAN LAW

Law is perhaps Rome's most important legacy. Roman law was fundamental to mediaeval intellectual culture, and played a crucial role in the Renaissance. It remains today the basis of many legal systems around the world. Mediaeval scholars knew it through the great compilations made for the sixth-century Byzantine emperor Justinian. His *Digest* is still our most important source for law, and hence also for Roman notions of the family, of citizenship and much else. There are also a number of documents, such as the records of a freedman family involved in trade in the port of Puteoli on the Bay of Naples, that show law being used by individuals well below the level of the élite.

The classical period of Roman law stretched from the late Republic until the early third century AD. In the second century BC there emerged for the first time in history legal experts (the jurists), and law itself appeared as a distinct discipline. Other ancient societies had laws, indeed many legal systems survived under the Empire and were used by those who were not Roman citizens. But the idea of law as a potentially coherent body of knowledge was new. Law was generated by popular assemblies, by the edicts of magistrates and also those of the emperors. The *Digest* consists largely of excerpted learned opinions about difficult cases, most of them hypothetical. Around two fifths of it comes from the works of Domitius Ulpianus, a praetorian prefect who wrote several hundred books explaining Roman law largely for the new citizens of the Empire. Most were written in the five years following Caracalla's *Constitutio Antoniniana* of 212 AD in which universal citizenship was granted to all free residents of the Empire.

Much of the law we have is concerned with property, hence the great amount that deals with slavery. Trade and inheritance, marriage, trusts, sales and leases also feature prominently. So too do the administrative duties of various magistrates, many of whom were themselves engaged in making law through the formulary procedure in which a magistrate resolved disputes by issuing a statement (a formula) of what was at issue and appointed an arbitrator. The jurists developed a range of flexible procedures and instruments, including standard contracts for sales and leases. Notions like 'legal fiction' and the idea that corporations have a legal existence of their own originate in Roman law. The greatest Severan jurists, Ulpian, Papinian and Paulus, sought order in the mass of statutes, edicts and earlier writings. They made

MAXIMIANVS

This sixth-century AD mosaic lies in the nave of San Vitale in Ravenna. It shows a haloed Justinian and twelve members of his court (thus reinforcing the concept of divine kingship). In 530 AD Justinian set up a commission of sixteen lawyers to order and codify the findings of legal experts (the *iurisconsulti*) who had been active during the second and third centuries AD. The result was the *Digest*. This work, along with a legal textbook entitled the *Insitutes*, formed the basis of a unified body of law which heavily influenced legal systems all over the world.

some use of Greek philosophy, especially Stoicism, and their writing was influenced by the rhetorical education of their day. Although their concerns were essentially pragmatic, they developed general principles such as equity, utility and natural law.

Law was the one great imperial science favoured by Roman intellectuals, and even after the jurists were drawn under the control of the emperors, legal education and the study and profession of law remained dynamic throughout late antiquity.

family member – including a slave – might treat as if it were his or her own. Burial inscriptions, house architecture and anecdotes from literature alike all strongly suggest that most Romans lived in nuclear families, and were close to their siblings and spouses even if they belonged to different *familiae*. Those historians and writers who tell stories of the strictness of antique fathers, or describe how a contemporary father convened a family court in response to some misdemeanour, do so because this sort of behaviour was exceptional in their own day. Finally, the low life expectancy that was common to everyone in antiquity made sure that few men lived long enough to torment their adult children for long.

All the same, the institutionalisation of the Roman family had a number of important consequences. Take the case of those women who remained in their father's family after their marriage. Each would take with her her share of the inheritance (as a dowry), but her husband had no access to it. If the couple divorced, she would take her property back with her to live on, or to serve as dowry for another marriage. If she died, it reverted to her birth family. Only if she had children would that property leave her own family and enter that of her husband, and then only through her children's inheritance of it. Remarriage was apparently very common, at least in those sectors of society the surviving evidence allows us to observe. Aristocratic women generally married for the first time soon after puberty, men not until they were in their mid-twenties. High death rates made it unlikely that both partners would survive to old age. Besides, divorce was easy to arrange and no stigma attached to it. It is not unusual to read of men or women with two or three marriages. Against this background, the continuing strong ties of each partner with his or her birth family was emotionally as well as financially practical.

A mural painting from Pompeii showing merchants in the city's forum. The lack of a legal institution in Rome that matched the modern company meant that most trade, industrial and farming enterprises were managed by families – which might include large numbers of trusted slaves with particular business or managerial skills.

THE FAMILY AS MANAGEMENT UNIT

Perhaps even more important was the fact that slaves belonged to a *familia*. As in many societies, buying slaves offered one way to change the composition of a family unit. Well-off peasants could use it to increase the workforce available for family-run farms or other enterprises. Cato the Elder, writing in the early second century BC, describes how richer farmers might employ twenty-odd slaves to work medium-sized farms. Archaeological survey has traced the extension and expansion of this villa-based agriculture in many parts of Italy through the last century BC, and a few examples, such as the villa at Settefinestre in Tuscany, have been excavated.

By the early Empire, members of the equestrian and senatorial elite generally owned multiple properties dispersed across Italy and sometimes the provinces too. These farms not only produced a vast variety of agricultural goods for sale, but might also exploit woodland or claypits or lakes. Coastal villas might have associated fish-processing plants, there were ranches on which large herds of sheep were kept for wool, and so on. Urban properties were also accumulated, *insulae* (multi-storey residential blocks) for letting, *tabernae* (retail shops and food-outlets) and productive enterprises like *fullonicae* where clothes were processed. The economic affairs of a wealthy aristocrat were potentially very complex.

It was in the slave *familia* that the wealthy found the means of managing these scattered interests. Probably it began in agriculture, where a trusted former slave might be appointed as a bailiff to manage the farm of the absentee landlord. Cato describes the bailiff's role in detail, supervising the workforce, making sure each task was done at the appropriate time and looking after the equipment and installations of the farm. The farm-manager would have to be literate and numerate. He also needed to be allowed limited financial authority, especially since these farms relied on equipment that had to be purchased in the market, and on casual labour for periods like the vintage when the slave staff was insufficient. The existence of trained and trusted urban slaves and ex-slaves provided landowners with the ideal managerial class. Slaves and ex-slaves also acted as resident managers for *insulae*, collecting rent and ensuring the building was kept in good condition. Others ran shops under arrangements that allowed master and slave or ex-slave to share the profits. The archaeology of the Vesuvian cities of Pompeii and Herculaneum show numerous examples of rich urban mansions hidden behind street fronts made up of rows of tiny retail outlets and food shops. Ex-slaves might even set up small businesses at a distance. Production of the red-gloss pottery known as Samian Ware or *terra sigillata* was mostly scattered into small-scale workshops, which shared the use of kilns and perhaps marketing. Slave labour seems to have been particularly important in the earliest stages of this industry.

Roman law was used by the propertied classes to extend even further the use of the family as an institution of management. From the mid-second century BC, landowners might appoint agents who could enter into contracts on their behalf. This reflected needs that were both pragmatic and ethical. Complex operations, such as the manufacture of wine and or clay containers on estates in Tuscany, their transportation down to the coast, then by sea to southern France and their resale

He also became involved in what is regarded as the most hateful kind of money-lending, that is funding maritime trade. He insisted those to whom he lent capital should have many partners. When the number of them and their ships came to be fifty, he himself took one share through his ex-slave Quintio, who was to sail with the adventurers, and take a part in all their proceedings. That way there was no danger of losing his whole stock, but only a small proportion, and that with a prospect of great profit. In the same way he lent money to any of his slaves who wished to borrow it, with which they bought other young slaves, whom, when they had taught and bred up at his charges, they would sell again at the end of the year. Some of them Cato would keep for himself, giving just as much for them as another had offered.

Plutarch describes some of Cato the Elder's business deals.

inland, could be achieved without the senatorial owner ever leaving his mansion on the Palatine. Equally, certain economic activities – the retail trade for example, or running a brothel or a tannery – were not those in which Roman gentlemen wished to be seen to participate. But a former slave could undertake them on behalf of a former master, using his capital and perhaps even his property.

The flexibility of the Roman family meant that even the largest enterprises could be efficiently managed without the need for corporations in a modern sense. Neither banks nor companies existed in antiquity on a scale larger than a family firm. Nor did a class of paid clerks or secretaries appear to help the rich manage their affairs. This does not mean, naturally, that being a slave was a privileged or comfortable position.

GOVERNING FAMILIES

It was only natural that when an aristocrat went out to govern a province he would often take with him trusted freedmen and slaves, along with his close family and perhaps the sons of his friends, who would act as his staff. For a slave, becoming the trusted assistant of a powerful master might offer the best chance available for advancement in the Roman world. But the Romans made use of slaves precisely because they did have such tight control over them. Slaves could be beaten or tortured, they were always sexually available to their masters and they had no rights to a family of their own. Cato explicitly recommends allowing male slaves access to female slaves for sex as an inducement to good behaviour. Slaves did have children, but masters decided whether to raise or expose them. And slave unions could be split up by sale, or simply by moving slaves between properties. Most of what a master could do to a slave he could do to an ex-slave as well. The relatively comfortable ex-slaves we see acting as managers, married and with children and slaves of their own, were the top of a social pyramid of the unfree that began much lower down. (For further discussion on slavery *see* Chapter 6, pages 128–135)

The family was the basic managerial unit of Roman society, so it is not surprising to see it playing a role in the running of Rome's Empire. It should be clear by now that the Roman state deliberately employed various mechanisms to prevent the emergence of anything resembling a civil service or bureaucracy. Public contractors remained important even after they stopped collecting the land-tax, and the landowning classes of allied and subject communities were given major responsibilities. Watching over all this were the aristocratic governors and procurators, promagistrates or imperial appointees serving short periods in each post. They took with them the skills they had acquired in military service, as junior officers and in running their own complex affairs. Unsurprisingly they also took with them portions of their families. Ex-slaves and slaves accompanied Republican governors, not just as attendants but as secretaries and assistants. Pompey's freedmen were accorded extravagant honours by Greek cities they visited on his behalf. If a governor had adult children, they might accompany him too, and a general would often take the children of his friends and political allies. Caesar's campaigns in Gaul provide a good example. The chance to participate was a chance to become rich, and Crassus's son and Cicero's younger brother both benefited. More controversial were the activities of governor's wives in the provinces, forming their own lesser friends and developing their own networks of influence. But the essential principle that governors acted through their own, rather than public, slaves and assistants was unchallenged.

A natural culmination of this was the part played by Augustus's own family in managing the Empire. Just as his adopted sons commanded the greatest armies, so in the early years his ex-slave procurators are found gathering taxes and acting as secretaries. Suetonius records how, along with his will, Augustus left a brief account of the whole Empire in which were recorded army strengths and deployments, the size of the Empire's reserves and what was owed in taxation. The emperor added the names of the slaves and ex-slaves from whom more information could be obtained. The *familia Caesaris* included within it a vast slave and ex-slave bureaucracy. The power of the greatest imperial freedmen, power that derived from the wealth they had been given and from their influence

with the emperors, was bitterly resented by aristocratic writers. Claudius, who had been made emperor by the army and against the senate's wishes, rubbed the aristocracy's noses in their powerlessness by having the Senate grant the freedman Pallas extraordinary honours. Aristocratic writers like Pliny and Tacitus retaliated (some decades later) by abusing Pallas's memory and claiming that Claudius's slaves had ruled him, even choosing his third wife for him after having her predecessor executed. But for the emperor, as for Republican magistrates, slaves were the perfect assistants. Many were well educated, numerate and experienced managers as well as trusted. More important, their power depended entirely on the emperor's will, so their loyalty was guaranteed.

A Roman marble plaque from Ephesus in Turkey, showing the adoption by Antoninus Pius (centre) of Marcus Aurelius (left) and Lucius Verus (right). The adoption as heir and successor of a distantly related or unrelated adult was not uncommon among Rome's rulers; it emphasises both the importance of family ties in Roman society and the instability of imperial succession.

IMPERIAL ROMAN SOCIETY

A funerary relief of a Roman couple found near the temple of Apollo at Scasato in the ancient city of Falerii (modern Civita Castellana, in Lazio). As this image suggests, the solidarity of the nuclear family may have been more important in practice for most Romans than the theoretical and legal ideal of an extended family with an autocratic *paterfamilias*.

Aristotle's *Politics,* written in the fourth century BC, had discussed the political composition of Greek society by building up the analysis from the family through citizenship and slavery to a discussion of the central institutions that made it a democracy, an oligarchy or a tyranny. Those categories remain good ones for looking at Roman society – as Polybius recognised – as long as some key differences are noted. The Roman family was structured in a unique way, focussed out from the partly mythic, but partly actual, figure of the *paterfamilias,* and using his connections with kinsmen and friends, slaves and ex-slaves to form a fundamental building block for Roman society. Although Roman law continued to evolve up until the period of the classical jurists that culminated in the early third century AD, these fundamental customs and principles were laid down early. In the conditions of imperialism – the only condition in which we observe Rome clearly – the aristocratic family in particular came to assume new roles. It is not an exaggeration to say it became the principle means through which large scale economic activity was coordinated.

Within the cities of the Empire, the families of the rich jostled for position. Formally, only Roman citizens could have Roman families. Most families in the Empire were therefore not technically Roman until the Edict of Caracalla. But Latin communities and many peregrine ones seem to have had Roman-style familial institutions, and so too did the Jewish communities of the Diaspora; Greek families also often behaved like Roman ones. Women, for example, often seem to be thrust into the limelight in the East and in the West as benefactors and priestesses, partly in order to represent their families when there were no males of suitable age to play those roles. Greek and Roman aristocrats intermarried, Greek dynasts like Herodes employed freedmen as agents, and so on. From the second century AD, more and more Greek aristocrats advertise their Roman citizenship, and a few serve as senators and even governors. Slavery remained ubiquitous, and Roman habits of manumission become widespread. Families and cities come together in the landowning civic elites, but sometimes clashed, as families spent in one city the money they had raised from several, or tried to shake off their civic burdens by moving their efforts to the centre of power. Emperors resisted this, but not completely effectively.

At the level of the Empire's landowning classes, this broad social uniformity contrasts with the persistence of cultural differences. Most obviously, there was the apparent survival of a strong sense among many Greeks that their Hellenic heritage in some way mattered more than current political loyalties. By the second century, there was a western echo, a community among Latin-writing intellectuals. It is very difficult to see, however, any cases where these perceived cultural or ethnic differences ever over-ruled class-based sympathies. Rich Greeks, in other words, acted as if they had more in common with rich westerners than with poorer Greeks. That community was based partly on the broad similarity of institutions across the Mediterranean world. Greek and Roman notions of the city, of family and of cult were not identical, but they were close enough. The subtle spread of Roman versions of these fundamental building blocks helped to engineer a social consensus at the top, against which diverse local practices and ideas further down the social scale had no chance of prevailing.

A wall painting from Pompeii, showing a group of elite Roman women at leisure. The ruling classes of Campanian cities like Pompeii were descended from a mixture of Oscan landowners and Roman colonists, their official documents were in Latin but their houses, dress, cults and pastimes included elements derived from Egypt, Greece, and Asia Minor as well. Campanian society is unique, but we still find in it typically Roman institutions including the family, slavery and imperial cult.

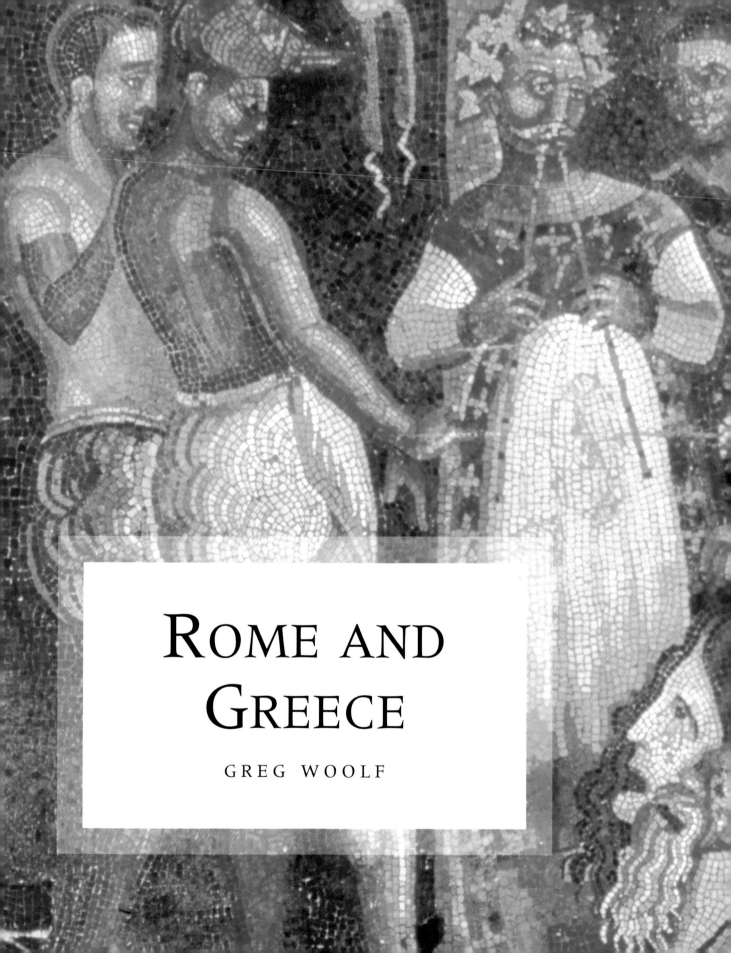

ROME AND GREECE

GREG WOOLF

ROME AND GREECE

There was no Rome before Greece. Objects of Greek manufacture have been found in the earliest levels of the city of Rome to be explored archaeologically, so the Romans can have had no sudden encounter with the Greeks. It could fairly be said that the world into which the Romans first appeared, through which they spread and over which they finally achieved domination, was always a Greek world. Yet the relationship between Romans and Greeks did change over time, until each identity had been remodelled largely in relation to the other.

The Mediterranean Sea was bound together by trade, travel and colonisation before the traditional date of Rome's foundation. Greeks were participating in these ventures from the eighth century BC, and Greek cities were common from France to Syria and on all the Mediterranean islands, wherever other urban civilisations, like those of the Phoenecians, Etruscans or Egyptians, did not exclude them.

Greek identity itself was not a fixed concept: it varied with time. Romans after the time of Varro believed that Romulus had lived in the middle of the eighth century BC. At this time, the Greeks had already explored most of the Mediterranean and were beginning to settle sites from southern France to the Black Sea. Every coast and island of the Aegean had had a Greek-speaking population for much longer. The Assyrian monarchs knew the Greeks as raiders and mercenaries; others had welcomed them as traders. Around the eighth century BC, the Greeks had begun to live in cities, some with lawcodes and constitutions. Rome's northern neighbours, the Etruscans, had encountered Greeks coming in search of iron and trading pottery, though they had never actually settled in

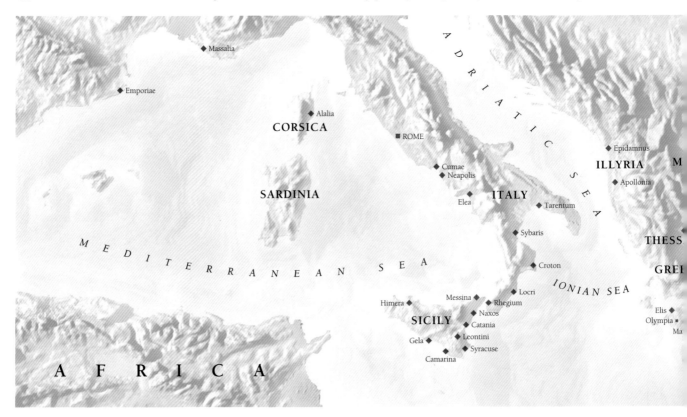

Tuscany. It seems that in general Greek settlement avoided, or was excluded from, regions where states were already established, including those settled by the peoples now known generically as Phoenicians, from whom the Greeks had acquired the alphabet and perhaps their navigational skills. But there were Greek cities just to the south of Rome in the bay of Naples, and Greek traders everywhere. Greece was never far away.

By the fifth century BC, the age of the early Republic, some of the Greek states were already regional powers. Struggles for primacy in Sicily had, by the end of the century, drawn several Greek cities into a lengthy conflict – the Peloponnesian War – which stretched as far as the Persian Empire and had at its heart the rivalry between Athens and Sparta for control of the Aegean world. This 'classical' Greek world was structured around city-states, all notionally autonomous and sovereign within their borders, just like nation-states today. Citizens of Athens and Sparta, Leontini and Ephesos and the rest had fierce loyalty to their own cities. Fighting together, sharing laws and participating to varying degrees in political life, the free adult males of these Greek cities celebrated local identities founded in myth and cult, in a geography of memory and a common history. Citizens were usually the only people allowed to own land in a city's territory or to hold office, and most free Greek men married women from their own community.

Much of this could be said of the Romans too, and probably of many other urbanised Mediterranean peoples. Most of their voices have been lost, either because they recorded little or because their eventual Roman conquerors did not value and preserve their traditions as they did those of the Greeks. One thing that distinguished the citizens of Athens, Sparta and the rest, however, was that in addition to local loyalties they shared a

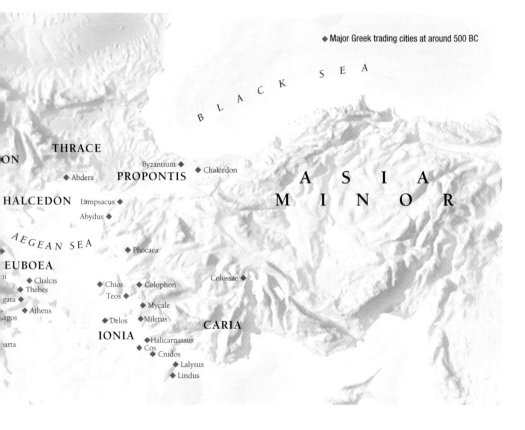

◆ Major Greek trading cities at around 500 BC

strong sense of being Greek. That identity, like their local civic identities, was founded in a shared myth-history and a belief in common descent. A shared language was also important for some, shared cults for many. But there was no complete consensus over which of these criteria were most important. Much of the prose and poetry written in the fifth century, was preoccupied with the question, 'What does it mean to be Greek?'.

Greekness might be manifested in different ways. There were common 'panhellenic' sanctuaries. Some were oracular like Dodona; others, like Olympia, the sites of great games. Delphi, for many Greeks the centre of the world, had both oracles and games. Greek writers shared a respect for Homer and Hesiod (even when it was manifested in criticism of them). And the Greeks shared more with each other than they did with those they regarded as non-Greeks – that is, as barbarians. The Mediterranean was a world of intense exchange, but somehow exchange had a different quality between Greeks. Institutions and festivals were often borrowed or adapted from neighbouring city-states; there were also periods of close cultural competition between them, for example in temple-building in the sixth century BC. When a Persian expeditionary force tried and failed to conquer the area we call mainland Greece, the Greek world at last found a national myth, despite the fact that many Greeks had fought on the Persian side and remained under Persian rule long after the war was over.

A portrait bust of Alexander the Great, now in the Capitoline Museum, Rome. The youthful, muscular appearance, head turned slighty to the left, leonine hair and upturned eyes are all standard features of Alexander portraits. Alexander fascinated Roman generals, and in their different ways Pompey, Caesar and Augustus all tried to rival him. Greek writers under Roman rule, on the other hand, might refer to him as 'our emperor'.

THE LIMITS OF GREEKNESS

The limits of Greekness – like those of any ethnic identity – were open to debate. Some Greek writers thought the Romans themselves were Greeks. The linguistic similarities between Greek and Latin, similarities we now regard as a feature of their common descent from Indo-European, offered some support for this theory: after all, there were several Greek language groups with distinct vocabularies and accents, and the Latin-speakers might simply be another such group. But this was a minority view, and it only emerged in Greek thought as a kind of rationalisation of the Roman conquest of the Greek world.

More controversial was the question of which of the peoples of northern and western Greece were real Greeks. They spoke languages related to Greek, but few lived in recognisable city-states or shared Greek festivals like the Thesmophoria (the ancient festival dedicated to Demeter and Persephone, in which women only could participate and staged throughout the classical Greek world), or sacrificed in the correct way. Notions of 'half-Greeks', of degenerate Greeks and of barbarian peoples ruled by Greek monarchies circulated among the Greeks of the fourth century BC. Such questions were heightened in importance by the rise of the most powerful kingdom of the northern Balkans, Macedon.

It was a Macedonian king, Alexander the Great, who destroyed this Greek world at the end of the fourth century. The great conqueror's

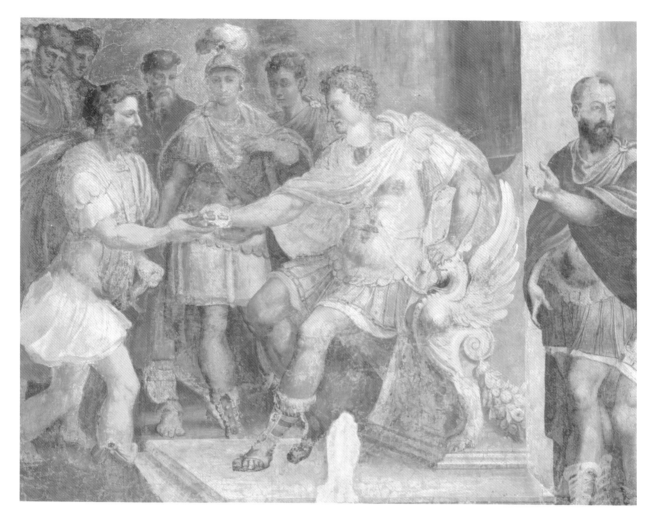

first victims were the Greek cities of the southern Balkans. Levying Greek troops to supplement his army, he made the Persian empire his next target. Greeks fought on both sides in every major battle fought by Alexander, but his victories were represented as a triumph of Greek culture. Around the edge of the Greek world – a border region that included southern Italy (sometimes called *Magna Graecia*, Great Greece) and Sicily – city-state politics survived, but for the rest of antiquity, most Greeks would be ruled by kings. After Alexander's death in 323 BC, his Macedonian generals divided up his great empire. Their successor states remained the superpowers of their day, and the Greek world now extended from the Hindu Kush to the Pyrenees.

The period from Alexander's death to the Roman conquest of the East is today known as the Hellenistic period. Kingdoms were created in Egypt and Syria, in Asia Minor and modern Afghanistan. Macedonia itself remained a great power, and some neighbouring nations – the Epirotes and Illyrians in the West, the Armenians and other peoples bordering the Black Sea – created kingdoms on much the same lines.

Most of these kingdoms combined features of Macedonian kingship with Persian institutions; the largest of them relied on hereditary Macedonian armies and many made considerable use of Greek colonists and mercenaries. At the centre of each

A fresco portrait of Alexander from the Spada palace, Italy, painted in the seventeenth century. The image of Alexander as a geat king remained a powerful one long after the end of the Roman Empire.

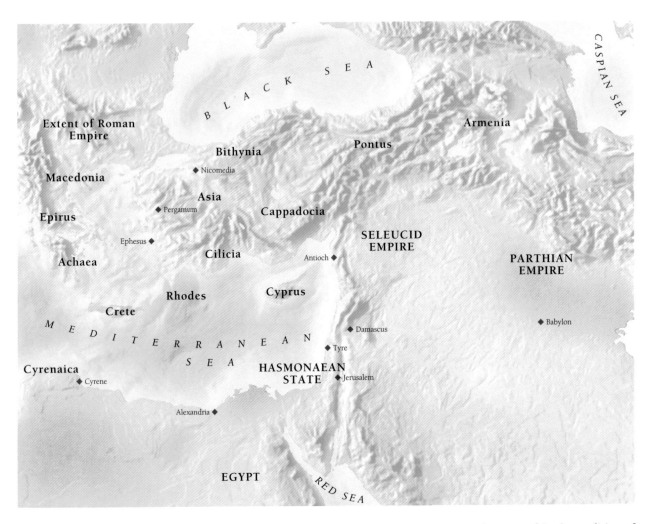

By the beginning of the first century BC, the Roman Empire had already made serious inroads into the legacy kingdoms of Alexander the Great. Macedonia was conquered in 148 BC and the rest of Greece two years later. Between 133–103 BC the Romans acquired a sizable chunk of western Asia Minor and subsequently, in 102 BC, established nominal control over the 'pirate coast' of Cilicia.

kingdom was the person of the king, always a great warrior general in the tradition of Alexander, loved by the army, worshipped by his subjects and surrounded by feuding relatives and courtiers. The most powerful of these kings built luxurious capital cities and patronised Greek scholars and poets, sculptors and architects. One explanation for the creation of the Roman principate is the argument that the Romans finally succumbed to the attractions of Hellenistic kingship. Certainly the Greek cities addressed the Roman emperors as *basileus* (the Greek word for king), paid them similar cult and inscribed their names alongside those of Macedonian monarchs, Republican generals and – in one case – a Persian king.

In the Egyptian kingdom created by Alexander's general Ptolemy, Greeks came to form something like a hereditary status group, distinguished from Egyptians by tax privileges and by their monopoly of posts in the government. When Augustus made Ptolemaic Egypt a province on the death of Cleopatra, he changed many parts of the country's government, but Greek speakers continued to dominate the administration and the cities. The same phenomenon occurred, in different ways, throughout Rome's eastern provinces. In effect, Rome ruled the East through Greek city-states, or rather through their propertied classes.

Where no Greek city-states were available, the Romans were prepared to create them, as Pompey did when he dismantled the kingdom of Pontus and Augustus did in central Anatolia. East of the Adriatic, the Roman army and a few colonists spoke and wrote Latin (although increasingly badly in some cases) but countless inscriptions demonstrate that Greek was in effect the official language.

GREEK CULTURE IN THE ROMAN EAST

The cultural life of the Roman East revolved entirely around Greek institutions. Rooted though they were in classical Greek culture, these institutions were not a simple reproduction of those of the fifth and fourth centuries BC. Democracy was missing, for example, as was inter-city warfare, while a standardised high culture, largely based on that of classical Athens, replaced many local variations. Greco-Roman culture included rhetorical displays given by touring sophists; the *gymnasium* where wealthy young men trained and were educated; and the *symposium*, an aristocratic drinking party that involved more or less serious literary and philosophical debates. From Cicero's day on, many young Roman aristocrats spent a year or so in one of the major Greek cities – Athens was the favourite – to study, participate in and become familiar with this culture.

Most splendid and socially inclusive of all these specifically Greek events were the great civic festivals. All Greek cities had annual festivals, but a growing number also hosted *penteric* games, which took place every four years and brought together rituals and processions, tax-free fairs and competitions in athletics, music, poetry and much else. Festivals were usually sponsored by the rich benefactors who seem to have dominated the political lives of many cities. Cities sent embassies to each others' festivals, which also attracted professional competitors, traders and country-dwellers into the town. By the end of the first century AD, several western towns, including Carthage and Rome itself, were staging games of this kind.

One consequence of the high status of Greek culture under Roman rule was that many of Rome's eastern subjects began to discover – or invent – Greek ancestors. Already in the Hellenistic era, there are signs of what some historians have called 'Culture Greeks', meaning those whose claims to descent from Greeks were less than plausible, but who behaved otherwise exactly like Greeks. (This is not to suggest that behaviour rather than descent became the defining feature of Greek identity: the ancient Greeks had a concept of racial identity that rivalled those of many modern racists. Rather, the insistence of some eastern provincials on biological descent from Greek ancestors is one of the clearest signs that they had internalised Greek values.) From all over Roman Asia Minor monumental inscriptions, local coins and festivals emphasised traditional beliefs that passing Greek heroes (Perseus or the Argonauts in the East, Herakles or Odysseus in the West) had founded their city, usually with the help of a local nymph or rescued princess. When cities of indisputable Greekness like Argos or Sparta could be persuaded to underwrite such a claim, their support was advertised prominently. Conformity with Greek cultural norms (as well as wealth) must have helped bolster such claims – but some were apparently adjudicated by the Panhellenion, a cultic association created by the emperor Hadrian, and based in Athens.

GROWING UP WITH THE GREEKS

Romans of the Republic might have been amazed to learn that a Roman Empire would one day spread Greek culture and identity to its greatest extent in the whole of history. After all, weren't the Romans ostentatiously non-Greeks? Didn't Romans celebrate the origins of their city in Virgil's epic story of the emphatically anti-Greek Trojan prince Aeneas?

Even Virgil, however, could not entirely conceal Greek influence in his account of Rome's origins. Much of the *Aeneid* tells the story of Aeneas wandering through the same landscapes as the Greek Odysseus, seeking not a return but a new home, his eyes fixed firmly on the future. Arriving at the site on the Tiber where Rome would once day be founded by his descendants, he finds a group of Arcadians from southern Greece already in residence, led by their king Evander. Nor were these the first Greeks here, for Evander shows Aeneas the site where Herakles (Hercules) had defeated and killed a local monster, Cacus. One reason these myths were incorporated into the *Aeneid* is that they were already well known in Augustan Rome, and like many myths of origin were closely connected with Rome's oldest cults, in this case that of Hercules at the Ara Maxima, the Great Altar.

The Greeks had always been there before. The reliance of the scholars of the late Republic on Greek writers is discussed in Chapter 1. The same applied to their predecessors in the middle Republic. Latin literature originated in the late third century BC. This was several centuries after the first religious inscriptions show that the Romans had first adapted Greek letters to write Latin. Literacy was, thanks to the Greeks, already widespread in the Mediterranean world by the sixth century BC, and Greek letters – themselves based on Near Eastern alphabets – were adapted to write Celtic and Spanish languages as well as Etruscan, Oscan and other Italian languages. Literary works were much rarer, even within the Greek world. It looks very much as if one generation of the aristocratic leaders of the city of Rome decided to create a Latin literature almost overnight. To do this they imported and patronised writers from all over Italy, engaged them to write first loose translations of Greek epic and drama, and then original works in these and other genres.

The prestige of literary production was immense, and we soon find leading Roman aristocrats composing works themselves. One of the most important was Cato the Elder, a much mythologised figure, not least by himself. Politically active through much of the early second century BC, Cato traded on his lack of noble ancestors to present himself as a defender of antique, non-aristocratic Roman culture and morals. The fact that he was one of the greatest orators of his day somewhat undermines this image, as does the clear dependence on Greek models displayed in many of his works. One, the *Origins*, collected foundation legends for a number of Italian peoples and integrated them into a historical account that mentioned no individuals. This is a major contrast with Fabius Pictor's history, written in the previous generation, in which a suspicious number of Roman heroes were members of the Fabian clan. Pictor wrote in Greek, but then Greek was the only language in which literature was produced in the Mediterranean world at that time. Cato's decision to write in Latin was equivalent in significance to the deliberate creation of vernacular literatures in

Concerning those Greeks, Marcus my son, I shall tell you in the proper place what I learned by my own experience in Athens: that it is a good idea to glance at their literature but not to devote yourself to it. I shall convince you that they are a most iniquitous and intractable people, and you may take my word as a word of a prophet; whenever that nation shall bestow its literature upon us it will corrupt everything, and all the sooner if it sends its doctors here. They have conspired among themselves to murder all foreigners with their medicine, a profession which they exercise for money, in order that they may win our confidence and dispatch us all the more easily.

Cato's view of the Greeks, as reported by the Elder Pliny

medieval Europe. Nonetheless, in order to research the *Origins*, Cato must have trawled through a mass of geography, ethnography and local history in Greek.

This cultural process is known as 'appropriation'. The Romans were plundering Greek culture not with the aim of reproducing or imitating it, but in order to make new uses of it and to acquire for themselves the cultural capital it represented. Cato was vociferous in his criticism of Greeks – all Greek doctors were poisoners, he claimed. By asserting that Roman *mores* (that is, traditions as well as morals) provided the basis for a discriminating use of Greek culture, Cato was making a claim that Roman authors would echo through the centuries: Greek culture had much to offer

The Roman poet Virgil composing the *Aeneid*, regarded by Romans as the definitive account of the founding of their city. The poet is inspired by the (Greek) Muses Clio (left), Muse of History, and Melpomene (right), Muse of Tragedy. This mosaic, dating from the early third century AD, is in the Bardo Museum in Tunis.

Rome, but being Roman was far preferable to being Greek. Cicero, producing a Roman version of Greek philosophy, played the same game as Cato. So, in different ways, did all those poets who claimed to be the Roman Homer, Theocritus, Alcaeus or whoever. The greater the amount borrowed, the more important it was to assert that Greek achievements were being surpassed, and that the selection made was a careful one that improved the original.

Many historians have been tempted to plot the story of Romans and Greeks in terms of a modern love story. A first encounter between the two parties makes an immediate impression, but is followed by tragicomic misunderstandings and expressions of antipathy that more and more obviously mask a growing attraction. Eventually there is a rapprochement (Roman literature's Augustan age) and despite last minute difficulties (Nero) there is an eventual happy-ever-after (Hadrian). The reality is more complicated: there were moments of rejection, imitation, appropriation and reconciliation at all periods of the relationship, from archaic Rome to the fifth century AD. Even in Hadrian's day we find Latin writers referring to their predecessors as *nostri* (ours) when they mean to distinguish them from Greeks. Besides, at no point did all Romans think alike about Greek culture, any more than all Greeks thought alike about the Romans.

Roman writers often tell a different – though equally over-simplified – tale of Greek and Roman culture. Horace provides a famous example in a series of poems that present Rome as a rude warrior nation conquering but then seduced by the Greeks, who were culturally more refined. The first Romans to imitate Greek literature had made a mess of it, he suggests, and only he and his contemporaries have succeeded in creating Latin literature that rivals its Greek counterpart. Recent research suggests that Horace, Virgil and even Cicero all claimed, explicitly or implicitly, to be the first reliable translator of Greek literary culture into Latin, partly in order to challenge the canonical status of their predecessors. After all, Ennius had written a great patriotic epic poem in the early second century BC that used the Greek hexameter metre instead of Italian Saturnians and was dedicated to the Greek Muses instead of the Italian Camenae. Ennius too had predecessors, one of whom had written a Latin *Odyssey*. Claiming Greek inspiration, in other words, was a way of establishing prestige in Latin literature. The same argument can be advanced for Horace's attempts to replace Lucilius as the classic satirist, and his predecessors as lyric poets. Interestingly, some of the poets of that earlier generation had called themselves *neoterikoi*, a Greek term meaning 'the New Ones'.

A portrait bust of Marcus Tullius Cicero, sculpted in the 1st-century BC and now in the Capitoline Museum, Rome. Cicero was one of a number of Roman literary figures who each claimed to be the first reliable translator into Latin of Greek literature.

So there was no single turning point, before which Rome was Roman and after which it was half Greek (or 'Hellenised' as some modern writers term it). Narratives of sudden contact nonetheless appealed to some ancient writers. Some postulate a sudden Roman exposure to Greek culture following the sack of Syracuse, the greatest Greek city of Sicily, in 211 BC. The city's Roman conqueror, Marcus Claudius Marcellus, had brought back hundreds of Greek statues to Rome (though this must have provoked controversy, since when Tarentum was sacked a few years later the Roman general responsible refused to do the same). Others suggest that Greek influence can be traced to the booty brought back from Rome's wars against Macedon and Syria, fought during Cato's lifetime. All these were turning points in a sense, but in fact the story of the relationship between Greek and Roman culture is a story made up of turning points. The Romans constantly found themselves 'suddenly Greek' because only by repeatedly being surprised at the foreignness of Greek culture could they remind themselves again and again that they were still Roman.

INCORPORATING THE GREEK

Roman interest in Greek culture was not confined to literature. Greek statues arrived in Rome as booty from at least the third century BC (and possibly a good deal earlier); Metellus Macedonicus created a portico including the first marble temples in the city in 131 BC; Pompey's theatre complex, dedicated in 55 BC, was supposedly modelled on monuments from the Greek city of Miletus, and included a quadriporticus in which were displayed a huge collection of exotic Greek statuary. Marble was the material of choice for civic monuments in the Greek East, where marble supplies were relatively abundant. Augustus boasted (inaccurately) that he had found Rome built of brick and left it built of marble. But it is true that much of the city was rebuilt in his reign in imitation of Hellenistic capitals such as Alexandria and Pergamum.

These were public monuments. Roman aristocrats had been privately collecting and commissioning Greek statuary for their villas throughout the first century BC (Cicero's letters provide evidence of this). The trend continued into the imperial period. Most of our knowledge of Hellenistic and classical Greek art comes from Roman imitations. Occasionally – for instance in a cave at Sperlonga on the Italian coast, at the villa of Chiragan in southern France or at Hadrian's palace at Tivoli – it is possible to observe the vast themed collections amassed by great Roman aristocrats and emperors. By removing these statues from their original context in Greek sanctuaries and public spaces, Romans in effect invented the concept of 'works of art'.

Roman sexuality was also influenced by Greek ideas. Sexual conduct was one of those areas of private life where moral transgressions could damage public reputation and careers. Marital monogamy was the ideal, and female 'virtue' (that is, chastity) in particular is celebrated in many of the myths of early Rome. Already in the middle Republic, some Romans were being more adventurous – at least when outside Rome. Many Republican generals had not only Greek mistresses but also younger male lovers. By the late Republic and Augustan periods, homosexual relations for men were probably common among the educated elite. What was shameful in this period –

to judge from jibes in Catullus and the satirists – was indiscretion, together with a number of specific practices, including being the active partner in oral sex or the passive one in anal intercourse. These attitudes were characteristic of Greek culture. By the early second century AD, conventions had changed again: Suetonius praised Titus for putting away his harem of boy lovers when he became emperor, but Trajan took his with him on campaign, while Hadrian had his most famous male lover, Antinoos, deified and founded a city in memory of him. Moral discourse in all periods revolved around regulating the behaviour appropriate to particular contexts. Suetonius' bad emperors are sexually incontinent, undergo marriages with male lovers, allow themselves to be penetrated. Good emperors may well have mistresses, but respect status and keep non-marital sex in the private sphere.

The history of Roman religion can be written along similar lines. Hercules was not the only Greek figure worshipped in archaic Rome. The temple of Diana on the Aventine was believed to be linked to Ephesian Artemis via a cult at Marseilles. More explicit introductions of Greek cults into Roman public religion begin in the third century with the worship of Asclepius, which was established on the Tiber island in 291 BC, and that of Magna Mater on the Palatine in 204 BC. Her public cult was accompanied by private worship, some of it distinctly un-Roman in character. Not all Greek cults were welcomed into public religion, however, or even tolerated in private. Livy and an inscribed version of a senatorial decree both record attempts to control the private cult of Bacchus in Italy. Greek cults, when introduced to public religion, were usually given a Romanised form. The temple of Magna Mater on the Palatine had an Italianate form, and the goddess was celebrated in traditional Roman games (the Ludi Megalenses); her Roman worshippers were not expected to castrate themselves in an ecstatic trance as her Anatolian ones had done. Yet elements of the alien and Greek were deliberately retained. The exotic costumes and musical instruments of the eunuch priests of Mater Magna can be compared to the sacrifice performed for Aesculapius according to 'the Greek rite' (in fact a Roman invention rather than a faithful imitation of Greek religion). Through all the incorporations of foreign gods that followed, right up to Constantine's innovation of public cult to Christ, elements of their alien origin were retained, even when many of the institutions that framed them were Roman.

This incorporation of Greek and Roman elements into a mixed culture, in which Romans nonetheless never lost sight of what was Greek, was common to many of these exchanges. Typically, new gods were introduced into Republican religion after some crisis or portent had led the senate to order a consultation of the Sibylline books. These oracles, reputedly dating back to the time of Rome's kings, were themselves written in Greek, but had to be interpreted by a college of Roman senatorial priests. Likewise, Greek art was placed in restricted contexts in the city and in the villa. Metellus' portico and Pompey's theatre were both built just outside the sacred boundary of the city. Greek art was often displayed in enclosed gardens of villas, many surrounded by Greek inspired peristyles. The main hall where business and cult was carried out, the atrium, had no images except those of the household gods, the *lares* and *penates*, and perhaps the busts of ancestors. This 'zoning' of Greek culture persisted into the Augustan period, when the emperor and aristocracy tended to play traditional roles in the city itself, but relaxed in Greek dress and enjoying Greek games and entertainments in the Bay of Naples.

The cultural life enjoyed by Romans of the imperial period was a complex mixture, one in which some parts were appropriately Greek. The distinction could be exploited in various ways. Greek-style poetry acquired a certain licence in its handling of sexual themes. Emperors worried about their standing in Rome could play the traditionalist, as Augustus and Vespasian did. Others might try to establish cosmopolitan credentials by making innovative use of Greek culture (Domitian, Nero… and Augustus again). Quoting Greek was a common tactic in Latin literature from Cicero to Pliny, usually for snob value. By contrast, a Latin inscription in a Roman colony in Greece or Turkey reminded those who set it up, and those who saw it, of the superior civic status of this community relative to its neighbours, even if none of them could read it.

The educated Roman was expected to be proficient in 'both languages', by which Romans meant Latin and Greek. Increasingly they also meant the 'classical' forms of each language, the Latin of Cicero and the Greek of Demosthenes. And proficiency included a knowledge of the canonical literary works of each of these classical periods. Perhaps few aristocratic Romans achieved this goal, even in the early empire. But this was the intellectual component of that complex of sophisticated values and moral judgement that Romans termed *humanitas* ('civilisation' rather than 'humanity'). These values transcended local Roman tradition just as they did Greek high culture. Barbarians, semi-educated provincials and the mass of the population, of course, were excluded. This was part of the point, as the imperial aristocracy defined itself more in terms of common aesthetic and ethical qualities than of noble descent or political pre-eminence.

The introduction of the Cult of Cybele at Rome, a cartoon of about 1504–5 by Andrea Mantegna. Cybele, an Anatolian mother-goddess, was one of a number of foreign cults introduced to Rome – in this case in about 205–4 BC. The cult was widely adopted in cities throughout the Empire, especially in Gaul and Africa.

The Sacred Landscape, a painting from Pompeii dated around AD 63–79 depicts an imaginary scene that reflects the Roman respect for Greek ideals and the assimilation of Greek myths into Roman culture. It is now in the Museo Archeologie Nazionale in Naples.

THE SEDUCTIONS OF HELLENISM

Yet are we any nearer to understanding the persistent Roman fascination for things Greek?

It helps, perhaps, to remember that the Romans were not unusual in the world of their time. Throughout the Greek world, we find peoples who seem enchanted with some aspects of Greek culture but were determined not to become Greeks. The political context was not always Greek or Roman political supremacy. The Etruscans imported Greek ceramics from the seventh century BC and seem to develop an interest in Greek myths. Much of the surviving Athenian painted pottery in museums today comes from Italian graves, just as most extant Greek silverware has been found in 'barbarian' contexts. The Lycians of southern Asia Minor were already re-imagining themselves in relation to Homeric epics in the fifth century BC. Several Persian princes and kings in the next century were apparently interested in Greek culture, as their Parthian successors were in the first century BC. Greek drama was performed for Parthian emperors and also imitated by Oscans and other south Italian peoples. The Greek alphabet spread in the West, often first appearing on coins modelled on those of Greek colonies and Macedonian kings. Hannibal's Carthage seems to have had largely Greek institutions. Within the Hellenistic kingdoms the range of exchanges is even greater. The translation of Hebrew scriptures into Greek started a major Jewish literature in Greek, the Phoenician cities re-invented their traditions on Greek lines and there were even exchanges between Greek philosophy and Buddhism in Afghanistan. And so on.

Probably no analysis of Rome's engagement with Greek culture will be convincing until this wider phenomenon is taken into account. It is certainly easier to understand the influence of Greek architectural and representational forms in Rome when we notice that they were also being copied by a number of central Italian peoples in the third, second and last centuries BC. Fabius Pictor's (Greek) history of Rome can usefully be set alongside the slightly earlier Greek history of Egypt written by the priest Manetho, and Josephus's much later rewriting of the Pentateuch in his *Jewish Antiquities* owes much to Herodotus. All these borrowings from Greek inspiration were different, but they looked to a common cultural centre and took place in broadly similar contexts.

Any explanation of this broader phenomenon might begin by asking why Greek things were so valuable to so many peoples. In part, the Greeks themselves were a conduit for the inventions of others. Writing, metallurgy, hoplite weapons, monumental statuary and perhaps even coinage originated elsewhere, but it was in their Greek forms that they became generalised. The Greeks connected up the Mediterranean's many lands and hinterlands. At a later stage, the Hellenistic empires, including that created by Rome, added political incentives to 'go Greek'. Perhaps too Greek culture was bound together in ways that made it easy to be seduced into taking on more than one intended. Greek myth led to cult as well as to art, the symposium linked wine to literature, and so on. Perhaps when one started to adopt Greek culture, it was difficult to stop.

One of the most obvious means by which Greek culture was interconnected was through Greek identity, a bond that survived thousands of miles of separation and centuries of separate development in the hundreds of cities of which the Greek world was composed. Greek identity was modified but certainly not eroded by Roman rule. The Romans played a hand in deciding which forms of Hellenism would be promoted, through institutions like the Panhellenion and through the patronage they gave to literary culture, Hellenistic art and festivals. The Romans nevertheless had no scruples about abolishing Greek institutions of which they disapproved: Spartan helotage and Cretan laws were, along with Athenian democracy, among the casualties of Roman rule noted by the early first-century AD geographer Strabo.

Yet many Greeks remained purists in relation to Roman culture. Roman gods were rarely worshipped in the Greek East, Latin literature was never cited and Roman loan-words, although frequent in daily speech and necessary in the administration of Rome's empire, were absolutely excluded from literary Greek. Greek writing often uses as its setting a Greece in which Romans are invisible. Was all this a form of cultural resistance? Many Greek writers, including Arrian in the early second century AD (who idolised the fourth-century BC Athenian Xenophon and wrote a gripping account of Alexander's conquests) and the historian Cassius Dio, born in 155 AD, were Roman senators. The modern search for a clear and fixed distinction between Greek and Roman culture is in the end as futile as the search for simple narratives of cultural change. This was a game the Greeks and Romans themselves played each for their own purposes and seemingly without tiring of it, throughout antiquity; we don't have to follow them.

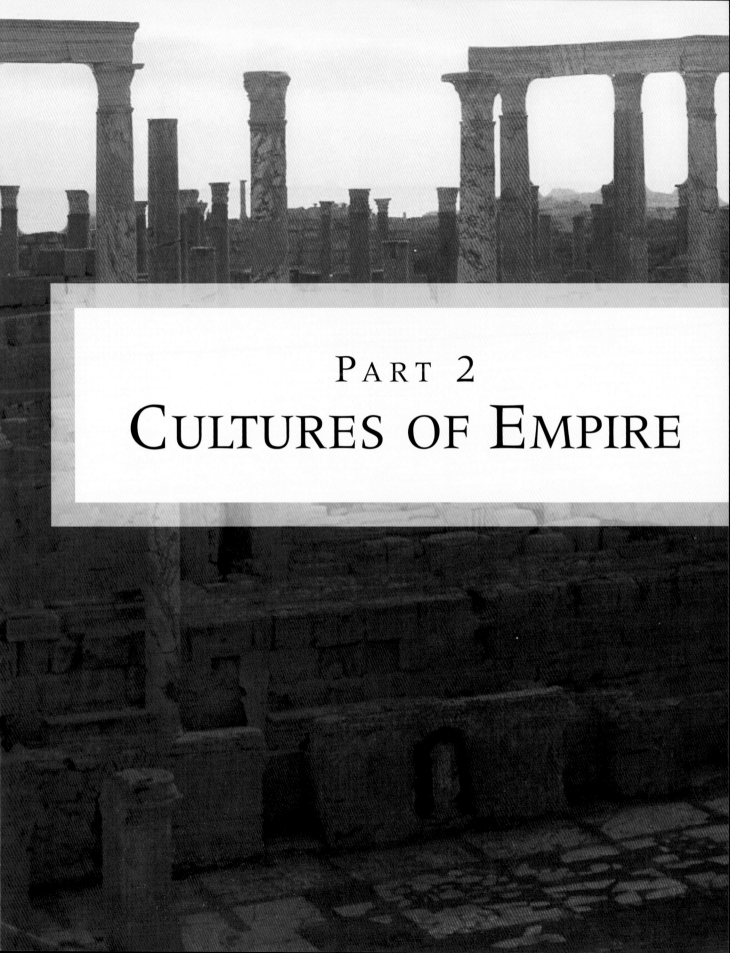

PART 2
CULTURES OF EMPIRE

DOMINATION

EMMA DENCH

THE ROMAN WORLD

DOMINATION

When we try to visualise the Roman world, most of us will piece together Hollywood films, picture-book ruins and museum collections of fine art, statues, jewellery and glassware. The images we are most likely to conjure up will probably include a culturally homogeneous, urbane society of gleaming monuments inhabited by wealthy men governing the Empire in purple-striped togas, and by elaborately coiffured women who share a taste for follies and passions. Hollywood obsessions with persecuted Christians and challenges to established power on the part of noble gladiators mean we are also more likely than not to imagine contrasting scenes of suffering, humiliation and hard labour – in the arena, in the mines or at the whim of cruel masters – undergone by those whose lowly status masks moral virtue, beauty and integrity.

This wall painting from Pompeii (which is usually interpreted as depicting two women and a younger female relative attended by a slave hairdresser) contributes to one of our stereotypical views of the Romans – that of a leisured and fashion-conscious elite, living in self-absorbed luxury, and insulated from mundane domestic cares by a multitude of household slaves.

Such images are primarily based on a combination of centuries of modern western fantasy and a curious mixture of political and religious identification with and rejection of aspects of Roman society. Nevertheless, they do reflect some genuine aspects of the culture and aspirations of wealthy Romans and their counterparts in the local communities of the Empire. While the people were acknowledged as a powerful political presence in the later Republic and feared as a source of violence and disruption during the imperial period, Roman political ideology was based on a hierarchy of wealth and status, with clear social, political, legal and moral distinctions between classes of people. The Empire was in many ways a loosely connected and by no means always tightly controlled entity. In order to function, it relied less on direct government by Roman officials than on the presence of loyal local elites, whose power was actively fostered and enhanced by Rome. Historical evidence tends to over-represent the aspirations of these wealthier and more privileged local elites and their urban, civilised culture: everywhere in the Empire, we find inscribed monuments to the dead in Latin or Greek; baths, theatres and amphitheatres; towns adorned with well-publicised benefactions.

In general, the structures and ideologies of the Roman Empire tended to exaggerate distinctions based on wealth and to widen the gulf between rich and poor. The Romans themselves were conscious of this, and in fact usually regarded the honouring of social distinctions and favouring of elite causes as characteristic of both the good emperor and the good Roman governor. At an institutional level, we see the formalisation in Roman law during the imperial period of a scale of penalties for crimes based on the peculiar blurring of wealth, status and morality that is common in Greco-Roman societies. Thus, *humiliores* – the more humble, poorer people – receive harsher penalties than *honestiores* – the better, wealthier people. At the political level, we can also see significant changes over the same period, not least in the very diminished role of popular assemblies both in Rome and, more generally, in local communities. The concept of democracy retained nominal power for a long time in the Greek cities of the eastern Mediterranean, but in practice the connection between wealth and the membership of councils was made increasingly overt by the requirement to undertake expensive public services, or indeed to pay admission fees.

This chapter concentrates on some aspects of the flip-side of this hierarchical and aspirational society. The Romans expected obedience from their imperial subjects, and were prone to see or imagine threats to themselves and their friends and to take drastic action against these. Women and slaves were automatically excluded from the institutions of political life, from voting assemblies and political office whether at a local or the Roman level. In Roman private law too, both women and slaves were in legal classes of their own, as were freedmen, who were debarred from local or Roman political office but whose continuing obligations to their former masters were enforceable by law. Only in the carnival world of the Saturnalia – when role reversal of masters and slaves was encouraged for a few days – could life be imagined to be any different. (This festival provided a metaphor for the reigns of 'bad' emperors, dominated by the women, freedmen and slaves of the household.) But the rules of normal life are only emphasised by making a song and dance about suspending them.

A first-century AD portrait fresco of Roman citizen Terentius Nero and his wife, found near Naples. This painting presents a different, more intimate, picture of ordinary Romans – a young and aspiring couple who gaze enigmatically down the ages. Their shared possession of scroll and stylus marks both as literate and educated, but whether the portraits suggest some joint literary endeavour, or merely the intention to write life's book together, remains unknown.

Beyond the traditional legal classes, attested as early as the fifth-century BC Twelve Tables, the historical sources regularly reveal elite annoyance at the presence and activities (or indeed the perceived inactivity) of 'the people', especially the urban people. 'The people' from this perspective are frequently an undifferentiated mass referred to as the *plebs*, but sometimes qualified by adjectives revealing much about the elite prejudices of Roman writers (such as the 'dirty' or 'miserable' *plebs*), or distinguished by depiction or institution (the 'worthy' or 'honest' *plebs*, or those who had the fortune to be eligible for the corn-dole). Distinctions such as these make clear the arbitrary nature of favour in the Roman imperial world, and the devastating effects for the poor of the withdrawal of such favour. The literary sources are significantly less interested in the ordinary people of the countryside than they are in either household slaves or the urban *plebs*. However, to some extent in Roman Italy, and markedly in some areas of the wider Empire such as North Africa or Egypt, we can gain valuable glimpses of rural people who were not slaves but who lived in vulnerable dependency on more wealthy individuals.

SOCIAL MOBILITY

While emphasis on hierarchy and aspiration is an important part of the story of the Roman Empire, it would be wrong to imagine the Roman class structure as static. Social mobility – both upwards and downwards – was a much-discussed feature of life in the Empire. As early as the late third century BC, the Romans were notorious in the Greek world for their practice of freeing slaves and incorporating them into their citizen body. The aspirations of freedmen and freedwomen, celebrating their transition from slavery to freedom, are very visible throughout the Roman world. One famous example is the so-called 'Tomb of the Baker', a proud commemoration of the dead freedman Eurysaces's trade that can still be seen today in the place where it was built in the last years of the Republic, at Rome's Porta Maggiore. General expectations of social mobility are reflected in evidence of all kinds, reflecting a broad cultural taste for sudden changes in fortune. These include gaming boards for *alea*, a popular game of chance that has something in common with Snakes and Ladders, and also the riches-to-rags-and-back-again romances that were particularly popular in Greek-speaking parts of the Empire. The snobbery that is a noticeable feature of Roman literature, with its acute interest in origins, accent and manners, is an attempt to make and state rules about belonging and not belonging in high society – but it is also a symptom of social as well as geographical mobility. A peculiarly Roman version of inverse snobbery also sometimes proclaimed the moral, social and even political superiority of 'non-noble' origins. Such attitudes both allowed the Roman elite to be constantly renewed and reflected the fact of its renewal.

It is hard to over-emphasise the importance of vertical links between social ranks in Roman society. Historians define some of these links as 'patronage', a range of reciprocal but unequal relationships that might be expressed in the euphemistic language of friendship, by the metaphor of fathers and sons, or by the more descriptive terms patron and client or landlord and tenant. Especially in the imperial period, it was above all the networks of patronage that allowed privilege of all kinds (ranging from high office to citizenship, from minor assistantships to high-ranking military posts, and all the way down to admission to the lists of those eligible for the corn-dole or other charitable schemes and individual hand-outs, to getting a casual labouring job on a farm) to be extended beyond immediate families or status groups, and in some cases even beyond geographical areas.

Historians have tended to see social mobility in the Roman world as a positive feature – but there are grounds for caution here. This was a society in which equality of opportunity was not even a philosopher's dream, in which concerns about slavery focussed more on the moral health and economic interests of masters than on the well-being of slaves, in which manumission was not a remotely probable outcome for the vast majority of slaves, and in which favour was arbitrary and charity and welfare chose its recipients on the basis of 'worth' rather than need.

Detail from a first-century AD Roman mosaic from Centocelle near Rome. The immediate impression is one of rather lurid sexuality, but this may be the fault of the mosaic technique, which allows only imprecise delineation. The artist may, for instance, have intended to portray a respectable matron giving instructions to servants.

ROMAN WOMEN

Much ancient evidence treats women as a single group, a class distinguished by gender alone. The Roman law of tutelage, the letter of which required (with a few, notable exceptions) the lifelong supervision of women's financial transactions, was attributed to Romulus's concern about women's 'weakness due to their sex'. Certainly, all women were excluded from participation in voting and office-holding, while appearance in other, normally exclusively male spheres of public life such as the courts caused amazement and distaste among (male) observers. During Tiberius's reign, the author Valerius Maximus noted that a woman called Maesia who had defended herself in court was known as 'Androgyne', 'because her female appearance concealed a man's heart'. Idealised female behaviour was proclaimed and advertised on tombstones, in Roman literature and in honorific inscriptions. Such ideals included chastity, modesty and proficiency at perceived 'female' crafts such as wool-working.

The imagery of empire reinforced highly differentiated gender roles. For example, at the end of the Republic, a kind of cosmic breakdown was widely believed to link the sexual immorality of the elite to civil war, neglect of the gods and impending disaster. The losing side at Actium was portrayed as both female and foreign, personified by Cleopatra and her oriental trappings: animal-headed gods and mosquito-nets. The Augustan resolution of the crisis emphasised both social and gender distinctions in opposition to the perceived blurring of boundaries at the end of the Republic. A prominent aspect of this resolution was legislation that made adultery a public crime and played on fears of female laxity, the illegitimacy of children and – increasingly – of palace plots.

However, we must be careful not to over-emphasise the significance of gender alone in the Roman world. The late first-century BC author Cornelius Nepos compared Roman women with their classical Athenian counterparts and emphasised that respectable women were sometimes present at Roman dinner-parties. In a society in which wealth and social status were highly prized, and in which there was considerable overlap between the public and private spheres of political life, elite women could enjoy social prominence and sometimes notoriety. The women of the imperial household were peculiarly prominent, a result of the inflation of the emperor's household into something like a court. Livia, much praised for her womanly virtues, already had a quasi-political role, and imperial petitions were openly directed to her. More broadly, emphasis on wealth in the Roman world had a profound effect on the prominence of women in the Greek cities of the eastern Mediterranean. Particularly in the imperial period, individual women were named as benefactors and honoured with statues, and even granted honorific magistracies and other offices, while being praised for their modesty, chastity, obedience and other traditionally female virtues.

Funerary monuments to humbler women tend also to suggest the aspirational nature of Roman society. In particular, women's work outside the home is frequently not mentioned by their husbands; instead, they are praised for their role as wives and mothers and for their womanly virtues. Sculptural portraits tend to show such women leading the leisured lifestyles of the wealthy. Commemorations offered by fellow-servants, Pompeiian graffiti and studies of the use of space in houses offer a grittier perspective on the lives of humbler Roman women.

A first-century AD wall painting of three women in conversation, from Herculaneum. This is the private and enduring inner world of women, where secrets are shared and the facts of life pondered and explained. Aside from a few minor details of dress, the scene depicted could easily be that of three well-to-do Athenian women from the fifth century BC.

STUDYING ROMAN SOCIETY

The images of the Roman world that we imagined at the beginning of this chapter are distorted partly by the kinds of evidence that has survived, and partly by centuries-old processes of selection, use and interpretation of aspects of the past in modern western societies.

Roman literature and the classical art of the Roman Empire, generally very narrowly defined in terms of period, culture and aesthetics, were the traditional bases of a classical education for the privileged classes of Europe and the English-speaking world in schools and in universities. Roman literature was written largely by and for wealthy and cultured men of leisure who, whatever their origins, were those most likely to have enjoyed the benefits of a hierarchical, imperial society. Our perceptions of classical art were determined in part by natural survival, which tends with some notable exceptions (such as Egyptian papyri and the whole slices of life preserved at Herculaneum and Pompeii) to include much stone, pottery, metals and glass, but little wood or paper. These distortions were hugely compounded by the aesthetic prejudices of early archaeologists, who favoured the 'classical' art and glorious monuments, overlooking or even actively discarding other material.

Well into the first half of the twentieth century, in the schools and universities of Europe and the English-speaking world, Roman literature was mainly used to provide the social and political framework for a history of great men, great works and the rise and fall of empire, while art and architecture was studied either as illustrations for this history or in purely aesthetic terms, often in a social and political vacuum.

More recent historians have, however, taken a more inclusive and holistic interest in the Roman world. From the 1930s onwards, 'daily life' has been a respectable subject for research. From the 1960s, theoretical approaches including Marxism, feminism, and postcolonial theory have all helped to uncover a very different kind of Roman history. Historians have looked at – and in some cases uncovered for the first time – different kinds of evidence, and asked different questions. For example, by the late 1960s there was considerable interest amongst archaeologists in rural settlement, and new surveying techniques were developed that encouraged the study of whole landscapes rather than just individually excavated sites. In recent decades too, the excavation of houses is as likely to consider finds of domestic implements and issues of how space was used (and by whom) as it is to focus on wall painting and *objets d'art*.

Archaeologically based regional studies are constantly challenging our generalisations about patterns of cultural interaction in the Roman Empire, and emphasising the diversity of its society, religion and culture. Changing assumptions and interests in social class are now raising fundamental questions about the structures of political and social life in the Empire, with great emphasis on the shifting membership and mobility of the elite, on reciprocal social and political relationships between richer and poorer people, and on the ways poor people survived.

Virgil's statement of imperial intent

Let others melt and mould the breathing bronze
To forms more fair, – aye! out of marble bring
Features that live; let them plead causes well;
Or trace with pointed wand the cycled heaven,
And hail the constellations as they rise;
But thou, O Roman, learn with sovereign sway
To rule the nations. Thy great art shall be
To keep the world in lasting peace, to spare
humbled foe, and crush to earth the proud.

Virgil Aeneid *Book 6*
(trans. Theodore C Williams, 1910)

IMPERIAL DOMINATION

For Polybius, what Roman rule was primarily concerned with was forcing those peoples under the sway of Rome to be obedient to Roman orders. Writing in Greek around the middle of the second century BC to explain the remarkable rise of Rome to a world power, Polybius had had first-hand experience of the consequences of being suspected of disobedience. As a young Achaean noble, he was taken as a prisoner to the city of Rome, but fortunately here he was befriended by members of some of the most powerful families. His account suggests both a keen appreciation of the grand achievement of Rome and a deep awareness of what it felt like to be subjected to Roman power.

This is a stark vision of Roman rule as all-embracing and universally intrusive. It is very different from the image presented in our own more traditional textbooks, in which great care is taken to delineate the supposed 'rules' that governed Roman conduct towards the provinces, in contrast to the much harsher impact of Roman force in those areas that were not subjected to direct rule.

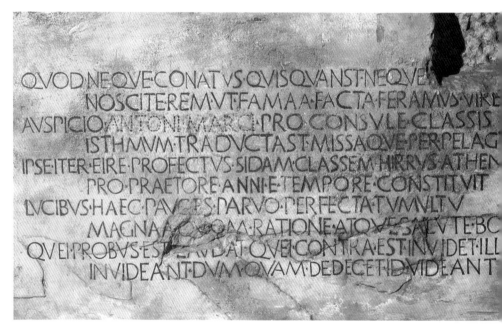

An inscription dating to the first century BC recording the passage of a Roman fleet through the Corinth Canal (across the 'ISTHMUM'), carrying a Proconsul en route for Athens. By this time the Romans had already become self-important about their overseas empire, and their officials even more so. They eagerly adopted the Eastern tradition of leaving an imperial graffito to commemorate their every action.

We might justifiably argue that there is excellent evidence to suggest that the Roman Empire was not in general as tightly controlled as it might sometimes have aspired to be: the continued presence of bandits, pirates and other outlaws in the heart of the Empire tells a different story. But it is hard to argue against the contemporary perceptions of a first-hand witness of what happened to states like Corinth that did not obey.

Polybius's perception of the character of Roman rule also seems to accord well with Roman thought about *imperium*. Our own term 'empire', which is vague and overused, derives from Latin *imperium*. The primary meaning of *imperium* is 'power' or 'sway'; it is a term that would usually be associated with high Roman magistrates, who were granted the power both to make orders and, if necessary, to force obedience to them.

Given the importance of the family as a social and legal unit in the Roman world, it is no accident that we can also find literary evidence of fathers being imagined to wield *imperium* over their dependents. This conceptualisation of 'empire' in the stark terms of force and obedience became important even before the end of the Republic, when Roman writers began to examine the 'benefits' that Roman rule brought to its subjects – benefits such as peace and the coming of 'civilisation'.

A fragment of wall painting showing a peace treaty (indicated by the shaking of hands) between the Romans and the Samnites. The painting comes from a third-century BC tomb on the Esquiline Hill in Rome. It seems very likely that the tomb's occupant had played a significant role at the conclusion of either the Third or Fourth Samnite Wars (or both).

ROME AND ITALY

Rome's acquisition of what was perceived even at the time to be world-rule was intimately connected with the Roman conquest and management of the Italian peninsula. Unusually for an aspirant state in the Hellenistic world, Rome's military power depended not on mercenaries but on a network of alliances with Italian peoples that required the regular supply of troops funded by the local community. This supply of troops made possible the almost incessant conquests of the third to first centuries BC (after which methods of recruitment began to change). Some historians suggest that the availability of troops itself encouraged overseas conquest.

Well into the second century AD, there were important distinctions between the Roman management of Italy and of the overseas territories – including the fact that there were no Roman governors in Italy. In this period, Rome's relationship with Italy was more intimate than that. As we shall see, in ideology and in practice, Rome could be distinctly proprietorial towards Italy, and Italy comes, particularly by the time of its full political integration in the mid-first century BC, to be seen as something of an extension of Rome, a large territorial state.

However, despite the distinctions between Italy and the overseas Empire, it is also true that Italy provided a model for wider imperial rule. Perhaps most significant of all are the precedents for legal and/or political incorporation. These include the extension of 'Latin rights' well beyond the original, ethnically Latin peoples, the subsequent systematisation of these 'Latin rights' as a half-way house towards the full citizenship, and of course the extension of the citizenship itself to the whole of peninsular Italy after the Social War. It was this policy towards Italy that ultimately facilitated a closely integrated overseas Empire, especially at the upper levels of society – making possible, for example, the entry of members of the provincial elites into the Roman senate and equestrian order.

With the benefit of hindsight, we might begin the story of Rome's distinctive way of ruling in 338 BC, when the Romans finally subjugated their immediate neighbours, including other Latin peoples and some of the northern Campanian and Volscian towns. They incorporated some of these peoples within the Roman citizenship, with or without the right to vote in Roman assemblies, and forced some of the Latin peoples into individual alliances.

All these arrangements had the effect of substantially increasing Rome's military strength against the other peoples of central Italy – the Samnites and their allies – with whom the Romans had already come into conflict over Campania as early as 343 BC. This was the beginning of a long series of campaigns that ancient authors refer to as an undifferentiated 'Samnite War', and modern historians tend to divide into the First (343–1), Second (about 328–1), Third (316–04) and Fourth (298–90) Samnite Wars. It was conflict with the Samnites that in turn embroiled Rome in the affairs of the Greek cities of southern Italy, and it was Rome's ultimate victory in these wars that made possible the conquest and subjugation of the whole of Italy south of the River Po by 264 BC.

It is probably in the later fourth century BC, at around the time of the first Roman experiments with new forms of legal status for conquered peoples, that myths of shared descent and ancestral blood ties between Romans and other Latins came to the fore. For example, traditional stories about Aeneas and his descendants link through family ties the foundation of a number of 'Latin' towns, including Rome, Alba Longa and Lavinium, while the story that we call 'the rape of the Sabine women' is in fact more accurately described as 'the rape of the Latin and Sabine women' – a more generalised account of the widening of the Roman gene pool. Roman assertions of blood-ties seem to chime in also with the juridical status that Rome granted to Latins who were not given Roman citizenship: they were still given rights of intermarriage and trade under the protection of Roman law, suggesting a socially and economically fluid relationship.

The new invention of the notion of Latin status that can be transferred to people who are not 'ethnically' Latin is highly significant. The establishment of colonies, both 'Roman' and 'Latin', was an important aspect of Rome's management of the conquest of Italy in the late fourth to early second centuries BC. 'Roman' colonies, composed of Roman citizens and remaining wholly within the Roman state, were small settlements that remained more or less exclusively military garrisons. 'Latin' colonies – such as

Livy justifies Roman expansion in Italy

Romulus sent envoys amongst the surrounding nations to ask for alliance and the right of intermarriage... It was represented that cities, like everything else, sprung from the humblest beginnings, and those who were helped on by their own courage and the favour of heaven won for themselves great power and great renown... There should, therefore, be no reluctance for men to mingle their blood with their fellow-men.

Nowhere did the envoys meet with a favourable reception.

Livy History of Rome *Book 1*

Fregellae (established 328), Venusia (291) and Beneventum (268) – were settlements made up of those who were originally Roman citizens, Latins and local people, and retained close links to the mother-city through the assertion of blood ties as well as through their possession of 'Latin rights'. Such colonies functioned as autonomous communities, but were obliged to provide manpower for Rome on a regular basis. Latin colonies often had at their origins very obvious strategic functions, being placed on major routes or between the territories of peoples allied against Rome. However, they were also an effective means of expanding Rome's dominion at a great geographical distance from the city, while still preserving the identity of the Roman citizenry as tight and participatory.

Rome's experiments with different modes of controlling and integrating its Italian subjects continued in the early third century BC. These included the activity of the consul Marcus Curius Dentatus in 290, who conquered and incorporated into the Roman state (initially as 'citizens without the vote', a somewhat enigmatic status) the Sabines and their eastern neighbours the Praetuttii, thereby extending Roman territory across central Italy as far as the Adriatic Sea. It is probable that the original intention towards the Sabines and Praetuttii was to punish them, both by confiscating large tracts of land and redistributing them to Roman settlers, and by removing political autonomy. However, this relationship was to become very different when the Sabines were later granted full Roman citizenship. By the early second century BC, Sabines had begun to be regarded not just as full members of the Roman community but, in some contexts at least, as morally worthier than the old Roman elite themselves. The integration of the Sabines on favourable terms

was no doubt sanctioned by myths of a close relationship between Romans and Sabines from time immemorial: the story of the rape of the Sabine women of course claims shared bloodlines. This incorporation of the Sabines eventually provided political, juridical and ideological precedents for the mass incorporation of Italians after the Social War of 91–88 BC.

The political incorporation of huge numbers of people into the Roman state was, however, rare in the period of the Roman conquest of Italy between the later fourth and early second centuries BC. The more usual pattern was that conquest was followed by the confiscation of land and its redistribution to colonists, while individual treaties were made between Rome and the conquered people requiring the regular provision of (and payment for) troops to fight in auxiliary units of the Roman army. While juridically Latin communities (including colonies) and the individual Italian allies of Rome remained politically autonomous, the effects of Roman domination would have been clear. The granting of individual treaties and differential juridical relationships with Rome, as well as the planting of colonies, disrupted existing networks and social, political and military relationships. The construction of a vast system of permanent roads, all leading to and from Rome, seems in some areas at least to have demonstrably changed local economies. Confiscated territory was reconfigured and redistributed by measuring out grids, some of which can still be seen today from the air. The building of Latin colonies often involved the importing of alien lifestyles, the manifestations of which might range from the very model of urban life itself to the use of Latin, and foreign religious practices, such as the dedication of votive offerings at sanctuaries.

The rape of the Sabine women as painted by Baldassarre Peruzzi in about 1525. The Sabine rape was a favourite subject for Renaissance artists, combining classical allusion with a frisson of prurient interest. For the Romans, this brutal action became part of their origin myth, dating back to a time when conquest was marked in far more basic ways than carved inscriptions.

THE OVERSEAS EMPIRE

The narrative of Rome's conflict with, and ultimate mastery of, overseas powers and territories in the third to second centuries BC is closely connected both with Roman embroilment in Italian affairs and Rome's increasingly proprietorial attitude towards Italy, to say nothing of the exploitation of Italian resources and military mastery of the peninsula. This is clear from some of the key moments of Rome's shift of attention overseas. For example, when the Tarentines called for help from Pyrrhus of Epirus, Rome's wars in Italy begin to take on a distinctly international significance. This is neatly reflected in second-century Roman claims to have reversed the outcome of the Trojan War, since Pyrrhus claimed descent from the Greek Achilles and the Romans from the Trojan Aeneas. It was Pyrrhus's involvement with Sicilian Syracuse that drew the Romans into Sicilian affairs, and ultimately led to their first war with Carthage (264–41 BC). For Rome, the most concrete results of this war were the subjugation and military occupation of Sicily, Sardinia and Corsica. Rome's wars with Illyria (229–8 and 219 BC) occurred because the Romans decided that it was their business to protect Italian traders threatened by Illyrian 'pirates' in the Adriatic, and it was this direction of military attention eastwards that brought them into conflict with the kingdom of Macedon.

The decision to interpret Illyrian harassment of Italian traders as Roman business is significant evidence of an increasingly proprietorial attitude on Rome's part towards Italy. Such an attitude was surely directly connected with the new management of the overseas territories, Rome's 'provinces'. Amongst the evidence for this changing attitude is a law prohibiting the pontifex maximus from leaving Italy – a sign that perceptions of the space within which Roman religion was efficacious now included the whole peninsula. If we take this example in conjunction with the growth in the second century BC of Roman interest in religious prodigies in central Italy, it seems clear that the whole of Italy was beginning to be understood in this period to be in some very real sense 'Roman'.

For some contemporary observers, it was not so much in the earliest days of overseas conquest but rather in the course of the second century BC that Roman rule took on its most distinctive, and even sinister, character for both the rulers and the ruled. This was connected above all with the elimination of the last of Rome's rivals in the rule of the known world. For Cato the Elder in 167 BC, the people of Rhodes could be forgiven for having contemplated joining the cause of Perseus of Macedon against Rome because they were afraid of being 'under our rule alone' if the counterbalance of Macedon were removed. For Polybius too, 167 was the true turning-point, with the defeat of the Macedonian kingdom and Rome's now unchallenged ability to exact obedience.

A detail from a Renaissance fresco showing a Roman colony neatly arrayed behind a strongly fortified wall. Unlike Greek colonies, which were established mainly to relieve population pressure and encourage trade, Roman colonies were essentially military in character. The first were set up as forward strongholds during the conquest of Italy; subsequently colonies were used for the wholesale settlement of veterans from the legions.

THE EXPERIENCE OF WORLD-RULE

In comparison with the closely woven but differentiated relationships between Romans and Italians, Rome's overseas rule seems in some ways much patchier. The direct rule of 'provinces' – originally meaning nothing more fixed or systematised than the sphere of command of a general with an army – is less usual in the Greek world than far more nebulous-sounding declarations of 'friendship'. But Rome's 'friends' were to find quickly that there was nothing benign about such a relationship: the Roman authorities expected to be kept fully informed of anything that might concern them, and in particular to be consulted in the case of local arguments. For those who were perceived to misunderstand the rules of friendship, the consequences were dire. Roman overseas rule worked also by distinction and differentiation: true friends were promised 'freedom', which sometimes (but not universally) included freedom from taxation. It is here that we can see the importance of the connection between taxation and subjection, long a theme of ancient consideration of imperial rule. Taxation in the Roman Empire often continued previous arrangements and was not necessarily restricted to areas of direct rule: while Macedonia remained autonomous after 167 BC, half the tribute formerly demanded by the kings was now due to Rome. The payment of taxes to Rome could be one of the most obvious and resented aspects of Roman rule at the local level, as we can see from the New Testament.

The experience of world-rule profoundly affected Rome's relationship with Italy as well as the shape of Roman politics. We can see a direct relationship between the economic prosperity of second-century BC Italy and the benefits reaped from Roman rule in the Mediterranean, not least as a result of measures to protect Roman and Italian traders in the east. This relationship may be illustrated by finds of Rhodian amphorae even in remoter areas of central Italy, by the monumental building of temples and theatres, and by the occurrence of the same family names among both benefactors of Italian towns and successful traders at Delos in Greece.

Nevertheless, the profits of world-rule had their greatest impact on the shape of Roman society, and it was this that increased tensions between Rome and the Latins and Italian allies. One of the major problems that Polybius associated with Rome's rise to world-rule was that empire disturbed the perfect balance of what he saw as the three key elements of Roman political life – monarchy, aristocracy and democracy. First, he condemned what he called 'courting the people' by members of the elite as a perversion of the role of the people in Roman politics. Roman experiments with democratic change are associated above all with the tribunates of Tiberius (133 BC) and Gaius (123–2 BC) Gracchus, who interpreted in somewhat different ways the principle of the sovereignty of the Roman people. Tiberius enacted the confiscation and redistribution of illegally occupied public land (beyond a very generous maximum) to the poor, probably exclusively Roman citizens. His bill seems to have set in motion a chain of events that created serious tensions with some of Rome's Italian allies, who are subsequently claimed to have been wronged by these measures. Connections between Roman world-rule and popular sovereignty were apparently made overt by Tiberius himself. In a public speech, he supposedly underlined the iniquity of the fact that the Roman people, who fought and died to line others' pockets, were called masters of the world, while having not a square metre of earth to call their own. When Attalus III of Pergamum left his estate to the Roman people later in 133 BC, Tiberius Gracchus set out, controversially, to use the bequest to benefit the Roman people directly by giving aid to colonists settled on the confiscated public land.

ENLARGING ROMAN CITIZENSHIP

Over the next forty years, Roman officials exploited the interests of the Roman people on the one hand and the Latins and Italian allies on the other. One major exception was the extraordinarily comprehensive legislation proposed by Gaius Gracchus, which (amongst other concerns) established the use of juries of *equites* in the trial of senatorial governors for extortion and provided for the sale of state-subsidised grain. One failed bill apparently proposed the extension of the Roman citizenship to those of Latin status and a lesser right, probably the *ius provocationis* (the right of appeal against heavy punishment at the hands of a Roman magistrate) to the allies. Following the failure of Fulvius Flaccus's apparently similar proposal in 125 BC, such extensions began to be seen as a possible means of addressing the grievances of the Latins and allies. Gaius Gracchus made use of incidents of overbearing and arbitrary behaviour by Roman magistrates and by private individuals towards Italians in his advocacy of the Italian cause. These

A ninteenth-century French bronze cenotaph for the Gracchi – the brothers Gaius and Tiberius Gracchus. After the murder of Tiberius at the hands of a gang of street-thugs employed by a political rival, the Gracchi became something of a Republican icon – revered by those who sought greater political power for the masses – both in Ancient Rome and also, some nine hundred years later, in Revolutionary France.

are interesting and chilling examples of what Roman domination might feel like, exercised here over those with whom Rome had long enjoyed a special relationship. A vivid sense of how such proposals could be presented as inimical to popular concerns can be gained from a preserved fragment of the speech of Gracchus's opponent, the consul Gaius Fannius, in 122 BC: 'If you give citizenship to the Latins, do you think that there will be room for you at rallies as there is now, or that you will be able to attend games and festivals? Don't you think that they will take up all the room?' Populist xenophobia was clearly a force even in the second century BC.

Whatever the original motivation was of the Italian allies who went to war against Rome in 91 BC, the ultimate outcome of the Social War was that Roman citizenship was eventually granted to all free adult males of peninsular Italy. Over the next two generations, this extraordinary act gradually had the effect of changing the whole balance of power within the Roman state. The effects of enfranchising the Italians were keenly felt in Rome precisely because the primary value of citizenship for the Italians was the right it conferred to participate in Roman politics.

In turn, however, the enlargement of the Roman state raised questions about the meaning of the Roman citizenship itself, and about the relationship between allegiances to Rome and to one's home town. In his *Laws*, Cicero prescribed an essentially hierarchical relationship: in the local fatherland are one's cults and the tombs of one's ancestors, but it is for the Roman fatherland that 'we give up our lives when necessary'. This early notion of 'dual citizenship' foreshadowed very different significance that Roman citizenship acquired when it became more common as a status overseas; citizenship primarily denoted privilege, often exercised within the local community, rather than participation in Roman political life. This issue, of course, was one only for the well-off: Paul of Tarsus, who in the mid-first century AD exercised his Roman citizenship by demanding to be tried at Rome, was typical.

The first century BC also brought a growing emphasis on individuals in Roman politics, initially in the form of military dynasts but ultimately in overt flirtation with ideas of kingship and the development of a carefully articulated, curious Roman compromise, the principate. This emphasis on individuals was closely related both to the growth of Rome's Empire and to changes in the balance of power in Italy. The grant of unprecedented powers to Pompey in 67 BC to deal with 'pirates' in the Mediterranean reinforced the link between Rome's ambitious imperial vision and individual power. The potential to build a huge power-base through the exploitation of Italian interests, first glimpsed in the later second century BC, is fully realised in the claims of Augustus to have come to power with the support of the whole of Italy.

The increased prominence of individuals in Roman politics had a major impact on the geography of integration within the Roman state. For example, changes in the pattern of army recruitment in the course of the first century BC, coupled with closer bonds between individuals and armies, made the settlement of veterans on lands assigned to them a crucial issue. While veterans were settled in Italy, the confiscation of Italian land to achieve this was highly contentious, as Octavian learned to his cost. Settlement in citizen colonies overseas was less politically sensitive. In the last decades of the Republic, grants of citizenship itself were beginning to be regarded as being in

A detail of the 'Claudian Table', a bronze plaque made in Gaul in about AD 48. Having added Britain to the empire in 43, Claudius was keen to promote closer ties between Gaul (which had already endured a century of foreign rule) and Rome. The tablet records the emperor's speech explaining his decision to allow Gallic aristocrats to stand for election to the Roman senate. The move was unpopular with some Italian aristocrats, who had dominated the senate until then.

he gift of high-profile individuals like Pompey, Caesar and Antony, and were used as a means of canvassing support or as a reward for loyalty. The increasing centralisation of Roman power on individuals was linked by contemporary writers to an increasing sense of imperial cohesion. In the last decades of the Republic, Rome's overseas Empire was regularly imagined in concrete geographical terms, with boundaries, or represented in stone or in words as a parade of peoples of the world.

It is in the last decades of the Republic that we also see the development of new ideas about Rome's relationship with the overseas Empire. In Cicero's advice on government addressed to his brother Quintus, there is a strong sense of Rome's duty to correct the character traits of its subjects: to curb the over-excitement and enthusiasm of Greeks and to civilise barbarous peoples. In Sallust's analysis of the Jugurthine War, there is a keen sense that what begins as an essentially Roman failing, corruption, is contagious, a nasty tendency that can be picked up by even the worthiest of North African outsiders. These perceptions reflect the development of a more integrated overseas Empire. The model for this Empire was usually the integration of the Italians; the emperor Claudius, for example, agreed (controversially) that leading Gauls should be made eligible for election to senatorial office. This agreement, he claimed in a rhetorical *tour de force*, was a 'natural' continuation of the whole of Roman history. His own family, he reminds his audience, were Sabines, supposedly admitted to the citizenship in the early years of the Republic, and the history of the Roman state is of the unbroken progression of citizenship, initially through Italy and now beyond the Alps as well.

It is easy to find in Roman literature arguments for preserving social distinctions at a local level. Pliny the Younger, always keen to promote models of good upper-class behaviour in the early imperial period, urged his friend Caelestrius Tiro, proconsul of Baetica in Spain, to maintain distinctions in class and rank, 'since nothing is more unequal than equality'. Something like an 'imperial culture' was emerging amongst Rome's urban elite – a culture not of homogeneity but of common aspiration. Similarly, in the sphere of religion, the so-called imperial cult provided a focus for the relationship between the individual local community and Rome, now personified in part by the emperor and his predecessors.

In political terms, the emperor Caracalla's edict of 'universal' citizenship for free males in the Empire (probably to be dated to AD 212) seems at first sight to reflect the global fulfilment of an idealised, integrated empire. The edict makes sense, however, only because the nature of Roman citizenship had itself changed profoundly. Certainly, with increasing numbers of Roman citizens overseas in the early imperial period, citizenship was no longer primarily about participation in Roman political and military institutions. In turn, the extension of citizenship to increasingly large numbers of people considerably diminished its use as a marker of social distinction at the local level, and it is no coincidence that we also see law-codes overtly differentiating penalties on the grounds of social status. It has also been argued that Caracalla's edict was concerned as much with the minority that was excluded as it was with the mass of people included. Some historians see the edict as foreshadowing the Dacian persecution of the Christians: a newly universal definition of what it was to be 'Roman' was may actually have been prompted by the rise of Christianity, a single category of 'un-Roman' behaviour.

From the late Republic, ancient writers tended to portray the enlargement of Roman citizenship in linear terms, as a policy of generosity traced back to Romulus. It is far from clear, however, that there was widespread interest in receiving Roman citizenship before the later Republic, and earlier grants may have been mainly punitive in intention. The early imperial period is characterized by parsimony with citizenship as much as by generosity. A corrective to this sense of linearity, however, can be gained from from scandalous stories of imperial freedmen selling citizenship.

A detail from Trajan's column in Rome, showing clean-shaven Roman recruiters signing-up hirsute non-citizens for service with the legions during Trajan's campaigns in Dacia early in the first century AD. Although they were confined to auxiliary status, military service was an important first step for outsiders (in this case almost certainly opportunistic Dacians) who wished to become Roman citizens.

THE ROMAN WORLD

A carved stone relief of a Roman trireme dating from the first century BC. The Romans had no seafaring tradition and, when they invented their navy during the First Punic War, slaves were the obvious means of propulsive power. This contrasts strongly with the Greek approach – the victorious Athenian rowers at Salamis were well-paid citizens, justly proud of their military prowess and consequent political clout.

SLAVERY

Within the ancient Mediterranean world, slavery had long been a metaphor for imperial rule, and imperial rulers were sometimes described as slave-masters or (virtually synonymously), as tyrants. Thucydides, in his account of the Peloponnesian War, written around 400 BC, had used the metaphorical language of enslavement to describe the beginnings of distinctive Athenian imperial rule as early as 466 BC. He referred to the enforcement of terms of alliance and the severe punishment of rebel states. This use of the language of slavery is ironic, given that playwrights and historians had explained 'Greek' success in the Persian Wars, and justified Athenian hegemony in the aftermath, in terms of the triumph of political freedom (associated with Athens's nascent democracy) over 'Asiatic' despotism.

The language of 'freedom' and 'slavery' continued to be much used and much manipulated in the history of rule and empire-building in the Mediterranean. When Roman imperial ambitions brought them at the end of the third century BC into conflict with the Macedonian kingdom, they loudly proclaimed the freedom of their Greek allies, in terms of the enjoyment of their own laws and the absence of garrisons and tribute. According to Polybius, writing on the rise of Rome some two generations later, the Aetolians, conspicuously excluded from the terms of the decree of 196 BC that made such claims, saw through its rhetoric: what was happening was not so much the freeing of Greeks from Macedonian rule as a mere change of master.

If the Roman Empire could be portrayed as slavery, so Rome itself, under the rule of the emperors, came to be depicted as enslaved. It is here that we see the development in literature of the image of the more or less noble northern barbarian opponents of Rome who see through the trappings of 'civilisation' to the realities of loss of freedom; this image was a commentary on the downside of empire that thoughtful Romans sometimes found deeply uncomfortable.

However, the connection between slavery and empire clearly went beyond metaphor; if nothing else, slavery was itself an important by-product of empire. Some historians suggest that the acquisition of slaves was in fact a primary motive for the almost constant Roman wars of conquest and expansion in the middle and later Republic, although neither contemporary nor later Roman evidence puts any emphasis on this. Over the long term, we might think of slavery in the Roman Empire as an important mode of integrating foreigners within the Roman state, due to the Roman custom of selectively manumitting slaves and making them citizens.

The early history of Roman slavery is closely connected with the process of 'state formation' in Rome itself. In the Twelve Tables, a late fifth-century BC codification of laws attributed by the late Republic to Romulus, the legendary founder of Rome, Roman individuals are to be sold into slavery only 'across the Tiber'. The Tiber here acts as a state boundary, and the connection between 'slaves' and 'foreigners' is codified in law.

The interest of the Twelve Tables in *nexum* (roughly translatable as 'debt-bondage') reminds us that warfare was only one of the ways of entering slavery. It is from the beginning of the third century BC that we begin to hear of very large numbers of prisoners of war being enslaved by the Romans. Livy gives figures for people enslaved as a result of the Samnite wars as up to eleven thousand at a time. However, such numbers pale into insignificance beside the proverbial cheapness of Sardinian slaves after sixty-five thousand of them were put up for sale in 177 BC.

It is notoriously difficult to calculate the numbers of the slave population of Italy or, for that matter, the whole of the Roman Empire, and what proportion of the population slaves constituted. However, modern estimates for Italy in the late Republic are around a third of the total population: two or perhaps three million individuals. A recent estimate of the proportion of slaves in the Empire as a whole is around ten per cent of the whole population. The relative proportions of imported slaves and 'home-grown' slaves, a category for which the Romans had a distinct name, *vernae*, is equally controversial. These proportions probably shifted from time to time, and in all likelihood the trade in imported slaves continued to be significant even after the early principate, when going to war was a less regular feature of Roman life than it had been in the middle and later Republic. Piracy and banditry were also important in the slave-trade – a reminder of the limits of Roman domination and the fact that the Empire was never as peaceful as its admirers imagined. It is very difficult to generalise from individual case-studies: for example, the use of slaves in agricultural contexts seems to have been common in Italy, Sicily, mainland Greece and areas of Gaul closest to Italy, but less common in, for example, North Africa and Egypt.

It has been argued that in the course of the second century BC, after the Second Punic War, the growth of huge agricultural estates dependent on slave labour displaced small farmers in the Italian countryside, causing them to flee to the towns. Some Roman politicians certainly seem to have found it possible in the later second century to manipulate perceptions of the prevalence of slaves on the land, at the cost of free labour: Gaius Gracchus told an anecdote about his brother Tiberius's journey through Italy to Numantia, in which he found the land empty of (free) farmers but farmed by 'imported barbarian slaves'. It is not clear, however, that this adds up to a nationwide picture of small farmers displaced from their land by slave estates. For a start, archaeologists trace the development of very large estates to around the mid-first century BC, rather than to the second century. While archaeology cannot by itself answer questions about the ownership of land or the status of people occupying farmsteads, the settlement patterns of a surveyed area of South Etruria suggest that here larger establishments did not displace smaller establishments. The interdependence of slave and free labour on large estates is also regularly assumed by Roman writers on agriculture.

The 'Mosaic of Dominus Julius', a late-Roman floor from Tunisia depicting a fortified country house surrounded by scenes from rural life. The agricultural workers harvesting and carrying crops are distinctively African, but are probably not slaves. In this part of the empire, the best results were obtained from waged labour paid either in cash or (more commonly) in kind.

More generally, slaves in the Roman world did not make up a single social or economic class: they did a huge variety of kinds of work and experienced a huge variety in their quality of life. Sustained group consciousness amongst slaves was more often feared than experienced: the Sicilian slave wars (136–2 and 104–1 BC), as well as the famous revolt of Spartacus (73–1 BC) were isolated incidents.

Roman law concerning slaves was primarily directed towards upholding the power of the *paterfamilias* to discipline and rule his own household, underlining the fragmented experience of slaves. Precisely because of the fear that group consciousness might develop, it was not in the interests of slave-owners that the common status of slaves should be marked in any obviously recognisable way. Two proposals that slaves should wear a kind of uniform were rejected by the senate in the imperial age.

It can be argued that the distinctions between slaves were easily as significant as perceptions of them as a single class in the Roman world. For example, there is plentiful evidence of slaves who supervised or even in all practical senses owned other slaves: farm-bailiffs, who might have huge responsibility for the estates of more or less absentee landlords, are sometimes slaves themselves. Historians have suggested that, particularly amongst domestic slaves and servants, the 'job-title' – and even in some cases a 'career progression' – was of great importance as a way of differentiating status, and it is this that is often mentioned on funerary inscriptions. In the third century AD, jurists even specify different kinds of food and clothing for different ranks of slaves. Even amongst slaves in the Roman Empire, status was paramount and minutely observed.

'BORN FOR SLAVERY'

The status of the Roman elite could be marked by the presence of slaves. In a famous passage, Polybius presents a speech of Cato the Elder in which he is horrified to note, after the fall of Macedon to Rome, that pretty boys and caviar are reaching higher prices than fields and ploughmen. His mention in the same breath of slave-boys and caviar gives a strong hint that slaves might be an imported luxury, a status-symbol for the wealthy and aspirant. Within an individual wealthy household, the number of slaves could run into hundreds, all with their distinctive job-titles. Inscriptions commemorating the deeds and lives of freedmen and slaves of the Julio-Claudian household show the degree of differentiation to be found in Rome's greatest household: the range of crystal-stewards, topiarists, cup-bearers and valets reflects favourably on the wealth and tastes of the house, as well as the potential for social distinction amongst the servants themselves.

As we have seen, the ethnic and cultural origins of slaves were very wide-ranging and Roman attempts to characterise slaves collectively as a group – such as by shared descent or as barbarian inferiors – were limited. This is one of the most important differences between ancient slavery and that of late eighteenth- and nineteenth-century Europe and America, which was linked to an ideology of racial superiority. In fourth-century BC Athens, Aristotle had rejected the idea that 'natural' slavery was manifested in physical inferiority: free men, he noted, were often physically inferior to slaves. Nonetheless, the cultural confidence of the Greeks allowed them easily to equate slaves with barbarians.

Even in the Roman world, however, ideas sometimes surfaced that slaves were distinguished by birth or descent from Romans. Roman writers occasionally characterised peoples like Jews and Syrians as 'born for slavery', a rhetorical exaggeration of the imagined connection between chattel slavery and subjection to imperial rule. More remarkable is the reported motive of Augustus for both his caution in granting the Roman citizenship to foreigners and the limitations he set on the manumission of slaves. According to Suetonius, Augustus considered it to be 'of great importance to keep the people pure and untainted by any influx of foreign and servile blood'.

The Romans regularly asserted that they themselves were of 'mixed' descent – from slaves and foreigners of various kinds, including among them Trojans, Greeks and peoples of Italy – and could regard this as a distinctive, and sometimes unambiguously positive, feature of Roman society. Nevertheless, the Augustan period in particular sees some emphasis on ideas of Roman identity based on descent – perhaps one response to a kind of identity crisis caused by large-scale political change in the first century BC. The passage quoted above may seem somewhat chilling to us: we can hardly avoid thinking of modern racism with its emphasis on blood purity. However, it is important to distinguish Augustus's meaning from modern racist ideology. The broader context shows that he was seeking to limit rather than stop admissions to Roman citizenship, and the emphasis of the passage as a whole is on foreigners 'qualifying' for citizenship, above all through cultural criteria.

MANUMISSION OF SLAVES

The Roman practice of selectively manumitting slaves and admitting them to the citizenship seemed to Greek eyes to be a distinctive and startling aspect of their culture. The percentage of slaves manumitted is very hard to determine, but manumission was certainly a well-advertised feature of Roman society. Pride in freed status is marked in inscriptions, and freedpersons are undoubtedly over-represented in surviving epigraphy precisely because they had cause to celebrate their newly acquired status. The practice of manumitting slaves in a dead man's will, a living advertisement of his generosity in life, is an example of how freeing slaves could be a statement about masters as well as about the slaves themselves. It has been argued that the well-publicised possibility of freedom worked as a form of social control, encouraging cooperation and good behaviour amongst slaves.

Detail of a first-century AD fresco from Pompeii depicting a group of wealthy Romans taking refreshments. Household slaves serve food and drinks, while another kneels to remove the sandals of a newly arrived guest. The overall lack of formality suggests that this is an everyday family gathering, rather than a ceremonial feast. However much an intimate part of the household the slaves might be, the demarcation between free persons and slaves was rigorously maintained when others were present.

We need to consider the practice of manumission in relation to ties of patronage, and also in the context of a society that imposed legal restrictions on some kinds of political participation even among citizens. A freedman or freedwoman's continuing obligations to his or her former master could as a last resort be upheld by legal process, and it is this relationship that encourages social integration (and even upwards mobility) as well as emphasising the liminal status of being freed. Perhaps most significantly, freedmen were barred from political office at either the local or the Roman level, although – importantly – their sons were not. The ban on being a local councillor was no doubt of great significance for some highly prosperous individuals. Interestingly, from the Augustan age, we see the development in Italy of a primarily religious office, the Augustales, attendants of the cult of the emperor's *genius*. Freedmen were not just eligible for this office but were the primary holders of it, and we see Augustales using their role as if it were a kind of magistracy, above all to participate in benefaction, a key activity for the urban elite. The chances of becoming local councillors for the sons and grandsons of Augustales were considerably enhanced.

The possibility of manumission did not, of course, make the world of the slave a rosy one. Manumission in fact emphasises the arbitrary nature of the world that all slaves inhabited: their dependence on the whims of a master or mistress for reward as well as punishment. Mobility and other social and status advantages available to slaves were far more likely to be experienced by those who worked closely or intimately with their masters of mistresses – to assistants, secretaries, children's nurses or doctors, for example. But even in these cases, intimacy could work both ways, and domestic slaves could equally incur the wrath of a master or mistress. In a notorious early imperial anecdote, the emperor Augustus intervened to save the life of a slave-boy when his proverbially self-indulgent master, Vedius Pollio, had threatened to feed him to the lampreys for breaking a glass.

In general, it was slaves condemned to the mines or mills, as well as certain kinds of agricultural slaves, for whom chances of manumission, privilege or even decently humane treatment were the slimmest. Inevitably, these are the kinds of slaves about whom we know least, in contrast to domestic slaves who might live in very close contact with their masters and mistresses and whose close relationships are reflected in their prominence in Roman literature. While the ancient world had no abolitionists, a somewhat sentimentalised realism is apparent in some Roman literature, such as Apuleius's *Metamorphoses*, a fantastical travelogue in the world of the Roman Empire undertaken by a character who has been transformed by magic into a donkey. The donkey's travels and vicissitudes of fortune take him into low-life situations, such as a mill worked by pitiable slaves who are scarred by beatings and brands on their foreheads, shackled, half-blind and dressed in bits of ragged clothing. Such slaves form the backdrop for a scene in the novel, but there is no reason to think that their conditions are exaggerated. We learn from writers on agriculture and from Pliny the Younger about gangs of chained agricultural slaves who lived in sub-human prison conditions. Unsurprisingly, such slaves had a reputation for being dangerous, difficult and less efficient than slaves who were more humanely treated. Equally chilling are finds of 'speaking' iron slave-collars, inscribed with instructions to the finder to return the slave to the rightful owner – a grossly uncomfortable and truly demeaning kind of dog tag.

A first-century AD tombstone depicting the tools and workshop of a metalsmith. The smith (shown seated) was a free man, but the hairstyle of his assistant suggests a slave captured in some foreign war. Depending on the relationship between the two, the slave might have been freed when the smith died, but he is more likely to have been sold by the widow as part of the workshop equipment.

TOWN AND COUNTRY

Just as domestic slaves are considerably more visible in surviving evidence of the Roman world than non-domestic slaves (by virtue of their intimate relationship with their masters and mistresses) so the urban poor are in general far more visible than the rural poor. The former were regularly thought of by socially superior Roman commentators as a highly annoying mass that needed to be appeased in order to keep the peace, and they became an increasingly pressing concern under Roman imperial rule. The *Orations* of Dio Chrysostom, writing in Bithynia between the end of the first and the beginning of the second century AD and the *Moralia* of his contemporary Plutarch both graphically illustrate the potential seriousness of social conflict within the Greek cities and the perceived dangers of this conflict coming to the attention of the Roman authorities. However, this annoyance is in large part a reflection of the close relations between rich and poor in the life of the city. This closeness was enacted both by large-scale benefaction (such as gifts from the rich of food, oil or games) and in reciprocal if profoundly unequal relationships between individuals of different social status (including landlords and tenants, or employers and employees).

Rural communities no doubt provided less of a stage upon which the wealthy might advertise their advancement and success; equally, popular political activity of all kinds was largely concentrated within urban centres. However, we should not underestimate the economic, social and political interconnections between town and country in the ancient world. Images of rural life functioned as powerful ideals for the Roman elite. The story of Cincinnatus, summoned from the plough to save Rome in

the early Republic, was full of powerful, culturally specific truths about worthy leadership, based on the values of frugality and hard work and the essential connection between farming and military prowess. A number of farming manuals survive from ancient Rome, each to a different extent an attempt to work through (by, and predominantly for, the leisured elite) ideologically important ideas about farming and country life by reference to its practicalities. For example, Cato the Elder's *De agricultura* (*On Agriculture*) prefaces advice on farm purchase, ownership and management by praising the traditional moral and military worth of the farmer-soldier. In doing so, he equates the experience of his readership – the prospective holders of relatively large estates – to that of small farmers. This creates some interesting tensions: his readers are expected to get their hands dirty by manuring fields and preparing medicine for sick cows, but they are also imagined to come and go, leaving their property in the hands of selected and closely monitored bailiffs. For the men who might read Cato's advice, farming was essentially a kind of hobby.

More concretely, the conscription of manpower for the Roman legions in the Republican period made the issue of farmland and its occupants a consistently hot political issue. The problem was how to increase the numbers of those who met the minimum census requirement for military service, measured in land-holding. This was addressed in various ways, including the establishment of colonies and Tiberius Gracchus's redistribution of illegally occupied public land. It is worth noting that, in the latter case, it is rural people who are said by the literary sources to be Tiberius' most visible supporters, thronging Rome to endorse his bill.

Two details from a 3rd-century AD Roman mosaic floor found in France, showing the harvesting of olives (left) and apples (right) by workers who are almost certainly slaves. Orchards and olive groves are a capitalist enterprise that require intensive labour only at certain times of the year. The slaves might belong to the landowner, or just be rented by him for the duration of the harvest.

COUNTRY RELATIONSHIPS

The memorial stone of the Roman citizen Lucius Aebutius Faustus, found in Italy. The artefacts carved below the inscription suggest that Faustus was a land surveyor (a highly regarded profession signified by the cross-shaped measuring gromma) who learned his skills in the army (military service is signified by the two swords). As such, he would have been in constant demand to settle boundary disputes.

At the individual level, it is important to note the importance in rural life of individual social relationships between wealthier and poorer farmers, as well as those between urban-dwellers and country-dwellers: it was such relationships that were crucial for prosperity (and at times for mere survival) in the Roman world. The surviving documents of such relationships give us great insight into rural life. In fact, most sources from the ancient world take an interest in the 'real' lives of the urban (or indeed the rural) poor only in terms of their relationships with the Roman elite. The reflections of Galen, a second-century AD doctor from Pergamum, on the diet of the rural poor are an isolated example of a specific, scientific concern with environmental matters. Galen observes, for example, that in times of famine poor country people eat acorns, a food normally given only to pigs, and that there is a regional variation in acorn recipes.

Most surviving documentary evidence reflects broadly social relationships between the richer and the poorer. This includes literary evidence in the form of the farming manuals mentioned above. The ostensibly didactic tone of these manuals contributes towards a somewhat stark but economically rational picture of relationships between landowners and the workforce: Cato prescribes a meagre clothing allowance for slaves, and recommends cutting the food rations of sick slaves. Varro recommends using casual free labour for working in unhealthy places, as the death of such people is a smaller loss to the landowner than the death of a slave.

There is a more paternalistic attitude towards tenant-farmers in the *Letters* of Pliny the Younger: he portrays himself holding audiences for their tedious complaints, making him more appreciative of his urbane leisured pursuits, and looks around in exasperation for new kinds of contracts that will address the large debts they owe to him.

Pliny seems keen to portray himself as a model senator of his time, with a paternalism that reflects the public image of the emperor Trajan. Trajan's so-called alimentary scheme in fact provides some important evidence of an attempt to foster a kind of social responsibility on the part of landowners.

Three documents provide evidence for this scheme, one from Veleia in northern Italy, one from Ligures Baebiani near Beneventum, and one from Ferentinum to the south of Rome. Landowners, the size of whose estates are listed in these documents, received an imperial loan of approximately eight per cent of the value of their property, and paid in perpetuity a five per cent interest on this loan, this interest to be used as grants for the maintenance of local children. As with all 'doles' in the Roman world, it does not seem that these grants were means-tested: perceptions of the moral worthiness of recipients seems to have been far more important than their actual need, and we can imagine the importance of patronage in deciding on the identity of recipients. Early imperial documents from Oxyrynchus in Egypt, however, sometimes suggest a relationship that seems rather different from either the rationalism of the farming manuals or the paternalism of the age of Trajan. For example, in 3 BC, one Aphynchis wrote to a potential absentee landlord in Alexandria, named Apis, to remind him of a conversation he had had with Aphynchis's son about leasing some land on which to plant animal fodder. Aphynchis is direct in his tone: he himself is too busy to arrange the lease, so Apis or his agent should do the necessary travelling and sort it out; Aphynchis has various other offers he might consider, but would 'prefer' to lease the land from Apis.

So far, we have concentrated on relationships between the rich and the poor in rural society. It is, in fact, possible to argue on the basis of some case-studies that such relationships did become more strongly polarised in later antiquity in rural society, one symptom of the sponsorship of the wealthy under Roman rule. However, rural social relations were of course generally much more complex and multi-layered than this schematic division would suggest. For a start, most rural household economies were probably highly fragmented. It is clear from the alimentary tables mentioned above, for example, that it was quite normal for the land-holdings of wealthier members of the community to be scattered into a number of individual plots, encouraging all sorts of complex relationships that might include several bailiffs and tenant-farmers.

Even when they discuss single, extensive estates, the authors of the Roman farming manuals regularly imagine the coexistence of slaves and free labourers of various kinds, reflecting the realities of fluctuating demands for labour in agriculture. The Egyptian 'Heroninos archive' suggests the presence of free workers engaged to work on the estate of the landowner Appianus on a whole range of contracts, as well as a permanent staff of servants and dependants.

Amongst less prosperous country-dwellers, we must imagine complex patterns of employment and obligation, as well as great variety in social and economic status. Even amongst landowners, grants of tiny allotments that were the size of small gardens rather than even subsistence farms are a recurrent feature of Roman landholding records, and it was probably the rule rather than the exception for such a landowner to play multiple roles in the rural economy. The roles of landowner, casual labourer and tenant-farmer must regularly have intersected.

We have already noted the importance of tenant-farmers in the context of the landowning patterns of the wealthy, but it is important to note also the range of statuses that were covered by the term *coloni*. *Coloni* could include both individuals working the land in return for the payment of rent or a percentage of the yield and also what we might call contractors in charge of teams of slaves or free labour. We can therefore imagine varying prosperity among tenant-farmers of different kinds and in different economic situations, covering the full social and economic range from wealthy prospectors right down to vulnerable individuals heavily indebted to and dependent on their creditors.

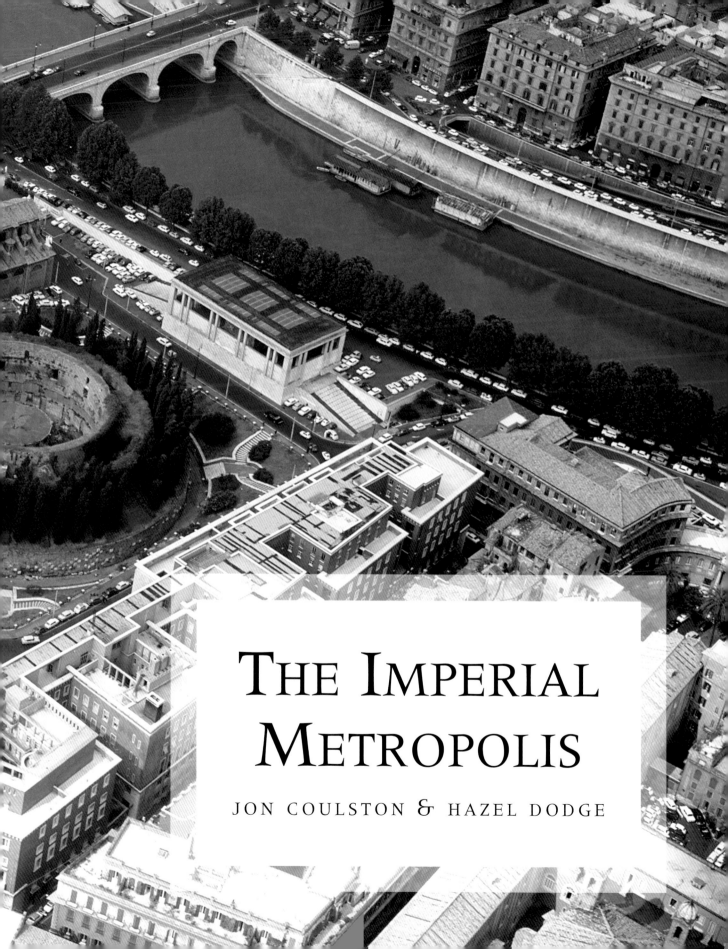

THE IMPERIAL METROPOLIS

JON COULSTON & HAZEL DODGE

THE IMPERIAL METROPOLIS

The growth of Rome from single city-state to pan-continental empire was directly reflected in the fabric of the city itself. The metropolis became a stage for elite display to an ever-growing population, and as the numbers of residents increased, their requirements for security (physical and spiritual), feeding, housing, entertainment and control were met by new forms of building. Rome's victories abroad enhanced the capital with artworks and financial resources. The advertisement of achievements by senatorial families and then the emperors was literally written across the city in the form of inscriptions on triumphal temples, arches and columns. No other city in the west before the Industrial Revolution came close to Rome in size, population and ornamental magnificence. Rome the city was the jewel in the crown of the Roman world, a model for urban emulation and an ideal of urban achievement almost to the present day.

An eighteenth-century German engraving depicting a reconstruction of a temple in Rome, based on the reverse of a coin. Temples were one of the prime 'adornments' of a city, enhancing not only its aesthetic qualities, but also its spiritual and (by implication) political authority.

Study of the ancient city since the Renaissance has yielded rich results and has been aided by some special classes of evidence. Ancient coins depict a range of monuments. An incised marble map with a ground plan of all the city's buildings has been recovered in fragments since the sixteenth century. This so-called *Forma Urbis Romae* had been attached to a wall (18 metres by 13 metres in size) within Vespasian's Temple of Peace, and dates to about AD 205–8. Although only some 20 per cent survives in pieces or antiquarian drawings, it does include a range of standing buildings (Colosseum, Circus Maximus), unexcavated monuments of known location (Temple of Claudius, Porticus Aemilia), unlocated public buildings, temples, houses, shops, gardens, streets, fountains, aqueducts and riverbanks. Two catalogues (the Regionary Catalogues) dating to the second half of the fourth century list classes of buildings and monuments organised in the fourteen Augustan regions, including obelisks, equestrian statues and colossal statues. Rome was a very epigraphically active city and has some 300,000 surviving inscriptions. From the Middle Ages, artists and architects have studied and recorded the ancient structures, many of which have since been destroyed. Photographers were

active recorders since the late 1840s, catching Rome before it became the capital of Italy (1870) and was transformed by a building explosion.

The archaeology of Rome also has some special features. The ancient city was cleared and renewed by frequent major fires. The perennial flooding of the River Tiber buried ancient buildings under metres of fluvial silt; terracing out of hillsides for optimum building space also filled up earlier buildings as revetments. Both processes resulted in deep stratification and good preservation – most notably in the wing of the Golden House of Nero with its rich fresco paintings, preserved beneath the Baths of Trajan. High population, linked with inflated land values, encouraged people to build high but also to tunnel deep into the soft tufa rock below. Underground cemeteries or catacombs are only the most famous product of this process.

An albumen print of the Roman Forum, dating from the 1860s. This early photograph, taken from the summit of the Capitoline Hill, shows the centrality of the forum within the old city; and this view would be readily recognised by a citizen of the fourth century AD.

THE SITE OF ROME

Rome's natural features were often cited in the ancient sources as reasons for its later greatness. The city's development itself transformed the site, at times dramatically, but it is possible to reconstruct the original landscape. Rome developed at the lowest fording place on the River Tiber (modern Tevere), made via a sand-bar island, with hills close to the river on either side, particularly on the east. Among these hills, the Palatine was steep-sided enough to be secure and large enough for a sizeable settlement. The Capitoline hill dominated the river crossing and was destined to become the city's acropolis and location of the most important temples. As the city grew it incorporated other freestanding hills, the Aventine, Velian and Caelian, rising to approximately 50 metres above sea level. Promontories such as the Quirinal and Viminal were also overtaken and the city mounted up onto the Esquiline plateau to the northeast, at a height of approximately 63 metres. These hills and promontories were originally thickly wooded and would have stood out more sharply, but over subsequent centuries they were levelled, terraced and quarried. Meanwhile, the ground level of low-lying areas between the hills steadily rose, naturally as a result of river inundations, or artificially through landfill operations. To the north and

Rome's earliest bridges across the Tiber were constructed of timber and were repeatedly destroyed in floods and storms. The first stone bridge was the Pons Aemilius (in the foreground) (179 and 142 BC); it has been known as the Ponte Rotto (the broken bridge) since its final collapse in 1598. The Tiber Island (at centre) is linked to the rest of the city by the Pons Cestius (at left) and the Pons Fabricus (at right); the latter is the oldest surviving ancient bridge in Rome (built 62 BC).

northwest of the Capitoline lay a part of the Tiber flood plain enclosed on three sides by a great meander of the river. In the middle of this area, known as the Field of Mars (ancient Campus Martius; modern Campo Marzio) because it was traditionally used for assembling the city's militia, the twenty-first-century ground level is some 8 metres above the first-century streets.

The Tiber valley, leading into the heart of Italy, was noted by ancient writers as beneficial for communications and trade, not least in the main local commodity, salt. However, flooding when the Apennine snows melted in spring was a major disadvantage for settlement in the valleys. The swiftness and force of the Tiber waters made permanent bridging difficult in early Rome. River navigation was problematic for both rowers and sailors, so boats were traditionally hauled upriver by human teams. The low-lying nature of parts of the city and the resultant flooding meant that earlier, less substantial architecture was undermined, if not swept away. In 193 BC the lower parts of the city were flooded, causing numbers of buildings to collapse, and in the following year two bridges were washed away. In 23 BC the Pons Sublicius was destroyed for the second time in forty years, and for three days the city was more easily navigated by boat than by foot. In AD 217 people were swept away in the very heart of the city, the Forum Romanum, by floodwaters.

Rome's location was advantageous on a larger scale, too. The city's bridges carried the routes overland between the Etruscan north-west and the Greek south-east, and Rome was close enough to the coast to control (ultimately) the equivalent sea route. The city's position on the Tiber helped the Romans to dominate their neighbours upstream, such as Veii and Fidenae. Later, with the development of roads and colonies, Rome's location halfway down the Italian peninsula made possible expansion both north and south. Italy occupied a central position in the Mediterranean as a whole once the latter had become the internal sea of the Roman Empire. On the other hand, when the problems of the Empire's northern frontier became acute from the later second century AD, Rome was inconveniently placed compared to more northerly centres like Milan, and less secure from invasion than Ravenna. Its position actually reduced the city's prosperity and political importance.

REGAL ROME

Under the kings, Rome emerged as a coherent urban entity, centred on the Palatine hill from the ninth century BC. At first the Palatine formed a fortified community with cemetery zones outside; sunken-floored huts from this period may still be seen on the west corner of the hill. By mid-seventh century the valley to the north-east was drained and raised with an immense (80,000 cubic metre) landfill to form a centre for ritual and economic activities, the Forum Romanum. Shrines gathered around it, as did the residences of the kings and the social elite. Market activities shifted gradually towards the Forum Boarium and Forum Holitorium near the river port – more convenient for landing supplies and separate from the high-status centre. As trade developed here so did structures associated with commerce, including storehouses and temples dedicated to the patrons of travel, notably Hercules. The Capitoline hill became the focus for the supreme deities of the city and a place for display commemorating victory. The valley south-west of the Palatine was conveniently shaped for holding horse-races and other sporting events, and gradually this area became monumentalised, with banks and seating for spectators, as the Circus Maximus.

REPUBLICAN ROME

Without contemporary written evidence from before 200 BC, scholars are heavily reliant on archaeology for information about Republican Rome's early development. After the seventh- to sixth-century Etruscan cultural dominance of the city, the fifth century BC reveals few substantial buildings and a reduction in rich funerary deposits. The emphasis of family commemoration was refocussed on the monumentalisation of temples. The fourth century was marked by Rome's Italian wars, the subjugation of Latium and the establishment of footholds in Etruria, and by much public building. The capture of Veii in 396 BC was quickly followed by the sack of Rome by the Gauls (around 390 BC). Whatever the destruction wrought by this event, it had a profound impact on future Roman perceptions of northern 'barbarian' peoples. It also encouraged the construction of new defences, the 'Servian' Wall.

Livy stated that the city rejuvenated quickly after the Gallic sack, but without rational planning such as the regular street grids of Hellenistic foundations. Roads followed valleys or the contours of hills, and so the city remained, as Cicero confirmed, 'perched on hills and propped in valleys, its tenements hanging aloft, its roads terrible, its alleys narrow'. The third century saw Roman control reach into northern Italy and Sicily, bringing the Greek culture of southern Italy much closer to Roman elite attention. This process advanced further in the second century, when wars around the Aegean brought more Greeks directly into the city. Each set of conflicts until the first-century Social War brought influxes of people, from Italy as refugees, and from abroad as slaves. As the population swelled, land prices in Rome increased and the urge to build upwards grew. High-density slum tenements became the lot of the poor. The senatorial rich became alarmed at the urban population growth. Various measures were taken to expel Latin residents, to export people to colonial foundations and to suppress 'foreign' cults and practices.

The second century saw more substantial stone and concrete building, new stone porticoes, bridges and paved streets. New classes of buildings also emerged, notably covered market basilicas (such as the Basilica Aemilia, 179 BC), triumphal columns and arches. Great riverside food warehouses such as the Porticus Aemilia (193 and 174 BC) and the Horrea Galbana were constructed on the flat space south of the Aventine outside the walls – an area which became known as the 'Emporium'. The first century was dominated by even larger structures, built under the auspices of military leaders like Sulla, Pompey and Julius Caesar, who harnessed the wealth of the Empire to their personal projects.

Either under the last kings or as a first 'victory' monument of the new Republic, an enormous Temple dedicated to Jupiter, Juno and Minerva was raised on the Capitoline. Its plan was Etruscan, its decorative roof terracottas were executed by imported Etruscan artists and its podium (raised base), measuring 62 metres by 53 metres, kept its dimensions through successive rebuilds until the first century AD. Sacrifice at this Temple of the Capitoline Triad was the culmination of triumphal processions. The temple was imitated in Roman colonies throughout the expanding empire.

A stretch of the so-called 'Servian Wall' now standing by the Stazione di Termini, well-preserved by a mound of spoil thrown up from creating cisterns for the Baths of Diocletian in the early fourth century AD.

THE FORUM ROMANUM

The Forum Romanum was the focus of public and political life and the site of some of the most important structures of the Roman state. Its site was originally a marshy valley between the Palatine and the Capitoline hills and the lower slopes of the Esquiline and Quirinal. It was developed as a communal area in the mid-seventh century BC, when a major landfill raised the ground level by up to 2 metres. This was clearly an attempt to counter the Tiber floods. The Cloaca Maxima was dug at this time. It crossed the Forum, draining the slopes of the Esquiline and Quirinal as well as the valley itself, passed through the Velabrum valley and the Forum Holitorium, and emptied into the Tiber. By the end of the seventh century BC the Forum was paved and the first Comitium and senate house had been constructed. On the edge of the Comitium was an important sanctuary, the Lapis Niger, named for the black stone used as paving; this was known to the Romans as the sanctuary of Vulcan. Votive deposits of the early sixth century BC date the development, and the base of a stone pillar survives with an Archaic Latin inscription.

After the expulsion of the kings, a number of important religious structures were built, notably the Temple of Saturn in 494 BC and the Temple of Castor and Pollux in 484/3 BC, both subsequently much rebuilt. Gradually the aristocratic houses that had surrounded the area gave way to more public buildings. The Sacra Via – the last stage of the processional way followed by triumphant generals – ran through the Forum. In 318 BC Gaius Maenius built porticoes and balconies on the shops on both the northeast and southwest sides of the square, which added not only architectural dignity but also extra viewing facilities.

Under the Republic, the Forum was also the traditional location for aristocratic funerals, which – from the mid-third century BC – often included gladiatorial combat. Such displays of elite status could sometimes get out of hand, however: in 52 BC, the Curia was burnt as a funeral pyre for Clodius and the Basilica Porcia was destroyed with it.

In the first half of the second century BC the Forum received Rome's first basilicas, the Basilica Porcia in 184 BC, the Basilica Fulvia and Aemilia in 179, and the Basilica Sempronia in 169 BC. The Forum was thus framed by important buildings and temples by mid-century. The next major work was carried out in the 80s BC by the dictator Sulla. The ground level was raised by nearly a metre and the central area was re-paved. Subterranean galleries, excavated in the 1960s, might also have been constructed at this time. Along the northern side of the Forum, the Curia was rebuilt, and on the slopes of the Capitoline rose a great cliff of masonry which may have been the state records office, the Tabularium, or the mint.

Under Julius Caesar and Augustus, the Forum achieved the form it maintained until the Late Roman period. Caesar started to rebuild the Curia and a great basilica on the south side, the Basilica Iulia. Both were completed by Augustus, who added a Temple of the Divine Julius at the southeast end, flanked by new triumphal arches. The Actian Arch, erected in 29 BC, commemorated his victory over Antony and Cleopatra, and the so-called Parthian Arch erected in 19 BC marked the recovery of the legionary standards previously lost to the Parthians by Crassus. Inscriptions listed the names of triumphorates from Romulus down to Augustus. The Rostra, the speakers' platform, was moved from the edge of the Comitium to the northwest end of the Forum to provide an axial focus and a place from which emperors could address a mass of Romans in the square. Thus the open space was completely surrounded by buildings constructed or rebuilt by the emperor, or by members of his family and faction.

A southwards view down the middle of the Roman Forum, with the ruins of the Basilica Julia on the right and, beyond, the three re-erected columns of the Temple of Castor and Pollux.

A serious fire in AD 283 allowed Diocletian to create a similar effect by rebuilding the Curia, the Basilica Iulia and the Rostra and erecting his own columnar monuments. When it was excavated in the nineteenth to early twentieth century, the Forum Romanum was predictably crowded with the latest display monuments, equestrian statue-bases of Constantine I and Constantius II and inscriptions associated with late-fourth to early-fifth century emperors. The very last addition came much later, with the Column of Phocas, a 50 Roman foot (15-metre) fourth-century column reused in AD 608 to honour the emperor who gifted the Pantheon as a store for relics of Christians from the catacombs. It was positioned so as to be viewed along the Argiletum road.

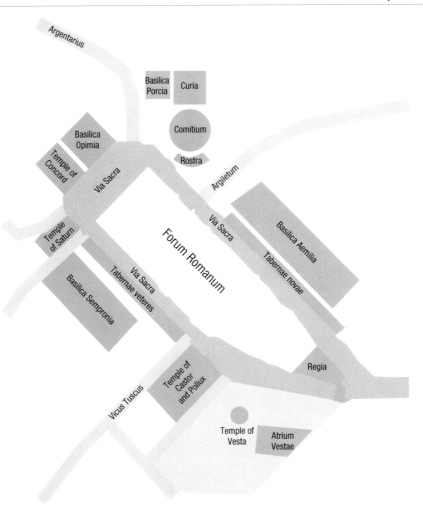

A plan of the Forum Romanum in the early second century BC. Following the founding of the Republic, a great number of public and government buildings were quickly erected to house the elite who had taken control of the various functions previously performed by the king and his court. Over time the role of the Forum itself changed from the central market to the site of public meetings and celebrations.

When the Republic was founded, the Roman elite took over and separated the king's functions as judge, general and priest. This prompted the further development of buildings associated with government and ritual around the Forum Romanum, such as the Regia and the Curia. Indeed, the open space of the Forum increasingly became less of a market and more of a stage for elite activities, such as public speaking, public honouring of individuals with statuary, and funerals with their associated processions, orations, cremations and games.

Long-existing cults were monumentalised with new temples, and new cults were added in association with important events, such as the Temple of Castor and Pollux after the Battle of Lake Regillus (about 496 BC) and the Temple of Concord after the patricians and plebeians had worked out new modes of political cooperation in 367 BC. Nearby crowded the houses of the Roman rich, around and behind the public buildings and up the slopes of the Palatine, so that they could be close to political life and – even better – so as to line the route taken by triumphs. The Aventine hill became the plebeian equivalent by the fourth century. From the third century, the focus for plebeian meetings was not the Forum Romanum but an open space below the Capitoline hill, outside the walls by the river, known as the Circus Flaminius.

One facet of Roman expansion was the importing of foreign deities, such as Diana from the Alban Hills and Juno Regina from Veii, set up in their temples on the Aventine. In response to plagues, Apollo was housed by the river (the Temple of Apollo Medicus) after 431 BC, and the healing god Aesculapius was established on the Tiber island in 291 BC. In the dark days of Hannibal's threat to the city, the cult of the *Magna Mater* (Great Mother) was brought from Asia Minor to the Palatine (*See also* Chapter 11).

Another facet was the importing of new and exotic building materials, the very availability of which symbolised Rome's spreading power. Fine white marbles came in from the Greek world in increasing quantities during the first century BC. With each rebuild, often following fires, temples were enlarged and 'updated' in new materials. Their larger podia enclosed earlier, smaller ones, rather like Russian dolls.

Victorious Roman generals were supposed to enrich the state treasury, reward their soldiers and enhance their family fortunes, but it also became customary to expend spoils on improving the city. New aqueducts were often constructed following wars, such as the Aqua Anio Vetus after the defeat of Pyrrhus (272 BC) and the Aqua Marcia after the sacks of Carthage and Corinth in 146 BC. However, the most characteristic monument was the 'victory' temple, often built in fulfilment of a vow made before battle. These were dedicated to deities appropriate to war and specific victories, and were intended to ensure an immortal reputation of achievement for the victor and his family (*gens*). Over time these temples tended to be placed in ranks, sometimes eventually in multiple-temple precincts, facing on to public spaces, principally along the triumphal way. One group even developed from about 300 BC in the central Campus Martius, at a spot now known as the Largo Argentina, so as to be close to where armies were assembled.

The triumph was one of the institutions of the Roman state that had most influence on the urban fabric. In the Republic, a triumph was an honour conferred by the senate on a victorious general; in some periods these were almost annual events, reflecting the expansion of the Empire but also the ambitions of individual senators. The main feature was a great procession through the city of soldiers, enemy leaders and other prisoners, booty, information placards, large framed paintings depicting war events and the triumphant general (*triumphator*) riding in a four-horse chariot. Processions could be held over a number of days, as was the triumph of Aemilius Paullus after his 168 BC victory at Pydna over Perseus of Macedon, described in detail by Polybius.

Over time the route became fixed. The triumphal procession began in the Campus Martius, where there was space to marshal those involved; its ultimate goal was the temple of Jupiter Capitolinus. Between these two points, the route led into the city by the Porta Triumphalis. It passed through the Forum Boarium and the Circus Maximus, up the valley between the Palatine and Caelian hills, over the saddle of the Velia and down into the Forum Romanum. Unless he had been spared, the enemy leader was here led off to execution, while the triumphant general mounted the Capitoline slope to make sacrifice and dedicate *spolia* arms at the temple. In passing around three sides of the Palatine, the route was similar to that run during the Lupercalia festival by young nobles with wolf skins. This followed the sacred boundary (*pomerium*) of the old Palatine 'City of Romulus'. The route ensured a maximum number of spectators, especially in the Circus Maximus. Temples and other monuments lined the way and triumphal arches spanned the route, added by Augustus and succeeding emperors (Augustus, Vespasian and Titus, Titus, Severus, Constantine). Even elite houses along the course joined in on triumphal days with façades decked with wreaths and captured *spolia* from previous triumphs awarded to the occupants' *gens*.

The start of the triumphal route in the Campus Martius, near the Villa Publica, was where Pompey chose to locate his theatre, dedicated in 55 BC. Its gardens were laid out with the Largo Argentina temple precinct acting like an entrance. The triumphal nature of the monument was further emphasised by dedication of the associated temple to Venus Victrix. The sheer scale of this complex, erected with spoils of war as a single construction by a single general, contrasts tellingly with the four small Largo Argentina temples that marked the earlier triumphs of various *gentes* over a period of two centuries.

These victory monuments became more and more elaborate and impressive as *triumphatores* sought to outdo their predecessors. From the late Republic, public spectacle became part of the victory celebrations. In 46 BC, when Julius Caesar celebrated a quadruple triumph, he put on gladiatorial shows in the Forum Romanum, races in the Circus Maximus, plays in the theatre (presumably the Theatre of Pompey) and a sea-battle re-enactment. For the latter, he had a special basin dug on the Campus Martius and a battle staged between Egyptian and Tyrian fleets. Suetonius noted that the crush was so great as people flocked to these entertainments that there were several fatalities, including two senators. Caesar made a number of other contributions to the city. He started to rebuild the Curia which had burned down during political rioting in 52 BC. He also constructed a new forum, the Forum Iulium, outside the Forum Romanum. Its axial temple was dedicated to Venus Genetrix, the divine ancestress of the *gens* Iulia, making it very much a family monument. In the Campus Martius he built a voting enclosure, the Saepta Iulia, which could also be used for public displays. Just as significantly, his sudden death left a number of well publicised plans and unfinished constructions to be completed by his heir, Augustus, including a new Basilica Iulia on one side of the Forum Romanum. His dominant position had allowed Caesar to plan for the city as a whole and to build on a lavish scale; his successors did both.

General view of the Forum of Julius Caesar with the axially placed Temple of Venus Genetrix (divine ancestress of the Julian Family).

CITY OF THE EMPERORS

With the accession of Augustus, a new era arrived for the city of Rome. From now on the emperors took responsibility for much of the city's administration, including policing, fire control, building regulations, food supply and prices. This was more efficient for a huge urban centre, but a concern for efficiency was secondary to political dictates. The emperors were determined that the instability of the late Republican period should not recur. This required measures to make food plentifully available and cheap, in order to avoid bread-riots. The emperors appointed equestrians, rather than members of the more politically prominent senate, to administer the corn supply. Emperors like Claudius, Nero and Trajan improved the harbours around the mouth of the Tiber (Ostia and Portus) and along the coast (Centumcellae, Terracina and Puteoli), while also attending to landing and secure storage facilities in the centre of Rome.

Augustus divided the city into fourteen regions, which helped administration on many levels. These were subdivided into wards (*vici*) where not only justice but also religious festivals linked with the emperor were administered by local officials (*vicomagistri*). The city was protected from fire by seven cohorts of military fire-watch personnel under an equestrian prefect, replacing the political gangs of Clodius or Crassus. Once major fires had taken hold, however, there was little that they could do except create fire-breaks. These patrols had powers of search and punishment. Other urban troops were also available to police events and provide riot control.

The emperors and their families required protection from the city population. Augustus maintained a bodyguard of citizen troops which Tiberius concentrated in one fortress, the Castra Praetoria. This Praetorian Guard increased in size, notably under Septimius Severus, who also changed the Guard's personnel from Italian soldiers to promoted legionaries from the Danubian provinces. Equestrians, not senators, were appointed as guard commanders.

The Julio-Claudian emperors balanced the praetorians with a cavalry guard of Germans, making it much more difficult for potential conspirators to suborn both formations. The cavalry guard, however, were disbanded during the 68–69 civil war, leaving emperors from Galba to Nerva rather less secure. Trajan resurrected a horse guard, the *equites singulares Augusti*, recruited from non-citizen frontier auxiliaries. Severus doubled this formation in size and stationed a newly raised legion of 5,000 troops close to Rome. There were marines based in Rome for communication and transport duties, but also to rig the awnings (*velaria*) used to protect theatre and amphitheatre audiences. These growing numbers of troops were stationed in fortresses around the city outskirts, where they would not seem like a tyrant's citadels.

In fact, there were more troops in Rome than in any other city or military base of the Empire: up to 8,000 under Augustus, 20,000 under Trajan, and 31,500 under Severus (excluding the legion). These men were highly paid and legally privileged, and they formed both a cosmopolitan element of Rome's population and a major source of financial patronage. Only very rarely, as with the death of Pertinax in 193, did these troops turn on their commander, the emperor.

The ruins of Domitian's great palace on the Palatine Hill in Rome. This wing of the building was known as the Domus Augustana, and housed the private appartments of the imperial family with views over the Circus Maximus, where chariot races were held.

IMPERIAL PATRONAGE

Rome was the main residence of the emperors, though some absented themselves from the city for long periods. Augustus supposedly lived a simple senator's life in his house on the west corner of the Palatine, although it was closely associated with the surrounding temples. Tiberius built a much more extensive residence across to the north corner, and Gaius (Caligula) linked this with the Forum Romanum below. Nero remodelled much of the Palatine and the valley to the north-east into a series of parks, water features and residences, known first as the Domus Transitoria, then rebuilt after the great AD 64 fire as the *Domus Aurea* (Golden House). This complex was innovative in architectural and decorative design, and unapologetically luxurious, exciting both awe and disapproval. The Flavian emperors were content to re-use it until Domitian constructed the greatest 'palace' of all (the word *palatium* itself coming from the location of this house, on the Palatine), the Domus Flavia. This presented façades towards the Forum Romanum and the Circus Maximus and consisted of multiple courts, audience halls, dining rooms, domestic wings and sunken gardens, all lavishly decorated with mosaics, marbles, stuccoes and an army of statuary, and supplied by dedicated aqueduct spurs. The Palatium was finished off by Severus with a great arcaded south wing and baths.

In addition to the Palatine properties, the emperors accumulated gardens (*horti*) and villas in a great green belt around the outskirts of the city, many known by the names of prominent republican owners, such as the Horti Sallustiani and the Horti Luculliani.

Emperors fulfilled a number of duties in Rome – sitting in the senate, meeting ambassadors, hearing legal cases, presiding at the games. They also held audiences, visited the Forum Romanum, threw dinner parties and enjoyed the baths. They followed the public and private activities of any other elite *patronus*, with the difference that this patron had the resources of the entire Empire at his command. It was as this supreme patron that the emperor interacted with the city population. Senators could sponsor public games, but could never compete with the lavishness of imperial entertainments. Senators could also erect buildings, but never on a scale which could serve the whole city. The *arcana imperii* (secrets of power) discussed by Tacitus included keeping the inhabitants of Rome happy with subsidised food, spectacles and other 'gifts'. Any emperor who built on a large scale not only provided new structures and facilities for the city, but also provided welcome employment for a significant element of the population.

The supply of building materials, such as fired brick, became more organised and supervised. From Tiberius onwards the emperors went to some lengths to ensure plentiful and economic supplies of decorative stone (marbles, limestones, granites and porphyries) for their massive projects in Rome. Indeed, the very polychrome range of stones used in the emperor's buildings symbolised the extent of Rome's hegemony over the natural world.

A good example of this combination of patronage, scale of provision and lavish decoration is the series of great imperial baths complexes (*thermae*). The first was provided in the Campus Martius by Agrippa under Augustus's auspices, followed by new *thermae* under Nero, Titus, Trajan, Severus, Caracalla, Severus Alexander, Decius, Diocletian and Constantine. These were not just Roman baths on an inflated scale: they provided a huge range of facilities. A modern equivalent, if one existed, would combine Turkish and Japanese baths, solaria, changing facilities, gymnasia, swimming pools, lavatories, restaurants, brothels, art galleries, shops, landscaped gardens, roof gardens, outdoor running tracks, libraries, lecture halls and religious shrines. Decoration included mosaic floors, marble veneered walls, stuccoed ceilings, statuary and sculpted, painted and gilded ornament.

Mosaic floors and massive vaults of the Baths of Caracalla in Rome. Intended to outshine the best of Caracalla's august predecessors, and overwhelm the citizens of Rome with his munificence, the baths reflect the scale of pan-Mediterranean resources available to an emperor.

THE WALLS OF ROME

The early city had a series of defensive wall circuits, sections of which have been traced on the Palatine and Capitoline hills. However, the first unified set of fortifications was constructed some time after the Gauls had sacked Rome in 390 BC. These defences, confusingly referred to traditionally as the 'Servian Wall', were constructed by imported Sicilian Greek masons, employing Grotta Oscura tufa quarried near Veii. They were 11 kilometres long and enclosed the traditional seven hills within an area of 426 hectares, access to the city was made through twenty-one gates. In common with many other fourth-century Italian town walls, the style was massive and monumental, and on the Esquiline plateau the wall was further protected by a huge ditch and backed by a great earth bank. This was the wall faced by Hannibal, and it protected Rome until the Social War, last being restored in 87 BC. Thereafter it lost its military function and became obscured by buildings, although some stretches on the northeast side became popular evening promenades. The armies on the imperial frontiers were now Rome's shield.

The military reverses and 'barbarian' incursions suffered by the Empire in the third century led Aurelian and Probus to re-fortify the city in AD 270–82. These walls were 19 kilometres long and built in brick-faced concrete, with 383 towers, eighteen main gates and numerous posterns, enclosing a total area of some 1,372 hectares. The walls themselves were heightened probably by Maxentius and further strengthened with massive gate structures by Honorius in the early fifth century, which are today especially well preserved at the Porta Appia, Asinaria, Ostiensis and Tiburtina. Along their course, which is still largely intact, the walls incorporated and thus preserved numerous tombs, *insula* facades, garden terraces, an amphitheatre and three sides of the Castra Praetoria. Their extent was generous, enclosing large open areas of *horti*, some not built on since. The successively raised levels of the curtain wall can be seen clearly at the Castra Praetoria, starting with the gates, towers, wall and parapet of the Tiberian construction. The Aurelianic Wall lined the Tiber riverbank and for the first time enclosed an area on the right bank up the slopes of the Janiculum hill (Trans Tiberim, modern Trastevere).

While the Vatican was joined to the river by a loop of 'Leonine' Wall in the ninth century and the Vatican and Janiculum were fortified with Renaissance gunpowder artillery defences in the sixteenth to seventeenth centuries, the Aurelianic Walls continued to protect the city on all other fronts until the nineteenth century. They were periodically repaired and the odd tower was added, but the only serious modifications were one large sixteenth-century brick bastion in the southwest, and earth bastions at the gates. In 1527 and 1849 Rome was successfully assaulted from the high ground to the west, where modern artillery could dominate the city. In 1870 the royal army made a symbolic breach in the Aurelianic Wall near the Porta Pia, the last occasion on which the Roman defences had a military role.

Exterior view of the Porta Appia (S. Sebastiano), first built in the later third century AD, but completed with square towers and upper storeys in the early fifth century.

MONUMENTS OF THE EMPERORS

The emperors had a range of other modes of communication with the city's inhabitants. In particular, the formal triumph became the emperor's sole preserve. In 19 BC Lucius Cornelius Balbus was the last 'private' senator to be awarded one; thereafter only emperors or members of imperial families rode in the chariot. Triumphal games became increasingly lavish. Those of AD 80 went on for a hundred days, involving 5,000 animals in a single day, and were linked with the opening of the *Amphitheatrum Flavium* (Colosseum), itself paid for by Titus' sack of Jerusalem. Trajan's games lasted 123 days, with 11,000 animals and 10,000 gladiators, celebrating his triumph over the Dacians. Coin issues were used to depict defeated barbarians and captured *spolia*, but also buildings – either to announce planned projects or to celebrate inaugurations. Advertising traditional achievements, principally victory in war, occurred through traditional monuments on a grand scale, such as the ever more imposing imperial arches that spanned the Via Triumphalis, or through gilded bronze statues, such as the massive equestrian Domitian that stood in the Forum Romanum. Figural sculpture was used to proclaim victory over the Empire's enemies and attentive care for Rome's inhabitants, as can still be seen on the arches of Titus, Severus and Constantine and the columns of Trajan and Marcus Aurelius. Painted and gilded, these must have been arresting sights, great information boards addressing the elite classes, soldiers and the urban masses alike.

One victory monument especially linked with the emperors was provided by the appropriation of red granite obelisks. These were either Pharaonic period items inscribed with hieroglyphs taken from temples in Egypt, or custom-made obelisks with plain shafts or non-sensical hieroglyphs. As ever, the first emperor set the precedent by placing large examples in the Circus Maximus and on his giant sundial in the Campus Martius. A smaller pair flanked the entrance to his mausoleum. This was a fitting act because obelisks were spoils from the newly annexed Egypt placed at the conqueror's tomb. Moreover, they were traditionally dedicated to the Sun, so in the Circus the imagery of sun and chariotry worked well, and on the Horologium the sun link was even more obvious. Gaius brought another huge obelisk to Rome for his circus alongside the Vatican hill. Many small obelisks adorned the Temple of Isis and Serapis in the Campus Martius, rebuilt by Vespasian, Titus and Domitian – for whom Egypt and Isis had special civil war resonances. Hadrian set up an obelisk as a memorial to his lover Antinoos, who drowned in the Nile.

A precedent had been set by Julius Caesar for building a new forum near the Forum Romanum, closely linked with the donor's family. His temple of Venus Genetrix was vowed at the Battle of Pharsalus (48 BC). Augustus built his own new forum on land he owned himself, adjacent to the Forum Iulium. This complex formed part of a much wider building programme aimed both at healing the rifts of civil war and at advertising victories. Its axial temple was dedicated to Mars the Avenger, originally for the elimination of Caesar's assassins and as a votive act following the Battle of Philippi (42 BC). Inside were statues of Mars, Venus and Julius Caesar. On the two long sides of the court were porticoes of coloured marble columns with large semi-circular *exedrae* filled with niched statuary. At the end of the north-west portico was a colossal Augustus statue; the *exedrae* contained statues of Aeneas and the kings

of Alba Longa on the one side, and on the other those of Romulus and the illustrious men of the Republic. In the centre of the court was a chariot carrying Augustus as *triumphator*. The emperor thus placed himself at the heart of Roman history, shoulder to shoulder with Rome's legendary heroes.

The Forum of Augustus in Rome. The axial temple was dedicated to Mars Ultor, avenging the murder of Julius Caesar. The was later used to display the standards lost by Crassus in 53 BC, returned by the Parthians in 20–19 BC.

Vespasian's Temple or Forum of Peace was built across the Argiletum road from the Forum Augustum. It was dedicated to the peace achieved after the 68–9 civil war, but was adorned with the more famous spoils of the sack of Jerusalem. Its court was decorated with long pools and its colonnades and rooms became a cultural facility, with artworks and libraries. In the south corner room, one wall was carved with the marble *Forma Urbis Romae*, first perhaps in the Flavian original building, but updated under Severus. The space between Templum Pacis and Forum Augustum was remodelled by Domitian to make the Forum Transitorium, the name derived from the Argiletum through-route between the Forum Romanum and the Subura quarter. This was traditionally an area for booksellers and copyists, and it was graced with a temple dedicated to Minerva, Domitian's chosen patroness. After Domitian's assassination, Nerva dedicated the complex and took the credit for the Forum Nervae.

The last of the Imperial fora was the largest and most lavish of them all (overall dimensions 118 metres by 89 metres). Dedicated in 112 by Trajan, this was paid for directly by Trajan's share of the spoils from the conquest of Dacia in AD 106. The term *ex manubiis* was used in inscriptions to specify the source, just as was done on the Colosseum. The unrelenting theme of this complex, expressed in relief sculpture, statuary and epigraphy, was the emperor's Danubian victories. The complex comprised an open colonnaded court with porticoes and paving of imported marble, the upper storeys of which were adorned with over life-size figures of captured Dacians. In the centre stood a colossal statue of a mounted Trajan. On one side was the largest colonnaded hall in Roman architecture, the Basilica Ulpia. Beyond this was Trajan's Column in its own court, flanked by a pair of libraries, a monument that not only depicted the Dacian Wars in sculpture but also provided a viewing platform above the whole complex, allowing further public appreciation of achievement. Trajan's Forum was used for legal cases, cultural activities such as poetry-readings, the public burning of debt-records and the manumission of slaves.

All these Imperial fora were dynastic monuments, designed to advertise individual and family achievement. All contained a temple, linking them closely with the republican tradition of 'victory' temples. In one sense they were also monuments built in competition – though the emperors competed with their predecessors, not with senators. Architecture was always politically charged in Rome. The Augustan Theatre of Marcellus, for example, was placed at one end of the Circus Flaminius so as to partake in triumphal route celebrations, but also so as

A view from Trajan's Forum up to the Markets of Trajan and the medieval Torre delle Milizie (top). This complex was terraced into the side of the Quirinal Hill constructed of brick-faced concrete with concrete vaulting.

to dominate completely the Temple of Apollo Sosianus, which had been rebuilt by a senator who was on the wrong side at the Battle of Actium (31 BC). The Colosseum was located so as to take advantage of a natural lake depression, but it also filled in the lake that had been a major feature of the Neronian Domus Aurea. Nero was unpopular for his personal use of so much urban space, but very popular for his *thermae* (the poet Martial asked 'What worse than Nero, what better than Nero's baths?'). Thus the Flavians made political capital in a variety of ways: they replaced the lake, they provided the greatest ever venue for gladiatorial games and they celebrated their defeat not of civil war enemies but of foreigners by using the Jerusalem *spolia* to finance the project. Lastly, by opening the Baths of Titus at the same time as the Colosseum was inaugurated, they diverted attention even further from Nero's reputation.

This all went wrong when a *damnatio memoriae* was served on Domitian by the senate after his assassination. His many triumphal arches were demolished and his equestrian statue in the Forum Romanum was melted down. Trajan could not directly outdo the Colosseum, remodelled in its completed form by Domitian, but he could address the even larger crowd capacity of the Circus Maximus (as celebrated on his coins). He could and did wipe away the memory of Domitian's triumphs and games with the lavish scale of his own displays. Trajan's *thermae* physically dominated and outshone the Baths of Titus below. The memory of Domitian's Forum Romanum statue was eclipsed by the statue of Trajan in his Forum. Through the latter, Trajan could emphasise victory over a foreign enemy, the Dacians (the Jews were, after all, unruly provincials inside the Empire), an enemy whose king Decebalus had defeated and humiliated Domitian. All these contrasts would have been plain to every intelligent reader of the inscriptions on the Colosseum and Forum.

THE RELIGIOUS ROLE OF EMPERORS

Emperors played a part in the religious and ritual life of the city by serving in priesthoods and by patronising traditional cults. Augustus's claim to have restored eighty-two temples in 28 BC was intended to signal a return to the traditional relationship with the gods after a lapse during the civil war. Emperors also supported favoured cults, such as the votive temple built by Augustus to Apollo Actiacus on the Palatine, vowed before the Battle of Actium (31 BC). The Flavians patronised the Iseum in the Campus Martius. Hadrian constructed a Temple of Venus and Rome between the Forum Romanum and the Colosseum to his own Hellenising design. He also rebuilt Agrippa's Temple to All the Gods (Pantheon) in the Campus Martius, perhaps personally designing its circular plan, which called for a 43-metre diameter concrete dome. Elagabalus infamously brought the Syrian sky god of his native city of Emesa to Rome and erected a temple for him on the Palatine (after his death the site was rededicated to Jupiter the Avenger).

The deification of deceased emperors also generated a good number of temples and new festivals, instituted by successors who could strengthen their own position by becoming the sons of gods. Augustus and Tiberius shared a temple in the Velabrum valley southwest of the Forum Romanum. Claudius's temple stood on a great platform amid spectacular fountains and gardens on the Caelian Hill. Vespasian and Titus shared a temple in the Forum Romanum, while Antoninus Pius was nearby on the Via Sacra. Hadrian, Marcus Aurelius and various female relatives of Trajan resided in the Campus Martius. This last area was effectively filled with temples, baths, theatres, porticoed enclosures, triumphal monuments and housing under the emperors. Many constructions took north–south or east–west alignments so that the Campus took on the look of a planned streetgrid, rather like the Emporium district, but unlike the rest of the city with its organic growth.

ENTERTAINING ROME

Bread and circuses (*panem et circenses*) were the two things yearned for by the Roman mob, according to the early second-century AD satirist Juvenal. Although they were religious in origin, Roman games quickly acquired secular and political importance. Such mass public entertainment took a number of different forms: chariot-racing in the Circus Maximus (*ludi circenses*), games with animals (*venationes*, also in the Circus, but later also in the amphitheatre) and theatrical performances (*ludi scaenici*). Gladiatorial displays were not part of the public games and had no institutional religious association: these were *munera*, public spectacles. The early gladiatorial games were associated with aristocratic funerals, and under the emperors took place in the amphitheatre, though occasionally also in other public spaces. Although the *ludi* and *munera* had very different origins, the political advantage to be gained from such displays had been fully realised in Rome during the last two centuries BC. In the imperial period it became common practice for the emperor to put on special games to commemorate victories and anniversaries.

Early dramatic performances in Rome were originally associated with religious festivals in honour of particular deities. The *ludi scaenici* are attested as early as 364 BC. Classical Greek tragedies and comedies and the works of the great early Republican poets (Ennius, Plautus, Terence and others) reached the height of their popularity in the second century BC. Nevertheless, it is interesting that Rome did not receive a permanent theatre building until Pompey built and dedicated his in 55 BC. Before this date all theatres in Rome were temporary wooden structures, usually in the appropriate religious sanctuary, dismantled after the festival for which they were erected. These temporary theatres became increasingly sumptuous in the late Republic as prominent politicians vied for public support. Marcus Scaurus became a byword for luxury, as a result of his extraordinary ostentation, which included a massively expensive temporary theatre built when he was aedile in 58 BC. According to Pliny the Elder:

This was his theatre, which had a stage arranged in three storeys with 360 columns; and this, if you please, in a community that had not tolerated the presence of six columns of Hymettus marble without reviling a leading citizen. The lowest storey of the stage was marble, and the middle one of glass (an extravagance unparalleled even in later times), while the top storey was made of gilded planks. The columns of the lowest storey were 38 feet high. The bronze statues in the spaces between the columns numbered 3,000... As for the auditorium, it accommodated 80,000.

The first recorded gladiatorial show in Rome is attributed to the ex-consul Decimus Junius Brutus Pera and his brother in 264 BC, who held games in the Forum Boarium in honour of their father. These shows, although part of an essentially private ritual, developed into public performances as aristocratic competition increased. Before specific buildings were constructed for them they were held in the social and ritual centre of the city, the Forum Romanum, from at least as early as 210 BC until as late as the early first century AD.

Rome's first permanent amphitheatre was built in the southern Campus Martius in 29 BC by Statilius Taurus, one of Augustus's generals. It was financed *ex manubiis* from his triumph in 34 BC, which celebrated his African victory. Very little is known about this structure, not even its exact location, since it burned down completely in the great fire of AD 64. This has led historians to suggest that while the foundations may have been of stone, the superstructure was predominantly wooden. In AD 57 Nero built a wooden amphitheatre on stone foundations in the Campus Martius; by all accounts this was a sumptuous construction despite its building materials. It had ivory and gold ornamentation and was covered by an awning the colour of the sky and studded with stars; exotic beasts were brought for the entertainment of the crowd.

However, it was not until AD 80 and the inauguration of the Colosseum that Rome received its first permanent amphitheatre. This was begun by Vespasian in 75 and dedicated by his son Titus. An impressive structure, the building stood nearly 50 metres high and could accommodate some 50,000 spectators. A recently discovered inscription clearly indicates that it was financed from the spoils of war from the sack of Jerusalem in AD 70, for which Vespasian and Titus celebrated the magnificent triumph described by Josephus. The inauguration itself was a further opportunity for imperial munificence in the form of one hundred days of games. These displays were commemorated by Martial in a series of epigrams that survive (partially, at least) in the collection known as the *Book of Spectacles* (*Liber spectaculorum* or *Liber de spectaculis*).

Chariot-racing was one of the most popular sports in both the Greek and Roman worlds; the circus and its associated events had a very long history in Rome. The most famous of the Roman world, Rome's Circus Maximus, was located in the valley between the Palatine and the Aventine hills. This area was used for public spectacles from at least the sixth century BC; the first structure is said by tradition to date back to the Tarquins. However, for centuries the circus was little more than

The interior of the Colosseum viewed from one of the lower seating tiers. In the middle, instead of the original wooden flooring, the modern visitor can see a labyrinth of passages which housed cells, preparation rooms and cages. Participants in the games and scenery were hoisted up to the arena floor by winch-powered elevators.

a flat area just over half a kilometre in length, with the starting gates and seating in timber and a simple central barrier around which the chariots raced. From the late Republic on, the structure was gradually monumentalised, with the greatest transformation taking place under Trajan. The new circus was 600 metres long and could accommodate 300–350,000 spectators, making it the largest single complex for public congregation in the world. The central barrier received monuments and sculptures over time; there were two lap-counting mechanisms: seven gilded eggs first attested in 174 BC, and seven gilded dolphins added by Agrippa in 33 BC. At either end was a turning point (*meta*) in the form of a large gilded bronze cone.

SUPPLYING THE CITY

Supplying food and water to an urban population that may have reached 1,000,000 by the second century AD was a constant challenge to Roman organisational skills; by the imperial period the provision of food in particular was considered the obligation of the emperor. A city the size of Rome was always faced with the threat of famine, particularly since from the late Republic more and more food, especially grain, wine and olive oil, was imported from other parts of the Mediterranean. This situation was partly caused by technological limitations in the transport and preservation of foodstuffs – but classical Athens had managed to maintain a continuous and steady supply despite heavy reliance on imports. Rome, however, was different on two counts. First, the size of the population meant the scale of the problem was much greater, and second there was growing political significance attached to the issue, especially from the time of Gaius Gracchus

The first recorded instance of state intervention in food supply was in 299 BC when high prices prompted the aediles to improve the grain supply. The acquisition of overseas territory, notably in Sicily, helped supplement supplies from Italy, and further measures were taken in 203 and 201 BC to distribute low-cost grain from Spain and Africa. The situation was not helped by fluctuating prices, speculation and profiteering, nor by changes in agricultural practice in Italy in the second century BC which saw a switch from grain cultivation to cash crops such as vines, olives and cattle.

The first major piece of legislation to address the supply of food to the poor of Rome was a food law (*lex frumentaria*) proposed by Gaius Gracchus (123 BC); the state would buy up grain in bulk and store it in public warehouses (the construction of which would provide much-needed employment). The state would then sell a monthly ration to qualifying Roman citizens at a low price. These measures had some success in the short term, but their political importance became clear in the first century BC, when they were transformed into a dole by ambitious politicians as a form of political bribery. As a result, the Roman population came to expect a guaranteed food supply. Julius Caesar made some attempt to address the issue by making some of the aediles responsible solely for the grain supply, but it was left to Augustus to formalise the process. He established an office of *praefectus annonae* (prefect of the grain supply), to be held by a man of equestrian rank. From the time of Claudius, this office was located in the Porticus Minucia Frumentaria on the Campus Martius. The Claudian construction of a new deep-water harbour at Portus also helped to improve supply. Nonetheless, there were still major problems – Claudius himself was waylaid in the Forum and pelted with bread by an angry starving mob.

Septimius Severus added olive oil to the *annona*, but olive oil had always been an important part of Rome's diet. It was a key source of fat as well as for lighting and bathing. The extent of Rome's consumption of olive oil in the first two centuries AD is graphically demonstrated by the enormous man-made hill known as Monte Testaccio, which comprises an estimated 53 million smashed *amphorae*, equivalent to an estimated 2,000 billion litres of oil, mostly imported from Baetica in southern Spain.

Until the later fourth century BC, Rome was furnished with water from wells, springs and rainwater collected in cisterns, as well as from the River Tiber. In 312 BC the first of Rome's aqueducts was built, the Aqua Appia, by the censor Appius Claudius Caecus; by the time of Trajan, the city had ten major aqueducts. Rome's greatness was measured by these vast facilities, which have left their mark on the Roman countryside even today. Ancient writers described them with admiration and amazement. Dionysius of Halicarnassus, writing in the first century BC, said 'In my opinion, indeed, the three most significant works of Rome, in which the greatness of its empire is best seen, are the aqueducts, the paved roads, and the construction of sewers'. The Roman geographer Strabo noted that 'water is brought into the city through aqueducts in such quantities that veritable rivers flow through the city and the sewers'. Perhaps the best-known acclamation of the aqueducts of Rome was made by Frontinus: 'With such an array of indispensable structures carrying so many waters, compare, if you will, the Pyramids or the useless, though famous, works of the Greeks!'

The arcades carrying the aqueduct channels of the Aqua Claudia and the Aqua Anio Novus to the south of Rome. For most of their length Rome's aqueducts took the form of a series of covered channels or tunnels cut through soft volcanic rock. However, it was necessary to build raised structures to maintain a steady gradient for the flow of water, especially across the flat countryside approaching Rome.

The Via in Selce, climbing up the slope of the Esquiline through the ancient Subura neighbourhood. The modern street follows the ancient basalt paving blocks. At the far end is the façade of a brick-faced *insula* block.

As Rome grew, water also became an important cultural symbol. The only historical source specifically on Roman water supply is Sextus Julius Frontinus, who was appointed water commissioner (*curator aquarum*) at Rome by Nerva. The water supply was as important a factor in the well-being of the Roman population as bread and circuses. In the Republic, the maintenance of the water supply had been one of the duties of the censors; the Aqua Appia in 312 BC and the Aqua Tepula in 125 BC were both their work. In 33 BC, Agrippa, as aedile, had not only built the Aqua Iulia but also repaired the existing aqueducts and maintained them with his own gang of slaves (240 strong); these he bequeathed to Augustus, who made them public property. From this beginning Augustus established the *cura aquarum*, a commission of three senators with a president, and a staff that included architects and surveyors, clerks and public slaves. The post of *procurator aquarum* was created under Claudius, with permanent authority over the water supply. The headquarters of the *statio aquarum* was probably at the Porticus Minucia from the later second century AD; epigraphic evidence suggests that from the fourth century it was at the Lacus Iuternae in the Forum Romanum.

From the construction of the first aqueduct late in the fourth century BC to the construction of the Aqua Traiana in the early second century AD, the amount of water brought to Rome was to increase fifteen-fold. This had less to do with a thirsty population than with an increased demand for bathing facilities and other amenities. From the time of Augustus, the construction of large imperial *thermae* became a determining factor in the provision of aqueducts.

LIFE AND DEATH IN ROME

To live in Rome was not always safe, even for wealthy people. A number of natural and unnatural events threatened the fragile urban infrastructure.

The Tiber's waters provided the easiest method of refuse disposal, either directly or indirectly via the sewers. This might involve anything from human waste to dead bodies, a fact of which the inhabitants of Rome were reminded every time the river flooded. The Tiber was both threat and benefit to the citizens. It was a major transport route, particularly for food brought from inland and elsewhere in the Mediterranean. The regular flooding was a constant threat to this food supply. Hadrian raised the ground level of the northern Campus Martius, effectively creating a raised bank as a flood barrier. Devastating floods continued, however, and it was not until the canalisation of the river in the late nineteenth century that they finally ceased.

Structural evidence for housing in the city, particularly for the Republican period, is rare. Scholars therefore have to rely on literary sources and comparative archaeological evidence from Pompeii, Herculaneum and Ostia. Typical upper-class housing by the late Republic took the form of *atrium* houses. Under Greek influence, many of these houses developed into luxurious buildings with a courtyard (*peristyle*), often at the rear. Despite later changes in domestic architecture, *atrium*-style houses still existed in the early third century AD, as seen on the *Forma Urbis* map. This type of house consisted of a series of bedrooms grouped around three sides of the central area, with an entrance corridor entering the *atrium* between the front rooms or shops. The main rooms of the house, the dining-room (*triclinium*) and day-room (*tablinum*), usually occupied the fourth side of the *atrium*, opposite the entrance. The *peristyle* was sometimes planted as an ornamental garden with fountains.

Aristocratic houses reflected the distinction of their occupants, both by their design and their location. The patron's morning audience (*salutatio*) was held in the *atrium* and *tablinum*, the attending clients being visible to anybody looking in through the front door from the street. A location fronting on to the Via Sacra or Via Triumphalis was the optimum address. The link between house and reputation is clearly shown by Cicero's Palatine house, which was pulled down by Clodius while the owner was in exile. On Cicero's triumphant return his house was rebuilt at public expense.

From the middle Republic another form of housing developed: the multi-storey apartment block known by the elastic term '*insula*'. This could refer to the 'island' of land bounded by roads, or to the building on it. The Regionary Catalogues of the fourth century AD list 4,602 *insulae*, compared with 1,832 *domus*. Blocks several storeys high had, however, existed in Rome at least as early as the third century BC. They were originally timber-framed with a rubble and mortar infill and, to judge from the ancient sources, were very liable to catch fire or collapse. With no building restrictions, owners built them higher and higher to maximise rents. Water could not be piped above the first floor (though connection direct to the city supply was unusual in any case) and many did not have purpose-built latrines. As a result, some – though by no means all – were infamously squalid and unhealthy. The situation was so bad that Augustus imposed a height limit of 60 Roman feet (18 metres, five storeys). After the fire of AD 64, various fire-prevention laws were passed. The height of *insulae* was restricted to 70 Roman feet (21 metres) and a 10-Roman foot (3-metre) space between buildings was required. The law also ordered that a flat-roofed portico be built across the facade of adjacent buildings so that firemen could gain access more easily. The threat of fire also brought about the large-scale introduction of brick-faced concrete as a construction material. Abuses continued, however, forcing Trajan again to restrict the height to 60 Roman feet. One example, the Insula of Felicula, built in the second century AD, was so high that it was listed among the sights of Rome.

Despite the regulations, unsafe buildings persisted. Juvenal, writing during the reign of Trajan, ridiculed Rome for its:

buildings supported for the most part by slender props: for that is how the bailiff patches up cracks in the old wall, telling the residents to sleep at ease under a roof ready to tumble about their ears. No, no, I must live where there are no fires, no nightly alarms. [The resident] below is already shouting for water and moving his belongings; smoke is pouring out of your third-floor attic above, but you know nothing about it; for if the alarm begins on the ground floor the last man to burn will be he who has nothing to shelter him from the rain but the tiles, where the gentle doves lay their eggs.

Single-room units were probably the lot of most of the poor. Some were shops (*tabernae*) with a mezzanine above for accommodation or storage. Property-owners of *domus* might let out shops fronting their buildings. Cicero owned some distinctly insalubrious properties that were dangerous:

two of my shops have fallen down, and the rest have large cracks, with the result that not only the tenants but even the mice have moved out. Others say that this is a disaster, but I think it is not even an inconvenience... However, on the advice... of Vestorius, a plan for rebuilding has been started that will make this loss profitable.

The remains of a few *insulae* have been uncovered in Rome, and a number are shown on the *Forma Urbis* map. Hadrianic blocks have been discovered beneath the Galleria Colonna on the eastern side of the Via Lata (Via del Corso). Between 1928 and 1930, an apartment block was uncovered along the northwest side of the Capitoline hill next to, and partially beneath, the steps up to the church of Santa Maria in Aracoeli. This block, built against the side of the hill, survives up to sixth-floor level. The ground floor comprised shops with a Neronian fire regulation arcade in front and mezzanines above. The third level, which has only partially been excavated, was divided into three apartments. On the fourth floor, and probably the fifth, were rows of single rooms reached by corridors, with those at the back only dimly lit by tiny windows. Whole façades of *insulae* are preserved by incorporation in later buildings, such as the Clivus Scauri side of Santi Giovanni e Paolo, a frontage along the Via in Selci, and in a section of the Aurelianic city wall along Via di Porta Labicana. Increasing use of brick-faced concrete and vault-supported floors in the first to third centuries AD reduced the fire hazard and improved the survival rate of such structures. Many more doubtless still stand, reused within later residential buildings.

Ancient satirists were happy to emphasise the dangers of life in Rome. Floods, fires, earthquakes, collapsing buildings, falling objects and muggings might shorten life, but far more significant were poor hygiene, very high maternal and infant mortality rates and communication of disease through crowding and public bathing. Plagues were a periodic visitor, 30,000 dying in AD 65 and 2,000 per day in AD 189. During the principate of Marcus Aurelius, pestilence was spread from the East by the army, a catastrophe that carried away too many people to calculate. Evidence suggests that malnutrition was also endemic, and malaria and other associated diseases were widespread.

How and where Romans resided in death depended upon their status, wealth and period. Normal Greco-Roman interment outside the sacred boundary of the city meant that as Rome expanded a bow-wave of cemeteries flowed ahead of settlement. The valley of the Forum Romanum had some of the earliest burials, but these were covered over by subsequent building. The Esquiline plateau and all the major approach roads to Rome developed cemeteries. In the Campus Martius, funerary monuments were established ever northwards as the area became built up and the *pomerium* moved on. The tomb of Gaius Poplicius Bibulus at the base of the Capitoline was perhaps first established in the early second century BC. The tomb of Aulus Hirtius who died in 43 BC has been found in mid Campus. The Mausoleum of Augustus was started in 28 BC and located right at the top of the Campus Martius, in the narrow neck between the Via Lata and the river.

Rear view of the Porta Asinaria (S. Giovanni) in the walls of Aurelian. Its single arch (centre), upper storeys, and rear enclosure wall (foreground) date to the reign of Honorius (early fifth century AD).

Emperors and prominent members of their families were cremated and their ashes placed in the Mausoleum from the time of Augustus to Nerva. Trajan was given the signal honour of burial within the *pomerium* in the base of his Column. Hadrian then constructed a great new mausoleum across the river, north-west of the Campus Martius, which served for imperial burials until the Severan period. Huge mausolea were constructed for members of the senatorial class, particularly in the later first century BC and early first century AD. The tomb of Caecilia Metella, granddaughter of the triumvir Crassus, on the Via Appia (with its 100 Roman foot (30-metre) diameter drum) and the tomb of Gaius Cestius by the Porta Ostiensis are two of the most prominent surviving examples. The Augustan tomb of the freedman baker Eurysaces, preserved by incorporation in the Porta Tiburtina, is a massive statement by a member of a class with wealth but not high status. The ashes of groups of freedmen were buried in large, multiple-niched mausolea (*columbaria*) and other people joined burial clubs to ensure some post-mortem commemoration. It seems as though the typical Roman vagueness about the afterlife was further compounded by the fear of anonymity within such a huge population. Soldiers are perhaps over-represented in inscriptions and figural gravestones because many were foreigners to Rome and thus particularly concerned to assert their identities and achievements.

Both cremation and the growing fashion for inhumation provided lucrative business for architects and sculptors, and the city's cemeteries have provided later generations with rich sources of marble *spolia* in the form of architectural decoration, statuary, gravestones, inscriptions, cinerary urns and sarcophagi. The third to fourth centuries AD saw massive development of underground cemeteries. These became predominantly Christian, but there were also traditional religious and Jewish examples. Catacombs had the advantages of community and cheapness, and for modern studies they provide high preservation levels of sculptures, frescoes and artefacts.

THE LATE IMPERIAL CITY

The short-lived emperors of the third century AD were increasingly absent from Rome, and their direct patronage of the city declined. The exploitation of fine stones around the Empire declined because of this slowing down of imperial construction. Administrative systems were maintained and older buildings were repaired. But some emperors, such as Aurelian, did contribute major new buildings to the city, not least his new set of urban fortifications.

However, the new Tetrarchic regime strove to emulate earlier emperors in their relationship with the city. Diocletian visited Rome for the first time in his life to celebrate the twentieth anniversary of his accession. New triumphal monuments came to dominate the Forum Romanum. New *thermae* were gifted to the city population. Rome continued to enjoy direct patronage when Maxentius, backed by the remaining Guard formations, made the city his base and adorned it with a new Temple of Venus and Rome, a great vaulted audience hall (the Basilica of Maxentius) and other dynastic buildings. This close identification with Rome meant that the civil

Scale model of Rome in the early fourth century, viewed looking northwestwards. Visible are the Flavian Colosseum (centre), the Temple of the Deified Claudius (to left), the Palatine palaces (top left), the Forum Romanum (top centre) and Imperial Flora (top right).

war opponent who vanquished him also had to pay attention to the city. Constantine I rededicated the basilica and constructed the last of the imperial *thermae*, the Baths of Constantine on the Quirinal hill. He disbanded the Praetorian Guard, which he had defeated outside Rome. Moreover, he shifted his own patronage to the Christian cult, building the first major churches, located on the outskirts of the city on his own land so as not to offend traditionalists.

The population of Rome may have been declining during the fourth century, but the senatorial class maintained its wealthy lifestyle. Imperial concern that the splendours of Rome should be maintained may be traced through the Theodosian Code. When Constantius II visited Rome in 357 he was no longer able to marshal the resources, or perhaps the skilled personnel, to build on a scale rivalling his predecessors. He toured the Forum of Trajan, viewed the city from the balcony of Trajan's Column and wondered at the equestrian statue of Trajan. His one act that did outdo those of the other emperors was to erect in the Circus Maximus the tallest obelisk (32.5 metres) ever brought to Rome.

The Empire of Letters

Simon Swain

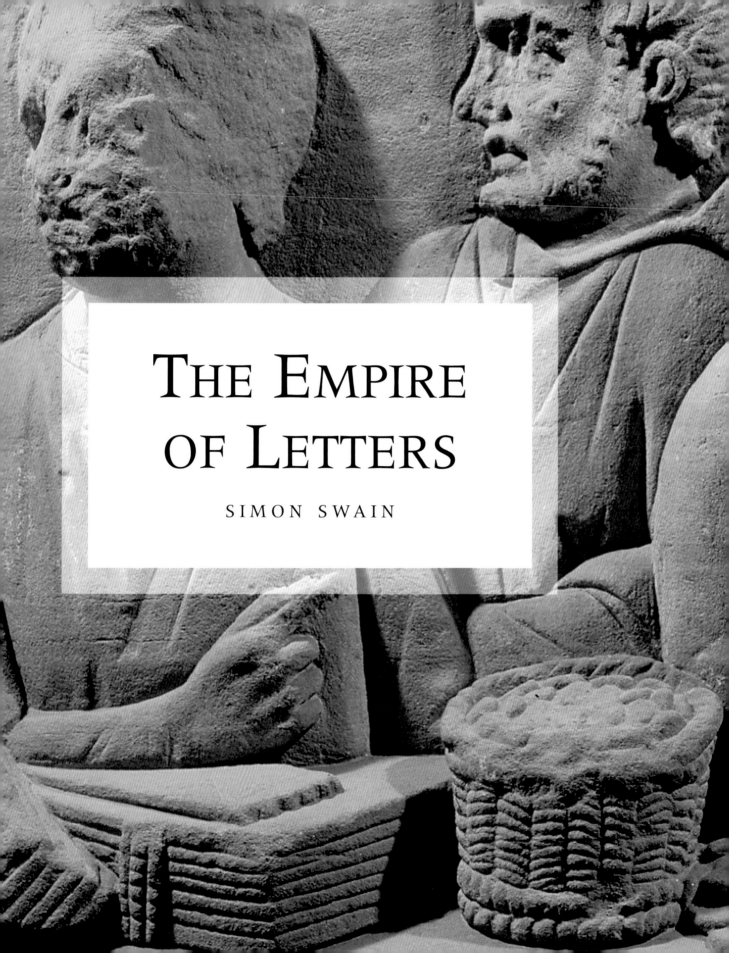

THE EMPIRE OF LETTERS

What do we mean by 'literature' in the Roman world? And what was its role? This chapter will attempt to answer both questions. It will look at literature in the conventional sense and consider its relation to Roman society as a whole, but it will also look beyond conventional definitions of literature to consider wider aspects of the literate culture that informed the Roman world.

Extant written material from ancient Rome comprises a huge variety of texts produced for different levels of society, from tax returns written on papyrus in Egypt to private letters to announcements, commemorations or orders inscribed on stone or bronze, to the longer books transmitted by generations of copyists until they could be printed. Most of what we might call Roman literature in the narrow sense is material that falls into the last category.

In ancient times books came in two forms: first the papyrus roll, then the 'codex' book familiar to us that replaced it. Papyrus was produced mainly in the Nile Delta.

A Roman wall painting of the Greek playwright Menander, the acknowledged master of the Athenian New Comedy. Menander is depicted wearing the laurel crown of a victor in literary competition, as befits an author of more than 70 plays, many of which were adapted for Roman audiences by Terence and Plautus.

Rolls were manufactured to a length of between 6 and 8 metres and the text was set out in columns. Recent work has tried to link the number of letters written on each line – some twenty-plus, without word breaks – with the way the eye moves and takes in characters; this seems to make some sense of what is otherwise a somewhat awkward format. Nevertheless, this sort of book made reading a very different experience from ours. Unfurling the roll might well require the assistance of a slave. Furthermore, it has long been believed (on the evidence of a few celebrated ancient references) that people usually read aloud.

As the Roman world developed, books underwent a radical change. The Roman business community pioneered the codex. At first, sheets of parchment (dried and prepared animal skin) were fastened together with thongs, in a manner derived from the wooden panels of the traditional wax writing tablets,. Books formed in this way were in use as notebooks for commercial records by the end of the first century BC. By the first century AD, literary texts were being produced as parchment codices – as cheap, 'pocket' editions of the normal papyrus rolls, according to the poet Martial. Books consisting of sheets of papyrus bound together with parchment covers were increasingly used for literary texts from the late second century AD. What really tipped the balance between roll and codex was the adoption of the codex by Christians. Codex books were physically easy to read, and their separation into pages made it easier to find particular text references. This new technology was ideal for promoting the sacred texts of the new religion. From the end of the third century AD, parchment codex books became the norm for both secular and religious works, except in Egypt, where papyrus remained in use until at least the sixth century.

Such books by ancient authors remain highly visible to us as one of the principal survivals of classical life. But book production was necessarily slow. There were some large private libraries in Rome (Cicero recorded his visits to those of the scholar Marcus Terentius Varro; Faustus Sulla, the son of the dictator; and Marcus Licinius Lucullus – and he is known to have assembled a large library of his own), but there is no evidence to suggest that members of the Roman elite in general normally maintained private libraries of any size. And though there is good evidence for public libraries in great cities like Rome, Athens and Alexandria, they were hardly common. It is important to understand, therefore, that Roman society was not based on writing, as our own is. Speech was at all times and at all levels the most important mode of discourse, even in the most formal situations. Even the works produced in Rome's lively literary circles were mostly never intended for written dissemination; they were aired in striking oral performances that were intended to impress potential patrons in the audience.

The link between literature and patronage is crucial. Literature, written or spoken, was largely restricted to the elite – the people (specifically men) who had control of the economic, political, and religious apparatus of ancient society. Literate culture was elite culture. Indeed, the close relationship between literate culture, wealth and social status meant that literature functioned as an instrument of competition in elite circles in Roman society.

A life-size marble statue of the Marcus Tullius Cicero, the greatest of the Rome's rhetoricians. Cicero's mastery of rhetoric allowed him an influential career as lawyer, a politician and a man of letters. Rhetoric lost much of its political power under the emperors but its cultural prestige, and so that of Cicero, outlasted the Empire in the West.

THE INFLUENCE OF GREECE

For a picture of the literary and high-cultural activity of the Roman world, we must begin by resuming the relationship between Latin and Greek and between Greeks and Romans that was sketched in Chapter 5.

One of the most important claims the Roman elite could make was the command of 'both the languages'. The phrase is Latin: it was important for Romans to advertise this dual knowledge, whereas Greeks had no reason to do so. Indeed, although we should assume that Latin was known in elite Greek-speaking circles, Greeks tended to keep quiet about it or to claim they knew no Latin. The rhetorician Quintilian recommended that rich Roman children should learn Greek *before* Latin. That this follows real life is clear from the ready assumption by Latin authors of a knowledge of Greek in their audiences.

This painting by Girolamo Batoni, entitled *Aeneas's Flight from Troy*, emphasises the personal nobility of Rome's founding culture-hero. Leading his young family from the burning city of Troy and the murderous Greeks, Aeneas demonstrates that most Roman of qualities – filial duty – by additionally shouldering the burden of his aged father.

The story of the relationship between Latin and Greek culture is one of appropriation, competition and mutual respect, but also of suspicion. At the heart of all ancient culture is the shared, common language of mythology. On one level, mythology was a Greek matter: most myths in the Greco-Roman world were Greek in origin. But mythology was a language anyone could learn. Many city-dwellers in the ancient Mediterranean world benefited from adapting the myths of Greek heroes to new use as foundation legends for their cities, integrating themselves firmly into Greek culture, with its marvellous package of literary, artistic, architectural, juristic, philosophical, political, religious and even military achievements. In Italy, Etruscan tomb paintings and artefacts demonstrate the popularity of the Aeneas legend from the earliest times. Aeneas offered two advantages: he was part of Greek myth (he is a major figure in the *Iliad*), but he was also a non-Greek, a Trojan. Already in the *Iliad* there was a prophecy that he would rule the Greeks. His wanderings in the west, which are also attested very early, made him a natural choice as a founding figure for budding western powers. When Rome began its military-political interaction with the Greek world in the third century BC, Aeneas was talked up by Roman authors. The culmination of this was the Roman national epic, Virgil's *Aeneid*, probably first recited publicly in the 20s BC. This Roman use of the Greek myth involves integration and distancing at the same time, and the same may be said of Roman relations with Greek culture in general.

As Chapter 7 has shown, ancient Rome was one of the most cosmopolitan cities in history. Among other foreign minorities, there was by the second century BC a very large and well-established Greek-speaking population in the city, mostly made up of people from lower status groups. The Roman elite were thus used to Greek-speaking slaves, or manumitted former slaves, rather than free Greeks of high status. This coloured their attitudes towards the inhabitants of the Greek-speaking provinces that Rome acquired during this period. Most elite Romans considered these Greeks on the whole incapable of self-government, and this political attitude had an important consequence in the cultural sphere. The Romans were quick to identify a golden age of 'classical' Greece, whose intellectual products they were prepared to imitate and value, in clear contrast to the apparently debased Greek culture they encountered in the present. This is particularly obvious in plastic art and painting: the reproduction of classical (Greek) art was originally prompted by Roman elite taste in the second century BC, and came to dominate Mediterranean artistic culture until the later third century AD. Art shows very clearly the Romans' determination to mould Greek culture according to their own preconceptions of the Greeks, but – in visual art, at least – they were never wholly confident in doing so. There must have been many Roman artists who produced classical-style Greek art, but none stepped forward to claim parity with the Greek artists of old.

Virgil's *Aeneid*, Book I (verses 1–18)

Arms, and the man I sing, who, forc'd by fate,
And haughty Juno's unrelenting hate,
Expell'd and exil'd, left the Trojan shore.
Long labors, both by sea and land, he bore,
And in the doubtful war, before he won
The Latian realm, and built the destin'd town;
His banish'd gods restor'd to rites divine,
And settled sure succession in his line,
From whence the race of Alban fathers come,
And the long glories of majestic Rome.

O Muse! the causes and the crimes relate;
What goddess was provok'd, and whence her hate;
For what offense the Queen of Heav'n began
To persecute so brave, so just a man;
Involv'd his anxious life in endless cares,
Expos'd to wants, and hurried into wars!
Can heav'nly minds such high resentment show,
Or exercise their spite in human woe?

(Translated by John Dryden)

176   A Brief History of Rome

LITERATURE AND POETRY IN LATIN

In literature, however, the situation was quite different. There is clear evidence of a feeling among Romans that they were here developing something new, in their own, different language and with a sufficiently independent agenda. Marcus Porcius Cato (Cato the Elder) has been called the founder of Latin prose literature. In the first half of the second century BC he wrote the first historical work in Latin, beginning its composition in 168, when Rome was poised to destroy the Greek kingdom of Macedon. Rome's tremendous military and political power clearly called for history in its own tongue. Cato was a crusty old figure, famous for his vituperative asides and his blanket condemnations (notably of Greek doctors, who he claimed were conspiring to kill Romans), but he was also far-sighted. His history was called *Origines* (*Origins*), and concerned not just Rome, but all of Italy. It expresses the nationalistic confidence of Rome based on its established dominance over the Italian peoples. *Origines* began a long tradition of works by Roman historians writing in Latin, including such eminent figures as Gaius Sallustius Crispus (Sallust) in the mid-first century BC, Titus Livius (Livy) around the turn of the millennium, and Publius Cornelius Tacitus in the later first and early second century AD. All these owed something to Greek models (the historians Herodotus and Thucydides in particular) in form, but in content they were unquestionably Roman discussing affairs from a Roman point of view.

Most early Latin poetry, including the famous comedies of Titus Maccius Plautus, who wrote between about 205 and 184 BC, and Publius Terentius Afer (Terence), who wrote in the 160s BC, adapted or translated Greek models. Latin poetry came into its own in the first century BC. But the major poets of the late Republic and early Empire, including Gaius Valerius Catullus, Virgil, Quintus Horatius Flaccus (Horace), Sextus Propertius, Albius Tibullus and Publius Ovidius Naso (Ovid), are still heavily involved with their Greek predecessors, and more noticeably than in the case of the historians. With poetry, the sheer quality of the Greek material imposed Greek metres on a different language with utterly different native traditions. The themes of Greek poetry also prevailed. But here we need to be careful. The thematic legacy became Roman, and this process is as much political and social as it is literary.

The wealth of the late Republic produced in these poets a class of young literary aristocrats who took the culture of the Hellenistic courts rather than that of early Rome as a model for their own writing and pleasure. Catullus, Propertius, Ovid and the others spoke in a new language. They talked of lovers' trysts in the fashionable spots of the new 'Hellenistic' Rome built from the mid-50s onwards. They laid their hearts bare on the subject of lovers' infidelities and rivals' successes. They portrayed family and friends. They rewrote Greek mythology for a laugh (Ovid's *Metamorphoses*). Their poems have endured because they say something general about the human condition, because of their technical brilliance and because of their sense of fun. Their public display of sexual independence was risky – Cicero complained that this *iuventus delicata* ('refined youth') put sex before country, and the straight-laced Augustus exiled Ovid for probably the same reason.

Catullus's well-known sequence of love poems provides a typical example. His poetic account of his involvement with a married woman he calls 'Lesbia' runs the gamut of human emotions in a love affair, from joyful exaggeration of her beauty, culture and self-assurance through celebration of his own good fortune in becoming her lover to despair at the discovery that she has continued her involvement with other lovers. The depth and honesty of his exploration of love goes far beyond the light-hearted approach of Hellenistic literature. Interestingly, this new fashion for treating personal affairs of the heart as suitable subjects for serious poetry also allowed the only female Roman voice of the classical era to celebrate her own love affair. Sulpicia, the niece of a prominent Augustan politician, stands as a reminder of the essential exclusivity of this new literature. Her 'Cerinthus' is a typically Greek pseudonym in Greek-style poems adapted for life at Rome:

I hate my birthday, that I have to spend
In the horrid countryside without Cerinthus –
For what's nicer than the City?

This was an exciting period. As Caesar said of Cicero, 'it was a greater achievement to push out the boundaries of Rome's culture than those of its empire'. Cicero had practically invented Roman philosophy and had established the authenticity and authority of Roman oratory. Virgil became the model of Latin poetry. All these authors together offered Romans of the Augustan Empire and after a sophisticated cultural underpinning of their right to rule.

A GROUNDING IN RHETORIC

A true understanding of the role of literature in the Roman world can only be obtained, however, by looking beyond the narrow definition of the term 'literature'. In effect, literature in the strict sense was only one aspect of a much wider literate culture.

In the late Republic and the Empire, this wider literate culture began with rhetoric, the art of persuasion. Roman high culture placed a premium on speaking well in public. This inevitably made education in rhetoric a largely male preserve, though it is clear that girls could benefit from some stages of the process. Formal training in rhetoric, as developed by the Greeks, had originally been regarded with suspicion in Rome (despite his own polished oratory, Cato the Elder had denounced those who claimed to teach rhetoric: 'engage with the subject, and the words will follow' was his advice). By the late second century BC, however, Greek rhetorical devices were becoming common in Roman public speech, and from the early first century formal rhetorical training was a part of the Roman education system.

The Roman system of education in rhetoric was very similar to the Greek. Pupils went to a *grammaticus* to learn to read and to do simple exercises. At the age of about thirteen, they went to a *rhetor*, a professional instructor of the five 'parts of rhetoric'. He taught first the different types of rhetoric (the oratory of praise, of debate, of the courts) and their appropriate structures and systems of proof, then 'disposition' (that is, composition), elocution (beginning with Latinity and moving

In one area, Latin literature not only broke free from the influence of Greece, but struck out in a new direction entirely. Satire (*satura*) was a literary genre that emerged in the Rome of the Late Republic and early Empire. The image is of an extravagantly illuminated page from a fifteenth-century manuscript of Decimus Iunius Iuvenalis (Juvenal). Although it is couched in the manuscript traditions of the Church, this is an entirely secular document. Juvenal depicted a Rome in which vice had reached epic proportions.

on to figures of speech, facility and so on), memory (recognised in the Classical world as a technique, not a gift of nature), and finally delivery (control of the voice and of the movements of the body).

Much of the theory of rhetoric was based on the world of the law courts, with detailed emphasis on proof and different types of evidence. In the late Republic, oratory had had its place chiefly in the senate and the courts (Cicero's legal speeches are a surviving example of some of the highest achievements of rhetoricians in the latter). But under the Empire the most widespread type of rhetoric was the oratory of praise and blame (called panegyric or encomium). These traditional forms acquired a new importance perhaps because of the Empire's more clearly defined socio-political pyramid, culminating in the office of emperor. There were many occasions when it was necessary or advantageous to speak formally to courtiers or military and civilian officials. Such interaction became crystallised around elaborate exchanges of courtesy, whether in speech or written in the form of letters. These exchanges, behind which lay years of practising formal rules of composition, can be considered a type of literature, and they represent a hugely important practical application of literary skills in the daily lives of the Roman elite.

The 'parts' of rhetoric outlined above represent the system of Marcus Fabius Quintilianus (Quintilian), the author of the enormously influential *Institutio Oratoria* (Orator's Education). Quintilian was a professional teacher and advocate in the Rome of the later first century AD. He was also highly placed in the court of the Flavian dynasty. The twelfth and last book of the *Institutio* puts forward the ideal of the consummate Ciceronian orator, and Quintilian claimed that identifying the qualities of such an orator was his hardest and most original task. His orator combined moral qualities, an ideal of educational breadth, a sense of career and choices of rhetorical style, resulting in an image of what Cato had called 'the good man skilled in speaking' – the consummate Roman. This image ensured the book's enduring popularity: every member of the Roman elite wanted to be seen to possess the high culture Quintilian had outlined.

GESTURES AND PHYSIOGNOMY

Quintilian's stylistic profile in this final book should be taken with the lengthy remarks in the preceding one on how to ensure *decor* (propriety) by employing the correct gesture and movement. He catalogues, for example, no fewer than twenty-three different gestures with the hand or fingers: 'the commonest gesture consists of bending the middle finger against the thumb and extending the other three'; 'if the first finger touches the middle of the right-hand edge of the thumbnail with its tip, the other fingers being relaxed, we have a gesture wholly suitable to approval'; 'there is also a gesture of insistence, which belongs to everyday use rather than to art, consisting of alternately closing and opening the hand with a rapid movement', and so on. This exhaustive advice is evidence of a wide concern with looking and being looked at in this period.

This cultural emphasis on looking, evaluating and assessing is perhaps not so surprising when we consider the carefully regulated Greco-Roman aristocratic society of the Empire. The property-owning class was small and competitive. A close observation of the character of one's peers and competitors was essential, and studying how they moved and spoke was a key to their characters. One of the greatest literary figures of the age was the Greek philosopher, essayist and biographer Lucius Mestrius Plutarchus (Plutarch), who lived between about AD 50 and 120. Plutarch understood the pressures Roman society imposed on a man of culture, and to reflect this he invented a new word, *dusôpia* ('being discountenanced'), to express what happens when social pressures require a man to behave in a way contrary to his own personal inclinations. Both Quintilian and Plutarch thus identified what modern socio-linguists call 'face' in linguistic interaction. In doing so, they identify for us a key feature of the educated culture of imperial Rome.

Another towering literary figure, the orator, super-rich aristocrat, and courtier of the emperor Hadrian, Marcus Antonius Polemo from Laodicea (near modern Denizli in southeast Turkey), concentrated on the face in a work that reflects aristocratic competitiveness. Polemo's manual of *Physiognomy* is a detailed exhibition of what different body parts – their shapes, colours and movements – tell readers about the sort of person they are looking at. The work was meant to appeal to the highly educated, and the introduction (such as it is preserved) discusses the physiognomy of Greek mythological heroes. Polemo starts in earnest with the eye. Indeed, his (to our minds) excessively detailed descriptions run to a third of the whole work:

If you see eyes which are turned upwards and show similarities to the eyes of cows, these are the signs of stupidity, carelessness and deficiency of intellect because they are people addicted to gluttony, sexual intercourse, and drunkenness. If these eyes shade towards green, this indicates a love of killing . . . if they are red and large, this indicates a devotee of drunkenness, conversation, and women: their owners are never free of lewdness, wickedness, love of disputation and laziness.

One of the most interesting aspects of the work is its several anecdotes describing Polemo's enemies from a physiognomical perspective. Polemo himself was immortalized in the series of descriptions of 'sophists' (or high-ranking teachers of rhetoric) written by a courtier of the third-century Severan dynasty, Flavius Philostratus, and it is a good idea to pause with Philostratus before returning to Polemo.

THE LIVES OF THE SOPHISTS

The *Lives of the Sophists* is an extremely important source for seeing literary high culture as an intrinsic part of aristocratic life. Philostratus' ostensible concern was to record the most famous teachers of the past two hundred years and to celebrate the rhetorical styles and themes they and he championed. But for him this entailed a description of aristocratic activity and much of the work is taken up with this. Aristocrats were mobile and the biography of Polemo and his oratory begins by stressing his attachment to the more important city of Smyrna and to Hadrian. 'Polemo was so arrogant that he conversed with cities as inferiors, emperors as not his superiors, and the gods as his equals.' Philostratus pays particular attention to Polemo's *skênê*, the 'scenic or theatrical effects' that wowed his audiences. These included his dress, his movements on stage, his delivery. Polemo himself compared his performances to those of a gladiator 'pouring with sweat and in fear of his life'. The even richer Athenian sophist and politician who became a consul, Herodes Atticus, recalled the effect on him with a line from the *Iliad*, 'The din of swift-footed horses strikes upon my ears.'

The lifestyle of Polemo can be illustrated by what Philosotratus says about a later second-century sophist whom he knew personally. Damianus was a major financial benefactor to his city, Ephesus. Philosotratus writes:

He was able to support the needy, to restore public buildings, and he connected the temple of Artemis to Ephesus by building a covered marble walkway a stade in length so worshippers would not be deterred by the rain. He dedicated this in his wife's name, but the banqueting hall he dedicated in his own. He built it to surpass all others and its finish in beautiful Phrygian marble is beyond description.

Damianus, however, did not neglect himself:

...all his estates were planted with trees to give fine fruit and abundant shade. In those by the sea he made offshore islands and protected harbours for his cargo vessels. As to his suburban homes, some were like town houses while others resembled caverns.

This is an evocative picture of well-watered landscapes that are productive and pleasurable at the same time, with their economic zones and their villas, those 'broken off pieces of cities', as one historian has called them.

Philostratus records that Damianus was buried in one of the suburban villas 'in which he had spent most of his life'. This love of place reminds us of Pliny the Younger's devoted descriptions in his *Letters* of two of his own villas in Italy, with their shady walks, topiaried gardens, beautiful rooms, and sea views. The ideal of the seaside villa in particular is shown on so many wall paintings from Pompeii that it was evidently ingrained in the imagination of the Mediterranean noble and his bourgeois imitators. But Damianus must have spent much of his time also in the council chamber, the auditorium, the theatre, and other venues where he would have come under the scrutiny of a Polemo. Polemo indeed finds his victims in a variety of private and public locations. The most notorious is another sophist in Philostratus' collection, Favorinus of Arelate (modern Arles). Favorinus was a millionaire. He had a high equestrian status and undertook the priesthood of the imperial cult in his home province of Narbonensis.

The unfortunate fact that he was a cryptorchid (that is, his testicles had never descended) attracted a good deal of publicity.

He had puffed-up eyes, his cheeks were slack, his mouth was broad, his neck was long and thin, his ankles were thick, with much flesh on the legs . . . He had a voice resembling the voice of a woman and slim lips. I never before saw looks like his . . . He went round the towns and markets . . . telling men he had the power to compel women to come to them and likewise the men to the women.

So Polemo. No-one would guess that this Favorinus is the same man as the highly respected expert on Latin and Greek language, customs, and history who appears in a number of scenes in the emperor's palace and private dinner parties in the *Attic Nights* of Aulus Gellius, an important Latin work of the mid-second century that celebrates the aristocracies' possession of high culture and high comfort at the height of the Empire.

Polemo's emphasis on sexual deviancy may attract our notice. In fact it accords with a major focus in the literature of this time on correct sexual behaviour, especially in the so-called 'Greek novel' (*see page 188*). The theme of correct relations leading to marriage is prominent in literature at least partly because of the importance of continuing the rule of the nobility. Thus one of the great political and literary figures of the turn of the second century, Dio 'the Golden Mouthed' of Prusa (modern Bursa), wrote a piece about rural life on the island of Euboea. The scene is a wedding celebration, and Dio 'was reminded of the marriages of the rich with their arrangers and considerations of property and family, the dowries and wedding presents, promises and deceits, agreements and documents, and finally all the abuse and hatred at the ceremony'.

Two of Polemo's examples of his contemporaries are brides-to-be who connived at being abducted on their wedding day, as he had predicted from physiognomy. But the descriptions read like passages from the novels. They are set-pieces where life reflects literature. Another of his themes is magic and poisoning. This too is prominent in the fictional literature of the age; but again in a world without modern science so much was inexplicable that belief in such practices was widespread. It was part of life, and accusations of involvement – often made by peer rivals – were taken very seriously.

The title page from a 17th-century edition of Quintillian. The illustration purports to show students of rhetoric practising their skills before the master himself. Although rhetoric evolved as a form of public performance, by Quintillian's time its exercise was confined mainly to the imperial audience chamber, and his manual of rhetoric can be seen as a courtiers' handbook and essential reading for all the aristocracy.

EDUCATION AND CULTURE

We have been looking at the various ways in which literature constituted a fundamental part of high culture and elite life in Rome, and specifically at how the oral culture of public performance – rhetoric – was a prized expression of education. Some idea of the importance of displaying such education can be gained from the observation of Galen of Pergamum, the greatest physician of antiquity, that the priorities of a gentleman of the second century AD were to 'know the families each of us come from, the education and culture we have received, and the property and attitudes and way of life we have'. Galen's 'education and culture' are summed up in the term *paideia*, another key concept in literate Roman culture. Although the term is Greek, Latin authors shared exactly the attitude it summed up. *Paideia* was not something that was inculcated at school and forgotten. Rather, it indicated a life that was lived according to the principles of high culture. It was a style, a public presentation based on display. In the second century AD, members of the Roman elite faced great pressure to be seen to conform to ideals of behaviour and education – hence the emphasis on *paideia*. The satirical writer Lucian of Samosata offers a guide to what was expected.

Lucian's sense of the competitiveness of high culture is acute. His surviving work trumpets the brilliance of his own achievements and originality – and with some justification, since his beautiful Greek and his observant eye made him a much loved author from antiquity to the Renaissance. He also launches bitter, scabrous attacks on enemies, written to be enjoyed. One emblematic piece concerns the 'ignorant book collector' – a figure whose very existence tells us a great deal about the importance in Roman society of an appearance of culture. 'You want to conceal your lack of *paideia* by the number of your books,' he comments, 'just like the most ignorant doctors use ivory pill boxes, silver cupping glasses and scalpels inlaid with gold – but when they're asked to use them, they haven't a clue'. He continues, 'If someone sees you with a book – for you always have one – and asks who it's by, you know the answer from the title; but if the conversation goes further, as it tends to, on the merits and faults of what's inside, you don't have anything to say. I'll bet you pray the ground will open up and swallow you!' The object of Lucian's satirical observation is the book chosen 'for its beauty'– in other words, he targets precisely his subject's affectation of a semblance of the educated culture that high society demanded.

Lucian's scorn for cultural charlatans was legendary. The sophist Hadrian of Tyre once dared to criticise his Greek. In the Greco-Roman world of the second century AD, the most highly-regarded style of public oratory in Greek was that that imitated the literary language of classical Athens. The educational investment that many people were prepared to make in order to be able to reproduce obsolete words and grammatical constructions sums up the preoccupation with literary display in the society of the time. Lucian tells us he was an Aramaic speaker by birth, and many of his works show how defensive he was about his Greek; perhaps this accounts for the vitriol with which he laid into his critic. His famously scabrous outburst at Hadrian heaped sexual innuendo on slanderous allegation, adding real venom to elite cultural competition.

Detail of an enigmatic Roman fresco depicting a group of obviously well-to-do women. The garlands suggest that this is no ordinary occasion, and the main figure is poised significantly in mid-step. It is unclear whether we are looking at humans or deities; at a theatrical performance, a religious ceremony, or a domestic celebration, such as betrothal or coming of age.

A Culture of Display

Later adaptations of Greek myth lie at the heart of the culture of social elites across the Roman Empire, both in life and in death. During the early second century AD burial came back into fashion among Romans. The 'flesh-eating stone' (*lapis sarcophagus*) of the Troad (north-western Turkey) gave its name to the newly fashionable stone coffins whose flat surfaces allowed artists to celebrate death with the same motifs noble men and women had enjoyed in life.

The battle of the Greeks and the Amazons is one of a number of favourite mythological scenes. In the sarcophagus illustrated here, the hero Achilles is shown clasping the lifeless body of his foe Penthesilea. Mythological heroes like these were carved on sarcophagi as representations of the deceased, so here we may assume that Achilles and Penthesilea represent a real-life husband and wife. If so, the artist and his patrons were able to turn a blind eye to the fact that in the myth Achilles has just *killed* Penthesilea. The squeezing of the myth into a contemporary frame can also be seen in the realistic Roman features and hairstyles of the central characters and the way in which the melée of fighters recalls another favourite motif – the victorious Roman army – which is found on the sarcophagi of battle-hardened generals from this same era.

In Roman elite life, the universal language of mythology was all around. For example, an account by the writer Flavius Philostratus of the private art gallery of a seaside villa outside Naples in the early third century AD includes descriptions of no fewer than sixty-five paintings of mythological scenes. Philostratus has the young son of his host guide us round the paintings while he carefully expounds the myths to the young gentlemen of the locality. No worthwhile painting has survived from this period, but we can get some idea of what Philostratus and his friends saw by turning again to

sculpture. The Spada reliefs are among the most perfectly preserved examples from the second century AD of the art of a private house, probably one near Rome itself. The eight panels include less well known stories such as the death of the child hero Opheltes as well as an interesting glimpse of one of their owner's homes overlooking the sea. Overall they demonstrate just how far the possession of wealth in Roman society involved the display of a classical repertoire and how these themes acted as a badge of belonging in a world where the nobility were on constant show to each other and in constant competition for social recognition.

The Trojan legend was central to Roman literature, art and life. One of the Spada reliefs (below) shows the theft of the Trojan 'Palladium', the little statue of Athena which became the guardian of Rome's fortunes. Most Romans said Aeneas took it. But a real connoisseur wanted a Greek version with Odysseus (in the cap) and Diomedes arrogantly holding the piece in his hand.

A Renaissance wall fresco from Italy depicting an embrace between Cupid and Psyche. Like much of Greek drama, this novel derives its plot from the interactions between mortals and immortals – Venus sends Cupid to torment the mortal Psyche, only to have Cupid fall in love with her and make Psyche his wife.

THE NOVEL: LATIN

Lucian is probably best known today for his *Alethe diegemata* ('True Histories'), the first account of a journey to the moon. *True Histories* was written for sheer pleasure, but also to satirise people who believed in the extraordinary fare of monsters and demons served up by contemporary travel writers and explorers. It is a sort of novel, and in terms of the history of literature in Western Europe perhaps the most significant literary development in the Roman world was the Greek and Roman novel proper.

The novel, in the sense of a long fictional narrative in prose, was probably created as a genre sometime between 50 BC and AD 50 in the Greek-speaking part of the Roman world; such novels seem to have been popular from about the first century AD, and to have remained so throughout the Empire. Today, the full texts of five Greek novels and one Latin (Apuleius's *Metamorphoses*, or *Golden Ass*) survive, along with parts of a second Latin work (the *Satyrica* of Petronius Arbiter) and fragments of others.

The term 'novel' of course encompasses many different types of writing. Among the fragmentary survivals are texts which were evidently quite raunchy, with accounts of sex, drinking and fighting. Both the *Satyrica* and the *Golden Ass* reveal the influence of a collection of racy Greek short stories translated into Latin as *Milesian Tales* by Lucius Cornelius Sisenna in the first century BC. The *Satyrica* is one of the most celebrated works of surviving Roman literature from the first century AD. It recounts the amoral adventures of a group of gay lovers in the Greek towns of southern Italy. There are many interesting aspects of this work, which in its original form must have been very long (perhaps 400,000 words). One is the placing of sexual deviance in a Greek setting with protagonists whose names are drawn from the Greek sexual lexicon, for the Romans were always ready to suspect the Greeks of wayward practices. The other is the evident pleasure in portraying low-life characters taken by the author, who was probably Nero's hedonistic 'arbiter of elegance' described in a fine portrait by the historian Tacitus. The *Satyrica* (the name is a deliberate reference both to satire and to the decidedly un-satyric sexual capacity of its main character, Encolpius) was clearly written as entertainment for upper class readers. It contains many satirical references to Homer's *Odyssey*, including a recurrent theme of Encolpius's sexual failures as a result of offending the god Priapus (thus parodying Odysseus's sufferings after incurring the wrath of Poseidon), and an encounter between Encolpius and a woman named Circe. The famous 'Dinner of Trimalchio' scene emphasises both the vulgarity of the rich freedman Trimalchio and the snobbishness of Encolpius, and it includes a series of (mostly bawdy) stories told by Trimalchio's freedmen friends as a kind of parody of the Platonic symposium.

We cannot be sure how far Petronius's work responds to contemporary Greek fiction, though the infidelity and general immorality of the central characters is almost certainly a deliberate parody of the fidelity and virtue of the (heterosexual) couples at the heart of contemporary Greek novels. Other influences almost certainly include the popular entertainment of pantomime and mime, which respectively enacted scenes from myth (focussing on the most theatrical and tragic ones) and domestic and contemporary sex and violence.

Apuleius was the archetypal showman and playboy. He seduced a rich widow and her relatives accused him of magic. His famous defence against the charge (the *Apology*) rests on the claim to intellectual community between himself and the judge in both Greek and Latin. He was sufficiently pleased with himself to publish four books of highlights from his display speeches which are full of diverse information on the exclusive social sphere he inhabited. His talents finally found a legitimate outlet in the comic novel about a man's life as an ass, the celebrated *Golden Ass*. This work, with its numerous inset tales and gaudy Latin, is actually an expanded version of an equally ribald anonymous short story written in Greek. The fact that the Greek background in the anonymous story is so coloured by Roman prejudices against Greeks (largely turning on sexual perversion and lack of good faith), that the language is the Greek of the ordinary educated man and not the tricky classicising form used by the major Greek authors, and that the hero is Roman make it clear that only a Roman could have written it. And there is only one candidate: Apuleius himself. It was evidently a prototype of the *Golden Ass*, and the two texts neatly encapsulate Roman use of a Greek background to suit their own cultural purposes. Apuleius certainly parades his own knowledge of Greek. Since he came from a small town in north Africa, his acquaintance with Greek (including a period of study at Athens) represents a considerable personal financial investment. It shows the gains to be had from displaying such knowledge in Roman society.

THE NOVEL: GREEK

The surviving Greek novels share themes of idealised heterosexual love and natural and human obstacles to its fulfilment. They all promote the idea of no sex before marriage (or not too much), fidelity within marriage, and marriage as the ideal solution in a world full of woe. Just as Petronius chose a Greek background for his account of homosexual lovers, so the Greek stories also find their settings in the Greek world – though the plots often involve travels through some of its more exotic, Middle Eastern parts. There is another difference in the settings, however: here the Roman Empire is written out of the picture altogether and we seem to be in a timeless world of independent Greek states. These stories were written by a literate class for a literate class, and it seems that the readers wanted their romantic escapism in a world familiar from their general reading and education. This

The Royal Ballet's production of Ravel's opera *Daphnis and Chloe*, based on the novel of the same name by the Greek writer Longus. His tale of young and completely inexperienced lovers can still be enjoyed for its comical peasants and referencing of earlier works, but the main thrust of its satire has been lost during the last two thousand years.

concentration on the world of earlier Greek culture recalls a similar phenomenon in the teaching of rhetoric, for there too fictional speeches based on stock situations – disputes between rich men and poor neighbours, the tyrant and the abused citizen, the morose man and his talkative wife and so on – are set in the same timeless Greek world. In the last example, which survives in the works of the fourth-century AD educationalist and politician Libanius of Antioch (and incidentally comes into English in Ben Jonson's *The Silent Woman*), the grumpy husband asks the town council for permission to kill himself to escape:

Before the wedding night was halfway through, she was grumbling out loud about the bed. Her speech caused me considerable disturbance – it didn't suit a bride. Then she said, 'Are you asleep?' and I was even more upset. Then she asked a third question and a fourth. I made no answer; I was too ashamed, she was shameless. The whole thing was upside down: a man silent, a woman talking.

These 'declamations', as they are formally called, were utilised as practice pieces by the trainee in rhetoric. The Greekness of their imaginary world is even clearer in those declamations based – often very loosely – on historical events such as the Greek victories over Persia in the early fifth century BC. Since writers and readers were brought up on this material, it is perhaps no surprise that the novels presupposed it.

The best of these Greek novels are Achilles Tatius's *Leucippe and Clitophon*, Longus's *Daphnis and Chloe* and the long, complex *Ethiopian Story* by Heliodorus. Longus has had the most influence: over 500 separate printed editions of his 80,000-word novel exist, as well as Ravel's famous opera. His story turns on the sexual naivety of the young couple at its heart rather than on external obstacles to their love, but whether the story is a cynical urbanite take-off of poor adolescent peasants or a genuine and charming attempt to purvey the burgeoning of innocent young love is difficult to say. That the young Daphnis and Chloe turn out to be mislaid scions of the aristocracy points to a satirical intention along the lines of Petronius, at least in part, since the peasants who make up most of the characters are obviously funny. The story is filled with other references to earlier Greek literature – so many that a detailed commentary is needed to enumerate them all – and the enjoyment of the text by its ancient readers must rest to some extent on these references.

Heliodorus cannot be done justice here. This the longest story (some 80,000 words) is inside out. What is striking is the accent on the faithfulness of the two betrothed youngsters whose separation forms the basis of the story. Many have suspected a religious dimension to such a tale of chastity, and indeed Christian authors claimed Heliodorus was a bishop, which is by no means impossible. Achilles Tatius probably appeals most to us for having fun with the genre. This extends to quite racy descriptions and a debate on the merits of 'male-directed sex'. Interestingly Christian sources also claimed Achilles as a bishop, albeit later in life. In the end the protagonists seem happy enough together. But Achilles certainly pushes the rules and gives his readers something to laugh about.

Mosaics from the tomb of a married couple, found near Sfax in Tunisia, depicting the husband and wife at a funeral repast. Although it comes from the later stages of the Roman period (the mosaic dates from the fourth century AD), the image is strongly reminiscent of the stylised terracotta sarcophagi with sculpted reclining couples that were popular with the Romans' Etruscan forebears.

MORALITY AND CHRISTIANITY

An important feature of these stories is their emphasis on heterosexual love and marriage at the expense of homosexual relationships between men. It may be that this is a response to a real social and moral priority amongst the Greco-Roman elite in the later Empire, as well as a reflection of a new emphasis in the Roman world on morality and good conduct. Similar themes are found in one of the most charming and successful works of literature in this period, the 'Eroticus' dialogue or *Dialogue on Love* by Plutarch, written in the early second century AD.

Plutarch's dialogue is shaped around a bride-kidnapping with a difference: here a younger man is kidnapped by an older and richer widow. The young man is beautiful and has many male admirers. The widow's behaviour scandalises the small town of Thespiae where the tale is set. Plutarch cleverly turns the Platonic idea of love as a power of exaltation from male-male love to male-female love. He builds in part on the more independent rights accorded to women in the Roman world after the classical Greek period. (Nonetheless, no equality of the sexes is envisaged here: Plutarch also wrote a very staid work of advice on marriage in which the ideal wife plays a very traditional part.) In the *Dialogue* married love and the physical union of man and wife are attractive and ennobling because of the reciprocity that is, Plutarch feels, less possible in the unequal relations between two men.

For married couples sexual relations are a foundation of affection, a communion, as it were, in a great mystery . . . No mutual pleasures are greater, no mutual services more constant, no form of affection is more enviable and estimable for its sheer beauty than "When man and wife in harmony of mind / Keep house together". And the law too helps Eros to assure society's increase.

The quotation, from Odysseus's wish for princess Nausicaa's future happiness, is an apposite invocation of a familiar passage, something we see often in the literature of this age.

Plutarch's attitude makes the ascription of Christianity to Heliodorus more understandable, for the novelistic recipe of travel and adventure combined with an emphasis on virginity was used to good effect by Christian writers in the second and

third centuries AD in the so-called Apocryphal Acts of the apostles. This interesting literature covers a wide spectrum of tastes and styles. There is every reason to believe that elite Christians read these stories, which were designed to fill in the gaps left by the Gospels and Letters of Paul and others. The period in which they were written is the age in which rich Christians first become visible in Roman society. Their needs are addressed in one of the earliest examples of a new form of literature, the homily. The word is significant: ordinarily it meant 'a conversation', but the Christians appropriated it and turned it to mean the conversation between a preacher and his audience, a monologue rather than a dialogue. It shows us a new element in the lives of the Roman elite, though – and this is the secret of Christianity – not an entirely new one.

Clement of Alexandria was a typical Christian writer, one of the most important authors of the later second century AD. Much of his work was directed towards a rich and educated flock, and he aimed to make Christianity safe and acceptable for them. In his little homily *The Rich Man's Salvation* he tackles the embarrassment caused to wealthy Christians by Jesus's famous parable about the rich man and eye of the needle. According to Clement, the important thing is to use one's money properly.

Another work by Clement, *The Tutor*, casts further light on the relationship between literature and real elite life in the later Empire. Purporting to offer Christian guidance on daily living, the book is well padded-out references to classical literature as well as scripture, indicating the educated audience Clement is addressing. The title does this too: it alludes to the 'tutor' who took rich people's children to school.

Smacking the lips, whistling, and sounds made through the fingers to call servants, are irrational signs, hence to be given up by rational men. Frequent spitting, too, and violent clearing of the throat, and wiping one's nose when drinking, are to be shunned . . . If any one is attacked with sneezing, just as when hiccupping, he must not startle those near him with the explosion, and so give proof of his lack of *paideia*; but the hiccup is to be quietly transmitted with the expiration of the breath, the mouth being composed becomingly, and not gaping and yawning like the masks used in tragedy.

Clement's views on shoes, earrings, laughter, and sex clearly respond to a real social need, and most of what he says would have been accepted (at least in theory) by non-Christians – indeed, comparable advice can be found in Plutarch or Galen.

The Apocryphal Acts themselves turn the Christian advice of a moralist like Clement into a narrative based on the famous figures of the Christian past. There is much on sexual continence, and abstention, including the breaking of troths, is a frequent theme. Clement's thoughts are mainly for men, though in the Acts the encouragement to chastity is more often directed at women. One of the most famous texts is the story of Paul and Thecla. Thecla is a young fiancée who hears Paul preaching and renounces her impending marriage. Naturally this causes all sorts of trouble, but her faith wins through in the end. Here we have familiar ingredients: a young couple, a mentor (also found, for example, in Heliodorus's novel), travel. The apostles were, of course, great globe-trotters. Such travel would have seemed familiar to the elite of the Roman world.

Another second-century Christian text, the *Acts of Peter*, has elements that look more like the pantomime and mime so beloved of all sections of Roman society. First comes the story of Peter's daughter, whom the apostle has prayed may be disabled so she cannot have sex with a rich abductor (the story was evidently written for Christian groups who went to great lengths to avoid 'bodily corruption'). The book also features the famous renewed battle between Peter and Simon Magus, which ends in a flying competition in which Simon is shot down by Peter on the main street of Rome and dies following surgery on his nastily broken leg. Entertainment – a 'good read' – here serves to promote serious Christian messages about faith, heresy and life.

A fifteenth-century painting by Benozzo Gozzoli depicting the victory of Saint Peter over the evil magician Simon Magus, who lies mortally wounded at the feet of the Roman emperor. A story that began as early-Christian 'agit-prop' has been enhanced by the centuries, and has become a fit subject for sacred painting.

THE RISE OF BIOGRAPHY

The emphasis on the human body that characterises all these texts parallels a growing interest in the imperial Roman world in individual human character and personality. Indeed, it is possible to see a profoundly biographical shift in the literature of this period. One feature of this shift is the emergence of dedicated biographies as a literary genre, like Plutarch's influential *Parallel Lives* which paired famous Greeks and Romans of the past as examples of how to live in the present. But the new emphasis on individuals is wider than this: all manner of texts from this period feature biographical sketches.

Writers of history like Tacitus and the Greek historian of Rome, Cassius Dio, focussed especially on the figure of the emperor. The rise of a fictional literature built round invented characters and lives is also part of this change of consciousness. But the experience of real, contemporary people was just as important – and perhaps a new manifestation of the culture of evaluation. Two very important texts in this context are *To Himself* (usually known as the *Meditations*) of the emperor Marcus Aurelius and the extraordinary account of the author's physical and psychological illness in the *Sacred Tales* of the aristocratic Greek orator Aelius Aristides.

The *Meditations* has long been admired, despite the fact that it is arguably one of the most depressing texts ever written. The genre seems to be that of the daily 'spiritual exercises' that were recommended by Stoic philosophers. Stoicism was a Hellenistic Greek philosophical response to an age of new empires and bureaucracies. It is not surprising that it was easily adapted to the Roman imperial elite, stressing as it did the idea of duty and rank. An early example of Stoic influence on literature can be found in the *Epistulae morales* ('Moral letters') of the philosopher, author and politician Lucius Annaeus Seneca ('Seneca the Younger') in the first century AD. These 'letters' are supposedly addressed to Gaius Lucilius, but in fact were simply Seneca's records of his own ideas on morals, which were heavily influenced by Stoic philosophers he had met as a young man in Rome. To a modern reader, these are moderately entertaining. Marcus, however, took philosophical introspection much more seriously – though it is highly unlikely that his private record of his daily thoughts was intended for publication. Reading the *Meditations* today, we can sense a depressive who was losing his grip:

These are your thoughts on bathing: oil, sweat, filth, greasy water, everything disgusting; such is every part of life.

Soon you will forget everything, and soon everything will forget you.
Alexander of Macedon and his muledriver were the same in death.
Everything is dissolving, changing, in a state of decomposition or dispersion.

There is a profound sense of the superficiality of the world of sense perceptions that for some makes the work a very religious one. There is also practical, Stoical advice on how to survive this world. In particular, Marcus addresses his own public life: 'Don't be caesarified'; 'Don't let anyone hear you grumbling at life in court, not even yourself'.

PERSONAL LETTERS

There is no doubt that the text is about Marcus's own experience, though historians must be disappointed by the lack of specific detail. It is difficult to generalise Marcus's pessimism, but we can put his mood in some kind of context by taking note of his letters. Some of these survive as part of the correspondence of Cornelius Fronto. Fronto was the leading orator of mid-second century Rome, though hardly anything of his speeches survives. He falls in the period after Tacitus and Juvenal, when Latin literature begins a decline that was not reversed until the later fourth century – in fact, from Fronto and Aulus Gellius until late antiquity, Apuleius's work is the only non-Christian writing to survive. In part, this may be because educated Romans wrote in Greek, the proper language for philosophical enquiry.

The letter in antiquity was a highly prized literary form. It was subject to theoretical analysis in the same way as rhetoric. Many letters were written according to formulae, for example the very common 'letter of recommendation'. Fiction and real life combined easily in this genre. In the hands of Quintilian's pupil Pliny the Younger, ten books of polished letters present us with the ideal Roman gentlemen – who is, of course, perfectly bicultural. Fronto's letters serve as examples for us of how the elite tailored a mannered literature to real needs. Fronto was the teacher of Marcus and his co-emperor, Lucius Verus. Most of the letters are to these imperial pupils-cum-masters. Those to Marcus and back are especially interesting. They discuss education and culture. Fronto tries to preserve Marcus for rhetoric as he sees him incline toward philosophy. But much more interesting for a cultural historian of second century Rome are the two discourses around which so many of the letters turn, love and health.

Marble bust of the second-century emperor Marcus Aurelius, who is sometimes known as the philosopher-emperor. His reign saw Rome celebrate its 900th anniversary, and also suffer the ravages of plague. He was a learned and scholarly man, surrounded by a coterie of sycophants and plotters; his personal experiences may have influenced his surprisingly modern and disengaged approach to life.

The language of love and affection is well known in Roman public life. But Marcus and Fronto take it onto a new level. 'I want to run at once to my most beautiful of souls, Fronto . . . to hold his hands . . . to massage his poorly foot, to warm it in the bath, to have my hand support you'. Fronto enthuses about Marcus' excessive love for him too. 'You wish to run to me, to fly to me, the peculiar behaviour of lovers'. Marcus' mother is envious, and Marcus should be ready to answer those who ask why he loves Fronto so much. 'Let them doubt, discuss, dispute, guess, puzzle over the origin of our *amor* as much they do about the sources of the Nile.' In a letter to Fronto during Fronto's consulship (142) Marcus begins, 'I surrender: you have won. Beyond question your loving has beaten all the lovers who ever lived. Take the crown and let the herald proclaim publicly before your own tribunal this your victory, "M. Cornelius Fronto, consul, is the winner. He is crowned in the contest of the Great Games of Love".' That the victory proclamation is expressed in Greek perhaps indicates some embarrassment. Greek is also used by Fronto in a fascinating 'erotic' letter (a known literary genre) in which he expresses his love for Marcus by rewriting discussions of love in Plato's *Phaedrus*. Fronto's pleasure in the exercise is clear: this 'erotic letter' is the third such Platonic pastiche he sent. This is strong stuff: classical literature and philosophy act as a code for exploring a very delicate relationship between a courtier and his imperial charge. Marcus's reply is equally interesting: he asserts that he is the senior lover, the Socrates figure, and Fronto his junior, the Phaedrus figure, as of course he was in terms of status.

An aerial view of a shrine to Asclepius, a demi-god of healing whom the Romans inherited from the Greeks, at Pergamum in Turkey. Those seeking his intervention were expected to spend the night in the shrine complex, the cure coming in the form of dreams.

AN INTIMATE JOURNAL

Very many of the letters mention health. For example, there are a series on Fronto's neck. 'I desire to know how you are doing, Lord. I myself have been seized with a pain in the neck. Goodbye Lord. Greet your Lady.' Marcus writes back, 'I seem to have passed the night without fever. I have accepted food willingly. Now I am doing absolutely fine. We shall discover what the night brings. But when I learnt that you had been seized by a pain in the neck . . .' This appears to have crossed with a more urgent *cri* from Fronto: 'I have been attacked by a grave pain in the neck. The pain has gone from my foot. Farewell, best of Lords. Greet your Lady.' Fronto is also keen to report accidents. 'When my slave boys were bringing me from the baths in a chair as usual, they were rather careless and dashed me against the boiling-hot entrance to the bath. My knee was badly grazed and scorched. Afterwards my groin swelled up. The doctors told me to stay in bed.' Once again it is very difficult to know how far we are entitled to generalize these concerns. We do not meet anything like this level of introspection in the letters of Pliny (turn of the second century), of Cicero (mid first century BC), or the great collections of later antiquity.

Whatever the truth of Fronto's and Marcus's medical concerns, in the second century AD healing cults were extremely important in the lives of rich and poor. One of the most influential was that of Asclepius. In the Roman period shrines to Asclepius (known as 'Asclepieia') were highly organised centres equipped with all the facilities visitors needed. A central part of the cult was the ritual of 'incubation', in other words sleeping within the sanctuary to enable the god to appear in a dream to advise and cure. Patients could spend a long time seeking this help. One of the best known sites was at the great city of Pergamum. This shrine underwent extensive refurbishment around the middle of the second century AD. We know from inscriptions and literary texts that many elite men came here to be cured or to display their wealth by making dedications and erecting buildings. The culture of healing was part of the culture of elite life. Pergamum was a good place to be seen.

It is not surprising that this ritual entered into literature, in the *Sacred Tales* of Aelius Aristides. Aristides's many surviving speeches, on classical mythological and historical subjects, contemporary political issues, the powers of his favourite gods, were highly regarded by contemporaries and later writers like Libanius who wrote his own work under a portrait of him. Aristides is a convoluted writer at the best of times. In the *Sacred Tales* he gives a lengthy account of the 130 or so extraordinary dreams given to him by Asclepius over a period of twenty-five years. For the most part the cures prescribed match those in contemporary medicine – enemas, vomiting, bloodletting – and Aristides typically used god and doctor in tandem. He also places much emphasis on bathing in rivers, though this must have been a more personal habit; river-bathing was not common in the Roman world.

The psychological self-portrait of Aristides has attracted a good deal of interest. As literature the texts are deliberately chopped up and chronologically disarranged. The introduction to the second tale speaks of the jumbling up of notebooks containing 'at least 300,000 lines'. This leads into the start of his troubles:

A detail of a fourth-century AD fresco from the catacombs of the saints Peter and Marcellinus in Rome. The image of Christ the Good Shepherd was very popular among early Christians, and may have its roots in the Greek pastoral tradition. The peacock was not an overtly Christian symbol, but was adopted from the Roman imperial cult, where it was closely associated with the goddess Juno.

When I was brought from Italy, after I had contracted many varied ailments from constant sickness and the stormy weather which I had experienced... the doctors were wholly at a loss not only as to how to help, but even to recognise what the whole thing was. The hardest and most difficult thing of all was that my breathing was blocked. With much effort and disbelief, scarcely would I draw a rasping and shallow breath . . . Here first the Saviour began to make his revelation. He ordered me to go forth unshod. And I cried out in my dream... 'Great is Asclepius!'

This was in the year 144, and in the next summer the god summoned Aristides to the Asclepieion at Pergamum. Here he remained for two years until coaxed out by dreams predicting his success as an orator. But the illness did not go away. Many years later he published an extract of a journal of his treatments for the period 4 January to 15 February of the year 166 during the Parthian War:

On the seventeenth no bathing after a dream, and on the eighteenth no bathing. On the nineteenth, I dreamed that some Parthians had got me in their power, and one of them approached me and made as if to brand me. Next he inserted a finger right in my throat… Then vomiting was indicated and the Parthian ordered that today I abstain from bathing… No bathing, and vomiting, and comfort.

The keeping of a diary is known from other sources. Marcus' *Meditations* probably rest on similar daily accounts, and the accent on physical symptoms reminds us of Fronto's letters. But the documentation of daily religious experience is unique in pagan antiquity.

THE CHRISTIAN FUTURE

Yet in spite of the originality of the form, there is something unsatisfying, too self-indulgent about the *Sacred Tales*. It is interesting to compare it with a very different sort of text which is a major representative of another new genre of literature in this period – the martyr act – and also contains a famous diary. Reports of martyrs' deaths begin in the mid second century and come in various shapes and sizes. The essential point is that this was literature for distribution designed to edify and encourage. Perhaps Aristides' *Tales* also had this function. Certainly his 'prose hymns' for various gods do. But his overblown, rich style is unattractive in comparison with the powerful and simple narratives of the Christian writers. One late second and one early third century Latin text repay our attention. The Acts of the Scillitan Martyrs purports to be an original record of a court hearing between a governor and a group of Christians. It is short and spare. The martyrs' end is left to the imagination – the same brilliant control that the author of Acts of the Apostles had exercised.

A more complex example is the Passion of Saints Perpetua and Felicitas. The most compelling part of this story is the prison diary of the 'respectably born and well educated' Vibia Perpetua 'as she left it written with her own hand and in her own words'. She was aged twenty-two, and still breastfeeding her baby. 'After a few days we were taken into prison, and I was much afraid because I had never known such darkness… There was a great heat because of the press, there was rough handling from the soldiers.' She asked for a vision and received one of a ladder to heaven. 'I went up, and I saw a very great garden, and in the midst a man sitting, white-haired, in shepherd's clothing, tall, milking his sheep… and he said to me, "Welcome, child (*teknon*)".' She ends the diary by saying, 'I have written this up till the day before the games. The deed of the games themselves let him write who will.' The image of the Good Shepherd is in fact one of the earliest known from Christian art in churches and catacombs. The use of the Greek word *teknon* reminds us of the debt of Latin-speaking Christianity to its Greek model, an indebtedness which parallels much of what we have been discussing.

Ultimately of course the future for Latin and Greek literature was Christian. As we have seen, this entailed the most radical development of the book as we know it. In fact the emergence of Christian literature may stand for the general theme of this chapter. For Christianity was a way of life. As it entered elite circles, it redeveloped slowly but surely the whole of Greco-Roman elite culture, including literature, which it adapted (history, epistolography, the novel) or invented (the homily, the martyr act) as necessary, showing as well as anything how culture is a matter of life and death.

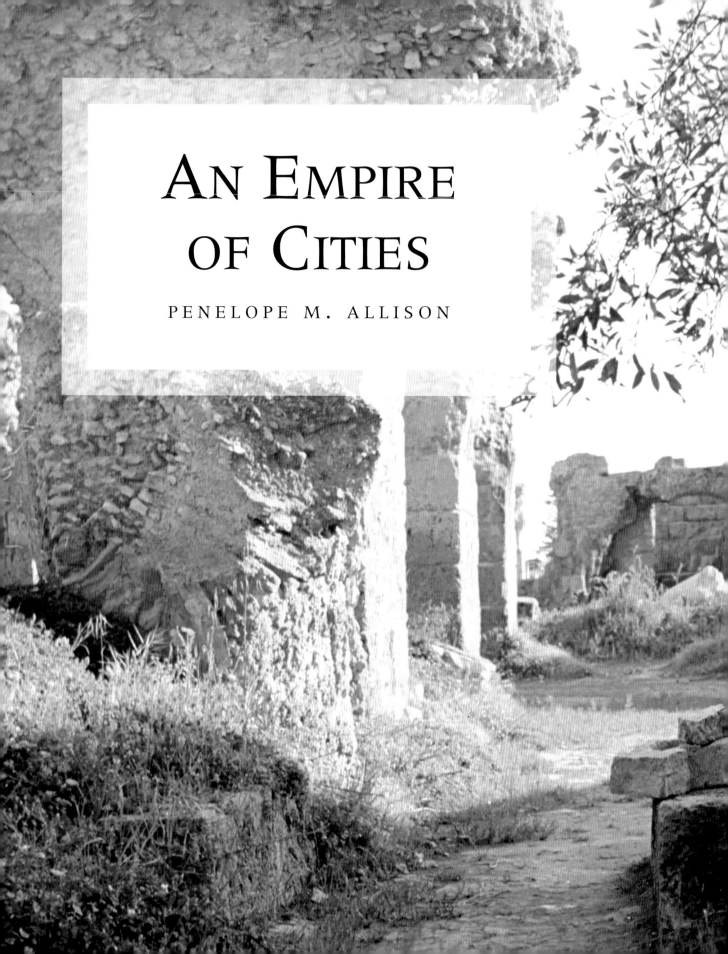

AN EMPIRE
OF CITIES

PENELOPE M. ALLISON

AN EMPIRE OF CITIES

The Romans are credited with bringing order to the western world, an order epitomised in the structure and organisation of their cities. These cities were often established for trade and military advantage, or to commemorate a victory and thus to advertise the power and prestige of Rome. Many, particularly in Italy, Africa and the East, were founded on pre-existing urban centres. In most cases the local population was incorporated into the new city, but in some they were expelled. Today, the Romans are heralded for the administrative, and military, skill with which they conquered the known world and established these cities.

The impact of Roman town planning on the layouts and functioning of the pre-existing towns has been much debated. However, it is now widely accepted that the orthogonal, chequerboard layout of many Roman cities was the result of Roman contact with the Greeks in southern Italy; the Greeks had been building cities with regular town plans since at least the sixth century BC. Depending on the terrain, the planned Greek cities were essentially laid out on a rectangular street pattern with one pair of main cross streets, or sometimes two. Besides blocks of houses, areas were set apart for an administrative centre and market space (the *agora*), for temples, theatres and exercise spaces (*gymnasia* or *stadia*). These basically Greek elements became the hallmarks of Roman cities.

The layout of each Roman city was usually based on the intersection of two main axial routes, the *cardo maximus* running north–south and the *decumanus maximus* running east–west, and secondary streets which formed blocks, called *insulae*. Most of these *insulae* were taken up by private housing but near the centre of this layout was also a civic centre (the *forum*), and temples, theatres and other areas for games, entertainment and leisure likewise formed part of the city. Like Greek and Near Eastern cities as far back as the Bronze Age, Roman cities often had fortification walls. Cemeteries usually lined the main roads, outside the city boundary.

So, like their predecessors, Roman cities not only provided accommodation and protection for their citizens but also political, administrative, economic, social and religious facilities. What is distinctly Roman, besides the particular administrative system, was the number and range of these physical amenities and the many building forms that are still preserved. Romans brought new building techniques to the established cities as well as to the new foundations. They introduced the use of concrete (first developed in Campania during the third century BC), which brought major technical and architectural advances, particularly in covering large spaces with vaults and domes. They brought Roman ideas of monumentality and symmetry to these cities, and the furbishing of buildings with lavish sculptural finishes in exotic white and coloured marbles and elaborate wall-paintings. They also brought specifically Roman building types, such as triumphal arches and amphitheatres, which were important to the social lives of the citizens and a reminder that their city was part of the greater Roman world. Relatively small-scale building projects were characteristic of the middle Republic, but from the mid-first century BC large-scale monumental planning began to emerge, as did a distinctive Roman architectural style based on domes and vaulting, more varied room shapes and the widespread use of concrete faced with brick. Cities throughout the Empire were being embellished with such architectural expressions of a distinctly Roman culture from around the first century BC onwards.

It was a duty of Roman public figures to provide Roman citizens with all the amenities required for their protection, administration, commercial needs, health and leisure. Leading citizens from Rome became patrons of certain cities, using their own money to build or restore particular buildings, thus enhancing their own prestige as well as that of Rome. In addition, eminent citizens often paid for public facilities in their own cities, competing with their political rivals to gain the goodwill and votes of the people in their aspirations for senior administrative appointments. Magistrates also often erected buildings and monuments to express gratitude to the townspeople for having voted for them in past elections. A city's walls, gates and streets were considered public facilities to be maintained by patrons willing to contribute. Water was also an essential requirement for city life. Its supply often necessitated the construction of aqueducts to bring water to the public fountains and baths, not to mention drainage and sewerage systems. Public baths, among the most important social and health centres of the cities of the Empire, also required good water supply; these too were often built, enlarged or embellished by such patrons.

An aerial view of the excavated ruins of Pompeii, with Mount Vesuvius looming in the background. At the time of its destruction, Pompeii was a small provincial city that enjoyed a more pleasant climate than that of Rome. It was a city not because of its size (which was quite small), but by virtue of its administration system not to mention being endowed with the full range of civic amenities, from temples and baths to theatres and brothels.

Even more so than their Greek predecessors, the Romans placed great importance on public entertainment and leisure. Not only did leading citizens vie to provide their cities with theatres, amphitheatres and exercise facilities, but they also competed to produce the shows, games and recreational activities that took place in them, and made sure that their efforts were recorded in inscriptions.

The peace, security and material prosperity of the first two centuries of the Empire, in particular, saw the development of many new cities and the elaboration of many former ones. Because of the diverse histories of the various parts of the Empire, the histories of the cities in each of these areas are also diverse. This chapter examines the development of one Roman city from each of the four main parts of the Ampire – Italy, North Africa, the eastern provinces and the western provinces.

POMPEII IN ITALY

Like many of the Etruscan cities in northern Italy and the Greek cities in the south, Pompeii was established as an urban centre long before the Roman Empire. The site was inhabited as early as the eighth century BC, and by the sixth century it

Pompeii was founded in the eighth century BC and ruled by among others Greeks and Etruscans before it was conquered by Rome in 89 BC. The city, one of the best preserved in the Roman Empire, was destroyed in AD 79 by a violent eruption of nearby Mount Vesuvius. The plan shows some of the more significant buildings and sites unearthed by a series of excavations that began in the eighteenth century.

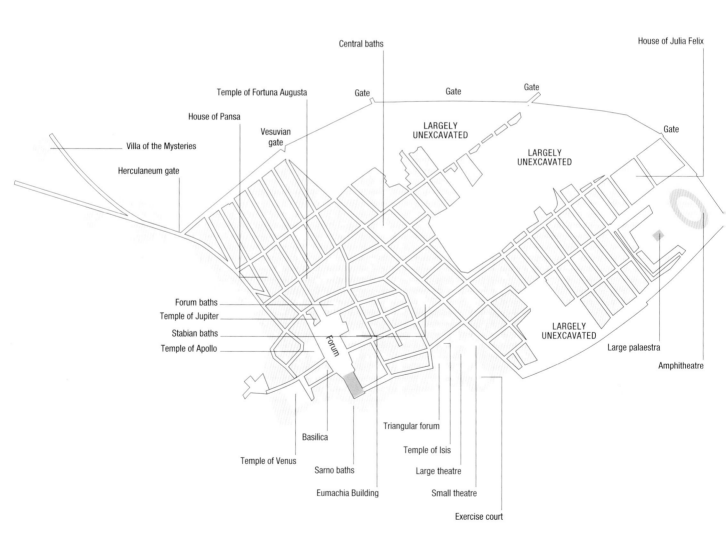

Central baths · House of Julia Felix · Temple of Fortuna Augusta · Gate · Gate · Gate · House of Pansa · Gate · Vesuvian gate · LARGELY UNEXCAVATED · Villa of the Mysteries · LARGELY UNEXCAVATED · Herculaneum gate · Forum baths · Temple of Jupiter · Stabian baths · Temple of Apollo · Forum · LARGELY UNEXCAVATED · Large palaestra · Amphitheatre · Triangular forum · Basilica · Temple of Isis · Temple of Venus · Large theatre · Sarno baths · Eumachia Building · Small theatre · Exercise court was a walled town, with solid fortification walls made from large blocks of local limestone and volcanic tufa, 3.2 km long and encompassing an area of some 66 hectares. We cannot be certain, however, that this whole area was built over with houses and public amenities as early as this. Indeed, recent research in the south-east part of the town has shown that many of the urban properties were still vineyards and orchards at the time of the city's destruction by the eruption of Mount Vesuvius in AD 79. The population of Pompeii has often been estimated at up to 20,000, but such estimates, based on the size of the city and analogies with city demographics in later periods, have not usually taken into account the considerable area of agricultural space within the city. It therefore follows that this particular Roman city probably had a population somewhat smaller than the number considered to constitute a city today. It was certainly never one of the great cities of the Empire.

Pompeii is important for us because its tragic demise has meant that it is better preserved archaeologically than any other city of the Empire. Our information on the city, in fact, comes almost exclusively from its archaeological remains, with very little from written sources. It thus provides more physical evidence of the layout and amenities of a Roman city than any other city in the Roman world.

Who actually controlled the city of Pompeii in its early years is still not well understood. There is evidence of both Greek and Etruscan presence here, alongside the indigenous inhabitants. In the sixth century BC, when the city fortifications were built, a temple to Apollo was built on the road leading from the waterfront to what became the forum, and another temple was built in the southern part of the city and dedicated first to the Greek god Heracles and then to Athena. Even so, the construction of these temples does not necessarily indicate Greek domination: these gods were also important to the Etruscans.

In 80 BC, after the Romans had defeated their former Italian allies in the Social Wars, the dictator Publius Cornelius Sulla established the colony *Colonia Cornelia Veneria Pompeianorum* on the site for the settlement of his veteran soldiers. It is from this date that we know the city's name was Pompeii. The establishment of this colony meant that some 4–5,000 Roman army veterans and their families took up residence here and took control of most of the city's administration, either expelling earlier occupants from their houses or occupying the land within the city previously used for agriculture. Because of this influx of Roman citizens, the construction of many of the public buildings and amenities, and important changes in the city's houses, are believed to date from this time. Certainly by the reign of Augustus, Pompeii had all the trappings of a proper Roman city, even if some of these had their foundation in the earlier pre-Roman town. For example, the area surrounding the forum does not conform to the regular street pattern that is one of the hallmarks of a Roman city, or even a Greek city. It is therefore likely that the foundation of this town centre pre-dates even Greek influence in the area. Nevertheless, many features still visible in this forum area today demonstrate how the Roman administration enhanced the pre-existing civic centre.

A RELIGIOUS CENTRE

In the first place, the forum was provided with temples for many of the gods and cults that were important to Roman citizens. Such temples were used for both public ceremonies and by individual citizens for their personal sacrifices and dedications. The first of these temples, as one enters the town from the seaward side, is the Temple of Venus, which stands majestically to the right. Of a standard Italian form, this temple stood within a wide precinct on a high platform, with a deep colonnaded front porch. The discovery of a marble statue holding a bronze rudder, found on the steps of the temple, has been used to identify it as the temple of the patroness of the city, Venus Pompeiana, whose cult may have been introduced by Sulla, as indicated in the name of the Roman colony. The Temple of Apollo occupied the west side of the forum, its precinct having been greatly expanded and monumentalised during the Augustan period. Inside the forum itself, pride of place is taken by the Temple of Jupiter, the father of the Roman pantheon. Its identification is based on the discovery within it of a colossal torso of a seated male figure. The temple occupies the northern end of the forum and is again of traditional Italian form. If these attributions are correct, then these three temples, together with that of Heracles and Athena in the south of the city, bear witness to the Pompeians' continuity of worship of the Greek deities that the Romans incorporated into their own pantheon.

Other sacred buildings within Pompeii's forum demonstrate the importance of the imperial cult in the lives of Pompeians. On the west side was the Sanctuary of the Public Lares. The Lares were household deities who protected the family and household. The public Lares performed this service for the whole citizen body of Pompeii, as one large household. This sanctuary, dating to about the middle of the first century AD, had an arched apse at one end, in which stood a statue, identified as the Genius, the representation of the ancestral family or line, of Augustus. Two flanking rectangular niches probably displayed statues of the Lares themselves. This sanctuary, in the form of an exedra, was undoubtedly inspired by such architectural forms in the Imperial fora in Rome. It therefore linked the security and welfare of Pompeii with the imperial family, and enhanced this association through its architectural connection with the central power of Rome.

Another building in the forum connected with the imperial cult was located in approximately the centre of the east side. It was a small temple with a wide colonnaded porch, in a relatively spacious precinct, in the centre of which was a marble altar. Sculptural remains on the façade showed the scene of a priest sacrificing a bull. Such sacrifices were often made to honour a living emperor. This temple was incomplete at the time that Pompeii was destroyed and was therefore very probably dedicated to the emperor Vespasian. Given its short life, it may not have been as important a feature of the lives of Pompeians as it would have become had Mount Vesuvius not erupted. The construction of this small but elegant temple reminded Pompeians of the control and patronage of the emperors in Rome.

A third temple, not far from the forum, also reminded Pompeians of the importance of the Roman emperors in their lives. This small marble temple on the road to the north of the civil centre has an inscription identifying it was the Temple of

Augustan Fortune, paid for by Marcus Tullius, who was magistrate three times and military tribune, elected by the people. These three temples in the vicinity of the forum demonstrated to the Pompeians that the emperor and power of Rome offered protection to the citizens, often through the instrument of the city magistrates, in exchange for their loyalty.

There were other cults that the citizens of Pompeii continued to worship. The Temple of Isis, found near Pompeii's two theatres and not far from the early temple to Athena, was probably built around the end of the second century BC. Dedicated to an Egyptian deity, the temple and its decorations illustrate that the spread of both Greek and Roman influence into Egypt also stimulated the spread of Egyptian culture and religion into Italy. This small but imposing temple demonstrates that such cults were tolerated – and indeed flourished – within the Roman Empire. An inscription indicates that this temple was badly damaged in an earthquake, probably that of AD 62, and was restored by Numerius Popidius Celsinus, the son of a freedman. His father, a freedman and therefore not a citizen, desired to advance his son's political career by linking his name with this temple and with this cult.

The excavated ruins of the Temple of Isis at Pompeii. The elaborate and exotic multi-cultural decoration – a mixture of Hellenistic and Egyptian styling – was executed mainly in stucco that was applied to the surfaces of stoutly built walls of mundane Roman brickwork.

THEATRES AND BATHS

While many secular public buildings in Pompeii also document the spread of Roman architectural and social forms into southern Italy, some such buildings preceded the arrival of the Roman colonists and probably belong to its Greek heritage. For example, the construction technique of the larger theatre in the southern part of the city indicates that it was built in the second century BC, some one hundred years before Rome received its first stone-built theatre. Pompeii's theatre is of traditional Greek form, although it was renovated on at least two occasions during the Roman period by citizens wishing to enhance their civic standing. This renovation of an essentially Greek building demonstrates the importance of Greek culture for the enhancement of the Roman administrative system. Indeed, adjacent to this theatre is a smaller one, referred to by modern scholars as the *odeion*, a covered theatre for musical events. Its masonry technique demonstrates that it was built after 80 BC, the foundation of the Roman colony, although it is again essentially a Greek theatre in form. Two magistrates, Gaius Quinctius Valgus and Marcus Porcius, claim credit for having constructed this covered theatre. Another inscription, in bronze in the pavement, tells us that the magistrate Marcus Oculatis Verus paid for a performance that was put on here for the public, no doubt to also gain their support.

Pompeii's citizens were amply provided with five different bathing facilities. Public baths are another civic amenity that had a Greek origin. The so-called Stabian Baths, which became the largest complex in Pompeii (covering over 4,000 square metres by the end of the first century AD), had at their core a much smaller complex consisting of a well and four small rooms with basins. This small complex served as bathing facilities for the adjacent exercise court (*gymnasium*) and was constructed at the end of the fourth century BC, long before Pompeii was colonised by the Romans. The final form of this bath was the standard type for a Roman bath complex, with two sections each of three rooms maintained at progressively higher temperatures – the *frigidarium*, the *tepidarium* and the *caldarium*. The duplication of this system, and Vitruvius's stipulation that male and female hot baths should be adjacent, has led to the identification of one section as the male bathing area and the other as the female. The origins of this extensive complex must also be dated to before Pompeii became a Roman colony, because an inscription indicates that the city magistrates restored and extended it shortly after the arrival of the colonists, paying for the addition of a sweat room (*laconicum*) and the restoration of the porticoes of the exercise court, the *palaestra*. In Pompeii's last years, other eminent citizens continued to embellish this bath complex (and, no doubt, their own reputations) by adding an elaborate plastered relief decoration to the west wall of the *palaestra* and repairing the smaller section of the baths. In so doing, they showed their goodwill towards the pre-Roman occupants of Pompeii as well as to the new colonists.

The other four bath complexes in Pompeii were built during the period of Roman control. One is located immediately to the north of the forum, opposite the Temple of Augustan Fortune; it is today called the Forum Baths. Its masonry construction has been used to date it to the early years of the colony and an inscription indicates that it was erected by three magistrates, possibly those who arrived in Pompeii with Sulla's army. The proximity of this complex to the public area of the forum no doubt meant it was frequented by citizens with business in the civic centre. A third bath complex, the Suburban Baths, located outside the city walls near the probable access road from the waterfront to the forum, was constructed in the first decades AD. The Sarno Baths, situated in the south-west of the city behind the municipal buildings of the forum, can also probably be dated to the early first century AD. Finally, the Central Baths were the newest public bath complex in Pompeii, probably initiated after the earthquake of AD 62 and never completed. So, while the provision of public baths dates to before Pompeii became a Roman city, the citizens were increasingly provided with new and upgraded bathing facilities in the Roman period.

Because Pompeii is situated on a high plateau of volcanic rock, the provision of adequate water to the city presented serious difficulties. In the city's early years, private individuals dug wells into the rock within their houses. In the first century BC, an aqueduct was constructed to convey water from a nearby river. The supply of water via this aqueduct not only meant the water was now a public commodity, but also that the range of public bath complexes described above could be amply supplied.

The *caldarium* (hot room) of the Forum Baths at Pompeii. This elegant space – starkly utilitarian, but with grace worthy of a temple interior – is situated only a few metres from the public turmoil of the forum. Here, in warmth and seclusion, the leading citizens of Pompeii would have relaxed and restored themselves before re-entering the melée outside.

THE AMPHITHEATRE

Most notable among the public buildings in Pompeii that did not share the Greek ancestry of the theatres, temples and bath complexes is the amphitheatre. Pompeii's amphitheatre is one of the earliest and best preserved stone-built amphitheatres in the Roman world. It was built in the south-east corner of the city, against the city walls, thus reducing the requirement for extensive earth banking to support it. This location also meant that the walls provided support for the awnings used to protect the spectators who came to watch gladiatorial contests and animal fights from the hot southern Italian sun. Amphitheatres are a quintessential Roman building, catering for typically Roman entertainment. The construction of this amphitheatre, in the early first century BC, indicates that the citizens of Pompeii had 'romanised' tastes in entertainment by this date, or were at least expected to have such tastes. A foundation inscription indicates that the same magistrates Gaius Quinctius Valgus and Marcus Porcius had this amphitheatre built so that the citizens of Pompeii might have a proper building in which to watch spectacles, but also to thank them for their electoral support and to ensure its continuation. The amphitheatre is estimated to have seated about 20,000 spectators.

Associated with the amphitheatre is a large open area (the so-called *palaestra*) with a central pool, covering some 1.5 hectares. This was built at public expense during the reign of Augustus and is thought to have served as a suitable space for young male Pompeians to meet and train to be fit for service in the Roman army.

GAMES (LUDI)

Juvenal's famous jibe (*Satire* 10.81) that all people were concerned with was bread and circuses highlights the significance of entertainment in Roman city life. An important feature of cities, therefore, was their provision of facilities for this entertainment – theatres, amphitheatres and circuses. By equipping loyal towns with entertainment facilities, and indeed the entertainment to stage in them, the Roman authorities both promoted the 'romanisation' of these communities and encouraged other communities to adopt Roman culture.

Responsibility for staging performances in these facilities fell on the municipal magistrates. These were expensive affairs, for which magistrates used both public money and their own; the performers were often slaves owned by the sponsors of the show. These shows included dramatic performances and recitals in the theatre, athletics and chariot races in the circus, and gladiatorial and wild animal contests in the amphitheatre. The theatrical performances drew on both Greek and Roman writers, but it was the chariot races and amphitheatre performances that were more popular. Charioteers and gladiators, although often slaves, frequently achieved hero status in the Roman world.

Games were attended both by townspeople and by people from the surrounding countryside. Often there was fierce rivalry between supporters of particular teams or performers. In AD 59, in Pompeii, a dispute over a particular gladiator resulted in a serious fight between the Pompeian spectators and the citizens of the neighbouring town, Nuceria. Consequently, the Pompeians were banned from holding any further such events for ten years, and the sponsor was exiled.

Many religious cults involved the celebration of games, either annually or every few years, with both magistrates and priests responsible. Sometimes a city would petition the emperor to hold international games. If the petition was successful, such games were a gift of the emperor. For example, in the third century, the Pythian Games were held in Carthage to honour the god Apollo. They attracted contestants from all over the Mediterranean and ambassadors from other cities were invited to pay their respects to Apollo and to Carthage.

Seating arrangements for theatre or amphitheatre performances reflected the social organisation of the city. Each segment of society had its own assigned area. Decurions, magistrates and senators sat in the orchestra, the front, most conspicuous part, of the theatre. The charter of Carthage imposed fines of 5,000 *sesterces* on those who sat in areas to which they were not entitled.

Above: Details of a fourth-century AD Roman mosaic from Spain (left and above) that portrays a sanitised view of gladiatorial combat as a carefully observed sport with nearly as many umpires as fighters. The implied importance of rules suggests the close involvement of the large Roman gambling fraternity.

Right: A view of the gladiator's barracks and training ground at Pompeii. Here, those literally without hope would practise with the sytlised weapon sets which made for a sporting contest in Roman eyes. The close presence of violence and blood made the barracks an attractive after-hours venue for all kinds of sensation-seekers.

The ruined colonnades of the Basilica at Pompeii. Elevated slightly above the forum (for both symbolic and practical purposes), the Basilica predates the official Roman presence by some fifty years. It housed some of the city's administration, and probably those offices concerned with the regulation of markets and trade.

ADMINISTRATIVE AND COMMERCIAL BUILDINGS

Besides religious buildings in the forum, a number of administrative and commercial buildings also formed part of this civic centre. To the right of the entranceway from the waterfront, beyond the Temple of Venus, is a large building now referred to as the Basilica. This building type has its origins in the colonnaded arcades (stoas) that flanked the Greek *agora*, in which people would shelter while discussing business and politics or selling their wares. The Basilica in Pompeii was a large building with a porch leading onto the forum and colonnades arranged to form three naves providing shelter for visitors. It was built in about 130 to 120 BC, before Pompeii became a Roman colony and before its counterparts in the Forum in Rome. It is, therefore, one of the oldest basilicas in the Roman world, adding weight to the argument that this building type, from which the form of the early Christian church developed, originally grew out of the Greek stoa.

At the south end of the forum in Pompeii are three smaller buildings, each with an apse at one end. While their actual function has not been verified, they are believed to have been administrative buildings. The easternmost is thought to be where the magistrates exercised their jurisdiction, that at the centre for the town archives (the *tabularium*), and the westernmost the meeting place for the members of the local senate, called the *curia*. The brickwork of all three of these buildings suggests that they were built during the Roman period, specifically to fulfil these municipal functions. Close by, on the east side of the forum, are the ruins of another building which had at least eight doorways and was probably where the municipal elections were held, the *comitium*.

Other buildings in Pompeii's forum were probably associated with its role as a centre of commerce. First, a colonnaded building with a large open central area occupied the space just across the street from the *comitium*. This building was dedicated by Eumachia and her son to Pietas Concordia Augusta. Eumachia was a public priestess and a member of an important local family, the Eumachii, and today the building is referred to as the Eumachia Building. Pietas (Piety) Concordia (Harmony) Augusta was a title that the Senate in Rome granted to the emperor Tiberius and his mother, Livia, the wife of Augustus. It is now believed that this building was the city's wool market; wool was one of the main products of the Pompeii region and its preparation was one of the main crafts identified in Pompeii itself. Whatever commercial activity took place here, the inscription indicates a clear link between local industry, the imperial cult and the role of the local elite, including eminent women, in the promotion of this link.

A large complex in the north-east corner of the forum consisted of a colonnaded area surrounded by numerous small rooms. This has been identified as the meat and fish market, the *macellum*. Numerous fish bones were found here and a water system in the centre was probably used for preserving this merchandise. At the east end is an altar, in which were found the remains of two statues that indicate that it too was dedicated to the imperial cult. Again, this building demonstrates that the commercial and sacred worlds in Roman cities, and the role of the emperor in these, were never separate.

The area around the forum also provided other facilities for the citizens of Pompeii, and displayed different symbols. Missing today are the commemorative statues that would have stood on the many bases still extant in the open space in the centre of the forum. These statues were already missing when the forum was excavated in the nineteenth century, so we will never know who was represented here; nonetheless, we may perhaps imagine that the statues included comparable images of present and past emperors, their families and city benefactors to those that were displayed in the fora of other Roman cities. In the north-west corner of the forum a number of storerooms and public latrines were found; these were again essential amenities for people using this public space.

This is not an exhaustive of list all the amenities that served the population of Roman Pompeii and provided their employment. Numerous smaller shops, workshops and perhaps taverns also lined the main streets of the city, and brothels have been identified in certain areas. But this list highlights that Pompeii contained the public amenities one might expect to find in almost any Roman city, and the role of such facilities in promoting the power of Rome. Some of these were already part of the city before the Romans took over but the Roman authorities adapted, renovated and monumentalised them, and used them, alongside the new buildings, to enhance their own power and prestige and to glorify the emperor and the Empire.

ATHENS IN THE GREEK EAST

While no other city offers such a wealth and diversity of surviving physical evidence of the Roman world as Pompeii, Athens is among the richest for its combination of archaeological, epigraphic and literary evidence.

Athens is also the foremost example of a city where the Romans built on an existing urban foundation. They were well aware of the importance of Athens as a principal Greek city and cultural centre, memorialising Greece's glorious classical past. Students and tourists from all over the Roman world flocked here to study Greek culture, perceived as essential to the acquisition of an image of sophistication in Rome. Many of Rome's subjects were Greeks, so it was also important that the Romans ensured that this centre of Greek heritage became a showpiece of the Roman world. Not only prominent Roman patrons but also emperors and other members of the imperial family lavished great fortunes on Athens. Roman authors have provided descriptions of extensive building programmes that can still be witnessed in the structural and epigraphical remains in the city.

But Athens was not always the pre-eminent Greek city. From the late fourth century BC, the growth of the new Hellenistic cities of Antioch in Syria, Alexandria in Egypt and Pergamum in Asia Minor meant that the centrality of Athens to the Greek world had diminished, though the rulers of these other cities paid tribute to Athens as their cultural centre by erecting buildings and monuments of their own there.

The Agora was the heart of ancient Athens – the centre of commercial, political, social and cultural activity. The Athenian Agora assumed its present rectangular shape by about the second century BC. Many of the existing buildings were 'romanised' by Augustus, however, his son-in-law, Marcus Aggripus also built monumental new structures including the 1000-seater Odeion and he is believed also to have been responsible for the Temple of Ares (the Greek equivalent of Mars).

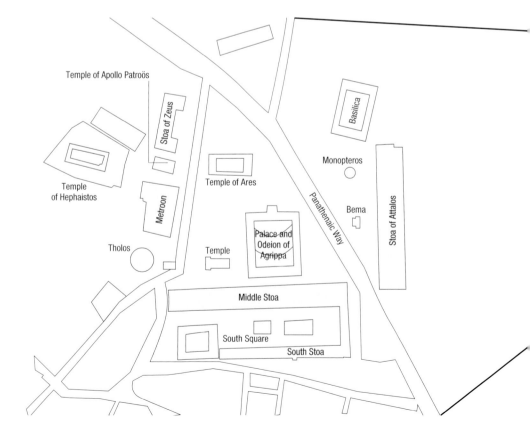

After it was sacked by Sulla in 86 BC and its defences largely destroyed, Athens became a political backwater. Under Augustus, however, it began to be 'romanised'. Julius Caesar had originally provided money for the construction of a new *agora* to the east of the old Athenian Agora, but it was completed and dedicated by Augustus. A paved rectangular court (82 metres by 69 metres in dimensions) was enclosed on four sides by Ionic porticoes, off which opened individual shops and, on its south side, a fountain house. It was entered from the west by a (still visible) monumental gateway which, according to an inscription, was originally surmounted by a statue of Lucius Caesar, Augustus's grandson. This gateway deliberately echoed the architectural form of the Propylaea, the monumental gateway to the sanctuary of Athena on the Acropolis, thus linking the Roman monument and trade centre with the city's patron goddess.

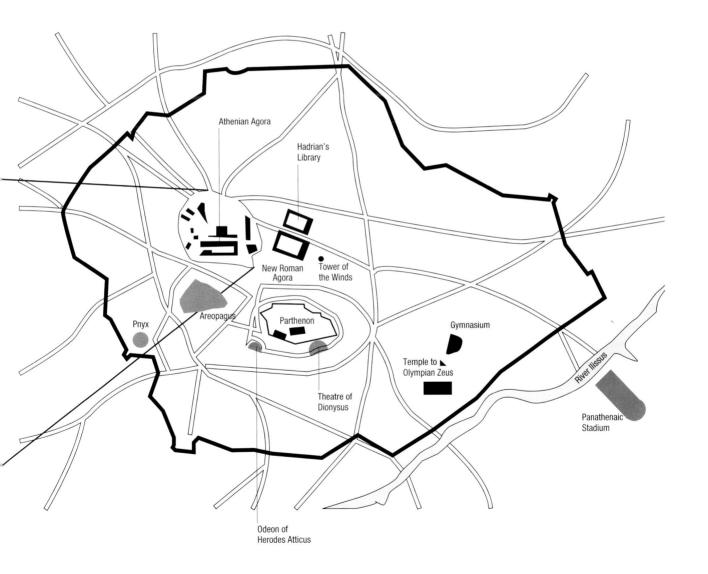

REDESIGNING THE AGORA AND ACROPOLIS

The Athenian Agora, the centre of Greek democracy, was also a centre of attention under Augustus. His son-in-law, Marcus Agrippa, built an *odeion* as a Roman focal point for the old Agora. The lofty, rectangular, gabled hall and the polychrome marble finish of this covered theatre, which could seat some 1,000 spectators, were comparable to the so-called *odeion* in Pompeii, but the difference here was that this theatre was located right in the heart of the Athenian civic centre. At the same time, the Temple of Apollo Patroös on the western side of the old Agora was adapted to house an altar to the imperial cult. Its northern neighbour, the Stoa of Zeus Eleutherios, was also adapted for the imperial cult, and here loyal Athenians offered sacrifices to celebrate the emperor's birthday.

Agrippa was probably also responsible for transplanting, from outside Athens to the Agora, the architectural elements of a fifth-century BC temple to Ares (the Greek god of war) to create a new Temple of Ares. This temple, now situated in the formerly open central space of the Agora, became the civic centre's biggest construction, and was symbolically connected with the Temple of Mars Ultor that dominated the Forum of Augustus in Rome. Thus, although the Temple of Ares was not directly associated with the imperial cult, it linked the traditional Athenian Agora with Augustus's imperial forum in Rome.

The building activities of Augustus and his relatives followed the tradition of the Hellenistic kings of erecting public buildings in Athens, but these Roman transformations also had a powerful symbolic impact: they filled in the Agora whose open public space was essential to Athenian democracy. They thus imposed upon Athens both a symbolic and a real Roman imperial domination.

The Roman Agora in Athens. Like new public spaces elsewhere in the Empire, this space built at the end of the first century BC, was planned as an ensemble. A rectangular piazza surrounded with porticoes and accessible through a monumental arch, it also incorporated shops, an office for the market official and a latrine. Beyond it is visible the octagonal Tower of the Winds, from the Hellenistic period, which housed an elaborate monumental clock.

Nero, in keeping with his theatrical interests, also associated himself with Athens as a Greek cultural centre by refurbishing its principal theatre, the Theatre of Dionysus, on the south slopes of the Acropolis. This refurbishment was dedicated to Dionysus and to Nero himself. In fact, the theatre had already been linked to the imperial cult under Augustus. An inscription on one of the seats attests to a priesthood of the cult of Augustus in Athens from about 27 BC. During the first century AD, gladiatorial shows, which in Italy and the west (after Augustus) would normally have been staged in an amphitheatre, were put on in this theatre, as was more normal in the east. Such shows were often associated with the imperial cult and were possibly offered by its priests as part payment for their office. Athenian enthusiasm for the imperial cult is difficult to gauge, but the citizens' enthusiasm for gladiatorial games is clearly attested in the Theatre of Dionysus; again, the Roman re-use of this existing institution successfully links a popular Roman form of entertainment with traditional Greek theatre, and probably also with the celebration of the imperial cult.

The only building that was actually erected in Athens specifically for the imperial cult is a small temple to Augustus and the goddess Roma on the Acropolis. The construction of this temple was a direct signal that Athens' religious centre, the Acropolis, was under the control of Rome. The style of the new temple was heavily influenced by that of the Erechtheion (the complex multiple temple to Athena, Poseidon and other Greek gods and heroes that stood nearby on the Acropolis), thus aligning it with classical Greek religion. The worship of the Roman emperor in Athens, however, appears to have been muted rather than enthusiastic – which suggests that the establishment of a new temple in this sanctuary of the patron goddess of Athens was perhaps a reflection of imperial anger at Athenian lack of obeisance. Only under Claudius and Nero did the imperial cult become more prominent in Athens.

The Theatre of Dionysus at the foot of the Acropolis in Athens. The city, and Greek culture in general, had a great champion in the emperor Nero.

HADRIAN'S IMPROVEMENTS

From this survey of Roman building activities in Athens under the Julio-Claudian emperors it is apparent that, even though the most enduring monuments were erected in the mid-second century AD by Hadrian, the great philhellene among the Roman emperors, the incursions of Romans into Athenian social, religious, commercial and political life were already well advanced in this earlier period – even if the Athenians, at first, were not very receptive. The Julio-Claudians and their officials absorbed, adapted and embellished the important components of Athenian civil life.

Because of his interests in Greek culture, Hadrian showed Athens special favour. In AD 130, he made Athens the centre for a cult organisation, the Panhellenion, which Greek cities from many provinces were invited to join. On his first visit to Athens, Hadrian ordered the completion of the Temple to Olympian Zeus that had been initiated by the tyrant Peisistratos in the late sixth century BC but abandoned in 510 BC when Athens became a democracy. This temple was finally completed and dedicated in AD 132, some seven hundred years later, an action seen by some historians and archaeologists as marking an association between the Roman emperor and the Greek tyrants of the pre-democratic era. A more practical addition under Hadrian was a new aqueduct, with a monumental façade of four Ionic columns, providing a vastly improved water supply. Under his patronage extensions were also made to the old city, to the west and to the south-east, where remains of private houses, baths and *gymnasia* are still to be found. In addition, Hadrian built a commemorative arch, which marked the transition between the old city and the new. This arch displayed statues of himself and the Athenian mythical hero Theseus. Hadrian also built a *stoa* and library next to the Agora of Caesar and Augustus which, in plan, copied Vespasian's Temple of Peace in the centre of Rome, with a porticoed garden enclosure and long pool extending down the centre.

In the period immediately following Hadrian, public works in Athens were dominated by Herodes Atticus, a wealthy patron of the arts who desired to thank the Athenians for the honour they showed him in putting him in charge of their most important city event, the Panathenaic Festival. He restored and enlarged the stadium, originally built in the fourth century BC, for the track contests of the Panathenaic Games. This now assumed a Roman form and was adapted for gladiatorial games.

The city of Athens continued to be a major centre of culture and learning until the Christian emperor Justinian closed the philosophical schools in the sixth century AD. Its pre-eminence was not, however, reflected in major building campaigns or monuments after the second century AD, although routine construction and some minor reorganisation of public spaces continued. In the mid-third century the Emperor Valerian built fortification walls, but these did not prevent the city from being laid waste by the Goths and Heruls in AD 267.

So, while Pompeii provides a wealth of archaeological evidence for the transformation of a Roman city, Athens is a foremost example of a city whose pre-Roman traditions were usurped and glorified under the Roman Empire. Many of Athens's imperial Roman buildings displayed a strong sense of nostalgia in their use of classical Greek forms. A temple to Augustus and Roma on the Acropolis and a Forum of Augustus in Rome which relied so heavily on these classical forms symbolised both the inclusive nature of the Roman administrative system and its religion and Rome's domination of its subjects. The works of the Roman emperors in Athens not only embellished the old classical and Hellenistic city but also provided it with a character and facilities that were essentially Roman. At the same time, however, Athens's stock of symbolic capital, both architectural and cultural, meant that it not only retained elements of its traditional appearance but also exported them to Rome itself.

CARTHAGE IN NORTH AFRICA

The archaeology and history of the Roman city of Carthage in North Africa presents a different picture from both Pompeii and Athens. The rich and romantic history of Punic Carthage provides tantalisingly little information on the structure and functioning of its Roman successor. Not only did Carthage continue to be built over after the Roman period but the expansion of modern Tunis and its suburbs, especially since the 1940s, has meant that little of the ancient Carthage, Punic or Roman, has survived. The search for Punic tombs and their contents has also added to the destruction of Roman Carthage. So, in 1972, the Tunisian government and UNESCO sponsored an international project to salvage some of the city's past. Teams from Bulgaria, Canada, Denmark, France, Germany, Holland, Italy, Poland, Sweden, Tunisia, the United Kingdom and the United States carried out archaeological excavations in various parts of the city, using modern stratigraphical methods, so that it is now possible to piece together something of the Roman city's life.

From at least the seventh until the mid-second century BC, Punic civilisation dominated much of the western Mediterranean. Carthage, founded (according to tradition) in about 814 BC by colonists from Tyre in Phoenicia, was its centre. The geographical limits of the Punic city are still unknown, but excavations have uncovered a monumental gateway, a defensive sea wall and a well laid-out city on a rectangular plan dated to at least the fifth century BC.

The age of Punic power in the Mediterranean and of Punic opposition to Rome ended in the spring of 146 BC, when the Roman senate ordered that Carthage be razed to the ground and a curse was placed on the site. Scipio Aemilianus's troops destroyed the fortification walls and advanced into the city centre – the citadel of Byrsa. Many of the tens of thousands of men, women and children who had taken refuge here were killed and Carthage's religious and civic buildings were destroyed. Among these buildings was the most celebrated temple in ancient literature, the Temple of Eshmoun, the Punic equivalent of Aesculapius, the healing god.

In 122 BC, despite this devastation and the curse placed on the city, the Roman tribune Gaius Gracchus attempted to found a small colony here of 6,000 colonists, *Colonia Junonia*. Each of the colonists was to be allotted about one-quarter of a hectare of land. While it is possible some of grid system (centuriation) still visible from the air belonged to this earlier colony, little else is known of it. Indeed, the record for Carthage for the next hundred years is blank.

THE ROMAN COLONY

Shortly before his death in 44 BC, Julius Caesar decreed that the city should be revived, but it was not until 29 BC, at the beginning of Augustus's reign, that *Colonia Julia Concordia Karthago* was founded on the old town site with 3,000 colonists. Augustus clearly intended to make Carthage the capital for the province of Africa and one of the greatest cities of his empire.

Augustus's surveyors mapped out an entire city grid system, as well as a centuriated agricultural landscape. Huge earthworks were carried out which obliterated the centre of the earlier Punic city. The citadel of Byrsa was levelled to produce a rectangular platform, of about 3–4 hectares, for a new civic centre for the Roman colony. Monumental buildings were set up here – a basilica, forum and temples – ostensibly erasing the symbolic focal point of Punic power. However, recent excavations have revealed traces of the Punic city and indicate that the alignment of this new Roman town followed that of its destroyed predecessor. Many of the new buildings were also constructed according to a Punic system of measurement, rather than the Roman. In other words, the myth that the old city was obliterated without trace is not substantiated by recent archaeological research. Like other Roman provincial cities, Carthage continued to be home to a mixed population of the original inhabitants and the recent Roman settlers.

RELIGIOUS CARTHAGE

Certainly, as was the case with other cities within the Roman Empire, the Roman conquerors imposed their own civil and religious order on the city. An altar of the *gens Augusta* was placed on this new platform so that, as had occurred in Athens, the former religious centre of Carthage became the location for observation of the imperial cult. This altar, with its garlands, wreaths, *bucrania* (symbolic bull's horns) and sacrifice scene, deliberately evoked the Altar of Augustan Peace, set up in Rome to celebrate the peace that Augustus had brought to the Roman world. Large classical-style temples were also built within this new centre.

It is unclear to whom the temples were dedicated but there survives documentary evidence to suggest that a temple to the Capitoline Triad – Jupiter, Juno and Minerva – was located at the western end of the forum. The Roman goddesses Ceres and Concordia (whose name appears on the title of the colony) also had shrines at Carthage, also probably located on this platform. Nonetheless, as was standard practice across the Empire, the Romans in Carthage remained tolerant of local religion.

Documentary evidence indicates that there was a temple to Caelestis in Roman Carthage. Caelestis was the Roman replacement for the patron deity of Punic Carthage, Tanit, whose sanctuary was located near the *tophet* (the site of sacrifices, which may have included child-sacrifice) to the south of the city. Recent excavations there have shown this ancient sanctuary continued to be the centre for the cult of the Roman goddess Caelestis. There is also evidence of a Christian community in Carthage by the mid-second century.

The excavated ruins of Carthage, near Tunis. Although the implacable logic of the hawks in the Roman Senate demanded that Carthage be obliterated, the site with its magnificent natural harbours was far too well-favoured to be long ignored. The Roman city prospered for nearly four centuries, (it boasted a branch of the imperial mint) until it was conquered by the Vandals.

PUBLIC FACILITIES

One of the most striking features of Roman Carthage was its two harbours to the south-east of the city, the outer rectangular harbour giving access to an inner circular one, within the city grid system (Cicero noted that Punic Carthage was surrounded by harbours). Archaeological excavations have found the remains of some thirty docks that date to the late Punic age, arranged in a fan-shape within the inner circular harbour. Again, it is clear that Roman Carthage relied heavily on its predecessor for much of its urban landscape.

But the Romans also provided Carthage with a range of new public facilities. Important among these was the essential amphitheatre on the west side of the city, measuring 156 metres by 128 metres, approximately the same size as the amphitheatre at Pompeii. Towards the end of the first century AD, a 516-metre long circus, or stadium, was built in the south-west corner of the city, where athletic events could be held. This circus had a seating capacity of 41,000 to 55,000 people and was only 80 metres shorter than the Circus Maximus in Rome.

During the second century AD, the province of Africa flourished and Carthage became the third-largest city in the Roman world, after Rome and Alexandria. The writer Apuleius, who was born in Africa, described the lavish furnishings of Carthage's Hadrianic theatre – its marble pavements and elaborate stage building with a brilliantly coloured coffered ceiling. Archaeological remains of this theatre, on the north side of the city, consist of fluted columns of granite, marble, porphyry and onyx, confirming Apuleius's picture of the opulence of Carthage's public buildings during the high Empire. Close to Hadrian's theatre, the largest *odeion* in the Roman world was also built during the late second or early third century AD.

The most imposing remains today, however, are those of the Antonine Baths, built facing the sea on what had previously been a small cove. This complex could thus have obliterated one of the old city's harbours. Covering an area of 17,850 square metres, it is the largest bath complex outside Rome. The complex has the familiar symmetrical plan of Roman baths, with identical facilities in each half and an octagonal central hot room. An inscription dates them to AD 145–162.

These baths were served by an aqueduct which brought water from some 56 kilometres away. The aqueduct, of which some stretches still survive, had an estimated capacity of 32

Little archaeological evidence remains of the Punic, or indeed the Roman city of Carthage. Its destruction in 146 BC at the hands of the Romans following the Punic Wars, combined with a large building programme during the mid-19th century has left very little remains of any ancient structure. What evidence there is, however, reveals a city based on a grid system, although we cannot be certain at what point in its history this centuriated system existed. We do know that the city was heavily fortified with over 23 miles of thick walls and that it featured spectacular harbours that were an integral part of the city.

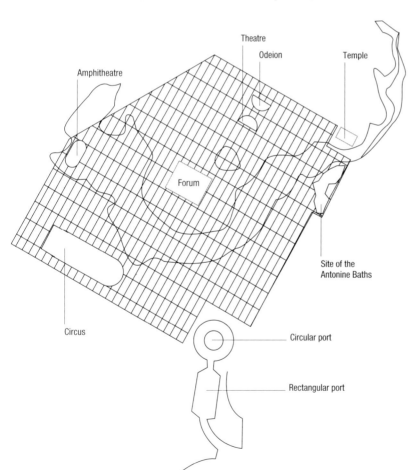

Amphitheatre

Theatre

Odeion

Temple

Forum

Circus

Site of the
Antonine Baths

Circular port

Rectangular port

million litres a day. It fed into the Bordji cistern, which held 25–30,000 cubic metres of water. The water was then piped into a U-shaped court to emerge in an ornate settling basin. This water system had already impressed the Roman water commissioner, Frontinus, who wrote about it in AD 100; the cisterns were original Punic constructions, re-used in the Roman period.

CHRISTIAN CARTHAGE

In the mid-third century AD, Cyprian, the bishop of Carthage, wrote that the mines were exhausted, the number of farmers reduced, the slaves had run away, the settlers had become brigands and the whole world was decrepit and at an end. But this image of Carthage seems to be contradicted by the archaeological evidence. In fact, much more significant upheaval is evident at the beginning of the fourth century,

Fallen columns within the ruins of the Antonine Baths in Roman Carthage. Their Etruscan-derived skills in hydraulic engineering enabled the Romans to rebuild Carthage as a 'modern' Mediterranean city, enjoying the same range of creature comforts that a citizen might enjoy in Rome, Pompeii, or Athens.

when Lucius Domitius Alexander, stationed at Carthage as the head of the diocese of Africa, revolted against Rome and destroyed the port, thus preventing grain exports and causing famine in Rome. Even so, this revolt was put down in AD 311 and there was a resurgence of building in Carthage.

Augustine of Thagaste, who lived in Carthage from AD 370 to 383, described a Carthage with ordered streets and squares, planted with trees and boasting no fewer than twelve churches and a hypostyle hall on the Byrsa. Elaborate mosaics in neighbouring villas also provide evidence for continuing prosperity in the fourth and fifth centuries. Despite the evidence of vitality, however, decline was clear in the early fifth century. Carthage was captured by the Vandals in 439, and became the capital of the Vandal king Gaiseric and his successors. The circus showed degradation by this date and went out of use by the seventh century. The Byzantine general Belisarius recaptured the city and destroyed the Vandal kingdom in 533–4, and the city remained a centre of Christianity and loyalty to the eastern Roman Empire for the next century. In AD 698, after 500 years of urbanisation and 'romanisation', Carthage fell to the Arab invasion that swept across North Africa.

The treatment of Punic Carthage by the conquering Romans is remembered as the most terrible annihilation of a nation in western Antiquity. However, Rome's political hatred of Carthage was directed at the annihilation of a state, not of a city or of a culture. Again, many features of Punic Carthage were transformed, revitalised and monumentalised in the Roman city. The local inhabitants were encouraged to keep their laws and religion, creating a multicultural city.

TRIER IN THE WEST

Unlike Pompeii, Athens and Carthage, Trier was a new foundation. On the banks of the Moselle River, it was inside the area controlled by the Treveri, an area roughly matching that of modern Luxembourg. The Treveri were a war-like Gallic tribe with a reputation for horsemanship, according to Julius Caesar. While pre-Roman hillforts are known in the surrounding area, Caesar mentioned no pre-existing town or fort on the site of the later Roman city, and archaeology has found no substantial pre-Roman settlement here. The lack of evidence for a pre-Roman name for the site also points to the lack of any earlier settlement.

A feature of Roman cities in the north-west provinces, in contrast to North Africa and the East, is that they were often founded without regard for pre-existing urban centres. Instead, they were usually founded for military reasons. Agrippa, Augustus's general and son-in-law, probably saw a need to control this fordable part of the Moselle and therefore chose this site for a military camp, strategically situated at the rear of the Roman frontier and the bases of Rome's armies on the Rhine. Such camps frequently attracted an accompanying settlement of non-military personnel. These included local people as well as soldiers' families and merchants following the army who, together with army veterans, often formed the nucleus for a new town. No veterans were actually settled at Trier, however, nor any large body of Roman colonists. Thus, while Trier was established by the Romans, its earliest inhabitants were largely the existing local population.

The Roman settlement at Trier was established according to the policies of Augustus, but it was not until reign of Claudius that it received its charter and the status of *colonia*, the *Colonia Augusta Treverorum*. Because of its economic importance on one of the main routes between Italy and the Rhineland, Trier developed rapidly to become the most prosperous city in northern Gaul. In about the mid-first century it became the residence of the provincial procurator of Belgica and Upper and Lower Germany. At the end of the third century, it became one of the sub-capitals of the Roman Empire. When Constantius Chlorus was nominated by the emperor Diocletian as one of the tetrarchs (the four joint emperors) in AD 293, he chose Trier as his capital and his residence; the city now commanded an area stretching from the Straits of Gibraltar to Hadrian's Wall and from the Rhine to the Atlantic. For the next century it was the leading city in the West, politically and culturally. It continued to be the residence of Constantius's son Constantine, and many members of their family, until AD 395 when the emperor Gratian transferred the court to Milan and the military headquarters to Arles. During the early to mid-fifth century, Trier was captured and sacked variously by Vandals, Franks, Burgundians and Alamanni. It is difficult to establish the actual end of Roman rule in the city, but the fifth century saw a decline in living standards as well as a decrease in population in Trier.

THE EARLY CITY OF TRIER

Because of its development in the later Roman period and its continued existence as an urban centre to this day, little remains of the first three centuries of Trier's history. The nucleus of its orthogonal layout was probably the original Augustan camp. A monumental inscription referring to Augustus's ill-fated descendants Gaius and Lucius indicates that at least one substantial building had been set up in Trier between 3 BC and AD 2. Also dated to the early Augustan period, by dendrochronology, is a timber bridge over the Moselle. This first bridge was replaced with a stone one during the reign of Claudius, the piers of which still support the modern bridge.

The earliest houses with stone foundations date to the mid-first century AD. The remains of a large rectangular hall and vestibule that have been uncovered to the west of the later 'Basilika' also date to this period. This building, decorated with elaborate mosaics and wall-paintings, was attached to an open court with porticoes and a garden, reminiscent of the palaces of Nero and Domitian in Rome. It is tempting to identify it as the residence of the procurator. A wooden amphitheatre may also have been built in the first century, sunk into the western slope of Petrisberg to the south-east of the city.

Thus, Trier was beginning to take the physical form of a Roman city at the time that it was granted the status of a colony. Not long afterwards, the street plan was extended and the *decumanus maximus* was replaced with a second major east–west road to the south. The amphitheatre was rebuilt in stone at about the same time. Seating up to 20,000 spectators, it would have provided entertainment for the citizens of Trier and the population of the surrounding countryside. During Constantine's reign these spectators would have seen captive Frankish princes being made to fight wild beasts here.

Built towards the end of the second century AD, the Porta Nigra in Trier acted as the monumental northern gateway to the Roman city. Built of sandstone, now heavily weathered (hence its name), the external decoration was never completed, adding to its practical defensive appearance. At 120 feet long, 76 feet wide and 100 feet high it is the largest Roman gateway in existence.

The remains of the so-called Kaiserthermen (Imperial Baths) at Trier. The early years of the fourth century AD witnessed the transformation of Trier from provincial city to seat of one of the co-emperors. Originally planned as a baths, the Kaiserthermen appears to have been coopted for another purpose, possibly to house the growing imperial bureaucracy.

TRIER AT ITS HEIGHT

Trier reached its full development as a prosperous Roman city in the course of the second and third centuries. Because the forum, which was about 400 metres long and 150 metres wide, was constructed over some of the earlier houses and over an early street, it was probably laid out in the early second century. Remains of a sunken corridor have been discovered to its west, as have further buildings that were probably the official *curia* and council meeting room. However, no traces have been found of buildings like a *basilica* or temple, though these are common in the fora of other Roman cities.

No theatre has been discovered within the city centre. Instead, a small theatre has been uncovered in the religious sanctuary of Altbachtal, to the south-east. This was built of wood and earth with stone seating, in the second century, and was probably connected with the rituals of this sacred place. Another theatre was also built during the late second and early third centuries on the opposite bank of the river, within the precinct of Lenus Mars. It was often the case in the West that theatres were more frequently connected with temples and sacred places than located in the city proper, and this seems to be the case in Trier.

Like their counterparts in Pompeii, Carthage and Athens, the citizens of Trier were well provided with bathing facilities – but only some time after the foundation of the city. The complex now known as the 'Barbarathermen', one of the largest and most imposing bathing complexes outside Rome itself, was probably built shortly after AD 100. These baths were elaborately decorated, with marble statues placed in deep semi-circular niches around an open-air swimming pool. While they had the symmetrical layout we have seen in other bathing complexes, the wings were not each a complete bath-suite, so they were probably not intended as segregated facilities for male and female bathing. Each wing does, however, have several heated rooms, an important provision in this colder part of the Empire. These baths, approximately contemporary with the Antonine Baths in Carthage, were on a huge scale compared with the bath complexes in Pompeii; this reflects a monumentalising trend in architecture characteristic of the later Empire.

By the fourth century, Trier was truly a capital city. We have both more substantial archaeological remains and surviving documentary evidence for this period. Amongst the latter, the poem *Mosella* by Ausonius and the Panegyrics praising Constantine provide much information on the city. These written sources indicate that Constantius started, and Constantine completed, a palace complex in the north-east part of the town. The remains of the so-called Basilika, which formed part of this palace complex, are one of the dominating features of Trier today. The building was destroyed in 1944, but its subsequent investigation and reconstruction have provided much information. It was constructed entirely of red tiles, without the more normal concrete core. It was 67 metres long, 27.5 metres wide and 30 metres high, with no internal supporting structures. It had an apse at one end and two rows of round-headed windows. The floor, with hypocaust heating underneath, was decorated with black and white marble, and the interior walls were furbished with a marble veneer. The exterior walls were covered with plaster. It probably served as the imperial audience hall of the palace complex, with its severely plain design perhaps intended to enhance the majesty of the emperor.

Trier also received a second monumental bathing facility, in all probability as another part of this palace complex. By the time of Constantine, therefore, the city was provided with two of the largest sets of baths known outside Rome. These 'Kaiserthermen' (Imperial Baths) were built sometime after AD 293, and occupied an area almost as large as that of Trier's forum. In comparison with the Barbarathermen, these baths show many advanced design features, such as more compactness, greater use of circular forms, extra heated rooms and more efficient drains. It is possible that they were not intended to function at the same time as the pre-existing baths, but rather to replace them. It is equally possible, however, that they were not intended as public baths at all: as a part of the palace complex, they may have been intended for the exclusive use of its residents and guests. However, the fact that no trace has been found of water pipes or of marble wall-covering suggests that the complex may never have been completed, and thus never actually came into use. Instead, they were subsequently reduced in size and converted into an official building, perhaps for use as a grander meeting place for the city council.

A RIVAL FOR ROME

Under Constantine, Christianity became the dominant religion in the Empire, and Trier became the first city in northern Gaul to receive a cathedral church. This early church was planned as a double church, which now forms the Trier cathedral and Liebfrauenkirche. The polygonal form of the latter was characteristic of fourth-century churches in Italy and the East, but exceptional for the West. Its design is thought to have been inspired by Constantine's mother, Helena, after her pilgrimage to the Holy Land.

The presence of the emperors in Trier also brought other changes. The already wide and spacious streets were now lined with porticoes, and their gravel surfaces were replaced with paving stones. Like Carthage, Trier now had a circus that vied with the Circus Maximus in Rome. Its precise location is not now known for certain, but it was probably built on the open space to the south-east of the cathedral, not very far from the amphitheatre.

Monumental limestone warehouses were built near the river on the other side of the city. These consisted of two buildings, each 70 metres long and 19 metres wide, and are comparable in size and grandeur to the Basilika. Their lack of ventilation suggests that they cannot have been grain stores; instead, they may have been used to store military equipment.

At some stage it was found necessary to build a city wall around Trier, but the date and reason for this are controversial. The wall cannot have been built before the second half of the second century, but it was certainly in existence by AD 355. It was built with a concrete core and was about 3 metres thick and about 6 metres high. The complete circuit extended over 6 kilometres, enclosing 285 hectares; the wall incorporated seventy-five towers. Rather strangely, this wall incorporated the structure of the amphitheatre, allowing it to function as a monumental gateway to the city. Another, still standing but unfinished, monumental gateway was the impressive Porta Nigra on the north side of the city wall, preserved because it became the cell of the holy man Simeon and remained a church until the nineteenth century. Its black colour – and hence its name – is the result of weathering of the stone. The design of this gateway demonstrates a deliberate return to earlier Imperial models of the first century, built to impress on the wayfarer the might of Rome. Such features suggest that these fortification walls may have been intended as a showpiece, symbolic of Rome's power, rather than for defensive purposes. The upper arcades of the wall are also too wide to have been useful in defence.

The austere brick-built Basilika in Trier (above) dates from the first half of the 4th century AD. It subsequently became a palace, first of Frankish kings, then archbishops, and it was extensively restored after the Second World War.

The interior of the Porta Nigra (left), with its relief-sculpted faux pillars, reveals something of the building's original Imperial magnificence; although it is unlikely that the building enjoyed anything more than symbolic power.

RELIGION IN TRIER

Roman Trier continued to be an important native religious centre. In keeping with Rome's policy of permitting, and even encouraging, local religions, many pre-Roman deities continued to be worshipped in the city, often alongside their Roman counterparts. The layout of the city thus took into consideration pre-existing sanctuaries of various local deities, particularly those in the Altbachtal valley. Over fifty shrines have been found here, packed closely together but varying in size, shape and orientation. Some of these are more local in form, while others are of a more Roman type. Many of these shrines showed little apparent change between the first and fourth centuries. This evidently sacred area also contained priests' houses and a small temple. The latter was abandoned in the second century and replaced in the third century by a building connected with the cult of Mithras, a cult originating in the East and particularly associated with soldiers, merchants and concepts of personal salvation.

On north slopes of Heiligkreuz Hill to the south of the city, looking across the Altbachtal valley to the amphitheatre, stood a magnificent temple, now known as the Herrenbrünnchen temple. This was a Roman-style temple, approached by a monumental flight of steps and decorated with acanthus spirals and reclining, draped female figures. The dedication of the temple is now unclear, but its commanding position suggests that it was devoted either to the Capitoline triad or to the imperial cult of Roma and Augustus. Two priests of Roma and Augustus are known in Trier from first-century inscriptions.

On the opposite side of the river, not far from the original bridge, was the precinct of Lenus Mars, a god who reveals a mixture of Roman and native attributes and styles. This precinct was sacred in pre-Roman times. The main temple, with a *cella* and colonnaded porch in front supporting a pediment, is of standard Roman type, however, and is dated to the second century. Lenus was a local deity of the people whose cult was here equated with that of the Roman god Mars. The offerings associated with this temple to Lenus Mars bear witness to powers of both gods: they include statuettes of children, connected with Mars as the protector of the young, and hooded dwarfs carrying money bags, connected with Lenus as the bringer of good luck. Trier's principal theatre was also within this precinct, indicating a well-organised Romano-Celtic cult. Interestingly, the two priests of Roma and Augustus noted above, were also recorded as priests of Lenus Mars, demonstrating again the mixture of traditional Roman deities, local deities, and the imperial cult. In the later third and fourth centuries, however, such local Gallo-Roman deities were considered a major source of opposition to the rising cult of Christianity so, under the emperor Gratian, their temples were destroyed.

Trier was a thriving Gallo-Roman city, owing much of its prosperity to its situation just behind the German frontier of the Empire and commanding one of the major routes, for both strategic military purposes and for trade between Italy and the north-west provinces. Strong native Gallic influences remained in the city's religious provision but Trier's public architecture was essentially of Roman imperial character, symbolising its administrative importance in the later Empire.

URBANISATION

The emperor Augustus was a major player in the foundation of the cities of the Empire, but it was only from the second century – by which time Pompeii had already been destroyed – that these cities begin to flourish as truly Roman political and cultural centres. From the early second century, regional differences between cities began to break down and monumental Roman building types started to dominate the urban landscape throughout the Empire. To the well-established cities of Italy, Africa and the East, the Romans brought new ideas and techniques, new materials and Roman concepts of monumentality, architectural composition and symmetry, as well as specifically Roman building types. In the West they used these same principles to create major new urban centres.

This architectural domination housed cultural and religious domination, but 'romanisation' was as much a desire on the part of the Romans to improve their subjects as to rule over them efficiently. Rome's power also depended on the cooperation of local elites, who exercised their own control over local religious and political matters. These elites, in turn, gained their own power through representing Roman power, so it was in their own best interests to ensure that Roman rule continued. Through such a system of control and tolerance the cities of the Roman Empire flourished as truly multicultural centres.

The ruins of the fourth-century Roman baths beside the River Moselle in Trier. Situated close to the border with unconquered Germany, Trier had a psychological, as well as strategic, significance to the Romans, and they endowed it accordingly with monumental buildings that earned the city the nickname, 'Roma Transalpina' (the Rome of the North).

P CAESARI
ERI PARTHICI
VI TRAIANI PA
BNEPOTI · MA
AX TRIB POTI
A VAS D VAS QVA
XISXXXN PONII
MATER ET HER

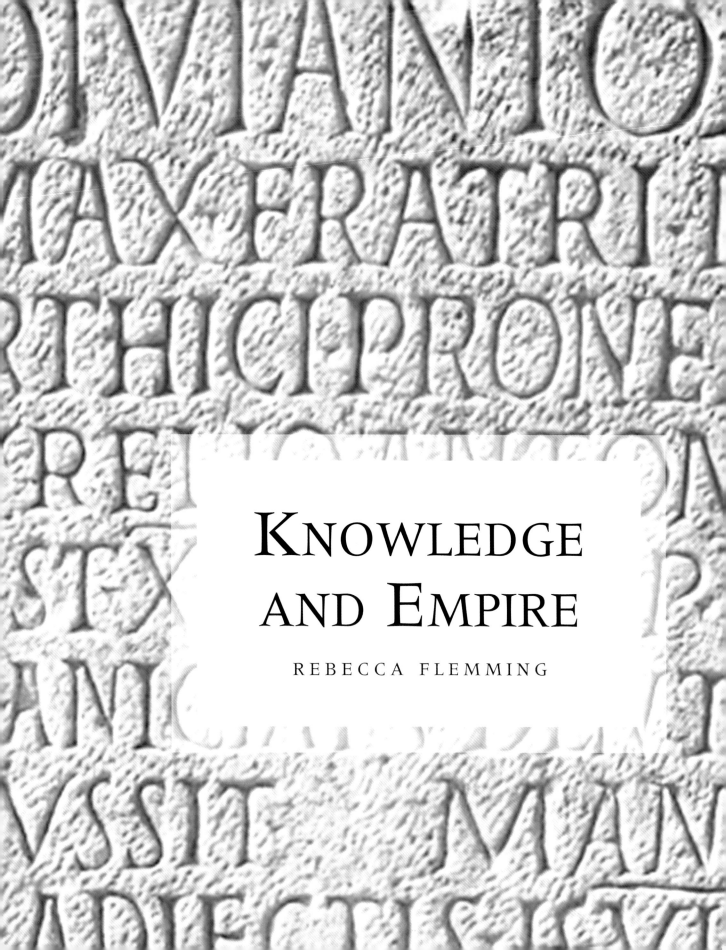

KNOWLEDGE
AND EMPIRE

REBECCA FLEMMING

THE ROMAN WORLD

KNOWLEDGE AND EMPIRE

As historians of modern European empires have stressed, colonial expansion is intimately bound up with the expansion of knowledge. Knowledge both enables conquest and is produced by it; knowledge is captured along with territories and peoples, and generated in the process of acquiring and establishing domination. Like these other new domains, it too must be ordered and organised, brought into line with the wider systems of imperial rule and productively managed – though these moves may be met with resistance and evasion.

A marble relief of Alexander the Great. The Romans saw themselves as the intellectual successors to the expansionist Greek hero-king. The multiple branches of science were to be conquered by Roman minds, and then welded together into an encyclopaedic empire of knowledge.

So, in the eighteenth and nineteenth centuries, for instance, disciplines like botany, zoology, ethnography and geography all greatly expanded along with the European empires that needed and sustained them. Empires depended not only on the information these disciplines produced (which facilitated conquest, settlement and the exploitation of colonial resources), but also on their ideological support, on the legitimacy they provided by linking imperial expansion with the expansion of knowledge. In the classical world too, the conquests of Alexander the Great, which extended from Asia Minor and Egypt to the Hindu Kush, led to an explosion in knowledge – about the world, its lands, peoples, plants, animals and minerals; about the human body, diseases and cures; about the structure of the cosmos itself, and more mundane mechanics – and to various moves to systematise that knowledge. The Hellenistic period saw, amongst its multitudinous intellectual developments, the creation of various literary corpora and canons, the solidification of several recognised bodies of knowledge. Many of these developments were, moreover, promoted and fostered by the ruling dynasties that succeeded Alexander. The most ambitious and expansive patrons were the early Ptolemies, as they strove to make Alexandria the new cultural capital of the now much larger Greek world and not just of their Egyptian empire; but all Hellenistic monarchs gathered at least some men of learning and imagination at their courts, for this kind of patronage became an integral part of their power.

The Roman Empire is no exception to this rule of expanding imperial knowledge. Nonetheless, it is a very particular case, most notably because of the ways in which the specific aims, methods and conditions of Roman empire-building combined to create a rather different set of attitudes to the cultures of the conquered than those that characterised either their Greek predecessors or later European successors. In particular, the long and complex relationship between Greece and Rome outlined in earlier chapters of this book had a part to play here. For, as the Romans made increasing military advances across the Hellenistic world, they subjugated people in whose culture they had already, in some senses, invested as the dominant cultural currency of the ancient Mediterranean, and they opened up vistas of knowledge unmatched by Roman traditions of learning. But Rome did, nonetheless, conquer the Greeks, and demonstrated clearly not only military superiority over the defeated but also the moral and religious superiority with which Roman martial prowess was bound up. The question was how would Roman power assert itself over such lofty cultural terrain, and establish a Roman Empire of knowledge alongside its political dominion.

POMPEY AND MITHRIDATES

The specific conditions of the encounter between Roman power and Greek learning can be seen in an episode from the end of Rome's wars with its great enemy, Mithridates VI Eupator, King of Pontus, a key set of conflicts both in Rome's military conquest of the East and in the development of Roman relations with its cultures. Mithridates was a monarch who, following the examples of Alexander the Great and the successor dynasties, took his role as intellectual patron very seriously. The outstanding botanist Crateuas, amongst others, was associated with his court and the king himself took a direct interest in scientific research: most famously in the field of poisons and their antidotes, but in a number of related areas also. A highly successful military conqueror in his own right, Mithridates collected information and objects from all over his vast realm, and consolidated and organised them around himself like his other dominions – as the great Roman general Pompey discovered after finally defeating him in 63 BC. Amongst the extensive royal booty were treatises on the medicinal properties of plants and on toxicology, together with examples of the plants in question and various other items of natural historical interest, perhaps including a whole zoo.

Pompey, like other Romans, also found Alexander an attractive model, as heroic conqueror and empire builder, and like Alexander he was accompanied on his Eastern campaigns by Greek friends (and freedmen) who would record not just his military achievements, but also the territories traversed, their peoples, flora and fauna. He was, therefore, already committed to the value and importance of his enemy's scientific activities, but no less committed to Roman victory and rule.

His response to these discoveries was, therefore, both respectful and assertive. Mithridates's achievements were recognised, but stripped from him and stamped with the mark of Roman (and Pompey's) authority. Pompey ordered his freedman Lenaeus to translate the medical treatises into Latin, and he arranged for a number of the more valuable and spectacular specimens in the collections to be transported to Rome. There, some (for example, a prized ebony tree) were carried in his triumph, some (the more exotic animals) ended up in the arena, and Mithridates's collection of precious stones was deposited on the Capitol. Knowledge had been captured along with the kingdom, its natural resources and plentiful populations; all were now – thanks to Pompey – subject to Roman power. Rome's expanded dominion in all these respects was variously demonstrated: through the encompassing of Greek medical and botanical texts as well as the more public displays of the triumph, games and temple.

By the end of the Mithridatic wars, Rome had acquired a vastly increased amount of Greek knowledge. This knowledge was accumulated in literary form in the libraries of great nobles like Marcus Licinius Lucullus; in the personal form of Greek scholars and teachers – slave, freed and free – who now made the imperial capital their home in much greater numbers; and in the form of more material booty. The encounter between Greek learning and Roman power was accordingly intensified, on both sides. Roman attempts to get to grips with this new intellectual territory became more systematic, as did Greek responses to the redrawn political map of their world.

A detail of a late-Roman mosaic floor from a Sicilian villa, depicting the capture of exotic wild animals (here, an Arabian oryx). Although they were taken for entertainment rather than for scientific enlightenment, the regular presence in Rome of ostriches, tigers, elephants and other rare beasts, increased Romans' sense of worldwide encyclopaedic knowledge.

THE BIRTH OF THE ROMAN ENCYCLOPAEDIA

The first attempt at overall mastery, and Roman recasting, of the Greek learned tradition was made by Marcus Terrentius Varro, the dominant figure in Latin intellectual life at the end of the Republic. A man who pursued a successful political and military career as well as a life of letters, Varro increased the scope of Latin literature in many directions, giving virtually all aspects of Roman life, customs and history a literary manifestation. He was supported in his efforts initially by Pompey, and then by a clement Julius Caesar. In much of this enterprise he was applying Greek methods – of subject definition and structure, research and presentation – to Roman materials, as also had (for all his anti-Greek rhetoric) Cato the Elder in the previous century. Indeed, in writing the treatise *On Agriculture* and in some of his historical ventures, Varro was following very directly in Cato's footsteps; but he went much further, exceeding previous Latin models in many ways, his literary horizons expanding with Rome's imperial boundaries.

A key work, not just of expansion but also of consolidation and organisation, was Varro's nine-book *Disciplinae*, written in the 30s BC. It is now unfortunately lost, but the influence of this endeavour is manifest from the large number of references to it found in the surviving literature. From these it is also possible to reconstruct the overall shape and structure of the work, as well as to recover at least some of the content. The *Disciplinae* aimed to encompass all the disciplines, or arts – that is, recognised bodies of knowledge and skills – that a Roman gentleman ought to master (though not in a professional sense, for it would of course be demeaning for a member of the Roman elite to make a living from any of these arts). But these were accomplishments that not only demonstrated a high degree of cultural formation, as befitted a rising imperial ruling class, but would also prove useful in the general business of being a Roman aristocrat. The disciplines that Varro considered vital in this respect were: grammar, rhetoric and dialectic (that is, roughly, an understanding of language, persuasion and argument), geometry, arithmetic, astronomy and musical theory (the mathematical subjects), and also medicine and architecture. The first seven topics broadly constituted the Greek *enkyklios paideia*, the general education from which more specialised, or advanced, teaching might follow. Medicine and architecture usually came into the more specialist category (and the most characteristic 'advanced' subject was philosophy, which Varro largely left to Cicero).

So, while Varro adopted Greek definitions of, and organisational approaches to, the disciplines, his selection of topics and coverage of them all within a single encyclopaedia is distinctive, and Roman as well as Greek sources and traditions provided his material. Indeed, if his extant treatise *On Agriculture* is anything to go by, the net was cast wider than that. For he counts the work of Mago the Carthaginian, originally written in his native Punic but abridged and adapted into Greek, as the most authoritative on the subject (Mago's work had also been translated into Latin). There was, then, a gathering up of useful knowledge, of whatever origin, using Greek models but Roman judgement; and the imposition of a unified order, as in the Empire itself.

THE ENCYCLOPAEDIC DYNASTY

Varro's encyclopaedic successors – Celsus and Pliny the Elder – developed his literary knowledge project further, albeit in distinct ways. Both were writing in the first century AD, after the political conflicts of the late Republic had been resolved by Augustus and a new imperial settlement established; both had similar social backgrounds to Varro, being gentlemen amateurs rather than professional players, and both also brought Roman values to bear on Greek (and Roman) learning in an ambitiously comprehensive manner. The divergence between their particular approaches within this overall framework, however, reflects the fact that much remained unresolved and unsettled in the early imperial era: the debate continued about the best relationship between empire and knowledge.

Aulus Cornelius Celsus, writing during the reign of the emperor Tiberius, follows most closely in Varro's footsteps. His collection of *Artes* – 'arts' – certainly covered medical, military and agricultural matters, probably also philosophy and rhetoric, and possibly jurisprudence too (though only his eight books on the medical arts survive). There is less here of the Greek general education, and more of a focus on specific arts that have a practical application. Rhetoric, however, does seem to remain a mainstay of Celsus's cultural programme, not only because it was an essential skill for the Roman gentleman, as oratorical performance was fundamental to a public career, but also because it was essential to any kind of literary presentation. Rules of rhetoric and dialectic governed the shape and structure of all kinds of writing: how material should be organised and arguments made, in technical or 'scientific' texts as well as more literary ones.

Celsus's own rhetorical and dialectical skills are certainly in evidence in what survives of his *Artes*. His Latin style is much admired, as are his compositional techniques, and his powers of persuasion have proved considerable. They can be seen at work most clearly in the preface to *On Medicine*. Here he articulates his approach to the basically Greek material that he is engaged in reworking for his Roman audience. Celsus represents himself as the inheritor of the learned Greek medical tradition, a tradition that began with the Hippocratic writings of the fifth century BC, passed through Hellenistic Alexandria, and has now come to Rome, the cultural capital of the known world, the imperial metropolis that contains the accumulated spoils of empire. The process of inheritance by conquest, Rome's dominant status in the world, places Celsus in a particularly privileged position in relation to this long, complex and conflicting tradition. He presents himself as an objective arbiter who stands imperiously above the contending currents in Greek medicine, above its sectarian disagreements and long-running disputes, who is able to steer a sensible middle course between them, selecting the best from each and organising it according to principles of clarity and utility.

Roman power, judgement and common sense are all invoked here, as is Roman practicality. Celsus's theoretical understanding of how the human body works and stays healthy, and how diseases are caused and remedied (an understanding based loosely on Hippocratic doctrines), is left largely implicit as he focuses on more concrete medical matters. Having covered how the healthy should conduct themselves in respect to all the key areas of life – food, drink, sex, exercise, rest and bathing – in order to preserve and improve their condition (that is, regimens for health), he moves directly to diseases and their cures, treating the three therapeutic categories of regimen, pharmacology and surgery in considerable detail. The social class of his audience is also made clear in the content of his advice on a healthy lifestyle: 'The healthy man... should lead a varied kind of life; sometimes in the country, sometimes in the city, but mostly on his estate. He should sail, hunt and sometimes rest.' For the vast majority of the Roman population such recommendations would have been entirely meaningless.

ROMAN APPLICATION OF KNOWLEDGE

Gaius Plinius Secundus ('Pliny the Elder'), writing some fifty years later, adopted a rather different approach to the encyclopaedic project. He took the Roman reworking of the Greek notion of dividing knowledge into distinct disciplines, or arts, a step further, integrating topics that had been dealt with separately into a single unified work that addressed a single, unifying, theme – 'nature, that is life'. For Pliny the arts – artificial and alien constructions as they are – create a barrier to real understanding of the world, to the kind of direct and practical understanding that is an important part of the Roman heritage, and to which Rome must return if it is not to succumb to luxury and lose its greatness. This return, however, must take into account Rome's expanded horizons, the fact that the Roman world is much larger and complex than it once was. Greek learning, or indeed non-Roman learning more widely, is not bad in itself (though it is certainly subject to scrutiny), but it needs to be removed from Greek hands, from the possession of specialists – to whom Pliny is often very hostile. It must become the property of all who can make use of it, most especially the Roman governing classes, who must rule this world. This is what Pliny attempts to do – to gather up all useful knowledge, radically re-order it, and place it as directly in the service of Roman power as possible.

A Greek stone relief from Italy, depicting a doctor examining a patient. Despite the military and political pre-eminence of Latin culture, most of the knowledge-base of the Roman empire (in disciplines such as medicine or engineering) still lay in the hands of Greek specialists during the first and second centuries AD. Some Romans saw the Latinisation of knowledge as an essential requirement of state.

After a dedicatory epistle to the imperial heir, Titus, and a book which lists not just the contents of the thirty-six volumes to follow but also the authors and works Pliny claims to be drawing on for each (and which makes his reliance on Greek learning most apparent), Pliny begins the main narrative of his *Natural History* with an attempt to describe the nature of things – both earthly and celestial – in its entirety. He then proceeds through the various parts of this whole, beginning with a geographical sequence, before moving on to delineate the peoples, animals, plants and minerals of the world.

The geography is clearly imperial, proceeding roughly province by province, and it draws on information produced directly by the military and administrative activity of the Empire, as well as more academic sources. Pliny frequently cites the work of Augustus's right-hand man, Agrippa, who seems to have undertaken to collect and collate the various measurements and descriptions of Rome's expanding domains provided by the reports of Roman generals and governors returning from far-flung lands, as well as the accounts of other travellers, in order (at least in part) to create a visual representation of the now mostly Roman world to display to the people of Rome. He also sometimes quotes directly from these reports – for example, from that of Aelius Gallus on his Arabian expedition – and from those of various intelligence-gathering missions too, such as the reconnaissance party of Praetorian Guards who explored the Nile southwards from Egypt when the emperor Nero was considering invading Ethiopia.

Pliny organises his information about the contents of the natural world more broadly, primarily according to their relationship with, and utility for, humanity. Almost ten books, for example, are dedicated to medicinal items derived from plants, animals and some minerals, while the cultivation of crops for food also receives considerable attention, along with growing flowers for garlands and the use of metals in sculpture. This too reveals Pliny's underlying imperial intention, since these are resources that Rome should make better use of – both in the sense of making more use of the simple remedies that nature has to offer, for example, and less extravagant use of gold – as the Romans assert their moral and political domination of the world. Indeed, Pliny asserts that one of the key benefits of Roman rule – 'of the boundless grandeur of the Roman peace' – is that it enables the free passage of medicinal plants from one end of the Empire to the other, so greatly contributing to humanity's well-being. This, he suggests, allows Nature's generosity to be fully realised.

The Empire surveyed by Agrippa already contained hundreds of cities linked by thousands of miles of paved roads, but did not yet completely encircle the Mediterranean. Augustus' successors completed that task, made minor adjustments to the German border, added Britain and Dacia (modern Romania), and extended the frontiers of the Empire to the Caspian Sea and the Persian Gulf. These easternmost gains were subsequently adandoned by Hadrian who considered them indefensible.

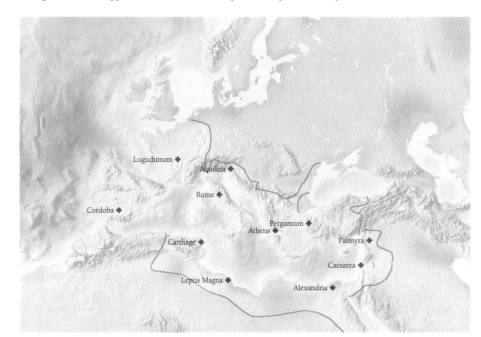

STRABO'S IMPERIAL GEOGRAPHY

The encounter between Roman power and Greek learning was not, however, entirely one-sided. Greek scholars were coming to terms with the new political reality just as their Roman conquerors were coming to terms with the scholarship they had captured, but not yet taken fully into their possession. There was a range of Greek responses to their changed circumstances in general and their Roman masters in particular, just as Roman responses to the Hellenistic culture they had conquered varied. The interactions between the two of course also occurred on a number of different levels and in a variety of different locations.

One Greek treatise of the early Empire that makes an interesting point of comparison with the Latin encyclopaedias of Celsus and Pliny is the *Geography* of Strabo. Born in Amasia (in modern Turkey) at about the same time as the defeat of Mithridates – an event that had significant repercussions for both himself and his family – Strabo journeyed to Rome as a young man, and returned to the imperial capital several times in the course of his wider travels. He wrote not just a *Geography*, but also a *History*, now lost; both were works of considerable size and scope, but focussed around a single discipline. Geography for Strabo included elements of historical and mythological learning, as well as concepts and techniques drawn from the mathematical arts and natural philosophy, especially astronomy and geometry. Though he has much to say about the theoretical geography of his Hellenistic predecessors – men like Eratosthenes and Posidonius (who also had important contacts with Rome) – his own contribution to the field is much more descriptive, and also political. He provides a detailed account of lands from Spain in the west to Assyria in the east, Britain in the north to Ethiopia in the south, which incorporates not just physical information about rivers and mountains and the rest but also data about cities and peoples, their history and government.

A detail from the Palestrina Mosaic, which shows the River Nile in flood. The mosaic, found near Rome, displays in graphic form the level of knowledge of foreign lands that the Romans had acquired by the beginning of the first century BC. The details of Egyptian life, such as the papyrus-bundle boats, are depicted with great precision.

Part of Strabo's description of Armenia

There are also large lakes in Armenia; one the Mantiane, which being translated means 'Blue'; it is the largest salt water lake after Lake Maeotis, as they say, extending as far as Atropatia; and it also has salt-works. Another is Arsene, also called Thopitis. It contains soda, and it cleanses and restores clothes; but because of this ingredient the water is also unfit for drinking. The Tigris flows through this lake after issuing from the mountainous country near the Niphates; and because of its swiftness it keeps its current unmixed with the lake; whence the name Tigris, since the Median word for 'arrow' is 'tigris'.

Strabo Geography *5.12*
(Trans. Horace L. Jones)

This political theme is part of Strabo's positioning of himself as an author between Roman power on the one hand and Greek learning on the other. He admired Rome's military and governmental achievements, particularly those of Augustus, in whose reign much of the *Geography* was composed. 'At no other time', he states, has the world 'enjoyed such perfect peace and prosperity,' now that 'peoples and cities are united in a single realm, under one political administration'. And his work was meant to be useful to rulers and generals as well as adding more broadly to the sum of human knowledge and understanding. Its usefulness to Roman rulers is based, he argues, on a contemporary deficiency in their geographical information, a deficiency that is not only generally evident in the superficial nature of Roman writings on the subject, but has also had damaging practical consequences in recent conflicts with the Parthians, Germans and Celts. Roman learning, Strabo suggests, has not kept pace with military successes. The scope for scholarly endeavour has been greatly increased by conquests, in both West and East – but these opportunities have not been exploited by the Romans with any thoroughness or rigour. He seeks to expand existing Greek knowledge right up to and beyond the boundaries of the Roman Empire, applying Greek geographical approaches to the spaces opened up by Roman force.

Strabo shared, therefore, the objective of placing Greek knowledge in the service of Roman power, but he also sought to place Roman power in the service of Greek knowledge. This is where his particular identity lay, and his own position in relationship to the scholarly traditions of Greek geography and ethnography was at least as important to him as finding a place in relationship to Roman rule. These two aims were mutually reinforcing, for it was Rome that provided him with the means to surpass his Greek predecessors, and thus to succeed in the competitive world of classical scientific endeavour, just as his version of Greek learning provided Rome with a means to strengthen the Empire.

Strabo's other point of contact with Varro, Celsus and Pliny is his social status. He also came from the social elite, albeit the elite of a conquered Greek city; he was well travelled not because he was a professional student of geography, but because matters of politics took him all over the Empire. As we have seen in earlier chapters of this book, one of the strengths of Roman imperial rule was its ability to draw in local aristocracies and involve them not just in the practicalities of provincial government but also in the wider, more ideological, processes of empire-building. Strabo illustrates various facets of these processes – of the ongoing imperial negotiation between Greece and Rome.

Strabo had Western counterparts, too. The most comprehensive and systematic *On Agriculture* to survive from the Roman world was written in Latin by Lucius Junius Columella, a Roman citizen – indeed a man of equestrian status – but born in Gades (modern Cadiz) in Spain. He may have served as a military tribune with the armies in the East before eventually settling in Italy in around AD 50 to cultivate his estates and his literary career; certainly he is knowledgeable about agricultural conditions in both East and West. His work builds on its two major predecessors – those of Cato and Varro – but, as befits Columella's time, expands and enlarges on them in a clearly structured way. It draws on all the resources and constituencies of the Empire.

PROFESSIONAL EXPERTS

This expansionist vision of various disciplines was not the sole preserve of the social elite. The professionals too might have imperial aspirations. Though they wrote at a remove, the works of Varro and Celsus had brought some improvement to the status of activities like architecture and medicine in the Roman world. They were effectively legitimated as recognised *artes* – that is, as comprising book learning as well as practical skills. There were a number of professional experts who sought to take this process further, to exploit both the cultural space thus opened up and the growth of Roman power in general in the interests of their own careers and of their art in itself. It is important to note the competitive nature of these disciplines in the Roman world, a characteristic shared with many other aspects of classical life but given an extra twist by the unregulated and informal way in which the professions operated in antiquity.

Today, the qualifications necessary to practise as a doctor, architect or engineer are well established and carefully policed, with both professional bodies and governments concerned to maintain standards of training and practice. In the Roman world, however, there were no formal qualifications for such professions. There were no exams, no institutions acting as gatekeepers, no legal requirements. Sets of cultural expectations did exist, about how, for example, a doctor should present himself (or herself), about the kind of learning and skills that ought to be demonstrated and so forth; but making a successful career as a physician depended basically on the number of people who could be persuaded of your expertise, and also their quality. The rich and respectable would not only provide the greatest rewards but also the best recommendations to their friends. Medical authority was not, therefore, contained in a framed certificate on the surgery wall, but had to be actively created, personally won, along with paying patients, in an environment where many others were attempting the same thing. All professionals were chasing the same clientele using the same methods, in what has been described by modern historians as a 'medical marketplace'.

A Latin funerary inscription for a female physician, Asyllia Polla, from Carthage in North Africa; one of many from the Roman Empire. Changes in the formation of the medical professions were eventually to force women out of their ranks, so that they then had to fight to gain re-entry.

A high-relief sculpture of a Roman pharmacy. Drugs and bizarre potions (the more exotic the ingredients the better) were commonplace in the Roman world, with little distinction made between cures for medical illnesses and those for other complaints, such as being unlucky in love. The woman at the front of the shop can be seen as the urban incarnation of a village wise woman.

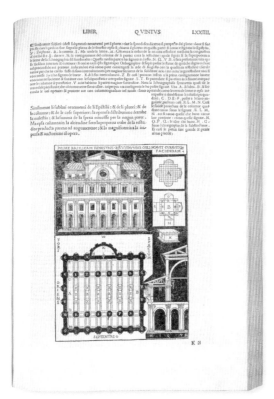

A page from an early printed edition of Vitruvius's *De architectura*. The text is the Latin original and the illustrations, although they have been added by the publisher, give an excellent impression of the techniques employed in Roman construction work. The building shown incorporates two of the principal Roman innovations – the arch and the dome.

VITRUVIUS AND THE ARCHITECTS

Others who tried to make a living through their expertise, like architects, were in the same situation. It is in this context, as well as the wider cultural milieu of the early Empire (the age of Augustus, in fact), that architecture's most famous Roman representative – Vitruvius – and his work should be located. Marcus Vitruvius Pollio seems to have begun his career in the technical section of Julius Caesar's army – amongst the *fabri*, or military engineers, who were responsible for tasks such as the construction and maintenance of artillery weapons (like catapults) and transport vehicles, as well as the building of structures like bridges and some fortifications. He then moved into civil engineering, apparently holding a salaried position of some kind under Augustus, the dedicatee of his ten-book *On Architecture* and the sponsor of the biggest building programme in Rome's history.

In these books, Vitruvius makes an ambitious series of claims for architecture (and, of course, his own position within it). His primary assertion is that the art of architecture requires not just craftsmanship but also extensive theoretical knowledge, drawn from an even more impressive range of disciplines than Strabo had claimed for geography. Rhetoric, the mathematical arts (arithmetic, geometry, astronomy, optics and music), history, philosophy (both moral and natural), medicine and law are all vital parts of architecture according to Vitruvius, in addition to the more practical skills. Most of the theoretical basis for this knowledge is, needless to say, Greek – but once again, the material to which Vitruvius applies it is more culturally heterogeneous, especially when he deals with building types. In his discussion of temple architecture, for instance, he uses examples from Rome – such as the Temple of Ceres by the Circus Maximus and the Capitoline Temple itself – as well as from the Greek world. His coverage of other public buildings includes the typically Roman forum and basilica alongside the (still) more Greek theatres and baths. On the domestic side too, Roman house-styles, which were quite different from the Greek, receive considerable attention. His engineering background then comes more to the fore in the last three books of the work, which deal with a series of matters related to building, from water supplies to the construction of mechanical devices such as cranes and hoists (and also siege engines). He also takes in sundials and water clocks, the two main ancient means of measuring time.

The expansionist character of Vitruvius's undertaking is clear. His architecture has colonised parts of various neighbouring disciplines, and so acquired a new intellectual scope and respectability. Architecture becomes an art that encompasses more than it did previously, both conceptually and materially, and is the stronger for it. Its growth, moreover, corresponds to the growth of Rome itself, as imperial power and imperial capital. Vitruvius makes direct reference to Augustus's building programme, a programme intended (among other things) to bring the city up to the standards of a Mediterranean metropolis.

GALEN AND THE DOCTORS

The true champion of this large-scale, expansionist approach to knowledge was, however, Galen of Pergamum, a physician rather than an architect. Galen was a man from the Greek East, not from Rome or Italy, though architecture was his father's profession and he was to spend most of his life in the imperial capital, the only place ambitions on his scale could be realised. By the time of Galen's birth in AD 129, Greece had a more assured place in the Empire than in earlier decades, and was enjoying something of a cultural renaissance.

There had not, of course, been any kind of hiatus in Greek medical writing prior to Galen. A range of texts, like the *On Medical Materials* of Dioscorides (the most influential classical work on medical simples – that is, drugs based on a single active ingredient) and the equally important *Gynaecology* of Soranus survive from the mid-first to early second centuries AD. They also bear the marks of the Roman Empire upon them.

Whether Dioscorides's reference to his 'soldier's life', made in the preface to his work, should be taken as meaning that he was actually a military physician, marching with the Roman legions, or as a more general indication of a frugal and well-travelled existence, he certainly describes plants from a range of imperial locations. Most are in the East (Dioscorides was born in Anazarbus and probably studied in Tarsus, both in modern Turkey), but Italy, Sardinia, Spain, Gaul and Britain all appear too, as do some of the more exotic places with which Rome traded, such as India. Similarly, whether or not the forename 'Pedanius' that appears in the rubrics of many manuscripts should be taken to indicate that Dioscorides had attained Roman citizenship, he certainly operated within the networks of Roman patronage more broadly. He dedicates his work to the physician Areius, who was probably his teacher in Tarsus. Behind Areius, however, stands the figure of the consular Laecanius Bassus, who is also clearly being addressed in the work.

Soranus, though also from Asia Minor (from the city of Ephesus), definitely spent much of his very successful medical career in Rome. His *Gynaecology* (the only Greek medical text entirely devoted to the treatment of women to survive from the imperial period) reflects its metropolitan, not to say cosmopolitan, setting. In addition, though most of it is lost (or is preserved only in later Latin translation), Soranus's literary output was impressive and extended from the specifically medical into the adjoining fields of philosophy and language. Galen, however, was to take this development much further.

A detail from Trajan's Column in Rome showing wounded soldiers being treated by army doctors. The Roman army, once composed entirely of citizens, was well aware of the importance of medical care on the battlefield: not only for saving the lives of those wounded, but also for preserving the morale of those still fighting.

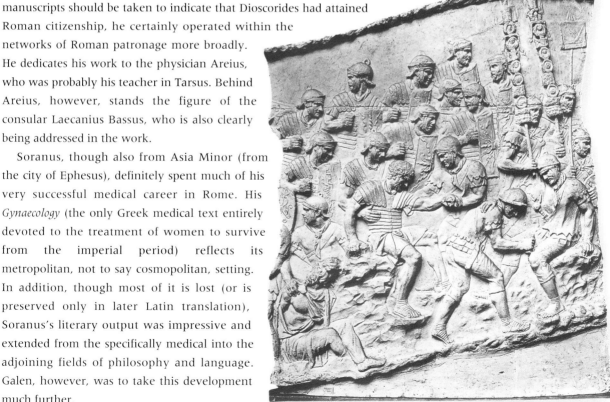

Galen pursued a twin path to success in Rome, which illustrates very clearly the competitive character of Roman medicine. He took on, and successfully cured, patients from the city's elite, such as the wife of the ex-consul Flavius Boethus. He also actively participated, and impressed, in various public debates and demonstrations on medical topics that seem to have formed part of the urban culture. There were, it appears, regular sessions in which he and his competitors in the field discoursed on passages chosen at random (by the method of inserting a stylus into a scroll with the eyes shut) from the works of the ancient physicians. Equally, anatomical displays might be organised on the demand of the rich and intellectually curious, such as that at which Galen demonstrated the nerves and muscles involved in respiration and the voice, by lecturing over several days on the dissection of pigs and goats. These more or less extempore rhetorical performances would then find their way into written form, either transcribed directly or in a more considered way. Galen's reputation and authority was built both through these texts (and the public demonstrations that lay behind them) and through his healing practice itself.

In time, his name reached the emperor Marcus Aurelius, and Galen became one of the physicians associated with the imperial household. With this position achieved, he could then withdraw from the more public aspects of his career and devote more time to literary composition (though he was persuaded back before the crowds to defend his magnum opus, *On the Usefulness of the Parts*, from its detractors). This appears to have been his main focus in the rest of a long life that saw him reach the service of the emperor Septimius Severus, if not his successors.

An illustration from the fourteenth-century scientific manuscript *De Herbis et Plantis* by Manfredus, depicting a hypothetical discourse between Hippocrates (left) and Galen (right). The lasting influence of philosophical Greek thought is implicit in the formal Socratic dialogue between the acknowledged founders of pre-modern Western medicine.

GALEN'S GRAND SYNTHESIS

The evidence of his vast literary output is still with us. Though far from complete, his oeuvre nonetheless occupies a hugely impressive place on library shelves, accounting as it does for about ten per cent of all extant classical (non-Christian) Greek literature. It includes not just a wide variety medical works (some of which are distinctly autobiographical) but also philosophical texts, of both a general kind (on questions of logical method or moral conduct) and more specifically focused on a particular set of teachings, such as those of Plato. Remnants also survive of his once much more extensive writing on rhetoric and language. This range reflects Galen's conception of the medical art as encompassing everything useful to its goal, human health. Medicine, for Galen, thus included not just the requisite knowledge of the way the body works, can go wrong and can be restored to full function, but also *all* the theoretical underpinnings and corollaries of that knowledge, the correct ethical formation and the right commitment to the art itself. One of his shorter treatises is entitled *The Ideal Physician is also a Philosopher* – but in fact he believed that the ideal physician is even more than this.

Even in its medical core, Galen's project could not have been more territorially ambitious. He wanted to cover everything, to master entirely the existing medical tradition. To this end, he constructs a kind of conceptual upwards spiral that has the 'divine Hippocrates', the father of Greek medicine, as its anchor. The Hippocratic writings represent the first attempt at the medical art, a sketchy route-map for his successors to follow and enlarge upon. Some of Galen's own predecessors did so in a rudimentary way, he suggests: the systematic dissection and vivisection of human beings undertaken in Hellenistic Alexandria by Herophilus, for example, added considerable anatomical detail that could be placed alongside the basic tenets of Hippocratic physiology. On the other hand, the other famous Alexandrian anatomist, Erasistratus, was gravely mistaken to try to establish new understandings of how the body worked based on his research. These and more recent errors have to be rejected, Galen asserts, and their perpetrators suitably chastised, while useful gains are incorporated and developed (there being rather more of the former than the latter). This whole process culminates, of course, in Galen himself. He has, again, gathered up everything of use and shaped it into a coherent whole that surpasses any previous medical treatise.

Galen's image of medicine was not, however, radically new; instead he offered a grand synthesis. The key Hippocratic understanding of health as bodily balance, with the humours in due proportion, and illness as imbalance caused by humoral disproportion that must be corrected by supplementing what is lacking or removing what is in excess, remained fundamental. But Galen succeeded in integrating this concept more tightly with the results of Hellenistic anatomical investigations, backed up by his own dissections, than ever before. Nor is anatomy the only post-Hippocratic development that his work encompassed. His synthesis is both exhaustive and systematic, it pays attention to detail as well as to the big picture, it is methodologically sound and theoretically sophisticated, persuasively presented and vigorously promoted; but it is not innovative. Indeed, it has a number of imperial predecessors, on a smaller scale, and it fits in with other intellectual developments of the time, such as philosophical 'eclecticism'.

Illustrations from a medieval manuscript that portray the four basic humoral temperaments – Sanguine, Phlegmatic, Choleric and Melancholic – in a matrimonial context. Galen's holistic view of corporeal personality was subsequently blown apart by the mind-body duality proposed by Descartes and other philosophers.

It also worked. Galen's overweening ambition paid off. He did effectively surpass in influence all earlier medical theorists, as is explicitly recognised by Oribasius, physician to the emperor Julian (the last pagan emperor) in the 360s AD. Instructed by Julian to 'collect together the principal writings of all the best physicians' and so compile everything that was useful to the medical art, Oribasius started from the summaries of Galen he had already completed, arguing that Galen was the very best of them all, dominating all the other writers. His encyclopaedia, and the notion of the medical art it embodies, is therefore constructed around a Galenic framework. Broadly speaking, this is the way medical thought would remain, at least in the Eastern half of the Empire (somewhat more diversity persisted in the Latin West, where, for example, Soranus remained more influential) until well beyond the Middle Ages.

So much of Galen's oeuvre has survived, in a range of languages from its original Greek through Syriac, Arabic, Hebrew, Latin and Armenian, because of the dominant position Galen attained in the classical medical tradition. These works continued to be read, taught, consulted, commented on, criticised and amended, praised and imitated for many centuries, in many different locations. In the West, Galenism – the medical system constructed out of his main concepts and doctrines by generations of doctors and teachers who sought to consolidate and codify his massive, sprawling, oeuvre – was only wholly displaced by modern, 'scientific' medicine in the nineteenth century, and there are still places around the world where Galen remains an authority, usually as part of the Arabic medical tradition – for example, on the Kenyan coast.

That neither human dissection in the Hellenistic period nor animal dissection in the Roman dislodged the fundamental assumptions of Hippocratic physiology demonstrates the way in which, in the classical world, empirical observation was subordinated to theoretical commitment. When Galen anatomised, he did so to demonstrate an existing hypothesis, and what he found would be interpreted in that light. He did not start from the data obtained through anatomy and build his understanding up from those foundations, as scientists today are meant to do. This, indeed, is held to be one of the key distinctions between modern science and ancient investigations into the world: the relationship between observation and theory is reversed. This perhaps explains why, though the classical world was the site of some activities that might definitely be described as 'experiments', these were never systematised into an experimental *method*.

PTOLEMY

This point is perhaps even more plainly illustrated by Ptolemy, the Greek mathematician (in the inclusive, ancient sense of the word), the only man who can seriously challenge Galen for scientific dominance in the Roman Empire in terms of both his own achievements and his legacy. Ptolemy was born a few decades before Galen, but we know much less about his life and career. It is, however, most likely that he spent his whole life in Egypt – indeed there is no contemporary evidence that he ever lived anywhere other than Alexandria. He never, therefore, made the journey to Rome, to the imperial capital, and although he certainly locates himself in the Roman Empire more broadly, there is an overriding impression that Alexandria is the centre of his world.

His surviving treatises span much of the classical mathematical domain, but at their heart is his first and largest work, which he called his *Mathematical Compilation* (or *Syntaxis*); it is more generally known (via an Arabic-Greek amalgam) as the *Almagest*. It is the ancient astronomical text that was to exert the greatest influence on the medieval world, being superseded by the work of Copernicus only in the sixteenth century. In it, Ptolemy provides a detailed mathematical theory describing the motions of the sun, moon and planets (Mercury, Venus, Mars, Jupiter and Saturn being the only planets observed in the classical era). As this would suggest, Ptolemy was an adherent of the earth-centred view of the universe, as proposed by Aristotle and followed by most classical astronomers, though not Aristarchus of Samos (who lived in the third century BC and postulated a heliocentric cosmos). Through a combination of continuous observation of the heavens (his astronomical observations can be dated precisely, from 26 March AD 127 to 2 January 141) and rigorous mathematical theorising, including the application of various new proofs and theorems, Ptolemy was able to produce a comprehensive account of heavenly movement within this model, an account that represents the complicated motions of the five planets fairly accurately.

It is, however, an account that involves a number of difficulties, a fact that Ptolemy himself recognised. Nonetheless, when faced with a choice between his observational data on the one hand and some of his most fundamental assumptions about the workings and structure of the universe on the other, he was not prepared to abandon the latter. He had, like Galen, a number of well-thought out methodological principles to which he was committed (outlined in his dissertation *On the Criterion and the*

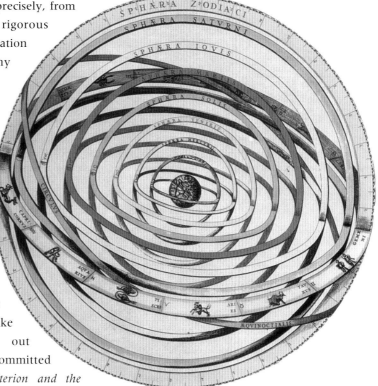

A seventeenth-century engraving of the Ptolemaic universe, showing the orbits of the planets around the Earth, with Saturn correctly identified as the most distant (then known). Although the orbits are depicted as the flat loops of an astronomical instrument, they were in fact (according to classical Ptolemaic theory) spheres of transparent crystal.

In this 1660s illustration, the 'terracentricity' of Ptolemy's universe is emphasised by the disproportionately large globe, embellished with a geographical detail that was beyond the grasp of the second-century AD astronomer. The implication is that the heavens were as accurately mapped and as closely confined, as the Earth itself.

Commanding Faculty) – but they are not those of modern science. On the other hand, his treatise *On Optics* (which survives only in a Latin translation from the Arabic) does involve systematic experimentation in reflection and refraction, for example, and even the construction of particular devices to assist investigation, though the results he obtained are disappointing to modern observers. And his *Harmonics*, a text that stands in a long tradition of highly mathematical discussions of musical theory, is also more experimental than we might expect. The book describes special instruments (various types of monochords), built according to precise principles and measurements, which produce notes in exactly the pattern of numerical relations his harmonic theory proposes.

As well as being surprisingly mathematical and experimental (at least to modern readers), Ptolemy's *Harmonics* is also surprisingly astronomical. In the third book he discusses the relationship between various musical and heavenly phenomena – for example: 'How the interrelations of the planets are to be compared with those of the notes'. Ptolemy followed the Pythagorean tradition in thinking that the same rational order underlies music, the heavens and indeed the soul; the same mathematical principles are expressed in each.

An astronomical theme unites the rest of his work. He produced various more popular and more technically useful spin-offs from the *Almagest*, as well as four books on astrology, his *Tetrabiblos*. For Ptolemy, the step from calculating and predicting the motions of the heavens to predicting their impact on the sublunary world in general, and on individual human beings in particular, is an entirely logical one. The interaction between the heavens and the terrestrial sphere is a natural one, based on the common possession of the fundamental qualities: heat, cold, wetness and dryness. Different heavenly conjunctions, therefore, bring a different combination of these qualities to bear on the sublunary world – being more or less drying, or more or less heating, and so on. These qualities affect places and people who themselves have their own individual constitutions, in which these same qualities are combined in different proportions, and so they are affected differently. Moreover, this system allows various prognostic possibilities; though these are challenging, they are valuable as foreknowledge helps humanity face the future calmly.

PTOLEMY'S WORLD VIEW

It was his astronomical activity that led to Ptolemy's other most famous work, the eight books of *Geography*. In particular, it was the need to fix firmly the place from which observations of the heavens were being made, in terms of latitude and longitude, and to relate different observational points, that led him into his elaborately mathematical approach to geography. This same need also led him to propose projections that would give a visual impression of the curvature of the Earth while preserving (as far as possible) the relative distances between localities, and thus led to his renowned maps. These are, as Ptolemy himself was keen to stress, world maps, not regional ones. He aimed to provide, 'an imitation through drawing of the entire known part of the world together with the things that are, broadly speaking, connected to it'. This known world was, more or less, the Roman Empire, together with its eastern and southern trade routes, but it is very noticeable that the amount and quality of information available drops dramatically the moment he passes beyond Roman control.

Ptolemy shares, therefore, at least some of Galen's imperial visions, but he retains a rather different focus, and so did many other creators and purveyors of knowledge within the Roman world. The large-scale, expansionist approach to knowledge was not the only one adopted in the imperial era. This was the age of the technical handbook as much as the encyclopaedia, of popularising treatises and beginner's guides as much as the specialist monograph. These various approaches reflected the many different audiences available throughout the Empire, the differences of perspective and purpose the Empire permitted and the spaces it created for a high degree of specialisation and professional development – as well as the drive to encompass and integrate.

PRACTICAL TECHNOLOGY

Although one typical example of the specialist, Hero of Alexandria was remarkable. He wrote, probably in the second half of the second century AD, a compact treatise entirely dedicated to artillery engines, a topic covered by Vitruvius in three chapters of his tenth book. Indeed it seems that Hero wrote at least two such texts. One (the *Belopoeica*), written in a more discursive style, was aimed, so he claimed, at the general public. The other, which survives only in fragmentary form, was aimed at the experts – at those, that is, who were actually going to build the new kind of arrow-shooting machine the work describes (the *cheiroballistra*, or 'hand-catapult', with its metal – rather than timber – frames to hold the springs). Hero's literary output also extended into other areas of mechanics, mensuration and mathematics, each treated separately rather than synthetically. He wrote in Greek, but made a number of references to the Roman world – to Roman weights and measures and Latin terminology – as well as to his own Egyptian environment. His *Pneumatica* (see below) was a similarly thorough and extraordinarily precocious examination of the principles of steam power.

Despite Hero's remarkable achievements, Roman society – particularly elite society – did not generally favour the practical application of technology. The most programmatic statement of elite attitudes comes from the Greek intellectual and local dignitary of the late first century AD, Lucius Mestrius Plutarchus ('Plutarch'), another

A mosaic copy (based on a second-century AD Roman original) showing the death of Archimedes in Syracuse at the hands of Roman soldiers. A polymath and perhaps the greatest thinker of his time, Archimedes was subsequently elevated to the status of Greek culture-hero, and his fate became symbolic of civilisation crushed by barbarism.

man actively involved in the mediation of Roman power and Greek culture. Amongst his *Parallel Lives* (paired biographies of famous Greek and Roman statesmen composed as part of this mediation) is a biography of Marcus Claudius Marcellus, the notable Republican general. Marcellus's victory in the siege of Syracuse in 212 BC was a key moment in Rome's conquest of the Greek world, not just militarily but also morally and aesthetically. According to Plutarch, the triumphant general took back to Rome with him not only a selection of the best Greek art Syracuse had to offer (art that Marcellus was to champion against contemporary Roman philistinism), but also the memory of perhaps the greatest ever Greek mathematician, Archimedes, who had been killed during the sack of the city despite Marcellus's best efforts to save him. Of Archimedes himself, Plutarch noted:

Considering the business of mechanics and all the arts that as a whole touch upon utility low-born and fit for vulgar craftsmen, he directed all his ambition only to the things in which the beautiful and extraordinary are not mixed with the necessary.

Plutarch's Archimedes disdained, therefore, many of his most famous inventions, including his notable contributions to Syracuse's military strength – and the city's ability to withstand Rome for so long – such as his innovative artillery engines, adapted to sink ships. Archimedes wanted instead to be remembered for his abstract thought, his theoretical achievements.

It is, of course, questionable whether Plutarch represents the opinion of the historical Archimedes with any degree of accuracy, rather than simply projecting his own prejudices onto a figure who had attained the status of Greek culture-hero. The surviving works of Archimedes contain no explicit statement on the matter, and their implicit positioning is much debated, without firm conclusion. The responses of the successors of Archimedes in the Roman imperial period to elite attitudes of this kind do not accord with Plutarch's view. Roman attitudes to technology and its practical application were, of course, far more varied than Plutarch implies.

Even Vitruvius, who can certainly be seen as responding to elite prejudices about the profession or expertise of the architect – and indeed as making concessions to elite values in his construction of his art – nonetheless stresses the importance of its practical application. He seeks to bring technical skill and experience together with theoretical knowledge, not to replace the former with the latter. Hero makes a much more dramatic claim for the mechanical arts – for the art of building war machines in particular – when he asserts, in the introduction to his *Belopoeica*, that its contribution to human tranquillity and happiness (the goal of all philosophical endeavour) far surpasses that of any theoretical speculation or abstract consideration. Powerful artillery ensures peace and security, he argued, acting both as a deterrent to potential aggressors and a guarantee of victory if conflict should break out. Philosophy, on the other hand, is an ongoing, irresolvable, argument. There is, furthermore, at least one member of the Roman aristocracy – a consular, no less – who did not consider technical details beneath him, but seemed rather to revel in them. Sextus Julius Frontinus's treatise *On Aqueducts* is a systematic study of the Roman water supply system, right down to the smallest pipe, composed by a man who enjoyed a successful

STEAM POWER
IN THE ROMAN WORLD

Hero of Alexandria is perhaps most famous for his *Pneumatica*, a two-book catalogue of mechanisms using air, water and steam under pressure, as well as an outline of some of the theoretical principles underlying these devices. Amongst over eighty separate devices described by Hero were a trick jug that could pour, depending on the whim of the operator, unmixed wine, wine mixed with water or just plain water; and a couple of suggested improvements to the bronze turnstile wheel mounted at the entrance to some Egyptian temples and turned by worshippers on their way in for the purposes of purification, one causing water to be dispensed when the wheel was turned and so doubling the purificatory effect and another that added the warbling of a stuffed bird to the proceedings. Hero's most famous inventions, however, were the closest the ancient world came to moving beyond human-, animal- and water-power by harnessing steam as a source of energy. One of these used the pressure of escaping steam to cause a small ball to jump into the air. The other was a more sophisticated invention, using steam power to produce rotary motion. The technological achievement here was remarkable, surpassing in many ways that of both the 'architron' (a sort of steam cannon) invented by Leonardo da Vinci in the European Renaissance and the steam pressure vessel invented by Denis Papin in the seventeenth century.

The site of the Roman mine of Las Medulas in Spain (main picture), where sophisticated force-pumps of the type described by Hero were used to raise water from otherwise flooded galleries. Three illustrations (inset) from a medieval edition of Hero's work entitled *Automata and Other Curious Machines*.

The device invented by Hero was the aeolipile, or steam sphere. A large, sealed metal cauldron of water was placed over a fire. As the water boiled, steam escaped through two pipes attached to the top, between which was pivoted a hollow metal sphere, able to rotate freely. Steam from the cauldron passed through the pipes into the sphere, and could escape only through small opposed L-shaped outlet pipes set in the exterior of the sphere, perpendicular to the axis of rotation. As the pressure built up within the sphere, the escaping steam caused the sphere to rotate rapidly on its axis.

That neither Hero nor any of his successors did actually go on to build a steam engine despite developing all the necessary elements (not just the boiler, but also, variously, valves, pistons and cylinders) has been taken as symptomatic of the weaknesses of classical technology. The fact that many of Hero's most innovative devices were entertainments, designed for their spectacular effects (the speed of the spinning aeolipile would have impressed as much as the height of the jumping ball) rather than everyday usefulness, is taken as even more damning. This was a society in which the entertaining, the marvellous, had a higher status than the industrial; it was also one in which an association with manual labour, with getting one's hands dirty, was considered demeaning. These attitudes have been held responsible by modern observers for putting severe limitations on the possibilities of technological advance in the Roman world, especially when taken together with other broadly conservative attitudes in Roman social and economic life.

In fact, the difficulty and expense of creating devices like those built by Hero meant that their practical and economic value was limited in a society where animal and human labour was cheap. Moreover, the theoretical basis on which Hero and his followers built their understanding of the physical world meant that they were not able to recognise the underlying principles of steam power that would have made further development possible. To Hero, the behaviour of the escaping steam was paradoxical, not a natural phenomenon that could be exploited systematically.

political and military career. He was made responsible for Rome's water supply by the emperor Nerva in AD 97, a position in which he was then confirmed by Trajan, to whom Frontinus was also twice a colleague in the consulship.

Moreover, to judge even Hero's surviving works by the more exotic contents of the *Pneumatica* – or indeed his short work *Automatapoetica* on automata, which describes the construction of two miniature puppet theatres – is misleading. His *Mechanica*, preserved only in Arabic translation (and some Greek fragments), is a much more utilitarian text, dealing first with the theoretical underpinnings of mechanics, then its basic devices, and finally some key applications of these fundamentals in machines such as cranes, hoists and presses. Hero also covers measurement very thoroughly, a matter of crucial importance not only in everyday life but also in governmental affairs such as the division and distribution of land, the settling of boundary disputes, tax assessment and the paying of taxes in kind (for example in grain), the planning of irrigation and the organisation of the water supply. In his *Metrica* he expounds an almost entirely geometrical approach to mensuration, while the *Stereometrica* is more practical, including, for example, calculations of the number of amphorae that can be stacked in the holds of ships of various sizes, and the number of tiles needed to roof buildings of different dimensions. His *Dioptra* is entirely dedicated to surveying (his other treatises, on clocks and the measurement of time, are lost).

TECHNOLOGY AND SOCIETY

These texts, and others such as the large collection of Latin works on land-surveying and related activities known as the *Corpus Agrimensorum Romanorum* and the ongoing tradition of writing on military matters (including military engineering) in both Latin and Greek – and also a range of archaeological evidence – should serve as a warning against overly simple, or overly negative, characterisations of Roman technological development. Roman engineering achievements extended far beyond the realm of the mechanical marvel or toy, and improvements continued to be made on basic designs over the whole period. One of the Roman developments in military artillery – the metal-framed *cheiroballistra* – has already been mentioned, and there were others. On the civil side, Roman technology brought significant inventions – concrete and glass, for example. Among mechanical advances, the use of water-power in flour milling and a range of other machines (from trip-hammers to saws) increased over the course of the Empire, as did increasing sophistication in water-pumps and water-management systems, associated with the supply of cities, with agriculture and with mining.

Indeed, some of the most impressive engineering achievements of the Roman Empire are to be found in the larger Spanish mines where water was one of the key tools used in the extraction process. Spain yielded the precious metals – gold, silver and copper – as well as tin, lead and iron – from mines that were owned by the Roman state, but might be leased to private enterprises. The scale of exploitation is manifest from the marks left on the environment by these activities, and some of the methods used were also on a grand scale. Large reservoirs were constructed above the

From Hero's preface to his treatise on pneumatics

For, by the union of air, earth, fire and water, and the concurrence of three, or four, elementary principles, various combinations are effected, some of which supply the most pressing wants of human life, while others produce amazement and alarm.

Hero Pneumatica
(Trans. Bennet Woodcroft)

A late-Roman water wheel at Hama in Syria. Repaired countless times over the centuries, these wheels preserve the scale and complexity of the Roman originals. For lifting water and providing rotary power – it was wheels like these that turned the Roman world in its later years. The banks of the Tiber were lined with wheel-powered grain mills; and in times of crisis, wheels were even mounted on ships anchored in the river.

workings, with sluices at one end; once the reservoirs had been filled, often via aqueducts, the sluices were quickly opened, releasing the great mass of water to wash over the workings, carrying away the spoil. Water might also be utilised in a more controlled manner in other parts of the process; and, of course, it also had to be removed from mines, by pumping systems that raised the water, on occasion as much as 30 metres (in the Rio Tinto mines, where a succession of eight pairs of large and sophisticated bucket-wheels, each driven by a presumably reasonably fit man, could pump, it is calculated, about 2,400 gallons an hour). Technologically, however, the Roman world saw few radically new inventions, and few interventions in previously untouched areas of life as were eventually to occur in the European industrial revolution. Instead, the Empire brought growth and intensification in technologies that mostly predated the Roman world. Technology kept pace with society, with Empire, rather than outstripping it. Ingenious solutions were found to specific technical challenges thrown up by the imperial enterprise – militarily, logistically and economically – but there was little generalisation from these solutions. Knowledge too expanded with Empire, and was systematised and synthesised along Roman imperial lines but not radically transformed. But then, the Roman world was not really a radical kind of place.

THE GODS
OF EMPIRE

RICHARD LIM

THE GODS OF EMPIRE

Despite their reputation for religious conservatism, the Romans adjusted their relationship with the gods as they acquired an Empire of their own. The many gods henceforth competed for pride of place and adherents within the *Pax Romana*. Local peoples responded to the Greco-Roman mythological scheme by renaming their own deities, while at the same time retaining traditional forms of worship. There was no central pagan religion in the manner of the monotheistic Jews and Christians, whose notion of one transcendant God converged with contemporary philosophical notions about the divine. After the fourth century AD, Christian monotheism began to capture the support of elite and commoner alike, thereby redefining the nature of the relationship between gods and men in the Roman world.

A relief from the Temple of Capitoline Jove (Jupiter) in Rome, showing the emperor Marcus Aurelius (hooded) performing a public sacrifice. Conforming to 'ancient' tradition, the careful observation of the sacrifice ritual (the age and gender of all participants, human and animal, being precisely specified) was considered an essential imperial duty. Since the inception of the Principiate, the emperor had also held the title of Pontifex Maximus (Chief Priest).

'Our state has always thought that everything should take second place to *religio*' – thus Valerius Maximus (1.1.9) calls attention to the emphasis Rome placed on the worship of the gods. For Rome to remain successful and to fulfil its destiny to rule the world, its deities had to be punctiliously cultivated according to ritual formulae set down by the ancients. What the gods required most of all was the sacrifice of animals, carried out by designated priests on sacred altars. The correct enactment of sacrifices and prayers as prescribed by the *mos maiorum*, the way of the ancestors, was the basis of the city's religious rites. The Latin word *religio* may best be translated as the scrupulous devotion to ritual acts that sought to establish a positive relationship between the human and the divine worlds; it therefore differs greatly from the more current Western notion of 'religion' as an individual's spiritual disposition and belief in a transcendental God. During the monarchy and early Republic, this religion was first related to the needs and desires of an early agrarian community that looked to the fertility of the soil for its survival. Worshipping the divine in the proper fashion ensured that the rain would fall and the crops would grow. The fertility of people and livestock mattered too, and for all these reasons the early Romans kept a keen watch over their relationship with the teaming yet unseen animating spirits (*numina*) that populated the landscape around them. Roman public religion represents in important respects the ritual practices of the farm and the house writ large. In time, gods and goddesses in human form made their way into Rome from adjoining areas. As the city grew from a small archaic community into the capital of a world empire, its relationship with the gods changed gradually, but many of the earlier features of its religion remained constant. Individuals and groups of non-Romans were continually brought in and accepted as citizens – some by the grant of citizenship to whole groups and others through first having been enslaved as individuals and later manumitted. These people brought the native cults of their original communities to Rome. In this and other ways, Rome's gods of empire were slowly transformed along with the character of the Empire itself.

GODS NATIVE AND FOREIGN

Originally the gods of Rome were the gods to whom the community of Roman citizens paid honour with ritual observances such as public sacrifices and prayers. Such a definition allows a certain amount of ambiguity and flexibility, since Rome was from the start an ethnically mixed city. Its original inhabitants had come from nearby towns and regions, as seen in the foundation myths of Romulus and Aeneas. The Romans held much in common with the Latins. In myth, Aeneas and his son had founded the Latin cities of Lavinium and Alba Longa, from which the founders of Rome would later come. Rome replaced Lavinium as the central place of the cult for the Latin League when its kings built a temple to Diana, one of the federal deities honoured by the Latins, on the Aventine Hill.

This commerce in the divine continued after Rome attained pre-eminence in Latium; it imported deities such as Juno Sospita from its Latin neighbours and learned religious rites from the Etruscans, who were famous for their expertise in the art of divination. With increasing contact with Etruscans and the Greek communities of Magna Graecia, the Romans turned their own abstract deities into anthropo-morphised gods and goddesses and established a set of nominal equivalents by which, for instance, Jupiter was equated to Zeus, Juno to Hera, Athena to Minerva, Mercury to Hermes, Mars to Ares and Ceres to Demeter. Roman religion became, in mytho-logical terms at least, assimilated to a Greek theological framework derived from Homer and Hesiod. However, this process left the rites of worship largely unaltered.

Romans in the classical period claimed to have a native pantheon, the *ius divinum*, whose worship was tied to the specific topography of the city and the earliest history of its people. Yet far from being fixed in some original form from the foundation of the city, the history of Roman religion unfolds as a story of adaptation and change even with respect to the city's patron deities. Rome under the legendary priest-king Numa revered Jupiter, Mars and Quirinus. In the sixth century BC this threesome was replaced by another triad honoured in nearby Etruscan cities: Jupiter, Juno and Minerva, for whom a great temple was built on the Capitoline Hill during the last years of the monarchy in Rome; this temple probably reflected the Tarquins' desire to broadcast their power by building a monumental temple in an 'international' (in this case, Etruscan) style.

If cultivating an image of power was one motive for innovation in Roman public religion, war and social crises were another. It was a common practice for Roman generals on the eve of battle to pledge to particular deities that, in exchange for victory, they would dedicate temples in Rome to them using the spoils of war. Among these are the four Republican temples found in Rome at a site now called the Area Sacra of Largo Argentina. A temple of Feronia, an Italic deity, here commemorated the Roman victory over the Sabines in 290 BC, while that of Juno Curritis was vowed after the defeat of either Falerii or Carthage in 241 BC. Not fulfilling such *ex voto* promises was impious in the extreme and the community as a whole largely accepted what one individual Roman had vowed to the gods in their name. The Romans were not always victorious on the battlefield and, given their belief that each community had its own protective gods, they saw defeat as a sign that the enemy's patron deities were simply too powerful. Under such circumstances, the Romans performed the rite of *evocatio*, in which the gods of hostile communities were invited to desert their native towns and come to Rome with the promise that a temple cult would be established there in their name. One of the earliest known cases was connected with Rome's long war with Etruscan Veii. In 396 BC, the Roman dictator Camillus made a vow to Apollo of one-tenth of the spoils and also promised to Veii's patron goddess Uni (now referred to as Juno) that a temple would be built for her in Rome. The Romans traditionally repeated this use of *evocatio* during the Punic Wars to summon Carthage's patron Tanit to desert her city and take up residence in Rome, which she did as Juno Caelestis. (By thus renaming a foreign god with a familiar name, the Romans were able to assimilate an otherwise alien deity within the existing collectivity of native gods.) These cases also show that the Romans did not translate their animosity towards human enemies into hatred for their gods. Yet this formula fell into abeyance after the Punic Wars, suggesting the Romans' growing confidence in the might of their arms and their right to empire.

Even though adding foreign gods to one's pantheon was for the Romans an accepted practice, there were times when deep crises demanded particularly direct imports from afar. In the fifth century BC, an epidemic prompted the Senate to turn to the Sibylline books, a collection of oracular writings, which instructed the Romans to establish the cult of Apollo the Healer in the city to safeguard the health of its people. In 293 BC another epidemic decimated the population of the countryside. Perplexed and despairing that the normal *res sacra*, or rites of divine worship, had not averted such disaster, the Romans resorted again to the Sibyl, who counselled seeking the help of the healing god Asclepius, son of Apollo, whose chief shrine was in Epidaurus in central Greece. The Romans' preoccupation with the war with Carthage meant that this exotic undertaking was put off for two to three years. But the plague raged unabated and the Sibyl persisted in her pronouncement. At last, a delegation of Roman dignitaries travelled eastwards and, having secured a sacred snake from the temple priests, returned with their mission accomplished. This snake, often represented entwined on a staff, was sacred to Asclepius and embodied the god's divine presence. According to one tradition, it slipped off the boat and alighted on the Tiber island, which the Romans then assigned to the god as his special precinct. A temple to Aesculapius (Latin for Asclepius) containing the divine images of the god and his daughter Hygeia, who later became associated with the native Italic deity Salus, was dedicated on 1 January 291 BC. Remains of this temple are still visible under the modern hospital for children on the island. In this instance, the Romans did not adopt a neighbour's gods but made a deliberate choice to send away for one whose healing touch was greatly needed in Italy at the time. The Sibylline oracle provided the legitimating voice for this endeavour and gave the new cult a respectability and place in Roman society that it might otherwise not have had. Yet Aesculapius, for all the help he rendered Rome, was kept at arm's length. The Tiber island was not within the *pomerium*, the sacred boundaries of the city of Rome, and the god thus continued to serve the Romans as a *peregrinus* living amidst the city's immigrant population on the banks of the Tiber.

Dionysius on the Sybilline Oracle

[An] exceptional piece of good fortune came to the city of Rome during Tarquin's reign, a blessing conferred by some god or power... A foreign woman approached the tyrant and offered to sell him nine books of Sibylline Oracles; Tarquin refused to buy at her price, so she went away and burned three... [this was repeated once.] Tarquin, now becoming curious about the woman's purpose, sent for the augurs, told them what had happened and asked them what he should do. They realised by certain signs that what he had rebuffed was a gift from the gods; so, they told him that it was a disaster that he had not bought all the books and advised him to pay the woman the whole price she was asking and to get the oracles that were left. The woman handed over the books, told him to take the greatest care of them and vanished from human sight.

Dionysius of Halicarnassus
Roman Antiquities 6.2

The ruins of a temple to an unknown deity
in the Largo Argentina area of Rome, where
the remains of three other temples dating
from the Republican period have been
found. Rome was dotted with hundreds
of temples and shrines in varying states of
repair, and with widely differing levels
of patronage. Some, such as the Temple
of Venus in the Forum, played a significant
role in the life of the city, while others
were local curiosities.

This was perhaps a fitting fate for a god of medicine, which in Rome was long the trade of Greek-speaking slaves. Greater esteem had to be accorded to another celebrity import from the East during the wars with Hannibal. The decade-long war in Italy sapped Roman morale and the uncertainty that many felt at the time was amplified by the widespread reporting of prodigies and omens. The Romans even took to sacrificing humans in public to appease the gods. The Sibylline books, again the last resort for a people in crisis, revealed that Hannibal would only be removed from Italy if 'the Idaean Mother of Pessinus' could be brought to Rome. This was taken to refer to the Anatolian mother goddess Magna Mater (Cybele in Greek), whose cult site was in Phrygia in central Asia Minor. The Romans dutifully sent a delegation and, after some politicking, obtained the divine symbol of the goddess – a black stone that was perhaps a meteorite. The Delphic oracle meanwhile instructed the Romans to greet the goddess with their best man, and the idol was introduced into the city and temporarily housed in the Temple of Victory with joyous ceremony. On 10 April 191 BC, Magna Mater witnessed the dedication of her own temple on the Palatine where her native cultic apparatus, including a band of eunuch priests (*galli*) brought over from Phrygia, was also installed. The Megalesia, a great communal festival which all Romans were supposed to attend and during which official business was forbidden, celebrated the cult of the Great Mother in Rome annually from 5 to 10 April. It comprised religious processions, Greek-style athletic competitions and theatrical performances held in the Circus Maximus. The religious ceremony was presided over by a Roman magistrate, an aedile in Cicero's time and a praetor in the late Empire, who made the initial offering of herbs at the temple of the goddess.

Yet the universal appeal and respectability of the Megalesia as a communal festival stood in strong contrast to the worship of Magna Mater in the city. Her cult involved castrated males and exotic paraphernalia that greatly offended elite Roman sensibilities. The *galli*, dressed in brightly coloured robes, stained with blood from self-flagellation, accompanied by flute-players, tambourines, drums and cymbals, often made spectacular processions through Roman streets while singing hymns in Greek. The Roman state in fact forbade its citizens to join the priesthood of Magna Mater and, according to a Greek writer, even banned them from walking in the processions. Thus, while Magna Mater was welcomed into the city and assigned a festival in the official calendar, she remained a foreign deity, outside the native pantheon, and her worship was confined to her Palatine temple.

A censorious reception of foreign cults was particularly in evidence when they entered Rome as a result of private initiatives rather than state action. One such incident concerned the worship of Dionysus (Latin Bacchus) who had long been revered in Rome as Liber Pater, an Italian god of fertility and wine. Romans celebrated the Liberalia annually on 17 March. Since Liber was a rustic deity, his major cultic presence in the city was in association with Ceres at a temple dedicated in 493 BC on the Aventine Hill, which was then outside the sacred boundaries of Rome. Ceres, Liber and Libera became known as the Aventine Triad, a Plebeian counterpart to the Patrician Capitoline Triad during the Struggle of the Orders. In the second century BC, Bacchic rites of worship involving ecstatic celebrations spread in Italy and came even to Rome, attracting a following of men and women of all social strata. Members of the senatorial elite became so concerned that a law was passed in 186 BC which resulted in what came to be called the 'Bacchanalian incident', the first organised Roman state persecution of a religious group. The consuls were ordered to suppress the cult and destroy all but the most ancient altars and statues of the god wherever they were found. An inquisition was carried out in all the country districts of Italy, but while the public manifestations of the cult receded for a time, it remained a potent force in Roman society afterwards. Why did the polytheistic Romans take such an action? It had nothing to do with the fact that a foreign god was being worshipped. The followers of Bacchic rites in fact offended Roman social and political mores much more than their religious scruples. Roman religion was utilitarian in outlook and served to reinforce corporate identities such as the family, *gens* and

A third-century AD mosaic from Tunisia depicting the triumph of Bacchus over the Indians. Although he was initially linked with indigenous rural deities, Bacchus (like his Greek incarnation, Dionysus) was an unashamedly oriental god. The emphasis on direct and enthusiastic personal involvement in his cult gave rise to concern among both Greek and Roman authorities.

other kinship groups, and the Roman state. In contrast, the Bacchic cult was tightly organised around particular leaders who exercised a strong hold over their followers, even to the point of influencing them to turn over their property. The fact that individuals were repudiating their ties to their families, kinship groups and the state in favour of these shadowy authority figures probably accounts for the unprecedented response of the state.

A delicate balance between religious conservatism and change existed throughout the Republic. The state continued to keep a careful watch over which gods could be brought to and installed in Rome, adjusting its religious practice to fit the particular needs of the city. At the same time, it strove to check more random religious innovations and periodically took steps to curb what it deemed excessive. Cicero described the attitude that proper-thinking Romans ought to have regarding the gods: 'no one shall have gods of their own, neither new ones nor ones imported from abroad, unless introduced [to Rome] publicly; their own private worship shall be for those gods whose worship they have duly received from their fathers' (*De legibus* 2.19). But the very fact that Cicero was moved to make this statement shows that his contemporaries often thought otherwise.

The ruins of the Temple of Mars the Avenger in the Forum of Augustus in Rome. The temple was the centrepiece of a major piece of dynastic monumentalisation by the first emperor who set up in it the Roman standards he had recovered from the Parthians. The temple continued to be used for meetings of the senate, the reception of embassies and many other formal occasions.

GODS AND MEN IN THE PAX ROMANA

The transformation from Republic to Empire altered the distribution of political power but ushered in no great religious change in the Roman world, the major exception being the rise of the figure of the emperor as Rome's supreme political and religious authority. The emperor became alternately the conservator of traditional religion and the agent through whom changes were made to Roman public cult. Julius Caesar had reformed Roman religious customs while holding the office of *pontifex maximus*, the chief of a college of priests who at this time became the head of Roman state religion as a whole. Augustus, inheriting this office (which became an imperial title), chose to pose as the defender of ancient Roman religion; according to his *Res Gestae*, the autobiographical statement of his accomplishments, he restored eighty-two temples and resurrected rites that had fallen into disuse.

He also built new temples, the most striking one being the Temple of Mars the Avenger (*Mars Ultor*), supposedly vowed on the eve of the Battle of Philippi, which served as the centrepiece of the new Forum of Augustus. The full complex articulates

Augustus's vision of the close ties between Rome's gods and its past and present. The association with Mars the Avenger suggests the god's care for the family of Augustus and the justice of the revenge he took against the killers of Julius Caesar, his adoptive father who had then become a god. The pediment of the temple featured Mars flanked by Venus and Romulus on the left and by Fortuna and Roma on the right. In the side porticoes were semi-circular exedras that housed images of Aeneas and Romulus, the two founders of the city, and selected great men from Rome's historical past: Latin kings of Alba Longa and members of the Julian clan accompanied Aeneas, their ancestor, while figures from the Republic surrounded Romulus. A statue of Augustus himself on a four-horsed chariot, the vehicle of a triumphant general, faced the altar at the front of the temple. This careful choreography, juxtaposing the human and the divine, presents a providential view of Roman history and highlights the special part that Augustus's own family played in fulfilling the role that the gods had destined for Rome.

Italia, a personified goddess whose image appears on the Altar of Peace (*Ara Pacis*), was promoted by the emperor to reassure Romans and Italians that they still counted as the core of Rome's growing Empire. Whenever Augustus and his successors restored ancient temples and re-established their cults, they were attempting to slow the normal processes of religious and social change. As we have seen, the Roman state and private religion were both in fact quite dynamic and open to innovation, and it was the scale and the nature of the new imports and not merely the fact that they were foreign that ultimately determined their acceptability.

The Hellenistic East had been a major source of cultural and religious imports to Rome. From the time of Cato the Elder until well into the Empire, the pace of Hellenisation and the immigration to Rome of Greek-speakers began to worry those who feared the loss of their native Latin culture and religion. Augustus's own emphasis on the values and cults of a national Italy was in many ways a repudiation of what he represented as Mark Antony's Hellenising ways. But even the defeat of Antony did not deter later emperors from overt Philhellenism: Nero and Hadrian are only the best-known examples of emperors who loved everything Greek and sought to introduce Greek customs to Rome.

Rome never opposed the spread of Greek culture as a matter of principle. Rather the Romans actively encouraged the further dissemination of Greek values and institutions from the Greek cities in the Mediterranean and Middle East to the hinterland. In the West, a parallel transformation of native communities took place through Romanisation. Imperial Rome made no genuine effort to export its gods, but colonies of Roman citizens naturally established the cults of traditional Roman gods in the new territories. Thus the worship of the Capitoline Triad spread to the western Mediterranean and elsewhere. Dominating local civic forums in towns such as Cosa in Etruria, and Thugga (Dougga), Thuburbo Maius, Thamugadi (Timgad) and Sufetula (Sbeitla) in North Africa, these temples to a triad of gods, originally worshipped by Etruscans and later adapted to Roman use, copied in miniaturised form the close proximity of the Capitol to the Roman Forum and the close relationship between the divine and the human that it symbolised.

THE CULT OF ROMAN EMPERORS

During the Empire, colonies and other provincial cities might decide to dedicate a temple to one of the emperors rather than to build a Capitolium temple. The emperors were worshipped in the Roman world in a variety of contexts that ranged from the state cult to individual families' worship of the household gods, with whom the emperors were associated. The Romans had come to power within a Mediterranean world in which the custom of honouring kings as divine beings had been well established since the time of Alexander the Great. Greek cities would vote to establish a temple, an annual festival, a set of sacrifices and a priesthood to honour the powerful kings; in turn they would usually be granted various concessions and benefits. After Rome emerged as the equal of the Hellenistic rulers during the middle Republic, the Greeks began to pay homage to the abstracted deity of the goddess Roma, and even to the Senate and the People of Rome, for reasons that ranged from gratitude to political expedience. They also greeted as divine saviours certain Republican generals and governors until the practice was abolished under Augustus, after whose reign divine honours became the prerogative of members of the imperial family. The Greek states readily assimilated worship of the emperors into the existing Hellenistic ruler cult, in which sacred images of emperors were prominently carried in civic processions and traditional religious festivals, and housed in the ancient sanctuaries of Greek gods. Temples for the imperial cult, such as the remarkably well-preserved Sebasteion in Aphrodisias in Turkey, became a common sight in provincial towns. Special priesthoods were formed of members of the local aristocratic elite, to whom the office of imperial priest was a sign of their connection with the ruling power. Cities vied with each other to offer more and more elaborate cultic worship to the emperors even in their absence. Thus Augustus was honoured with sacred hymn singers at Pergamum and Tiberius fêted by the people of Gytheum in the Peloponnese with a festival consisting of musical competitions. Generally the emperors deferred to the locals' need to express their love for them rather than encouraged these forms of celebrations. At the beginning, there was little regulation or centralised control over such cults – though the emperors from Augustus onwards sought to control visual representation of their own imperial images by sending out models from Rome for copying in provincial workshops.

The citizens of Hellenistic cities, long used to the worship of divine rulers, welcomed the opportunity to form a direct link with these personifications of Roman power. On the other hand, the imperial cult was a novelty in other parts of the Roman world, including Rome itself, where the suspicion of monarchy even after the Republic caused the aristocracy in particular to regard the deification of a living person as a sign of tyranny. Augustus made no effort to introduce the cult of his own divinity in Rome, choosing instead to allow his household gods (*lares*) and his own life-force (*genius*) to become the object of worship instead. At first only deceased emperors would receive deification by decree of the Senate. When Caligula dressed up as Bacchus, Apollo and even Jupiter, and insisted that he be worshipped as a divine being, his histrionic gestures were attributed to madness. Domitian's assertion that he should be addressed as *dominus et deus*, 'lord and god', was read likewise as evidence of egomania. Most of the early Roman emperors had to wait for a posthumous apotheosis. The process became formulaic: after the body was cremated on the funerary pyre, priests would preside over the consecration while released eagles, symbolising the soul of the deceased, took wing in simulation of its ascent to the heavens. For all this, the Romans were not unaware of the wide gulf that separated men from gods, and outside official circles a certain amount of cynicism greeted the practice. The apotheosis of deceased emperors might even be met with some irony by the emperors themselves. On his deathbed, Vespasian famously joked, 'I think I'm turning into a god!'

Augustus and Trajan actively tried to dissuade their subjects from granting them excessive divine honours; this was a sign of their virtue, their *civilitas*. In fact, there are few instances of imperial worship being imposed from above upon unwilling subjects. And in antiquity there were no more unwilling subjects than the Jews. By

A Roman cameo depicting the apotheosis of Claudius – a winged Victory places the wreath of godhood on the head of the deceased emperor. The original sardonyx jewel was carved in the first century AD, and was placed in its present setting during the seventeenth century. Imperial attitudes to godhood ranged from the blithely pragmatic to the downright insane.

long-established custom, Roman authorities recognised that the Jews' ancient religion forbade them from worshipping any deity but their own, and acknowledged their right to worship after their own fashion. Nonetheless Caligula, who probably knew very well that the Jews' strict monotheism would not allow them to worship the emperor in the manner of their Greek neighbours, ordered his own cult statue placed within the Holy of Holies in the Temple in Jerusalem. This outrageous proposal might have been a reaction to recent riots in Alexandria and Judaea, where the Jews destroyed an altar to the imperial cult provocatively erected by their non-Jewish neighbours. Appeal after appeal by Jews and Roman notables finally moved the emperor to rescind his unprecedented order, saving both Jews and Romans from much bloodshed.

In the West, the introduction of the imperial cult into a newly established province became an integral component of the Romanisation of territories such as Gaul, Germany and Britain. Altars to the imperial cult were made into focal points for the expression of loyalty towards Rome. A Great Altar to Rome and Augustus was established in Lugdunum (Lyon), and representatives of the three Gallic provinces came here for their annual show of devotion to Rome and the emperor. A similar plan was envisaged for Colonia Agrippinensis (Cologne), the former capital of the client Ubii and later provincial capital of Lower Germany. The provincial councils were political and religious bodies, and the presidents of the councils were often also the chief imperial priests. In this way, members of the native nobility became Roman aristocrats whose tenure as imperial priests represented one aspect of their public service to their local communities. Such a formula satisfied the need of this elite to demonstrate their new identity as Romans and that of the Roman authorities to secure concrete signs of provincial loyalty.

Having an established imperial cult in one's city was for some a sign that it had attained a certain level in the competitive hierarchy of Roman cities. For others, particularly within the first generation of Roman conquest, it simply signified foreign oppression. Following the Claudian invasion of Britain, a new provincial capital was established at Camulodunum (Colchester), where a monumental temple of the deified Claudius became the focus of the new provincial assembly that met annually in the city. Some Britons found themselves exploited by corrupt Roman officials who spared not even former Roman clients. Among these were the Iceni, who saw the lands of their nobles expropriated without compensation – contrary to expected Roman administrative practice. The outcry against Roman injustice led to a major revolt, under their queen, Boudicca. Camulodunum was taken and its population of Romans and Italians killed while the Temple of Claudius was targeted for destruction. The symbol of the emperor's divinity thus became a focus for the sense of outrage of the rebels. Similar local rebellions in Germany and Gaul involved a native assertion of local, including religious, identities – but nonetheless there is no reason to believe that resistance to the imperial cult was ideological or common in the West. The new Romanised aristocracies happily and enthusiastically participated in the imperial cult to mark their own Roman cultural identity, status in society and close ties to the ruling power.

The Roman theatre in Lyon, France. The theatre was part of the monumental apparatus of the Roman colony. Lyon also housed a federal sanctuary around the Altar used each year for collective cult of Rome and of Augustus. The elecion of an annual priest, the gladiatorial games associated with the festival and the meeting of the provincial council at this time, made Lyon a centre for monumental benefactions by the richest of the Gallo-Roman nobility.

Steam rises from the naturally heated waters of the restored Roman baths, at Bath on the River Avon. Known to the Romans as Aquae Sulis (after Sulis, the local Celtic deity), the town has been a medical spa for more than two millennia. Springs have an ancient tradition (pre-Roman and pre-Greek) in Europe as sacred places. The warm waters at Bath lent the site additional significance.

A WORLD FULL OF GODS

The Roman world was a place full of gods, reflecting the multi-ethnic character of the Empire itself. These deities were not all equal, of course, just as not all inhabitants of the Empire were equal. While references to the names of Greek and Roman gods abound in imperial literature, this does not mean that either Hellenisation or Romanisation succeeded in effacing the identity of the native gods of other communities. For centuries, the Greeks and the Romans had sought to establish correspondences between their gods and those of their neighbours. This process, referred to as *interpretatio graeca* or *interpretatio romana*, allowed native religious traditions to be assimilated, in the imagination if not in practice, within a Greco-Roman mythological narrative. This might enable a Greek or a Roman to regard a diverse religious world with a sense of familiarity and their counterparts to see their native cults as somehow linked with the dominant literary mythological discourse of the Empire. While this helped fit local deities into a uniform intellectual framework in a world full of gods and diverse ritual practices, the situation on the ground was much more complex, and the plurality and distinctiveness of the gods remained a fact of life. A very strong sense of religious particularism and identity prevailed in most places as everyone, including the Romans themselves, continued to regard religious cult as the inviolable right of local communities. Rome's own elaborate ritual laws and its *ius divinum* were not relevant to those who were not Roman citizens. They were not imposed on non-Romans because there was no reason to do so. Just as the Romans differed from others and lived according to their own set of civil laws, they worshipped their gods in accordance with their special traditions. Others could be expected to honour their own native deities in the same way.

In the western Mediterranean world, the Romans encountered established Middle Eastern temple cults, native religions with tribal gods akin to classical Greco-Roman deities, as well as the worship of a variety of local gods of nature. The religion of the Carthaginians was in many ways similar to that of the Romans, even though the former was adapted from Phoenician civic cults. Faced with gods and goddesses whose counterparts existed throughout the Mediterranean and Middle East, the Romans could employ the same technique of translation by which the Greeks had earlier turned Roman deities into their Greek equivalents. Thus the Punic deities Baal Hammon, Tanit, Shadrapa and Melqart became known respectively as Saturn, Juno Caelestis, Bacchus and Hercules. But the change of name did not mean the wholesale replacement of Punic religious beliefs with Roman ones. In Roman religion, Jupiter was the supreme god while Saturn, an old Italo-Roman deity associated with King Numa, was an obscure deity known chiefly on account of the Saturnalia, a merry-making festival in mid-December. In North Africa, however, the importance of even Jupiter paled considerably in comparison with that of Saturn, in whose honour many children were named, showing quite clearly the continued relevance of the basic framework of Punic religious beliefs and practices even after the names of the gods had been Latinised. One should not over-estimate the ability of either Punic or Roman temple religion to transform the religious beliefs and practices of those living in the countryside either. In North Africa, neither the Carthaginians nor the Romans completely altered the indigenous Berber people's devotion to local nature spirits, who according to Augustine of Hippo were still widely worshipped even by Christians in the fifth century AD.

The well-known example of the cult of Sulis at Bath demonstrates a typical encounter between the Romans and gods of nature. A goddess of the sun (Irish *suil*), she was the local deity who presided over hot springs on which a world famous spa was built during Nero's reign. The *aquae Sulis* became an international site for healing, and Romans who frequented it associated it with the healing Minerva, *Minerva medica*. The Celtic goddess fused with the Roman Minerva in the official nomenclature: Sulis Minerva. But this dual name is no evidence that the way the deity was worshipped at Bath necessarily resembled pre-Roman religious practices at such a major site.

Gods of nature also abounded in Gaul. Historians and archaeologists know of some four hundred pre-Roman Celtic deities, patrons of tree groves, springs, caves and tops of mountains and the like. Caesar and other later Roman observers typically employed *interpretatio romana* to turn these deities into the more anthropomorphised forms familiar to their Greco-Roman readers. Thus Teutates became Mercury, Belen Apollo, Esus Mars, and Taranis Jupiter. This form of syncretism did not so much make a hybrid out of the existing religious forms of worship as lead, in time, to the thorough Romanisation of the native deities until very little of the original beliefs and practices remained. Interestingly, many of these sites later became the locations were local (Christian) Gallo-Roman martyr shrines would be built during late antiquity.

Julius Caesar on the gods of the Gauls

Among the gods, they worship Mercury in particular. There are numerous images of him; they claim that he is the inventor of all crafts, the guide for all roads and journeys; they consider that he has especial power over money-making and trade. After him, they worship Apollo and Mars and Jupiter and Minerva. On these deities they have roughly the same views as the other nations – that Apollo dispels sickness, that Minerva bestows the principles of arts and crafts, that Jupiter holds sway in heaven, that Mars controls wars. It is to Mars, after deciding to enter battle, they normally vow whatever spoils they may take in the conflict.

Caesar Gallic War 6.17

INTERNATIONAL GODS

The worship of these Romanised Punic and Celtic deities was for the most part restricted to their own home regions. Such gods had little power further afield. Yet from the Hellenistic period to the Roman, several originally indigenous deities managed to become internationally known and revered. Many of these were of eastern extraction, coming from Asia Minor, the Middle East and Egypt. It may seem odd how well these deities competed with the original gods of Rome, the imperial power, but religious change was inevitable within an emerging world empire. Roman cities became cosmopolitan places to which different groups brought their own native gods and forms of worship. Roman rule made possible, and at times inevitable, a high degree of internal migration.

Among the migrants were ethnic Greeks, many of whom came to Rome either as war captives or as entrepreneurs seeking opportunities in the new centre of power. Hellenisation created an even larger pool of Greek-speakers whose importance as traders, soldiers and conduits of culture became increasingly evident under the Empire. Among these were Syrians who brought their religious cults with them to the western Mediterranean. The wide diffusion of a large number of gods who claimed Syrian descent during the Roman period had as much to do with the general reputation of the East as a potent source of religious authority as with the entrepreneurial spirit and geographic ubiquity of these Greek Syrians.

Among the Syrian gods who attained universal fame was Baal Haddad, who with his consort Atargartis-Astarte was worshipped in the ancient Phoenician city of Baalbek in modern Lebanon. The Romans renamed the city Heliopolis when they made it a colony, and this local Baal became henceforth known as Jupiter (or Zeus in Greek) of Heliopolis. The giant monumental temple complex containing his golden image came to be honoured by those outside the region as a site of a powerful oracle consulted even by Roman emperors. The god, known as Jupiter Optimus Maximus Heliopolitanus, was himself transformed in the popular imagination to a cosmic deity who wielded power over all things. Still, even a more obscure Baal from a far less prestigious site could aspire for greatness in this world of equal religious opportunity. By origins a Hittite sky god, Jupiter Dolichenus hailed originally from a humble town in Commagene, now in south-east Turkey. In the Roman period, this former Baal took on the appearance of a warrior god wearing a breastplate and wielding a double axe. He also sported the grandiose title of Jupiter Optimus Maximus Dolichenus, a not-so-subtle hint that this provincial deity claimed equality in importance with Rome's chief god, not to mention his Syrian cousin from Heliopolis. This Dolichene god even had as his consort an Anatolian mother goddess, known in Latin as Juno Dolichena. His cult spread throughout the Empire and two temples were dedicated to the god in Rome by priests and eager devotees. His followers were mainly easterners, many of whom were soldiers; they were later joined by others in the army. These adherents of the cult transported it with them whenever they moved from one part of the Empire to another. Jupiter Dolichenus was sometimes combined with Jupiter Heliopolitanus, and evidence for the veneration of both can be found as far away from their Syrian home as Britain, Gaul and Germany.

THE GOD OF THE JEWS

The Yahweh of the Jews also of course numbers among the Syro-Palestinian deities who were successful in appealing to a wide audience. The Jews were known since the Hellenistic period for the antiquity of their religion. The eastern wars of Pompey introduced large numbers of Jewish captives to Rome and, together with the settlement of Jews in the coastal cities of the Roman world and in Mesopotamia, they comprised a far-flung Jewish Diaspora united by a shared temple cult. The Jewish revolt of AD 66–70 was a traumatic event that ended in the destruction of the second Temple of Jerusalem, the centre of the Jews' national sacrificial cult; after this Jews continued to meet in local synagogues and worshipped according to rituals that derived their symbolism from the lost temple. Interestingly, even non-Jews sought to tap into the power offered by the God of the Jews, some even becoming 'god-fearers', a category of gentiles, or non-Jews, who practised some but not all the tenets of the Jewish law in the Roman world. The power of the Jewish god is also invoked in other ways such as in magical spells found on papyri in Egypt; Jews themselves, particularly the figure of Moses, were commonly regarded as powerful magicians.

THE JEWISH REVOLT

The Roman authorities honoured the Jews' religion and gave them freedom to practice it. But recurring tensions between Jews and their non-Jewish neighbours and unhappiness about the Romans' support for an aristocratic, theocratic state in Judaea eventually led to the revolt, violent repression and a temporary Roman effort to circumscribe the practice and spread of Judaism.

As the Roman Empire took an ever firmer grip on the Mediterranean region so to the Jewish Diaspora became more widespread. From the first century BC, at which point many Jews had settled in the coastal regions of the eastern Mediterranean to the end of the third century AD, towards the end of the Empire, Jews moved progressively westward.

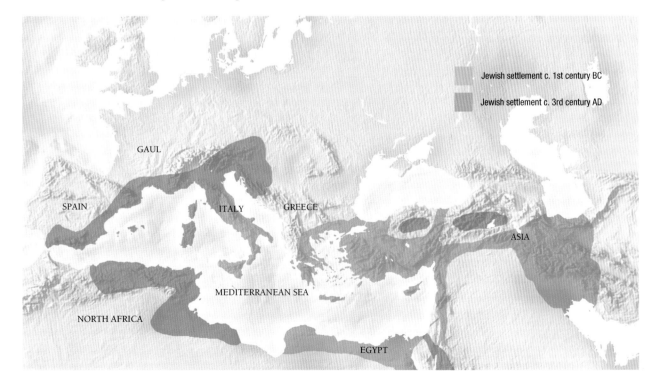

Jewish settlement c. 1st century BC

Jewish settlement c. 3rd century AD

GAUL

SPAIN

ITALY   GREECE

ASIA

MEDITERRANEAN SEA

NORTH AFRICA

EGYPT

EGYPTIAN GODS

The Egyptian religion was another native tradition that struck the Greeks and Romans as both very ancient and rather odd. Ever since the time of Herodotus in the fifth century BC, visitors to the Nile had been awed by the monumental architecture they encountered and by the great antiquity of the land and its customs, safeguarded by a long line of temple priests by hieroglyphics, an arcane sacred script. Alexander the Great's famous visit to the Oracle of Ammon in the Siwa Oasis in modern Libya established the reputation of this particular Egyptian god as an authoritative source of prophecy on a par with the Delphic Apollo or Zeus at Dodona. Despite the attempts by Herodotus and others to read Egyptian religion by means of *interpretatio graeca*, Greeks and Romans regarded most of the gods of Egypt as very different from their own. Many Egyptian deities had animal attributes and were represented in zoomorphic form, alienating Greeks and Romans who preferred anthropomorphic deities. Certain local religious rituals likewise seemed bizarre to outsiders: the embalming of crocodiles and other sacred animals was taken to mean that the Egyptians worshipped dead animals, which – to the Greeks and Romans – was a sure sign of the superstitious folly of Egypt's people. But then Egypt had long enjoyed the reputation as the country in which all customs were the inverse of those practised by other nations. This essentialist premise made Greeks and Romans alike unwilling to meddle in native Egyptian religious traditions, however bizarre and repulsive they seemed. Instead Hellenistic Greek rulers and Roman emperors carefully cultivated the many Egyptian cults. In return they were seen by locals as native pharaohs and legitimate rulers of the land of Egypt.

THE CULT OF SARAPIS

The great reputation of Egypt as the fount of an impressive alien wisdom meant that in time a number of its deities would find worshippers among even non-Egyptians. Sarapis was one such deity. A conflation of the god Osiris and the sacred Apis bulls, Osor-apis, a god of the underworld, became Hellenised as Sarapis in the Hellenistic period. He came to Alexandria under the auspices of Ptolemaic kings who associated their own royal power with the god, who was henceforth given the title of 'Zeus Sarapis'. The Sarapis who showed up in Mediterranean cities appeared as a stately bearded male god strongly reminiscent of the portraiture of Zeus, whereas in mythological terms the Greeks had trouble fitting him in precisely with known Greek gods, identifying him variously with Zeus, Dionysus, Asclepius and even Pluto. Healing remained Sarapis's main function and to his temples came individuals eager to receive divine cures through healing dreams, a process known as incubation. While a hereditary Egyptian priesthood continued to maintain the cult of the Apis bulls at Memphis, the cult took a different form outside Egypt and had devotees in voluntary sacred associations. The Hellenised cult of Sarapis became the first Egyptian religion to find support among the non-Egyptian population of the wider Mediterranean world. Hellenistic kings and later Roman emperors paid homage to Sarapis, and Vespasian even proclaimed himself a 'New Sarapis' in his bid for imperial power and legitimacy.

THE CULT OF ISIS

Isis was another major Egyptian deity who broke into the international scene; in the first century AD Vitruvius took it for granted that all Italian cities would have temples to Sarapis and Isis. Mother of Horus and consort of Osiris, Isis in Egyptian sacred lore searched the earth to recover her husband's dismembered body, a myth that clearly had to do with fertility and the annual 'death' and 'rebirth' of crops. Her story was recast by Hellenised Egyptian priests in Greek form and the goddess began to gain currency as a cosmic saviour wielding great powers over the elements. First established in Alexandria on the island of Pharos, Isis appeared as the protector of those who travelled by sea and in Rome her annual festival celebrated the opening of the sailing season. In all the places where her cult took root, including at her well-known temples in the Campus Martius and Pompeii, Isis was accompanied by personnel and cult objects featuring Egyptian-style motifs to underscore the fact that she encapsulated all the awesome religious aura of the Egyptians. Isis balanced her image as an Egyptian goddess with a broad reputation as a transcendent goddess whose power to protect and save extended far beyond her native land. A Latin inscription invokes her as the 'one who art all things', while Apuleius concocts an even more elaborate set of praises for her in his *Metamorphoses*: 'first of heavenly beings, the single appearance of the gods and goddesses, the Mother of the gods, Minerva, Venus, Diana, Prosperina, Ceres, Juno, Bellona, Hecate, Nemesis; her true name, known in Ethiopia and in Egypt as Queen Isis.'

Isis and Mithras are often paired in modern accounts as the two eastern deities most popular among the Romans. Represented in iconography as an easterner in Persian dress and donning a Phyrgian cap, Mithras is often shown in the act of killing a bull, a scene that served as the central image in his shrines (*mithraea*) throughout the Roman world. His origins remain in dispute. Current theories suggest he originated as the proto-Indo-Iranian deity Mithra, known from the Vedas, or see him as a creation of Stoic intellectuals in Hellenistic Tarsus in response to an observed astronomical anomaly in the heavens, or as the invention of people of the Rhineland or Rome's eastern frontier (Commagene). Some even contend that Rome itself gave birth to this 'foreign' god. Whatever his provenance, Mithras appeared to the Romans as a universal saviour figure whose triumph over the elemental forces of an otherwise fatally deterministic universe is symbolised by the familiar bull-slaying scene. His cult was popular in the second and third century AD, particularly along the Rhine and Danube and in Rome and Ostia. Like the cult of Isis, Mithraism was a religion of graded mystical initiations through which an adherent would advance to an ever closer union with the god. In the late nineteenth century, the historian Ernest Renan famously claimed that the cult of Mithraism was the functional equivalent of Christianity and would have conquered the rest of the Roman world had it not been for the latter's triumph, but the fact that Mithraism drew exclusively from the male population rendered it much less universal in appeal. As a fraternal organisation, Mithraism's strong hierarchical structure is reminiscent of the Roman army and administration from which it drew most of its followers. When certain men from these groups rose to positions of higher authority it was inevitable that the worship of Mithras would eventually attract imperial support and become associated with the solar cult of the Unconquered Sun (*see* page 283).

A carved stone relief from the Circus Maximus in Rome, with the central image of Mithras killing a bull. With its emphasis on personal and individual 'salvation', Mithraism was an ideal barrack-room religion. Unlike the state cult, the essential elements of the belief system could be reduced to a few symbolic graphic icons, such as the scorpion, that were easily understood by illiterate converts.

IN SEARCH OF AN IMPERIAL RELIGION

In AD 212, Caracalla granted Roman citizenship to all the free inhabitants of the Roman world with the expressed goal of unifying all people in common religious worship of the Roman gods. A more careful examination of the law's context shows that the Antonine Constitution was meant to raise state revenues by increasing the number of people liable to Roman estate taxes. Even so, this change effectively made the religion of the Romans the religion of everyone in the Empire, so that the Capitoline Triad now made an appearance even in the Egyptian countryside where little Romanisation had previously taken place. But this change was not meant to undermine worship of the local gods since it was assumed that all provincials, now also Romans, would continue to revere them as well as the gods of Rome. In a similar way, individuals did not give up citizenship in their local cities as a result of Caracalla's grant of Roman citizenship but were henceforth at once citizens of Alexandria, say, and Rome – their *communis patria* – having obligations to both.

The attempt to create a unified pantheon in the early Empire did not create a universal imperial religion. Nonetheless, there emerged deities whose adherents claimed for them greater and greater honours, thereby creating in effect a category of universal gods and goddesses whose powers were regarded as extending to all inhabitants of the Roman world. An awareness of the collectivity of all the gods in the Empire was amplified by the perceived need for their care in a time of troubles. Efforts to cultivate a *pax deorum*, a Peace of the Gods, united the religious and political interests of the Empire's people, from the emperors down. Syncretism became a means of pooling the power of the gods – there could presumably never be too many gods on one's side. According to the *Augustan History*, Severus Alexander had images of the household gods and deified emperors placed in his private chapel in Rome, alongside those of Apollonius of Tyana, Christ, Abraham and Orpheus.

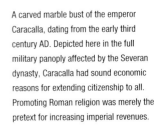

A carved marble bust of the emperor Caracalla, dating from the early third century AD. Depicted here in the full military panoply affected by the Severan dynasty, Caracalla had sound economic reasons for extending citizenship to all. Promoting Roman religion was merely the pretext for increasing imperial revenues.

The philosophical speculations of the elite had long given credence to a growing belief that behind the plethora of polytheistic gods lurked a more fundamental, single divine power. Philosophers were also the first to oppose seeing the gods in anthropomorphic form and to read the adulteries of a Zeus as a spiritual allegory rather than a story about how divine beings truly behaved – that is, immorally. Some found it difficult to accept that people would worship idols fashioned by human hands, choosing to see particular native gods rather as emanations of a unitary divine force underlying all things in the universe. But these non-traditional views about the nature of the gods caused no public conflict. Polytheism valued participation more than belief, and generally ancient philosophers did not forsake the practice of public religion even though they might emphasise private, spiritual prayers and sacrifices in their writings or in their own private lives.

The political and philosophical tendency to seek a unifying divine power in the universe culminated in the worship of Sol, the sun. Sol Indiges was an early Italic deity worshipped by the Romans as well as their Latin neighbours. The Greek Helios was of course also known in Italy; so too was Apollo. Augustus had a temple dedicated to the solar Apollo on the Palatine while Nero often styled himself as Helios. In AD 102, the first Middle Eastern sun god came to Rome and honorific mentions of the Unconquered Sun (Sol Invictus) first appeared in the middle of the second century. Septimius Severus had added a radiant solar nimbus to his own imperial image and henceforth emperors of the Severan dynasty were addressed as *invicti*, a title normally associated with the sun god Sol.

The decisive influence might have come from Septimius's wife Julia Domna and her sister Julia Maesa, daughters of the high priest of the sun god Elagabal in Emesa in Syria. Septimius's grandson Varius Avitus had been a priest of Elagabal prior to assuming the purple, so that when he came to Rome in AD 218–19 he brought with him the god's famous black baetyl, or stone stele, which he installed with the sacred symbol of Carthage's Tanit, or Juno Caelestis, in a temple on the Palatine. This zealous emperor, better known as Elagabalus, renamed the Temple of Jupiter Ultor the Temple of Jupiter Victor, thereby merging the native Roman cult of Iuppiter with that of Sol Invictus in a process we might call *intepretatio syriaca*. Under Elagabalus, Sol Invictus became briefly the chief god of Rome. His act of making a foreign god not only the equal but the superior of Rome's indigenous pantheon offended the sensibilities of the Romans of Rome so much that after Elagabalus was assassinated, his successor Alexander quickly rededicated the temple to Jupiter Ultor and struck a medallion on which Jupiter himself is represented as electing Alexander emperor of the Romans.

Alexander Severus underscored his image as the restitutor of *res antiqui* by repatriating the baetyls of Elagabal and Tanit and at the same time restoring traditional shrines and cultic sites in Rome. But Sol Invictus would not be denied his due for long. In AD 274, Aurelian installed another Sol Invictus, with a new priestly college dedicated to the god, as the primary object of public and imperial worship in Rome and the Empire, making 25 December, the god's birthday, a public holiday (the same date was of course later adopted by the Christians as the birthday

of the Son their own God). Given the difficulties the Empire was facing at the time, the Romans generally found it more expedient to imagine all their gods as working in concert to promote and secure the welfare of their state, in which the gods of Rome still played a large role.

The imperial promotion of Sol Invictus in the late Empire was at times balanced by efforts to channel devotion to Jupiter. Trajan had long ago shown himself as having been given the right to rule by Jupiter on the Arch of Beneventum. In the tetrarchy of Diocletian, the reigning emperors were associated even more closely with the gods Jupiter and Hercules, so that the two emperors of the senior imperial house held the title of *Jovii* and those of the junior one that of *Herculii*; the explanation offered was that just as Jupiter ruled the heavens and Hercules maintained peace on earth, together these two imperial houses cooperated to protect the peace and tranquillity of the *pax romana*.

Detail of a badly weathered stone relief from the arch of Trajan at Benevento, Italy. The scene depicts the dead emperor being welcomed into the pantheon by Jupiter (at left) and other gods. Trajan (at right) is hooded beneath his laurel crown. According to Roman artistic tradition, deceased citizens of all social classes were portrayed wearing a hood.

THE GOD OF EMPIRE

Issued in AD 297, Diocletian's first edict of persecution was aimed at the Manichaeans, whom he portrayed as Persian fifth-columnists who misled the people and endangered the safety of the Roman state. In 303, the emperor turned his attention to another group of religious sectarians, the Christians. With its founder executed in a manner befitting criminals, Christianity began as a dissident splinter group within Judaism but quickly became a popular urban religion among gentiles or non-Jews. Their neighbours long regarded the Christians with suspicion, not so much because of their beliefs – though these seemed outlandish enough – as on account of their refusal to participate in civic religious rituals. The failure to worship the gods of the ancestors seemed to traditional Romans the very essence of atheism, and at times local tensions escalated into conflicts and persecutions. Many rumours circulated that portrayed Christians as engaging in orgies and cannibalism, distortions of the Christian celebrations of the *agape*, love feast, and the eucharist.

While the Roman authorities did not on the whole believe these charges, they began to take the initiative in persecuting Christians towards the end of the third century AD. Before that, Roman officials had opted to punish only those brought to their attention and who, even after repeated invitations to recant, persisted in professing their faith. It was the sheer obstinacy of these followers of Christ that led even enlightened Romans such as the governor Pliny the Younger and his emperor Trajan to sentence them to death.

For all this, the Christians were not actually rebels against the Empire, having been taught to 'render unto Caesar'. Christian worship shared many similarities with the Greco-Roman voluntary religious associations devoted to the mystery religions of Mithras and Isis – except that, rather than claiming that theirs was the best of the gods, Christians as well as Jews claimed that theirs was the *only* God. But whereas the Jews could claim the antiquity of their religion as justification for their strict monotheism, the Christians tried but failed to convince the pagan authorities that they were in fact the 'True Israel', rightful heir of the Jews' sacred books and of Judaism's status. Christians, mostly converts from polytheism, were left with a grim choice: return to the religious custom of their ancestors and worship the gods, or face the charge of atheism. Those who chose the latter underwent what Christians called martyrdom, a form of witnessing for Christ, by which, according to some contemporaries, they gained immediate entrance into Paradise.

A massive stone head of Constantine the Great in the Museo del Palazzo dei Conservatori, Rome. Intended to overawe through its sheer size, the portrait reveals little, if any, personal detail. Under the Tetrarchy, art served to convey the uniform and unvarying authority of the Augustii and Caesars, rather than any quirks of individual appearance or personality.

The persecutors of the Christians believed that the Christians' refusal to give the many gods of the Empire their due placed everyone in jeopardy, for they had breached the *pax deorum*. The precarious state of the Empire in the late second to the third century increased this anxiety. Now angered by neglect, these gods showed their displeasure by afflicting the Roman people with numerous woes. In many ways, this was a classic case of scapegoating and yet it also suggests a fear of Christianity's ability to redirect individual loyalties to new, non-legitimate social bodies and ideals. In time, it became clear that even concerted state persecution was failing to achieve its purpose of making Christians abandon their folly. Thus Galerius gave up the campaign in 311 and issued an edict of toleration asking Christians to pray for the emperors and the Empire for the common good of all. The Empire needed the corporate protection of all the gods, including that of the Christians.

On the eve of the battle of the Milvian Bridge in 312, Constantine, according to later statements, received in a dream the instructions to display the insignia of Christ, under which he was to conquer his enemies. His subsequent victory over Maxentius seemed to confirm the belief that Christ was a bringer of victory in battle and a worthy patron deity for an ambitious ruler. Constantine prevailed upon his eastern colleague of the time, the pagan Licinius, to issue a joint statement confirming the

The pediment frieze on an Italian villa designed by Andrea Palladio, depicting the execution of Christians at the feet of a Roman emperor. Christians were easy scapegoats from the time of Nero, and their new religion was not accorded the same grudging toleration as that of the Jews, which the Romans considered to be sanctified by its antiquity.

toleration of Christians throughout the empire. The basic idea that all the gods could somehow work together did not survive long, but some of its underlying notions were remarkably persistent. Years after he accepted Christianity in 312, the first Christian emperor continued to issue coins with images of Sol Invictus, which he associated with the glory of the Roman state, and even erected a statue of himself with a crown of solar rays and a thunderbolt in his hand in Constantinople, his new city. This might have been syncretism at work or, more likely, evidence for how Constantine cleverly adapted traditional symbols to represent his new god in a manner fit for public consumption. Yet in the long run the strict monotheism of Christianity made any pragmatic accommodation impossible, since the God of the Christians would tolerate no equal. To Christians, the many gods of the polytheists were not gods at all but evil demons. Yet while Constantine did institute certain changes to favour Christians, he took few real steps to sever the bonds between the Empire and its many gods. There was certainly as yet no decisive alliance between Empire and Church.

Many decades elapsed before Christian emperors finally established Christianity as the Roman Empire's state religion. Some of the first steps taken were those against religious practices that Christians found most abhorrent, such as the sacrifice of animals. At first there were to be no public sacrifices; later private ones were also banned. Without them, the *res sacra* could no longer be carried out and the notion of magistrates and emperors as priests who sacrificed on behalf of the community at large became an untenable one. The whole fabric that united the Roman state and the worship of the gods was slowly unravelled. Constantine had once granted Christian clergy the same tax exemptions as those enjoyed by holders of priestly offices; in 396, his successors moved to strip the pagan priests of their immunity from taxation. The marginalisation of traditional priesthoods was underscored when Gratian renounced the robes of the *pontifex maximus*, an office held by all his imperial predecessors since the time of Augustus. The same emperor caused the Altar of Victory in the senate house in Rome to be removed, much to the dismay of pagan senators such as Symmachus the Elder who, as prefect of the city, pleaded for its return by arguing that even a Christianising empire had need of victory. But ultimately the arguments of his opponent Ambrose, bishop of Milan, prevailed and the altar was never restored.

Taking many forms, the worship of the gods had long been an integral part of Roman society so that it was impossible to separate out neatly what was religious, political, social and cultural. Yet Christians persevered in singling out certain elements of the old society as pagan and therefore to be destroyed. Even the physical landscape changed as temples, once the houses of the gods, were condemned as places of demonic possession and pollution. Christian vigilantes took the lead. In 392, under the direction of Bishop Theophilus of Alexandria, local Christians decapitated the statue of Sarapis and destroyed his famous temple. When this illegal act went unpunished, other Christians followed suit elsewhere. Now even the many shrines and temples to deities in the Egyptian countryside, which had survived the coming of the Greeks and Romans, were demolished one after another. It was the same outside Egypt. Soon the emperors declared an open season on temples in the countryside, while temples in the cities were shut down but not destroyed. Taken as a whole, such events in the last decades of the fourth century marked a watershed when Rome's public officials turned their collective back on its ancient gods, pronouncing the customary rite of sacrifice to be an abomination and traditional religion itself to be *superstitio*. But not everything was changed overnight. The festivals of the gods had long defined the annual rhythm of many communities, and these communal rituals persisted in many places well after the closing of temples and the end of sacrifices. Some were renamed to remove any damaging association with pagan religious cults. Others, such as the Kalends of January or the festival of the New Year, became increasingly regarded as 'secular' holidays devoid of religious meaning.

These transformations took place during a time of uncertainty as the Empire suffered one humiliating setback after another: Valens was defeated and killed by the Goths at the battle of Adrianople in 378, Rome was sacked by the army of Alaric in 410 and Carthage, that 'Rome in Africa', fell to the Germanic Vandals in 439. Some bemoaned the coming of evil times, blaming the widespread abandonment of sacrificial rites and the breach of the *pax deorum* with the disappearance of the divine protection that the Romans had enjoyed. The whole history of the relationship between Rome and its gods came under review in the polemical exchanges that ensued. Augustine of Hippo's monumental *City of God* gave voice to one side of the debate by using Roman antiquarian and historical texts to show how the Roman gods had never been very good at aiding the Romans in the first place. But his argument turned from asserting that the Romans often suffered reverses, even while offering sacrifices to the gods, to the far more radical claim that no necessary correlation existed between divine favour and earthly prosperity. According to Augustine, God allowed bad things to happen even to good people in order to teach them spiritual lessons and wean them from any attachment to the transient City of Man. His willingness to abandon the comfortable traditional religious paradigm underlying the *pax deorum* was not widely shared at the time. Most people clung to the belief that the new God of the Roman Empire was also a saving god who answered prayers and protected his people. Local Christians continued to consider Christ and martyrs as their own special protectors and in the city of Rome itself the apostles Peter and Paul were promoted as the new Dioscuri and joint patrons of *Roma aeterna*. A Christian empire eventually emerged under the protection of the *pax Dei*, the Peace of God. One of its earliest proponents, the church historian and Constantine's biographer Eusebius of Caesarea, saw providence at work in joining the fates of the Empire and Christianity, as clearly seen in the birth of Jesus during the reign of the first emperor, Augustus. Constantine's reign began an alliance that deepened over the next century. By the later fourth century, religious nonconformity had become a civil offence punishable by the state. Pagans and Manichaeans bore the brunt of these laws, while Jews were more restricted in their religious practice than before. Under Theodosius I, Christians whose beliefs did not match the orthodoxy defined by the state were persecuted as heretics. Holding a prescribed set of correct beliefs about the divine had become the mark of a good Roman citizen. With this, the spirit of religious toleration that had once existed within the multi-ethnic and polytheistic Roman Empire began to give way to the zealous enforcement of a single monotheistic creed.

Prudentius prays for a Christian Rome

Grant, Christ, to your Romans that the city through which you have granted that all other cities shall be of one mind in worship may be Christian. All the parts of the Empire are allied in faith; the world it has subdued grows gentle. May its capital too grow gentle. May she see that lands far apart are uniting in one state of grace; may Romulus become one of the faithful and let Numa himself now believe… Depart adulterous Jupiter, defiled with sex with your sister, leave Rome free and flee from its people who are now Christ's. Paul exiles you from here, and the blood of Peter drives you out, and the deeds of Nero, for which you put the sword in his hand, redounds on you.

Prudentius Crowns of Martyrdom *2.4.33*

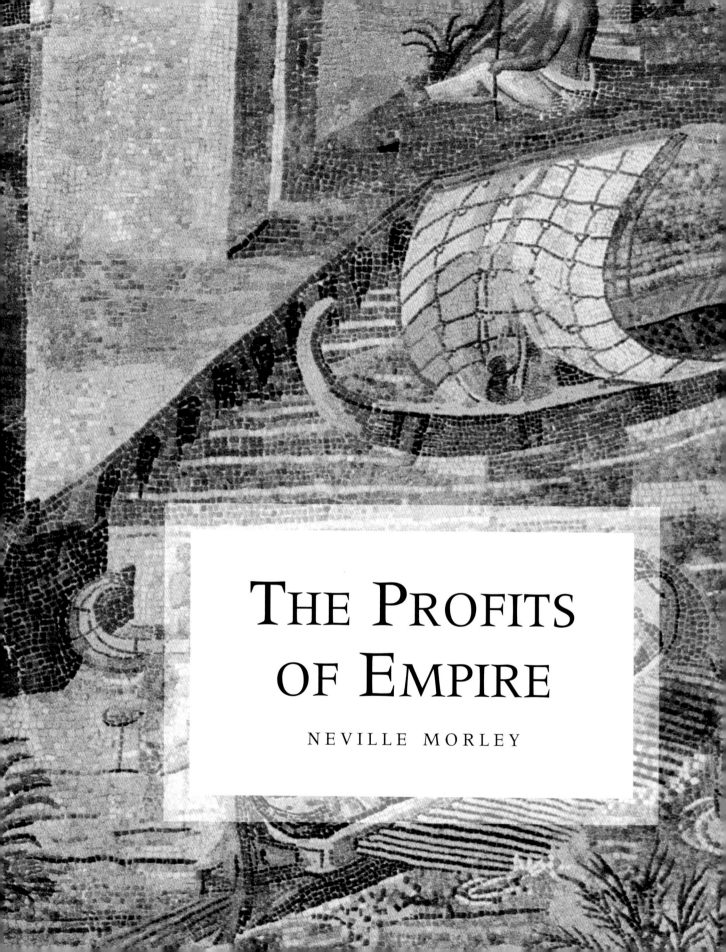

THE PROFITS
OF EMPIRE

NEVILLE MORLEY

THE PROFITS OF EMPIRE

Successful conquest was extremely profitable. The figures are astonishing: the defeat of Macedonia in 167 BC, for example, brought in 120 million sesterces of booty. It is difficult to quantify this in modern terms, but 120 sesterces could buy enough grain to feed someone at a basic level for a year; the annual wage of a Roman soldier was 1,200 sesterces, while the minimum property qualification to become a member of the Augustan Senate was one million. Macedonia also brought in an annual revenue of 2.4 million sesterces; the Spanish silver mines brought in 36.5 million every year; the cities of Greece and Asia were required to pay 720 million in tribute in 70 BC; the treasury of Mithridates, captured by Pompey, contained some 860 million. There is little wonder that Rome came to be known as *aurea*, golden. A passage in the Jewish *Talmud* remarks: 'Ten portions of wisdom descended to the world: nine were taken by Palestine and one by the rest of the world… Ten portions of wealth descended to the world: nine were taken by Rome and one by the rest of the world.'

A Renaissance fresco by Francesco Cecchino depicting the triumphal procession of the Roman general Marcus Furius Camilius at the end of the fifth century BC. At this early time, Rome's wars were fought mainly to ensure the continuation of the state as an independent entity. Nevertheless, economic benefits did accrue in the form of tribute and booty.

The profits of empire were shared – very unequally – among all Roman citizens. The state received taxes and tribute in money and goods (grain from Sicily and Egypt, for example), at first irregularly and then, from the first century BC, through a regular system of direct tax; it also collected revenue from mines, quarries and confiscated land, and income from customs dues and other indirect taxes. Ordinary Roman citizens benefited from the abolition of the *tributum*, the direct land-tax, after the conquest of Macedonia. Those who lived in Rome itself might receive a share of the grain collected as tribute, which was at first sold at below the market rate and later (from the first century BC) distributed free. They could also enjoy the aqueducts, sewers, theatres and other public buildings built with the proceeds of conquest.

Some individuals profited to a spectacular degree. The successful general controlled the distribution of booty, collected gifts from conquered cities hoping for favourable treatment and received the proceeds from the sale of captives into slavery – Caesar's campaigns in Gaul produced perhaps one million new slaves. Junior commanders, centurions and soldiers received a share of the booty, while some Romans profited from war before, or even regardless of, victory; they signed lucrative contracts to supply the army with food, clothing and equipment. Peace brought more opportunities. Members of the political elite could hope to receive millions of sesterces in gifts and bribes while serving as provincial governors, with only a limited risk of prosecution for extortion when they completed their term of office. Cicero makes a show of his honesty and integrity as governor of Cilicia, and still admits to receiving 2.2 million sesterces; he accuses Verres, the governor of Sicily whom he prosecuted for extortion in 70 BC, of amassing 40 million in three years. Other wealthy Romans bid for the profitable contracts for tax collection (these contractors, known as *publicani*, became widely hated for their alleged greed and extortionate practices) and for the exploitation of public assets like mines. Still others made their fortunes by lending money, at high rates of compound interest, to provincial cities to help them pay the tribute demanded by Rome. Many acquired extensive estates in the provinces; by the time of Nero, half of Africa was said to be owned by just six men.

Roman conquest was of course devastating for the conquered, at least in the short term. Populations were reduced through death and slavery, cities and regions were plunged into debt by the need to pay tribute, and large quantities of wealth were simply carried off – the percentage of precious metal in Gallic coinage collapsed over the course of Caesar's campaign. The picture over the long term is less clear, especially once Rome moved to a system of regular taxation at a reasonable rate instead of punitive exactions of tribute. In many provinces, the level of taxation was no higher than it had been before the conquest – although the taxes were now being spent outside the region, mainly in Rome and Italy, so that provincial wealth was being steadily drained away. At the same time, Roman rule brought about various changes in provincial societies, not least by incorporating them into a Mediterranean-wide imperial system. The loss of political independence was, perhaps, balanced by an increase in economic opportunities. The aim of this chapter is not to provide a balance sheet of Roman imperialism but to consider how far the expansion of the Roman Empire transformed the traditional structures of the ancient economy.

A PRE-INDUSTRIAL ECONOMY

The ancient world is often described by historians as 'pre-industrial', to emphasise the enormous differences in economic organisation and performance between it and a modern industrial society like our own. Sometimes, indeed, antiquity is described as 'underdeveloped' or even 'primitive'. This may seem to be an excessively negative judgement, given the achievements of the Greeks and Romans in architecture, art, literature, philosophy and other areas of culture; but of course it is not intended to apply to classical civilisation as a whole, just to its economic structures. The level of economic development of a society does not necessarily determine its level of political or cultural sophistication. However, the economy does produce the surplus wealth that allows people to do more than just survive, that enables them to build an empire and a culture. The development of classical civilisation seems all the more remarkable because it was achieved on the basis of relatively primitive and inefficient techniques of production and a relatively low level of technology, which set strict limits on the potential for economic growth.

One of the most important characteristics of a pre-industrial economy is that it depends on the produce of the land not only for food but for many raw materials (wood, wool, hides) and for most of its sources of heat and power (wood, charcoal, food to support human and animal workers). Land, especially land that is fertile and easily cultivated, is a finite resource, which sets a theoretical ultimate limit on how far the economy can expand. Under pressure of an expanding population, less fertile land can be brought under cultivation, but the costs of farming it may be greater than the resulting yields. Moreover, the expansion of agriculture onto marginal land generally involves the displacement of activities like herding and hunting, which may have serious consequences for the lives of some members of society. The alternative way of increasing overall production is to increase the yield from the land already being farmed, either by increasing the amount of labour used to cultivate it or by investing more money (to buy an ox, for example, or to bring in extra manure). However, before the invention of chemical fertilisers, there is a limit to how far yields can be increased in the long term without exhausting the fertility of the land. Ancient farmers often had to leave their land fallow every other year, to allow it to recover its fertility; this was vital for long-term survival, but it put another limit on the level of production in the ancient Mediterranean, and hence on the number of people that could be supported at a given level of prosperity.

Another important characteristic of the pre-industrial economy is that the sources of power available to perform any task were 'organic' – above all, human and animal muscle – rather than the mineral energy (coal, oil, gas) that underpins the modern economy. The productivity of human muscles, the amount of work that an individual can do in a given time, is low; it is even lower if, as seems likely for most people in the ancient world, the worker is undernourished. The productivity of a man driving an ox-drawn plough or leading an ox-drawn wagon is much higher. However, a pre-industrial society may not be able to support a large number of oxen, since they compete with humans for the produce of the land. The rich landowner could afford to keep them, and would benefit not only from their labour but also from their manure, replenishing the fertility of his fields. The poorest peasants did not own enough land to feed an ox as well as their families, and they could hardly make their families redundant in favour of an ox. The result is a low average productivity of labour, which means that surplus production, the amount produced above what was needed to feed the farmer and his family, must also have been low. Today, a farmer with a tractor and a combine harvester can produce enough food to feed one hundred or more people; in a pre-industrial economy, the labour of nine or ten farmers and their families was needed to produce enough to feed one additional family of non-farmers.

The limitations of organic power affected other areas of the economy. Virtually all manufacturing was carried out by hand, and most craft production took place in small workshops or in the household. Larger workshops did exist, but they simply contained more workers carrying out the same tasks; there was little scope for economies of scale, whereas in the modern world it is normally much more economical to produce hundreds of items than to produce dozens. Some division of labour was possible in larger enterprises, so that a pot might be made by one worker and decorated by another, and the different stages of producing cloth from raw wool were separated and allocated to different workers. This gave the specialised workshop a small advantage in efficiency over household production, and its product might be

Detail of a carved stone sarcophagus from the Vatican Museum, dating from the fourth century AD. This wealthy Roman capitalist has combined the 'new' stone sarcophagus with the descriptive imagery of a traditional funerary stele. Beneath the upwardly gazing bust of the proprietor (the pose was popularised by Constantine the Great) the sculptor has depicted employees (or slaves) working at the ancient equivalent of a production line.

superior in quality. On the other hand, the peasant family with a small surplus might still prefer to expend labour rather than money, and carry on making its own textiles. Even if the manufacturing sector had the technology to expand its productivity, there was limited demand for its products and therefore limited incentive for anyone to invest heavily in equipment or labour.

Third, reliance on organic power made travel and transport slow and expensive. Over land, horses were fast but could carry little and were costly to maintain, and so only the wealthy and the agents of the state could afford them. Oxen could carry or pull much heavier loads but were slow, so that over any significant distance the value of the load could quickly be eaten up by the costs of feeding the draught animals. Humans were faster but could carry less, and were more expensive to maintain over long distances (needing shelter as well as food). Most land transport, therefore, tended to be short-haul: to the nearest town, river or coast. Water transport was much cheaper, especially for transporting bulky goods. However, only the largest rivers in the Mediterranean were suitable for regular transport; the others were raging torrents in the winter and sank too low in the summer months. Sea travel was risky – traditionally the Greeks and Romans avoided sailing during the winter months for fear of storms – and unreliable, since if the wind was contrary or lacking a ship could be stuck in harbour for days or even weeks.

RESPONSES TO RISK AND UNCERTAINTY

Agricultural productivity was limited further by the production strategies followed by many ancient farmers. Agriculture is always a risky activity, as suggested by 'Agathias the Astrologer' (actually a satire, dating to the sixth century AD): 'If your bit of land receives sufficient rain, and grows no crop of wild weeds; if frost does not break the furrows; if hail does not nip off the tops of the sprouting ears; if no deer grazes down the crops and if it meets with no other disaster from air or earth, I prophesy that your harvest will be excellent and you will cut the ears with success – only beware the locusts.' One of the features of the Mediterranean climate is its unpredictability and

Renaissance fresco by Jacopo Rip depicting Marcus Atilius Regulus advising the Romans not to make peace with the Carthaginians. Regulus was a Roman general and consul captured by the Carthaginians during the First Punic War. Released on condition that he negotiate a peace, Regulus did exactly the opposite, and then honourably returned to Carthage where he was tortured to death.

tendency to extremes, especially in its seasonal patterns of rainfall. The amount of rain varies enormously from year to year, from region to region and even within regions – in much of the Mediterranean, we find microclimates, variations in the weather even between adjacent valleys. The timing and the amount of rainfall are critical for the success of different crops; flood and drought could be equally fatal.

Most ancient farmers responded to these uncertain conditions by adopting a strategy of minimising risk. They tended to farm scattered holdings rather than a single consolidated plot; choosing to expend labour on travelling between fields, thus reducing their productivity, in the hope that if disaster struck one field the rest might escape. Rather than seeking to maximise their possible gains and economise on labour by growing a single marketable crop, they chose to make more work for themselves by growing a whole range of crops suited to different conditions, in the hope that a bad year would never leave them with nothing at all to eat. Both strategies are sensible, and well adapted to the environmental conditions of the Mediterranean and the level of available technology – but by modern standards such an approach is inefficient, limiting surplus production and the possibilities of expanding output.

Ancient farmers aimed as far as possible at self-sufficiency, producing what they needed themselves rather than relying on the market, and storing as much as possible so that they could get through a bad year. Again, by modern standards this is costly and inefficient; far better to specialise in a cash crop and purchase the goods you need from other specialist producers. That only works, however, if the market is reasonably efficient in ensuring that goods are available to meet demand. Ancient markets were not so efficient, since information could travel no faster than a ship or a horse. Cicero, in one of his philosophical discussions, uses the example of a grain merchant arriving in Rhodes in the middle of a famine; the moral question is whether the merchant should tell the Rhodians that more grain ships are on the way (causing the price of grain to fall), or keep quiet and make a fortune. It seems unlikely that a real merchant would hesitate for long over such a choice, but the situation is intended to be credible. This is a world in which it might take weeks before anyone outside a region would know that there had been a poor harvest, and weeks more before merchants could arrive with additional supplies.

At best, therefore, markets in different parts of the ancient world were poorly integrated with one another, and slow to respond to changes in demand. In some cases, they might not respond at all. For regions that were distant from the sea, the cost of transporting a bulky, cheap commodity like grain over any distance overland might be too great to leave sufficient margin for profit for the traders. This seems to have been the problem in AD 362, when the city of Antioch suffered from a severe food crisis while grain stocks were available less than eighty kilometres away. On that occasion, it took the intervention of the emperor to force traders to bring in supplies (not unfairly, since it was probably the arrival of his entourage in Antioch that caused the problem in the first place). The residents of other cities often had to rely on the generosity of the local aristocracy to solve food crises. In general, it was much safer, if you were able, to produce and store your own food, rather than producing a cash crop and then finding that there was no food in the market to purchase.

Pliny the Younger on the similarities between farming and the law

On my farms I cultivate my fruit trees and fields as carefully as my vineyards, and in the fields I sow barley, beans and other legumes, as well as corn and wheat; so when I am making a speech I scatter various arguments around like seeds in order to reap whatever crop comes up. There are as many unforeseen hazards and uncertainties to surmount in working on the minds of judges as in dealing with the problems of weather and soil.

Pliny the Younger Epistles *1.20*

LIMITS ON TRADE

Craftsmen and traders had no such insulation from the vagaries of market prices, since they had to buy their food. The size of most cities was therefore limited by the 'carrying capacity' of their immediate hinterlands, the number of people who could normally be supported from local produce. The capricious Mediterranean environment meant that every region, even if its population was below the carrying capacity of the land, sometimes had to find food from elsewhere, and sometimes had a surplus to export. Comparative evidence from the Mediterranean suggests that the wheat harvest might fail in a given region one year in every four.

The task of moving food supplies between areas of surplus and deficit provided a living for significant numbers of traders, but it was a precarious one. It was as risky to rely on the market for a living as it was to rely on it for food. As Cato argued, in the preface to a work urging Romans to stick to farming: 'The trader I consider to be an energetic man, and one bent on making money; but it is a dangerous career and one subject to disaster.' Not only was there the danger of losing the ship and cargo to a storm or to pirates, but there was also the difficulty, in an age where demand was unpredictable and information travelled slowly, of finding a market where the prices would repay the merchant's investment.

Regions were generally more or less self-sufficient in other goods as well, which further reduced the level of demand for traded goods and increased the risks for merchants. Most raw materials for manufacturing were found almost everywhere in the Mediterranean. Demand for manufactured goods was generally low, since surplus production was limited, and it could usually be satisfied from local sources. No region had any technological advantage that would enable it to produce goods cheaply enough so that, when exported, even with the added costs of transport they could undercut goods produced locally. A certain quantity of goods, especially those of higher quality, might find an overseas market, but hardly enough to support a significant specialised export trade. A number of essential resources for which there was a small but steady demand, such as metals, pitch and stone for millstones, were distributed unevenly through the Mediterranean, and so some trade in these commodities always took place; but most merchants in the ancient world operated on a small scale, carrying mixed cargoes from port to port, hoping to sell at least something at every stop.

Only a city like Athens, on the coast and with a reliable source of wealth in the Laurion silver mines, could afford to grow far beyond the capacity of its territory and support a higher level of industrial activity. The demand for foodstuffs in Athens was consistent, so that traders could always count on selling their goods there for a decent price and collect a cargo of manufactured items for the return journey. Few ancient cities had Athens's advantages, and even so the Athenians had to protect their food supply with laws regulating merchants. It was too risky to rely wholly on the free market.

This first-century AD wall painting (opposite) of the Roman harbour at Stabiae, near Naples, is a masterpiece of ancient perspective and a worthy expression of the importance of sea-trade within the Empire. The harbour, an essentially functional structure, is adorned with statues on tall columns, numerous shrines, and a gated ceremonial way leading to the city.

Ambrose on maritime trade

God did not make the sea to be sailed over, but for the beauty of the element. The sea is tossed by storms; you ought, therefore, to fear it, not to use it. The innocent element does no wrong; it is man's own rashness that brings him into peril. He who never puts to sea need fear no shipwreck. The sea is given to supply you with fish to eat, not for you to endanger yourself upon it; use it for purposes of food, not for commerce. But how insatiable is the greed of merchants! The sea itself gives way to them, the ocean cannot endure their restlessness. The element is wearied with the merchants who plough their paths across it, to and fro, continually. The waves themselves are not so restless as these men; the winds themselves are not so violent as their desires.

Ambrose On Elijah and Fasting *70–1*

THE GROWTH OF DEMAND

The ancient economy's low level of productivity, and the cost and speed of transport, meant that demand for manufactured and traded goods was limited and only a small non-agricultural sector could be supported. This was a vicious circle, since it meant that the market for agricultural produce was small and unpredictable, and farmers lacked any incentive to increase their productivity. However, the bleakness of this picture should not be exaggerated. The examples of other pre-industrial societies, not least early modern England, show that growth is possible within such constraints, even if the sustained growth characteristic of the modern economy is unachievable. From antiquity, the example of Athens shows that the pattern of self-sufficiency and low demand can sometimes be broken. It is in this light that we can consider the impact of the Roman Empire on the economy of the Mediterranean.

A detail from Trajan's Column, showing Roman soldiers harvesting wheat during the Dacian campaign – an example of the Roman army's self-sufficiency. Some military enterprises, such as the manufacture of roof tiles, became permanent industrial complexes.

If we consider the aggregate wealth of the Mediterranean as a whole, the Roman conquests were initially disastrous. They destroyed lives and property, and the exaction of tribute left regions impoverished and indebted – though it is difficult to know whether the effects lasted decades or only a few years. Rome did not create wealth; it appropriated the wealth of others. However, from the point of view of the economy, what is significant is that the Romans concentrated this wealth in particular locations. The two groups who came to control the greater proportion of the Empire's surplus, the state and the great landowners, spent their new revenues in such a way as to create centres of demand for foodstuffs and other basic materials that could never be fully supplied locally. This necessitated the development of more elaborate systems for distributing goods between different regions, leading to an expansion of trade; in due course it had an impact on systems of production as well.

THE ARMY

The first such centre of demand was the army. Army costs were the most important item of state expenditure, absorbing 450–500 million sesterces per year (over half of the estimated imperial budget) by the mid-first century AD. Most of these troops were stationed in the sparsely settled margins of the Empire, where they could obtain at best only part of their basic requirements locally. It has been estimated that the four legions based on the Rhine frontier in the first and second centuries AD would have consumed the equivalent of a tithe on 100,000 square kilometres of land, whereas the region comprised only 52,000 square kilometres. Over time, the army might hope to be able to obtain a greater proportion of its grain supplies locally, as producers responded to the new demand. This certainly seems to have happened in Britain; the volume of imported *terra sigillata* pottery, generally agreed to be a 'marker' for food imports (since it was imported in mixed cargoes rather than traded in its own right), declines significantly by the mid-third century from a high point in the early years of the Roman occupation. However, many frontier regions, especially in the East, were at the margins of successful cereal cultivation, and so in those regions it must always have been necessary to import grain from elsewhere.

The army consumed more than just cereals. The soldiers' diet included wine or *posca* (a mixture of water and vinegar), olive oil and pork, not to mention condiments like *garum* (fish sauce) and pepper. They needed horses, pack animals and animals for sacrifice, all of which required fodder. The replacement of equipment called for leather (the army of northern Britain needed 12,000 calves per annum simply to repair and replace its tents) and metals (a single legionary fortress has yielded 20 tonnes of iron nails). The supply of some of these goods followed a similar pattern to that of grain; mass imports in the early years of occupation followed by a shift towards local supplies as domestic production developed. Other goods – notably, in the case of the northern frontier, Mediterranean products like olive oil and wine – always had to be imported. Feeding the army involved significant investment in the task of distribution, in infrastructure and personnel, and represented a net transfer of resources from the wealthy, tax-producing inner provinces to the frontiers.

THE CITY OF ROME

The second centre of demand was the city of Rome, whose population grew dramatically in the last century of the Republic from around 200,000 – already an impressive figure for a pre-industrial city – to about one million. This expansion of Rome as a city was due entirely to its role as the capital, symbol and showpiece of the Empire, the focus of the political ambitions and conspicuous consumption of the Roman elite, including the emperors. Their activities, especially the grandiose building projects undertaken in the city, required an astonishing quantity of raw materials. Some could be produced locally; for example, brickworks were set up in the immediate hinterland of the city. Others had to be transported hundreds of kilometres: marbles from Egypt and the Aegean, not to mention thousands of tonnes of lead for aqueducts and bathhouses, tens of thousands of slaves and animals and a cornucopia of exotic foodstuffs, spices and textiles.

The building projects and lavish lifestyles of the elite employed large numbers of people who themselves needed food, housing and services, and the task of

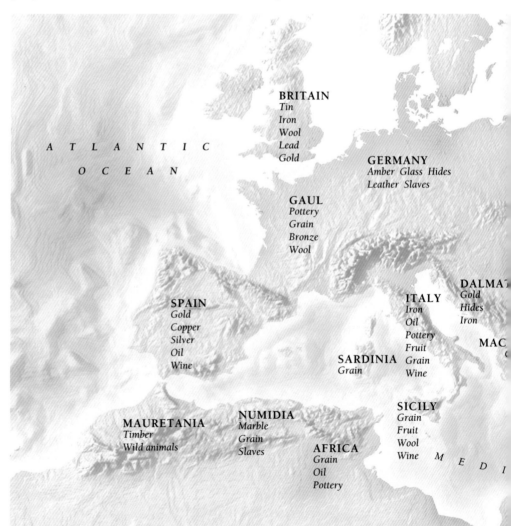

supplying their needs employed still more people. Rome's demands for grain have been estimated at a minimum of 150,000 tonnes per year; its consumption of wine at perhaps 75 million litres per year, with a million litres of olive oil for lighting and twenty to thirty million litres for cooking and washing. These demands could never be met from the city's immediate hinterland. Rome drew in grain from Italy, Sardinia, Sicily, Africa and Egypt; wine from Italy, Gaul, Spain and the Aegean; olive oil from Italy, Spain and Africa; other goods from every part of the known world. Some of its needs were met through state distribution, but the *annona* did not cover all of Rome's grain requirements, let alone its demand for other goods. Most of the city's supplies were brought in by merchants because they were assured of being able to sell their goods at a premium price. Rome was the archetypal consumer city, the majority of its population supported directly or indirectly from taxes and rents rather than from industrial production for export – but a consumer is not necessarily a parasite, and Rome's demands created and supported a level of trading activity that had not been possible before.

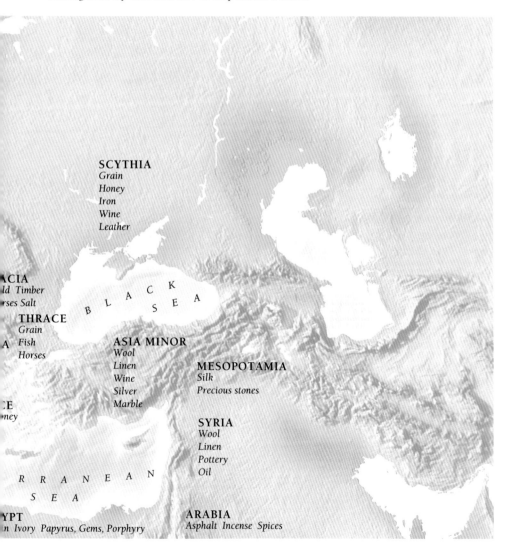

SCYTHIA
Grain
Honey
Iron
Wine
Leather

CIA
ld Timber
rses Salt

THRACE
Grain
Fish
Horses

BLACK SEA

ASIA MINOR
Wool
Linen
Wine
Silver
Marble

MESOPOTAMIA
Silk
Precious stones

E
ney

SYRIA
Wool
Linen
Pottery
Oil

RRANEAN SEA

YPT
n Ivory Papyrus, Gems, Porphyry

ARABIA
Asphalt Incense Spices

The Roman Empire and its hinterlands produced a variety of agricultural and mineral resources – sufficient to meet all but the most outlandish desires of its inhabitants. The economic, and to some extent political, security of the Empire depended on the redistribution of these resources, mainly through sea-trade. Rome's own stability hinged on the city's resident 'mob' being fed a dole of imported grain.

LUXURY AND THE EASTERN TRADE

Not everything the Romans required could be found within their Empire. As the Greek orator Aelius Aristides noted, hyperbolically, 'cargoes from India and, if you will, even from Arabia the Blest, one can see in such abundance as to surmise that in those lands the trees will have been stripped bare and that the inhabitants of those lands, if they need anything, must come here and beg for a share of their own'. Incense and other aromatics, perfumes and unguents, spices, silks and pearls were imported from beyond the Eastern frontier, to such an extent that the Elder Pliny feared the Empire was being drained of gold and silver to pay for them.

Originally this trade was in the hands of Arab merchants, but in 116 BC a sea-captain in the service of the Greek rulers of Egypt discovered the route to India. A Roman handbook for merchants, the *Periplus Maris Erythraei*, shows how ships set out for India from the Red Sea in July to catch the monsoon winds, and returned in December or January on the north-eastern monsoon; others headed for Arabia for the frankincense harvest. The volume and value of this trade increased enormously under the Romans. Papyri relating to the financing of trading expeditions show how lucrative it was. One describes a consignment of ivory, textiles and nard worth about three million sesterces, and a large boat might carry a hundred such cargoes. Cities like Alexandria and Palmyra become rich through their strategic locations on the trade routes (Alexandria was also a centre for processing imported raw materials), and the state collected substantial customs dues.

For many writers, this flow of exotic goods into Rome was disastrous. The proud and virtuous Roman people was being corrupted, weakened and effeminised by decadent foreign habits. The Roman elite's sense of their own identity as frugal peasant soldiers survived their acquisition of vast slave-run estates, and created

anxieties about the effects of wealth and prosperity on their society. *Luxuria* was blamed for the decline of Rome – 'luxurious banquets and elaborate dress are indications of a disease in the state', according to the philosopher Seneca – and used as a weapon against political enemies, since someone unable to control their appetite for exotic food, perfumes and citrus-wood tables was clearly unsuited to wield power.

Historians have often dismissed this trade as irrelevant to the development of the economy, since it served only a minority of wealthy consumers. Pliny's calculation of the wealth it drained is certainly exaggerated, based on the price of goods in Rome after the costs of transport, processing and the merchants' profit had been added. However, not all the eastern trade was in superfluous 'luxuries'; incense was essential for sacrifices and funerals, while spices were used (in small amounts) by large numbers of people. We can see the growth of demand for such goods as evidence for the development of the economy. As Seneca said, 'prosperity has spread luxury far and wide'.

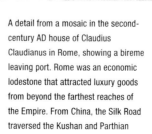

A detail from a mosaic in the second-century AD house of Claudius Claudianus in Rome, showing a bireme leaving port. Rome was an economic lodestone that attracted luxury goods from beyond the farthest reaches of the Empire. From China, the Silk Road traversed the Kushan and Parthian empires delivering costly fabrics to the markets of Alexandria (via the Red Sea port of Berenice), Antioch, and the Roman trading outpost at Dura Europus. Spices were shipped directly from southern India and also through the northwest Indian port of Barbaricon.

A mosaic pavement from the Piazzale delle Corporazion in Ostia, the port of Rome. Merchant ships – wide, round-bottomed, and powered by sail – were as essential as the legions to the city's existence. Without regular grain shipments from Egypt, Cyprus and Sicily, Rome would literally have starved. The object depicted on the other side of the ship is a modius, a traditional measure for grain and other dry goods.

URBANISATION AND 'ROMANISATION'

The Romans spent the profits of their conquests in the capital and at the frontiers, creating a demand for goods that could only be met from outside those regions, through trade or some other form of distribution. This was not the result of any economic policy, but of the self-interest and self-indulgence of the state and its rulers, and yet its economic impact was enormous. Other aspects of Roman domination had equally unintended economic consequences.

The first is the increase in urbanisation, especially in the western half of the Empire (the eastern half was largely urbanised before the Romans arrived). The ancient city was a means of establishing and reinforcing political, ideological and economic power; a theatre for conspicuous consumption and the display of culture and newly-acquired *Romanitas* and the arena for the competition between members of the local elite. The Romans encouraged the development of cities, and preferred to govern their Empire through cooperation with local civic elites; the city thus became a place of mediation between local society and higher powers, and a stepping-stone for the more ambitious who sought to ascend to the great provincial capitals or to Rome itself. The establishment of Roman rule thus gave an impetus to the development of cities, especially in regions that were not heavily urbanised before the conquest. Certain cities also prospered because of their role in the major supply routes to the army and the capital. Ostia, the port of Rome, grew from a minor town under the Republic to a city of 30,000 or more people by the second century AD, complete with a monumental forum, temples, a theatre, an amphitheatre and at least seventeen public bathhouses. Cities located on major rivers and at the junctions of major roads towards the frontiers, like Arles, Lyon and Vienne on the Rhône, London, Amiens and Trier, also grew dramatically in population size and acquired a range of public buildings and civic amenities. (For further information on urbanisation *see also* Chapter 9)

The cities became, or continued to be, the main focus of expenditure for the local elite. As in Rome, upper-class habits of consumption and building projects gave employment to craftsmen and other workers, whose needs then also had to be supplied. Most of these cities obtained most of their basic supplies from their immediate locality, except when a poor harvest forced them to look for supplies elsewhere. Even in a normal year, however, the fact that the population was concentrated in a single location created a need for investment in means of distributing goods between city and countryside; cities are more costly to maintain than a dispersed rural population. The great cities of the East like Alexandria and Antioch (and perhaps even medium-sized regional centres in the West like Trier, Arles, Lyon and Milan) always had to import food and other materials from a wide area on a regular basis.

The second significant consequence of Roman rule was, again especially in the West, a change in consumption habits among the population as a whole. In the process of cultural change often referred to as 'Romanisation', provincials articulated their new identity as Roman subjects and citizens through new patterns of consumption. This is most visible in the case of the elites who could afford to invest heavily in the process of acculturation – building large and elaborately decorated villas, for example, or purchasing litres of the best Italian wine – but it was not confined to them. An individual peasant in Gaul might be able to afford wine only occasionally, and to buy a single piece of fine Italian-style pottery once a year, but if every peasant spent a little on such 'refined' goods, the resulting increase in aggregate demand would be sufficient to support a greater volume of inter-regional trade. This can be seen clearly in the archaeological evidence; for example, the distribution of Italian wine containers in Gaul, where the remains of tens of thousands of amphorae have been found along the major river valleys, and the finds of glossy red-glazed *terra sigillata* throughout the western Empire. In some cases this trade rode piggy-back on supplies to the army, which effectively subsidised the costs of transport – while the demand for these goods also made army supply contracts more profitable. In many cases local production eventually expanded to meet demand; Gaul again provides a good example, as Italian Arretine pottery was succeeded by a series of local fine wares in a similar style. For several centuries, however, Roman rule once again created a demand for goods that could not be satisfied locally.

THE EXPANSION OF TRADE

A wide range of different kinds of archaeological evidence reveals the impact of these new demands for foodstuffs and other goods on the economy of the Roman Empire. For example, there are the numbers of ancient shipwrecks discovered in the Mediterranean: far more are datable to the period of the late Republic and early Principate than for any other period before the sixteenth century. As with any piece of evidence, we cannot take this completely at face value. The known wrecks are not evenly distributed throughout the Mediterranean, but cluster in certain areas, especially the south coasts of Spain and France; this reflects where archaeologists and divers are active as much as it reflects ancient trade routes. Moreover, wrecks containing large pottery containers like Roman amphorae are much more likely to be detected than those that carried their cargo in more perishable containers. More data, from the African coast or the eastern Mediterranean, might alter the picture – but, since we know from other evidence that Roman ships were active throughout the Mediterranean, data from these regions would probably reveal equally large numbers of Roman wrecks. Improved surveying techniques, capable of identifying wrecks that did not carry amphorae, would probably discover as many Roman ships (those carrying grain loose or in sacks, for example) as ships from other periods. There is no evidence for a drastic decline in the quality of Roman shipbuilding that would have increased the likelihood of shipwreck, so the figures for wrecks imply that many more ships were making voyages at the height of the Roman Empire than in any earlier period, a number that was not surpassed for over a thousand years.

There is also the evidence of the vast quantities of amphorae and other pottery dated to this period, much of it recovered from shipwrecks but much more found on all kinds of sites throughout the Empire. The most spectacular concentration is Monte Testaccio, a hill in Rome that rises about 50 metres above sea level, made up entirely of fragments of olive oil amphorae. Amphorae came in a variety of shapes and sizes, many of which can be precisely dated and their point of origin identified by archaeologists. The wide geographical distribution of certain

An encrusted amphora at a Roman shipwreck site near the island of Ustica. Although they are mainly associated with agricultural staples such as wine and olive oil, amphoras were versatile shipping containers that could also be used for more exotic produce such as pepper, cloves, alum or incense, that might otherwise become spoiled during a long sea voyage.

Detail of a mosaic from Ostia showing an amphora flanked by two palm trees. Perhaps 'MC' was a merchant engaged in African trade, who owed at least some of his wealth to the demand for imported palm oil, palm sugar or palm wine.

forms is impressive; for example, Lamboglia 2 amphorae from the south of Italy are found throughout the western Mediterranean, while some African amphorae occur almost everywhere from Britain to Egypt. Amphorae were ideally suited to transporting goods over long distances and were designed to stack neatly in ships' holds – another indicator of the regularity with which goods were now being moved around the Mediterranean. The standardisation of regional types, so that you could recognise Spanish oil or Greek wine from the shape of the container (except when some regions started to imitate the containers of their competitors), also points to the development of regular large-scale trade.

Amphorae were used to transport goods like wine, oil, olives, fish sauce and other foodstuffs; relatively cheap, relatively bulky in relation to their value, relatively ubiquitous in the Mediterranean. This represents a change in the nature of the goods being distributed between regions: not just expensive rarities like incense and silk for the very rich and a few essential but scarce resources like metals, as we would expect from the high cost of transport, but foodstuffs that were staple but not essential. These are precisely the sort of 'mass luxury' products that were within reach of a significant proportion of the population. Many were destined for the city of Rome (especially in the shipwrecks along the coasts of France and Spain) or for the armies, but many more were being shipped to the cities of the Roman Empire and the surrounding countryside.

THE PROCESS OF DISTRIBUTION

Goods were distributed through the Empire in lots of different ways, by lots of different people. At one end of the scale we find simple, small-scale, local exchange, as peasants bring their surplus into town and trade directly with urban consumers; Italian towns held *nundinae*, regular weekly markets where local farmers could sell their produce, buy whatever goods they needed from urban craftsmen and make use of the town's facilities. Sometimes goods were not traded at all, but simply moved to where they were needed; rich landowners transferred supplies from their estates to their urban residences, and the state regularly redistributed grain collected as tax in kind, as well as the produce of imperial estates, mines and quarries, from the place of production to the city of Rome and the frontiers. At the other end of the scale, we find goods being moved through a complicated series of transactions, with a succession of intermediaries taking a share of the profits.

For example, we can consider the process by which the produce of a villa estate on the western coast of Italy, like the large complex known as Settefinestre, near Cosa in Etruria, reached the consumer. The wealthy men who owned such villas needed money to fund their luxurious lifestyles and to advance their political careers, and so, as we can see from the advice given in Roman textbooks on agriculture, the bulk of the produce of the villa was sold: this might include olive oil, olives, fruit and vegetables, poultry, pork, grain and – the product for which the villas of coastal Etruria became famous – wine. Some landowners marketed their produce themselves: some owned ships for the purpose of taking their goods to market (one senator was accused of using state funds to build a quay near his villa), while the Appianus estate in Egypt owned asses, oxen and a corps of camels for transporting goods. More commonly, villa owners sold directly to merchants at the farm gate, choosing to make a smaller but more reliable profit by passing on the costs and risks of transporting and marketing the produce. The evidence of the agricultural manual written by Cato in the second century BC and of the writings of Roman lawyers shows that it was common practice to sell crops even before they were harvested (the original futures market): the landowners passed on even the risks associated with an unreliable climate to the traders, who gambled on the likely success of the harvest. Roman law offered detailed rules for such contracts, allocating responsibility for making and storing the wine, checking its quality and trying to sort out compensation if it turned to vinegar before the buyer collected it, but if the harvest failed the buyer lost everything. The fact that landowners were able to find purchasers even on these unfavourable terms suggests that there was fierce competition between merchants for the produce of estates, which must therefore suggest that the profits that could be made in the market were worthwhile.

Sometimes the villa provided the amphorae in which the wine was transported – some estates had their own clay-pits and kilns – and sometimes the merchant supplied them. The amphora might be stamped to indicate the name of the producer of the contents or the owner of the workshop that made the container; the stopper might be stamped with the name of the producer or of the merchant. Once the wine was ready, and had been tasted and accepted by the buyer, it was transported to the coast by mule, wagon or river barge, and loaded onto a ship. Some merchants owned their own ships; in a shipwreck known as the Dramont A, found off the coast of France not far from Cannes and dating from the first century BC, the same name appears on both the ship's anchor and the lids of the amphorae that it was carrying. Others rented space on board a ship that was carrying a number of different cargoes; Roman lawyers wrote extensively on the problem of trying to allocate liability if such a ship sank during the voyage, or if the captain wanted to throw some cargo overboard during a storm to keep the ship afloat. The stamps on the amphorae helped to identify which goods belonged to which merchant; amphorae might also have further information painted on them (known as *tituli picti*), often including the name of the *navicularius*, the shipper – who might or might not also be owner of the goods being transported.

Some merchant ships sailed from port to port, selling whatever goods they could at each stop to consumers, local retailers or other merchants who carried the goods further inland. Wine amphorae from near Cosa stamped with the name of Sestius are found all along the southern coast of France as far as Ampurias in Spain and inland up the valley of the Rhône as far as Basel and Poitiers; such wide distribution shows that more than one merchant must have been involved. Other ships had clear destinations: Ostia, the port of Rome, where (as we can see from inscriptions) there were societies of merchants specialising in the import of particular goods and of the produce of particular regions, and the armies on the frontier. The pattern of distribution of some amphorae, such as the oil containers from Baetica classified as 'Dressel 20', corresponds closely to army supply networks and areas of military activity along the Rhine, while most of the inscriptions commemorating *negotiatores* in Gaul are found along the Rhône-Rhine supply route.

Such patterns reflect 'redistribution' rather than free-market trade – which is not to say that private merchants were not involved. The Romans never had a state merchant fleet, but had to arrange for the transport of state-owned goods like grain and marble by requisitioning transport animals and setting up contracts with shipowners. They offered generous concessions, grants of citizenship and exemption from local civic dues, to persuade people to sign up for the grain supply to the city of Rome, simply because they had no other means of getting the goods to where they were needed. Historians have sometimes argued that the importance of state redistribution under the Roman Empire meant that market trade was unimportant. Clearly, however, the Roman system presupposes the existence of privately-owned ships which could be recruited to supply the needs of the state. Transport contractors were paid at market rates, and could make additional profits by transporting private goods alongside their official cargoes (and occasionally attempting to claim tax exemption on such goods as well as on state supplies). State demands for transport more or less guaranteed that shipowning would be profitable, and encouraged further construction – and those ships were then available for private enterprise as well. The emperors also invested in the transport infrastructure, above all in developing the port facilities at the mouth of the Tiber. All this created a more hospitable environment for the development of trade in the Empire.

Suetonius on Rome's grain supply

On one occasion, after repeated poor harvests had led to a shortage of grain, Claudius was held up in the Forum by a mob who, hurling insults as well as crusts of bread, attacked him so fiercely that he was scarcely able to escape into the palace. He then left no means untried of importing supplies, even in the winter season. For he offered traders guaranteed profits by undertaking to cover any losses himself, if there should be an accident as a result of bad weather, and to those constructing merchant ships he offered large incentives, corresponding to each person's status.

Suetonius Claudius 18–19

FINANCE AND ORGANISATION

Most Roman traders were of relatively low status and middling wealth, perhaps because the process of distribution was so fragmented and so many intermediaries were taking a share of the profits: the emperor Hadrian passed a law to control fish prices in Attica by limiting the number of intermediate traders, to put an end to 'shameful profit-seeking'. However, we should beware of judging Roman trade by the standards of later medieval developments, and condemning it because of the absence of merchant princes and grand trading companies. The existing structures were adequate for the purpose of keeping the army and the cities regularly supplied, and the same can be said of the institutional structures that supported distribution. The Romans lacked certain practices (limited companies, for example, and bills of exchange) that have sometimes been identified as prerequisites for the economic development of early modern Europe. It is not clear, however, that they lacked the commercial structures that they actually needed. As mentioned above, Roman law offered clear rules on contracts, on the sale of wine, on compensation for lost cargoes and so forth, essential for the management of complex trading ventures. There is little evidence of established commercial companies, but that is largely because the Romans preferred to keep business within the family, or the *familia* – many business arrangements were based on the close legal and social ties that persisted between freedmen and their former owners. (*See also* pages 80–86)

As far as finance was concerned, the organisation of maritime loans (in which the lender carried the risk of the cargo being lost, and so charged much higher rates of interest) had changed little since the fourth century BC. Large-scale trading ventures required extensive credit; the risks were large, but so were the potential returns, for the merchant but even more for the lenders, and so credit was generally forthcoming. The Murecine tablets, lacquer-covered writing tablets found at Pompeii, include details of commercial loans and show that some of the money was advanced by slaves or freedmen of the imperial household. Members of the senatorial elite must similarly have been involved in lending money through intermediaries. There is almost no evidence for the existence of 'merchant financiers' both operating and financing trade (the Sulpicii of Puteoli, who appear on the Murecine tablets, may be the exception). The vast sums of money that financed trade remained largely in the hands of the landowning elite, which any successful 'entrepreneur' would seek to join as soon as possible.

THE ROLE OF THE STATE

As noted above, the state played an important role in creating centres of demand for goods supplied by merchants, in subsidising the transport infrastructure and in developing rules for settling disputes in the market-place and in other business transactions. Other aspects of its activities also had economic consequences. Most obviously, Rome brought peace to the Mediterranean; the region became a single unified space (*mare nostrum*, 'our sea') where once it had been a battlefield. To protect its own supplies, the state invested resources in dealing with pirates, which benefited all traders and shipowners. It built roads to move troops, but there was nothing to stop other people using them to move their goods more easily.

The state issued coinage for its own purposes, to pay soldiers and officials and to purchase supplies, rather than pursuing economic policies by regulating the money supply. This still had the effect of promoting trade by providing a standard medium of exchange and measure of value accepted through most of the Mediterranean. Bronze and silver coinage circulated widely at regional level, while the development of gold coinage under the Principate made it easier to move large sums of money between regions. The fact that the volume of silver coinage increased significantly during this period, without any apparent effect on prices, suggests that there was an increase in overall market activity.

Gold coins (aureii) of the emperors Claudius and Nero found in the ruins of Pompeii. During the first two centuries of the Principate, the Romans used a trimetallic currency system (gold, silver and copper). This became impossible during the third century, as inflation spiralled and supplies of precious metals dwindled, through hoarding and trade. Gold coinage ceased altogether, and 'silver' coins were chemically silvered rather than being made from silver or silver alloy.

A fragment of a Roman mosaic floor dating from about 400 AD, showing a villa surrounded by a manicured parkland inhabited by game birds and waterfowl. Behind this idyllic facade of rural paradise, the agricultural villa was an economic and cultural powerhouse in late-Roman Europe, prefiguring the role of the medieval manor house as mutually convenient locus for everyday transactions between community and government.

INCREASED PRODUCTION

At first, the increase in goods moving around the Mediterranean world was no more than a redistribution of existing wealth, as taxes and rents flowed to the state and the rich landowners, and thence into the pockets of individuals involved in the supply network. The expansion of the cities, with a larger proportion of the population now working in non-agricultural occupations, might suggest that agricultural productivity had increased – or alternatively it might simply be evidence that farmers were being exploited more efficiently. In time, however, the Empire's demands did lead to changes in agriculture and industry, as producers – or some producers – responded to the incentive of higher market prices (or the need to pay their taxes) by striving to increase their marketable surplus.

The clearest evidence for changes in agriculture comes from the region immediately around the city of Rome, the *suburbium*. The combination of high land prices and rents on the one hand, and the profits to be made in supplying the city on the other, led farmers to cultivate their land as intensively as possible. The region produced costly perishable goods: fruit, vegetables, flowers, honey and a wide range of luxury meats (dormice, snails, songbirds and game). Archaeological survey shows the intensification of settlement in the region, though not all the sites were market gardens: horticulture had to compete for land (and water) with the suburban villas of the urban elite and with the demand for burial plots for the urban dead. The economy and society of the *suburbium* was shaped by the wealth and the various demands of the city.

In central Italy, we find the 'villas' described in the writings of Roman agricultural writers like Varro and Columella. The villa was a medium-sized estate using slave labour, large enough to support a number of animals and to benefit from their labour and manure. It did not specialise in a single crop – growing a variety meant that the workforce was kept busy all year round, as well as making the villa almost self-sufficient in food and raw materials – but was intended to produce a large surplus of wine, oil or grain for sale. Some of the wine was exported to Gaul; amphorae from the town of Cosa on the coast of Etruria have been found all the way up the River Rhône. However, most of the produce of these villas was intended for the insatiable market of the city of Rome itself.

Archaeological survey in Italy identifies certain sites as 'villas' on the basis of the size of the scatter of pottery found by the surveyors and by the presence of objects that suggest wealth, such as pieces of mosaic. The type of labour used on these sites, free or slave, is archaeologically invisible, and so it is risky to assume that all such large, wealthy sites were managed in the way advised by the Roman agronomists. However, it is striking that these sites appear in large numbers close to transport routes, in regions of Etruria, Latium and Campania that lay within easy reach of Rome. In more isolated inland areas the pattern of settlement was much less disrupted, with less evidence of such large sites. This does fit the idea that agricultural change was most likely to be seen in areas that had good access to the Roman market.

However, more distant regions also saw changes in agriculture. Elsewhere in Italy we find the development of some spectacularly large flocks of sheep, which were moved long distances between summer and winter pasture. Traditionally, herding was small-scale and local; these large flocks indicate sizable investment in land and animals, undoubtedly with the aim of making large profits in the market. In the western provinces, vine and olive cultivation gradually spread, at first for local consumption and then, as shown clearly in finds of amphorae from the port of Ostia and the Rhine frontier, for export to Rome and the army. By the third century, African oil amphorae and pottery are found all over the western Mediterranean. The strongest evidence for agricultural specialisation in North Africa is the archaeological evidence for olive presses; not only the total numbers (one for every two square kilometres near Lepcis Magna, for example) but also the 'factory complexes' of four or five presses (or, in one example, seventeen presses), capable of processing huge quantities of olives. Again, this indicates major investment in production for the market by wealthy landowners, who were in the best position to take advantage of new market opportunities; as well as having capital to invest, they could afford to store produce until prices rose in the market, and could risk specialising in particular crops. Poor farmers were in a much weaker position, and may indeed have found their position deteriorating as the wealthy sought to buy up the best land for their villas and flocks.

TECHNOLOGY AND PRODUCTIVITY

Specialisation was one way for a landowner to increase his income; the other was to increase the productivity of the land or the labourers. The Roman agronomists offer advice on maintaining and improving the fertility of the land: they recommend not only animal manure (collected from the cesspits as well as from the stables) but also the use of 'green manure', plants which protected the soil from erosion and the leaching of nutrients while they grew and were then dug in to restore fertility. Such techniques may have enabled some farmers to increase their yields or to avoid the need to leave the land fallow every other year. The store of farming knowledge increased with experience and was recorded in books; the range of varieties of crops was extended, so that the farmer could chose one best suited to his soil and situation; techniques of grafting trees and training vines were refined.

There is little evidence for the introduction of advanced technology into cultivation, apart from a Gallic reaping machine that was apparently not widely adopted. In fact there was little scope for such improvements in the Mediterranean; the cultivation of vines and olives is, even today, poorly suited to mechanisation, while mechanised harvesting is really desirable only if there is a serious risk that bad weather will spoil the harvest. Roman agricultural technology was 'appropriate' for its environment; more intensive cultivation might have accelerated the erosion and exhaustion of the best soils – and there is some evidence that this was already a problem in antiquity.

The way that slaves were used in the villa may have brought an increase in productivity; there was some division of labour, with slaves developing expertise in specialised tasks like vine dressing, while close supervision and the threat of violence might also have increased their work rate. This is impossible to prove, and comparative evidence from nineteenth-century American slavery is equally controversial. The Roman agronomists never seriously consider hiring free labourers, except for temporary work at harvest time, but that could be because everything the slaves produced beyond the minimum for their subsistence was pure profit, rather than because they were more productive. The downside of slave labour was the need for constant supervision of the slaves by the *vilicus*, the overseer, and the need for the owner to supervise the supervisors. Slaves were an expensive investment, which had to be exploited intensively; the villa was a success as long as market prices were high enough to justify the costs, but by the second century AD the landowners of Italy were turning to less intensive and laborious means of managing their estates.

A detail of a mosaic from a third-century AD Roman villa in Gaul depicting two men pressing olives. The cultivation of olives for high-quality oil was one of the ancient foundations of agrarian capitalism in the Mediterranean. Olive trees produce a valuable annual crop.

INDUSTRIAL PRODUCTION

One indication of the development of crafts and industry under the Roman Empire is the number of different occupations recorded in inscriptions: 85 from Pompeii, for example, 110 from Corycus in Cilicia and over 284 from the city of Rome. Demand for goods was large and sophisticated enough to support increased specialisation – and this must also reflect the development of specialised skills. The edict passed by the emperor Diocletian in AD 301 to try to regulate prices in the Roman Empire shows the range of different goods now available to the consumer: twenty-two kinds of boots, sandals, shoes and slippers, and twenty-one varieties of shirt, varying in quality and place of manufacture – part of a list of 139 different categories of linen goods.

Production became more specialised, but was otherwise little changed. Most goods were still produced by small workshops, with little division of labour and limited efficiency gains; where slaves were owned, they were employed in exactly the same tasks as free workers. Carvings on the tomb of a prosperous baker from Rome, Eurysaces, show the different stages of the bread-making process, and are perhaps evidence for a division of labour on his premises; but the archaeological evidence from Pompeii suggests that most bakeries were much smaller operations, with a single donkey-mill and little space for lots of workers. There is evidence for large numbers of textile workshops in some cities, such as Thamugadi (Timgad) in North Africa, which stood on the boundaries between arable and pastoral regions. As Diocletian's Edict shows, cloth from some regions was widely distributed, but most areas continued to produce most of their own textiles and imported only higher-quality products; there is no ancient counterpart to the Lancashire cotton industry, exporting cheap, mass-produced goods across the globe.

The Romans did make significant innovations in two areas of production. First, they improved the processing, storage and transport of foodstuffs, with the development of presses and mills, granaries and standardised storage containers. In particular there is evidence for the widespread introduction of water mills into western Europe from the second century AD. The Barbegal complex near Arles in southern Gaul had sixteen millwheels and was capable of processing enough grain for half the local urban population. The mills on the Janiculum in Rome, fed from the Aqua Traiana, may have been even larger. Water power could drive a millwheel at least five times faster than a donkey, and the mills had lower running costs – once they had been built, which required investment, almost certainly from the state.

The other area where technology developed was mining: the contractors working silver and gold mines on behalf of the state used water power to expose deposits of ore, water-lifting devices to drain mineshafts, and animal and water power to crush the ore. The aim was not to save labour – slaves were regularly worked to death in the mines – but to maximise extraction. The success and scale of the operations can be seen from the evidence for atmospheric pollution caused by smelting ores; analysis of ice cores from Greenland shows a sharp rise in lead and copper traces over the first century BC. The state's demand for metals, like that for grain in Rome and other cities, promoted a significant technology-driven increase in productivity. The demand for other goods was not sufficient to prompt major investment in their industries.

THE LIMITS TO GROWTH

The growth of the city of Rome, the expansion of the Empire and the 'Romanisation' of the provinces were made possible by, and created a need for, efficient distribution of goods, underwritten by the purchasing power of state and elite. The state and the elite had only their own interests in view, but the way they deployed their wealth nevertheless created conditions favourable to the development of market trade and improvements in agricultural and industrial production. The archaeological evidence – the number of shipwrecks, the sheer volume of goods distributed across the Empire, the level of material culture even on poorer sites, the growth in the money supply – suggests that the period from about 200 BC to about AD 200 marks the high point of economic activity for centuries to come.

However, this evidence also raises the question of why growth was limited. The numbers of shipwrecks from the first two centuries of the Principate are only slightly higher than those from the late Republic, and thereafter they decline rapidly. The rise in industrial activity reflected in the Greenland ice cores is not sustained after the first century AD. There is no sign of the sustained expansion of economic activity which is seen in the European economy from the early modern period onwards. Although the Principate brought peace and stability to the Mediterranean, economic growth slowed and then began to decline; the great expansion took place under the Republic, despite almost constant wars.

This reflects the limits on the expansion of demand in a pre-industrial economy. The stimulus of military and urban demand promoted the development of more localised production in the provinces. Goods which during the Republic had to be imported could now be obtained more cheaply from local sources, and there were no alternative markets for the goods that had previously been exported. The most striking example of this process is the development of wine production in Gaul, so that the region ceased to import Italian amphorae by the second century AD and began to export its own products to Rome (which could happily absorb them in addition to Italian supplies). Similar patterns of local production replacing imports (and sometimes being exported in turn) can be seen in the pottery evidence from Gaul and Britain. The frontiers became increasingly (if never completely) self-sufficient by the third century, and so one of the key drivers of inter-regional distribution declined in importance. The cities of the Empire could also rely on local production for a wider range of goods. Rome continued to draw in goods from a vast area, but it ceased to expand, in part perhaps because the infrastructure (in particular the bottleneck in the city's supply network formed by the River Tiber) could not sustain a larger population.

The patterns of distribution and the new developments in production in the Roman Empire were not autonomous and self-supporting; they reflected the needs of the state and the elite. The emperors were concerned with supplying the army and the city of Rome, not with promoting economic activity. When the incentives offered to shipowners failed to attract enough contractors to ensure the reliable supply of Rome – which perhaps reflects the declining profitability of inter-regional exchange – the state turned to compulsion, regardless of the consequences for market trade.

Diocletian's Price Edict, and an increasing reliance on requisitions in kind from the fourth century, reveal a similar lack of faith that merchants could be relied upon to further the state's interests. When a single capital city became a less effective means of maintaining imperial power, the emperors had little hesitation in redirecting their expenditure to centres like Arles, Milan and Trier – each of which became, for a time, a significant centre of demand, but far smaller than the concentrated demands of Rome and one that could be more easily satisfied from local sources. Similarly, as civic duty and benefactions became a less effective route to power in the later Empire, the elite redirected their resources to their landed estates and to legacies to the Church, regardless of the consequences for the urban centres – let alone the knock-on effect on demand for goods and hence on the prosperity of the economy. Different parts of the Empire were affected to different degrees and at different times. In most areas of the West, urban building had more or less ceased by the third century, but even here there were significant exceptions like Marseilles and Carthage; meanwhile some cities in the East were still expanding in the sixth century. Nevertheless, the overall trend is clear: smaller centres of demand, and a move away from dependence on the market.

Effective mobilisation and distribution of surplus production had for centuries underpinned the power of Rome and its ruling elite and ensured the stability of the Empire. It may also over time have undermined it. The landowning elite profited greatly from the state's investment in maintaining the integrity and connectivity of the Empire. They were involved in every stage of the process of supplying Rome and the armies, from agricultural production to maritime loans to collecting rents from workshops and retail outlets. They acquired extensive lands and enormous wealth: the average senatorial fortune in the early second century AD was twice or three times that of the late Republic, and by the fourth century it had risen another seven- or eight-fold. By this stage the power of the elite was restricting the ability of the state to raise enough taxes to hold the Empire together. Moreover, the concentration of wealth in the hands of the few left the mass of the population with a smaller share of the surplus, reducing overall demand for goods. The economy failed to 'take off'; it remained dependent on organic energy, and when demand declined it returned to a lower, more sustainable level of activity, with low productivity, limited trade and a lower level of material culture. Compared with a modern economy, the Roman Empire was under-developed; compared with the early Middle Ages, however, and with many other pre-industrial societies, it was sophisticated and dynamic, and brought an improved quality of life for many of its inhabitants

Empire brought vast wealth to Rome's rulers, as noted by admirers and critics alike. Less attention was paid to the fact that Roman power depended on its economy, on the effective production, mobilisation and distribution of resources.

An early Christian view of the economic power of a great city

The merchants of the earth will weep and mourn over her [Babylon after its sack] because no one buys their cargoes any more – cargoes of gold, silver, precious stones and pearls; fine linen, purple silk and scarlet cloth; every sort of citron wood, and articles of every kind made of ivory, costly wood, bronze, iron and marble; cargoes of cinnamon and spice, of incense, myrrh and frankincense, of wine and olive oil, of fine flour and wheat; cattle and sheep, horses and carriages; and bodies and souls of men...

Every sea captain, and all who travel by ship, the sailors, and all who earn their living by the sea, will stand far off. When they see the smoke of her burning they will exclaim, 'Was there ever a city like this great city?' They will throw dust on their heads, and with weeping and mourning cry out: 'Woe, woe, o great city, where all who had ships on the sea became rich through her wealth! In one hour she has been brought to ruin.'

Revelation 18
[The identification of Rome with Babylon was a common theme in Jewish and early Christian texts.]

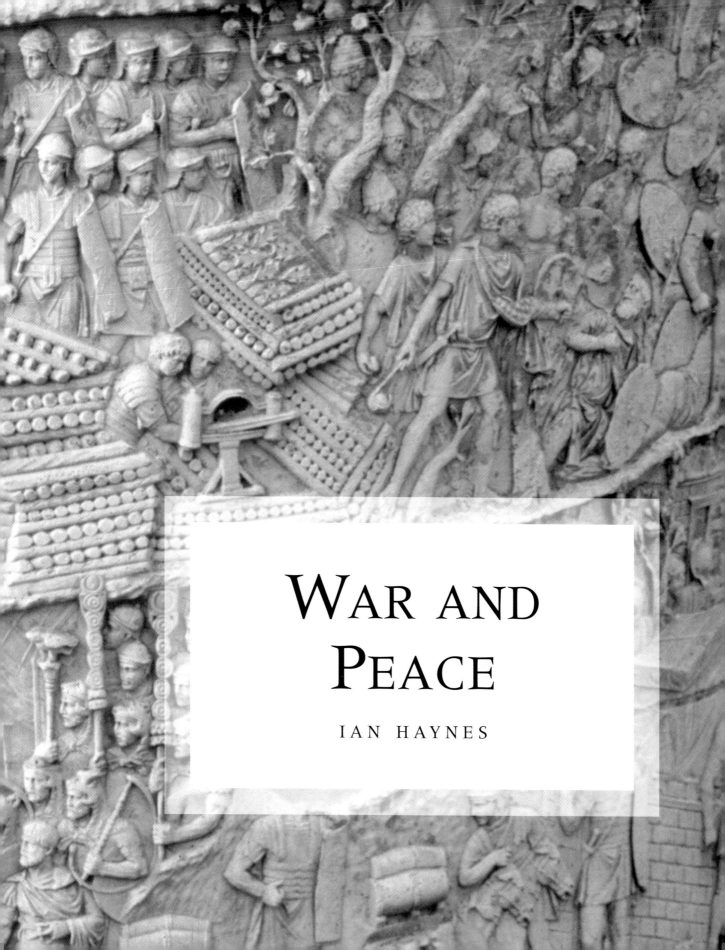

WAR AND PEACE

IAN HAYNES

WAR AND PEACE

Rome's origin myths celebrate martial glory. Romulus, founder of the city, was one of the twin sons of the war god Mars. In adulthood he and his brother led a war band that sustained itself through raiding. His life and actions reflect a world-view where legitimate authority and martial prowess are intimately linked. However far Rome's reach stretched, this association was preserved – and indeed perpetually reasserted – in the life and body of the city itself.

The Field of Mars, with its great altar to the god, long served as the location for political assembly and census registration. As new monuments jostled to adorn the Eternal City, military prowess was everywhere celebrated. The third and second centuries BC witnessed the emergence of a cluster of temples to Victory as Rome's armies emerged triumphant from ever more distant battles. Divine favour was understood to be a prerequisite of conquest and there was therefore due attention to the maintenance of proper cult in all matters pertaining to conflict. Ancient rituals of

The surviving remains of the Temple of Mars Ultor (Mars the Avenger), in the forum of Augustus in central Rome. Dedicated in 2 BC, this temple to the god of war was the centrepiece of the forum. Its descriptive name was a reference to the death of Julius Caesar, Augustus's adoptive father, whose cult statue it housed.

war and peace were dutifully enacted as Roman warfare underwent its bloody transition from local skirmish to world conquest. Yet in all this there was scope for adaptation. The Fetiales, a priestly order whose launching of a spear into enemy territory marked an ultimatum for peace or war, came to make do with enacting their rites on a small square of symbolic enemy territory in the heart of the evolving city. There were also times when the divine favour of deities alien to Roman tradition was required. Thus following an interpretation of the famous Sibylline oracle books Cybele, the Great

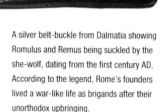

A silver belt-buckle from Dalmatia showing Romulus and Remus being suckled by the she-wolf, dating from the first century AD. According to the legend, Rome's founders lived a war-like life as brigands after their unorthodox upbringing.

Mother, was brought from Turkey to Rome in the last years of the exhausting Second Punic War. Significantly when her image arrived in 205 BC, it was housed in the temple of Victory on the Palatine until a suitable temple for it could be completed next door. Cybele was not to be the last foreign god or goddess to aid Rome. Indeed, the Romans came to recognise in the defeat of many of their enemies the defection of the opponents' deities to Rome.

It is no exaggeration to say that monuments proclaiming Rome's military superiority transformed the city's appearance. The first permanent theatres constructed within the city were all built in the first century BC in celebration of the triumph of Roman arms. Triumphal arches, found in virtually every Roman province, were a regular urban feature and were still being constructed there in the fourth century AD. Still more dramatically, under the Principate the spoils of victorious generals – the emperors – funded the construction of such mighty monuments as the forum of Augustus with its temple to the war god Mars the Avenger, the Colosseum and the forum of Trajan. It is only really in the first century AD that we see Peace (*Pax*) featured in this landscape, with the construction of Augustus's celebrated Altar of Peace (*Ara Pacis Augustae*) in the Field of Mars. To the Roman mind there was nothing ironic about this juxtaposition. For *Pax* was as much a symbol of Roman dominion as Victory. To understand why, we need to examine the particular and evolving relationship of Roman society to war.

HOPLITE AND CITY-STATE

In the earliest days, the influence of Greek thinking upon Rome was as profound in matters of war as in those of peace. Underpinning the armies of Greek city-states and Rome alike was the notion that military service was both a citizen's privilege and his duty. In the twilight years of Etruscan dominance and in the early Republic, Romans took for granted that those with sufficient wealth would serve their city in both the public square and the battle line. Military reforms were thus an integral part of social and political reforms.

Livy and Dionysius of Halicarnassus believed that Servius Tullius, king of Rome around 579–34 BC, was responsible for a package of reforms (the 'Servian Constitution') that profoundly influenced the development of the Roman state.

Central to this was the census. This device, which was to play a fundamental role in Roman economic and military life for generations, required the registration of citizens in wealth-based classes. How far Tullius was actually responsible for the full complexity of the arrangement attributed to him is open to debate. It seems, however, that some form of classification was deemed necessary for both the organisation of voters in the political arena and the effective marshalling of the state's combined resources for warfare. The 'century', or group of one hundred, was the unit in which men voted at the Assembly and, traditionally at least, fought on the battlefield. Those who lacked property were registered only by head-count; they could not afford to participate in the main battle line, because they could not purchase the military equipment required.

Certainly the defining feature of Italian warfare in the sixth century BC, the introduction from Greece of the hoplite phalanx, demanded a significant outlay from those involved. Equipped with a circular shield, heavy armour and a long spear, the

A tomb painting from Paestum (modern Pesto, near Naples) dating from the fourth century BC. It shows Greek-style hoplites, with greaves, breastplate and a large round shield, and a cavalryman with similar equipment. The Greek colony at Paestum was taken by the Lucanians, an Oscan people, in 410 BC, and became a Latin colony of Rome in 273 BC.

hoplite embodied new ideals on the battlefield. Old heroic ideas of single combat and martial display were increasingly undermined by an emphasis on highly disciplined teamwork and anonymity. To contemporary observers the desired effect of this teamwork, with the spearmen advancing together in tight formation eight or more ranks deep, resembled a roller (*phalanx*) and it was from this evocative metaphor that the formation took its name.

Though traditional forms of conflict – such as raiding – undoubtedly continued, the ascendancy of hoplite warfare on the battlefield had significant social implications. The ranks of the *phalanx* were not composed for the most part of aristocrats – these served as cavalry – but rather of ordinary farmers. For these men a bigger role in the army meant a bigger role in the Assembly. Yet, to judge from the more extensive evidence from Greece, such a system naturally imposed limits on the extent of hoplite warfare. Farmer-soldiers could not leave their fields unattended for long periods, and thus bouts of formal campaigning were limited to a matter of a few days at most.

ROMAN WARFARE COMES OF AGE

Such a pattern of warfare could be sustained as long as the enemy was close and the conflict short, but in the changing circumstances of fifth- and fourth-century Italy, there was a growing pressure to innovate. In particular, Rome's conflict with the neighbouring city of Veii and subsequently with Gallic migrants provoked the emergence of new, more distinctively Roman, forms of warfare.

Reading the epic ancient accounts of the long-running conflict between Rome and Veii, it is easy to forget that the two cities lay little more than 15 kilometres apart. Yet even conflict so relatively close to Rome could put an almost unbearable strain on the city's military resources. Farmer-soldiers could not afford to participate in the drawn-out siege that culminated in Veii's capture in 396 BC without some form of recompense, so for the first time the state began to pay its soldiers. Also of profound significance to the changing character of army was the growing size of the citizen body. The populations of several neighbouring Latin communities became citizens once their cities had fallen under Roman hegemony. Crucially, therefore, as Roman power grew, Rome was able to call on a growing pool of citizens to fight for further expansion. In the build-up to the final onslaught on Veii, the Roman army increased in numbers by a half, to 6,000 men. Quite possibly this expansion also necessitated innovations in Servius Tullius's class system, with men now called to the colours who were not able to afford a cuirass or greaves. Such men, it appears, compensated for their lack of body armour with the adoption of a long curved shield (*scutum*) in place of the smaller circular model represented on depictions of Roman soldiers from previous centuries.

Still less well understood at this time are the soldiers of those communities with Latin and Allied status (*socii*) that provided a crucial part of Rome's field armies. As non-citizens, these shadowy figures were of less interest to Roman writers. The name of the allied equivalent to the legion, *ala sociorum*, emphasises the fact that these soldiers were not seen as central to proper warfare even if in reality they played an essential role. The term *ala*, meaning 'wing', reflects the location of allies in the battle line. They served on the flanks, a position of great tactical importance, but one less prestigious than that occupied by the legionaries. The increasing dependence of Roman forces on non-citizens was to have major consequences for the shape of both war and peace in the Roman world for centuries to come.

The Gallic onslaught on Rome in 390 BC stamped the Roman psyche with a deeply rooted fear of the 'northern barbarians', but it may also have provoked reforms that ultimately gave the Romans the crucial edge over their opponents. Much of this new thinking has been attributed to Camillus, the *dictator* responsible for both the capture of Veii and later struggles against the Gauls, but the reality is probably more complex. It may have been in the free-flowing battles with the latter, or decades later in operations in the Apennine highlands against the Samnites (343–290 BC), that the Roman phalanx proved unwieldy and an alternative was sought. Commanders found a solution in the use of maniples, formations two centuries strong that were able to manoeuvre separately, yet within the main formation. This more flexible style of combat complemented wider adoption of the *scutum* and a growing emphasis on missile weapons. Now able to operate with greater flexibility than a Greek phalanx, but with greater cohesion than a Celtic war band, the Roman army blazed a tactical path that was to contribute greatly to Rome's dominance in Italy and beyond.

At a higher level, Roman military organisation at this period reflected an enduring concern of Roman politics. The body of men levied for service, or *legio*, was now divided up first into two legions (by 362 BC), then into four (by 311 BC). A consul, elected for a year at a time, commanded each half of the army; six tribunes led each legion. The division of command, the shortness of tenure, and the fact that the Assembly elected the holders of all of these posts reflect the characteristic Roman system of checks and balances. It also reflects the integral relationship between war and peace in the Roman world: the consuls were the supreme magistrates in both military and civil affairs.

By 265 BC this essentially citizen force had conquered Italy. In an intensive period of expansion spanning rather less than a century, Rome defeated the Samnite tribal confederation of the Apennines, the Etruscans, the Gauls south of the River Po and the diverse peoples of southern Italy. To secure their peace, the Romans used two devices that were to characterise the stamp of Roman imperialism for centuries to come. All-weather roads essentially shrunk the distances to and within conquered territories, enabling Rome's armies to project power at speed to the heart of any dissent. And colonies, filled with citizens loyal to Rome, ensured safe havens and secure bases within previously hostile territory.

Roman soldiers of the early second century AD, arrayed in close order with their rectangular shields at the ready. The image comes from the relief band that decorates Trajan's Column, erected to commemorate Trajan's campaigns in Dacia (modern Romania). The discipline and determination of the well-ordered and well-equipped Roman legionary troops is strongly conveyed.

THE COST OF WAR AND THE PRICE OF PEACE

Again and again in Rome's rise to Mediterranean hegemony, Roman military policies affirmed with brutal pragmatism the same core principles: never capitulate, exploit manpower reserves ruthlessly, emulate your enemy's most effective strategies (but if possible do so on a bigger scale) and show mercy only when it serves your purposes.

To those schooled in Greek warfare, Rome's refusal to come to terms was at first exasperating and then terrifying as the army showed its capacity to rebuild, reform and return to combat. Not by chance does our term Pyrrhic victory preserve the name of one of Rome's greatest opponents. Impressed by the discipline of his adversaries, King Pyrrhus of Epirus, one of the finest generals of his day and commander of an outstanding professional army, won repeated victories against Roman forces, yet ultimately it was he who withdrew from Italy; Rome endured.

A detail of Giovanni Battista Tiepolo's *The Continence of Scipio Africanus* (1745). The image represents Scipio's magnanimity after his defeat of Hannibal at the Battle of Zama (202 BC), which ended the Second Punic War and led to Scipio receiving the honorary title Africanus.

A capacity to endure was also a defining feature of Rome's confrontation with Carthage, its most dangerous rival in the western Mediterranean, during the three Punic wars. In the carnage of Cannae in 216 BC, some sixty years after Pyrrhus, 50,000 Roman and allied soldiers allegedly died at the hands of Hannibal's Carthaginian army in a single day. Yet Rome not only refused to negotiate, it refused to ransom Roman prisoners and even banned the prisoners' families from raising money to do so privately. Rather than sue for peace, the Romans showed their astonishing resolve by taking extraordinary measures to raise and arm troops. To equip four new legions they stripped their temples of displays of weapons captured in previous wars and purchased 8,000 slaves, freeing them and enlisting them. This last action is particularly illuminating: even in these difficult conditions there were certain standards to adhere to and the Romans could not accept the idea that slaves might fight on their behalf. In the course of time, the Romans revenged themselves on their Carthaginian adversaries several times over. At Zama in 202 BC, Scipio Africanus utterly defeated the Africans on the battlefield. Unlike the Romans, the Carthaginians were then prepared to sue for peace.

During the long conflict with Carthage, Roman beliefs regarding the proper conduct of war were necessarily extended to battle in a new and terrifyingly different milieu, the Mediterranean Sea. In an incredible surge of building activity, they created a fleet by copying a captured enemy ship. They also introduced a new device for naval combat. This remarkable innovation was the *corvus* (crow), a bridge with a spike that could be lowered from the deck of a Roman vessel onto that of its opponent, holding the two ships together and allowing Roman soldiers to board the enemy with relative ease. Extremely successful, the *corvus* could, however, make ships top-heavy in rough seas. It may well have contributed to the dreadful loss of men and ships suffered by Rome's fleet in a series of severe storms in the mid-250s BC. The Romans replaced the thousands of drowned sailors and carried on. Otherwise they took to water remarkably well, repeatedly defeating the navy of their experienced maritime opponents. Their only major defeat at sea was at Drepana in 249 BC. Interestingly, Roman commentators blamed the impiety of the commanding consul for the catastrophe. If chickens ate well, it was believed, the gods favoured Roman military action. Unfortunately, the consul's chickens did not oblige and, with a flourish, he hurled the luckless birds into the sea, observing that if they would not eat, then they would drink. The conduct of Roman warfare, for all its brutal pragmatism, never ceased to be wedded to complex religious beliefs and practices.

In his account of the Second Punic War, the Greek writer Polybius provides an account of both the Roman constitution and the Roman army. The juxtaposition illustrates that he too recognised the importance of the link between state and soldiery. His description, written in about 160 BC but drawing on earlier material, offers good insight into the organisation of the legions during the war with Hannibal. All men with property worth over 400 *denarii* were eligible for enlistment, but once on campaign they received an allowance from the state. The poorest recruits became *velites*, light troops who went into battle with little more than a circular shield and sword to protect them. They wore wolfskin covers on their helmets, served as skirmishers and numbered about 1,200 men in every legion. Wealthier soldiers formed the heavy infantry and were further divided on grounds of age and experience. The youngest of these, the *hastati* (1,200 men per legion), were placed closest to the enemy. The next in age formed the *principes* (1,200 per legion) and the most senior of all, the *triarii* (600 per legion) stood at the rear in reserve. Equipment for these three categories of soldiers was broadly similar, consisting of a breastplate, helmet, greaves and *scutum*. Soldiers threw heavy javelins at the enemy before closing for battle with the short sword (*gladius*). Integral to each legion was a contingent of 300 cavalry. Despite the importance of mounted soldiers in many of the battles of the Punic Wars, the number of cavalrymen serving within a legion seldom rose above this figure and indeed, in later years became smaller still. Citizen soldiers were primarily infantrymen; non-citizens provided most of the cavalry.

This, then, was the army that won the Punic wars for Rome. Yet while the destruction of Carthage in 146 BC gave Rome mastery of the Mediterranean, it did not bring peace. Retaining and exploiting this far-flung territory led to conflict on many fronts. By no means all of these were of Rome's own choosing.

THE MULES OF MARIUS

Lessons hard learnt by the veterans of the Punic wars were often forgotten in the years that followed. The long-term limitations of a citizen army became increasingly apparent in the closing decades of the second century BC as one battlefield humiliation followed another in quick succession. Notions of Roman military pre-eminence suffered one blow after another in Africa at the hands of the Numidian Jugurtha; a sorry saga of incompetence and corruption culminated in the surrender of a Roman army. In Gaul, Roman armies endured defeats at the hands of migrating Celtic tribes. Roman losses at one of these confrontations, at Orange in 105 BC, were at least as great as at Cannae.

The era also witnessed attempts at reform. The Gracchi, brothers who were each to hold the post of tribune of the *plebs*, advanced revolutionary reforms that had both civil and military implications. Tiberius Gracchus, the older of the two, advocated land redistribution, noting that such a policy would not only benefit poorer citizens, but would increase the number eligible to serve in the legions. Ten years later, Tiberius's brother Gaius argued for several changes to service conditions, including payment by the state for soldiers' personal equipment, restrictions on magistrates' rights to inflict draconian punishments upon soldiers under their command and, apparently, a limit on the duration of military service. Significant as the ideas promoted by the Gracchi were, however, the figure that looms largest in accounts of military reform during these troubled years is Gaius Marius, an accomplished war leader who defeated both the African uprising and the migratory Celts. As so often with alleged military reformers, it is hard, however, to determine the extent to which Marius was really responsible for all that was attributed to him.

In Sallust's account of a speech credited to Marius at the beginning of his first consulship (107 BC), the need for professionalism in military affairs emerges as a key theme. Roman 'greed, incompetence or vanity' are blamed for recent failures, but Marius assures his listeners that his election will transform the command and training of the army. Certainly Marius was prepared to innovate. Much has been made of his decision to open his army's ranks to the *capite censi*, those once considered too poor to be able to undertake military service. This was, however, neither as innovatory as is sometimes suggested – we have already seen something of the flexibility of recruitment strategies in the aftermath of Cannae – nor necessarily intended as a long-term model. Yet with it, and the long tenure of command (an unprecedented six consecutive consulships) enjoyed by Marius himself, the Roman army took on an increasingly professional appearance.

For the army, the hallmarks of Marius's tenure were hard fighting, hard training and hard marching. It was the latter that came to characterise the new legionary soldier. Slumped under the weight of their own equipment when on the march, the soldiers in his army came to be known as 'Marius's Mules'. The chore of carrying not only his weapons but also his entrenching and cooking equipment conveyed something of the peculiar status of the Roman fighting man. In many respects a privileged being and a powerful warrior, he was nonetheless expected to do hard manual labour away from the battlefield.

Credited to Marius with varying degrees of certainty are two other changes that were to have a lasting influence on the shape of the legions. The first was a development in tactical doctrine, involving a switch from maniples to cohorts of approximately 480 men as the basic battlefield unit. Each legion now consisted of ten cohorts. This change, which was certainly in place by the mid-first century BC, retained the century as a military administrative unit, but complemented changes in the social structure of the army. With state support, it was now possible to assure soldiers of broadly similar levels of equipment. Fighting men were no longer drawn up in lines determined by their ability to furnish their own equipment.

The other innovation of note was the decision to make the eagle the legion's chief standard. Military standards were to play an important role in the life of Rome's soldiers; increasingly venerated in their own right, they stood at the heart of every camp and at the centre of any battle formation. Up until the time of Marius, the armies of Rome had carried a variety of standards, but from this time onwards it was to be the eagle – the symbol of Jupiter – that was to be the legion's rallying point and its soul. The loss of its eagle was the greatest disgrace a legion could suffer.

Following his successes over Jugurtha and the Celtic tribes threatening Cisalpine Gaul, Marius's career encompassed two further episodes that were to have lasting implications for the relationship of army and society. The first, in which Marius served as legate, was the Social War. Italians living in Rome received citizenship in 94 BC, but many of Rome's allies elsewhere in the peninsula did not enjoy this privilege. Resentment over their inferior treatment boiled over into open warfare from 91 to 89 BC. Resolution of the conflict involved a mixture of violence and diplomacy, but ultimately resulted in the extension of citizenship to much of the Italian peninsula. A legacy of the crisis, however, was that many lost their homes and farms. These developments led to a change in the make-up of the legions. Henceforth, in both economic and geographical terms, Rome's citizen units were raised from an altogether larger pool of Italian manpower than before.

It was the final appointment of Marius's career that triggered an ominous development in the relationship between army and state. Mithridates, King of Pontus (in the modern Turkey), invaded Greece. The consul for 88 BC, Lucius Cornelius Sulla, was ordered by the Senate to launch operations against him, but shortly afterwards the command was transferred to Marius. Sulla's reaction was terrifying: he marched his army of six legions on Rome to ensure that he retained command. It was a lesson, soon to be repeated, on just how dangerous the army could be to Rome herself, and of how increasingly it came to look to its own commanders, not the Senate, for leadership. With Marius dead, Sulla went on to assert his will over much of Italy. His veterans were duly settled on confiscated lands in the territories that had resisted him.

Marius appeals to ancient values

My words are not carefully chosen. I attach no importance to such artifices... It is my adversaries who require oratorical skill to help them cover up their turpitude. Nor have I studied Greek literature; I have no interest in a branch of learning which did nothing to improve the characters of its professors. The lessons I have learnt are such as best enable me to serve my country – to strike down an enemy, to mount guard, to fear nothing but disgrace, to endure winter's cold and summer's heat with equal patience, to sleep on the bare ground, and to work hard on an empty stomach. These are the lessons I shall teach my soldiers. And I shall not make them go short while enjoying the best of everything myself, nor steal all the glory and leave them the toil. This is the proper way for a citizen to lead his fellow citizens. To live in luxury oneself while subjecting one's army to rigorous discipline is to act like a tyrant instead of a commander. It was by conduct such as I recommend that your ancestors won renown for themselves and for the state.

Sallust The Jugurthine War *85*
(translated by S. A. Handford)

GREAT MEN, PRIVATE ARMIES

Others were to follow Sulla's precedent. The first century BC was marked by the ascendancy of powerful individuals whose Roman armies owed their first loyalty to their commanders. So great indeed was this loyalty that it could motivate armies to fight against their fellow Romans. The charisma of the war leaders, so apparent in the literary accounts, only explains this phenomenon in part. Many soldiers now came from the landless classes: they had nothing on which to live after discharge unless their commander negotiated land for them from the Senate. Furthermore, long periods of service in distant lands served to reduce the ties these men felt to civil society. This situation had major implications for the Republic and for the evolving character of Roman imperialism. As the Senate's power crumbled, new strongmen emerged to extend the reach of Rome far beyond the shores of the Mediterranean.

The rise of these strongmen must, however, be seen against an Italian background. Their actions were designed to translate into the political capital that only Rome could provide. Furthermore, many of them made their mark by confronting threats in the Republic's heartlands. Marcus Licinius Crassus, for example, suppressed the famous slave revolt of Spartacus, a gladiator who famously challenged Roman authority from Capua from 73 BC. Accounts of the conflict reflect various key themes in Roman warfare. First, we learn that Spartacus had previously served in the Roman army as an auxiliary, a non-citizen soldier. In literature, and probably also frequently in reality, particularly dangerous enemies appear as men who once served Rome – learning the tricks of their fighting trade before turning them against their former masters. Second, we see the familiar pattern of Roman defeats until a disciplinarian commander brings victory. In this case Crassus proceeded with vigour and savagery, decimating two of the defeated legions he inherited from his humbled predecessor. For future generations this form of punishment, by which a proportion of a Roman force was selected for execution by its own commander, came to symbolise the draconian nature of military discipline, however rarely it was actually put into practice. Underpinning this ruthlessness was a sense of ownership. Crassus observed that nobody could consider himself rich unless he could fund an army from his own resources. Sometimes, as with the alliance of Crassus, Caesar and Pompey, these powerful commanders might pressurise the Senate to sanction military initiatives. Equipped with large armies such men were well placed to embark on riskier ventures than the Senate might desire.

Also making his mark on both battlefield and political stage in this period was Gnaeus Pompeius (Pompey). While ancient accounts tend to reflect the view that war essentially concerned conflict between armies and cities, for many ordinary people the greatest threat to life and liberty came from organised crime. Banditry was a widespread problem, and piracy had reached epidemic proportions in the Mediterranean. When pirates had the temerity to snatch two magistrates travelling on the Appian Way, the Senate decided to act – granting Pompey extraordinary powers and a fleet of two hundred ships. In three months, contemporaries claim, he resolved a problem that had made shipping in the Mediterranean a nightmare for at least a century. Though his campaign was undoubtedly a major achievement, piracy and brigandage continued to trouble travellers throughout the Principate, albeit on a smaller scale. Fresh from his campaigns against the pirates, Pompey went on to victory over Mithridates, the annexation of Syria and a series of important and lasting initiatives in provincial organisation across the Roman Middle East. Amongst the latter, a notable feature was the establishment of 'friendly kings', client rulers of buffer states on the fringes of Roman territory. Returning to Rome, however, Pompey encountered difficulties in getting land for his veterans, men who looked to him for their future. When the Senate proved uncooperative, Pompey formed a political alliance with Crassus and a less celebrated third partner, Gaius Julius Caesar, to form what we now call the First Triumvirate.

A typical Roman war galley, from a relief dating from the first century AD. Pompey's fleet, authorised by the Senate ostensibly to clear the Mediterranean of pirates, consisted of two hundred such ships, each with its contingent of heavily armed soldiers. Command of a major military force with such freedom of action gave Pompey a strong political powerbase in Rome.

This junior partner, Caesar, went on to exemplify the spirit of the time. Though no military reformer, he brought his forces up to an extraordinary level of efficiency. Retaining experienced soldiers and developing them through his exceptional powers of leadership, he exploited to the full the sense of personal loyalty to a commander that characterised armies of the period. This crucial relationship was underpinned by a soldier's oath (*sacramentum*) to his commander. It was also reinforced by the distribution of booty. In the ancient world, warfare could be profitable. A successful campaign brought wealth for both commanders and soldiers; Caesar's men benefited accordingly. In the larger scheme of Roman history, however, it was less Caesar's conduct as a war leader, bold and resourceful as it was, that marked him out but rather the extent to which his own ambitions led him to expand the limits of Roman territory. No single figure did as much to extend the reach of Roman power. Within a decade of becoming consul in 59 BC, he had crushed the migrating Helvetii, conquered Gaul, taken two expeditions to Britain and cowed the Germans. His operations in Britain, strictly speaking beyond his official remit, exemplify the way the motor of imperialism operated in the twilight years of the Republic. His own commentaries on his campaigns, sent to Rome to keep himself in the public eye, recall expeditions of uncertain military value that nevertheless won him great acclaim. In crossing the Channel, Caesar could assure his readers that Rome's armies were able to cross safely beyond the limits of the world they knew.

In this new Roman world of strong men and faltering Senatorial authority, it seems with hindsight almost inevitable that conflict between the great commanders and their armies would result. Caesar's confrontation with Pompey in 49 BC was to mark the beginning of a series of shattering confrontations as Roman army met Roman army. Caesar was assassinated in 44 BC and the ongoing Civil Wars accelerated the demise of the Republic. Order was only truly imposed on the Roman world with the victory of Caesar's nephew Octavian at the naval battle of Actium in 31 BC.

Despite changes in leadership, there was broad continuity throughout much of the first century BC in Rome's adherence to established principles of military service. With campaigning armies retained for longer periods, however, there are signs of increased professionalism. Some soldiers ended up serving for very long periods indeed, well beyond the six-year minimum, their extra experience making them especially formidable opponents on the battlefield. Changes in the officer class also foreshadow later developments. Consuls were no longer permitted to campaign abroad in their year of office – a legal measure that transforms the citizen character of military leadership. Furthermore, we begin to see junior officers progressing through the chain of command in a more systematic manner. How widespread a practice this was is difficult to assess, but the career of Marcus Petreius, one of Pompey's officers, is illuminating. He went from being the tribune of a legion, to a *praefectus* (probably commanding non-citizen soldiers) to legate.

Alongside the legionaries, the Romans continued to use non-citizen soldiers – a practice well established in earlier generations. There was a difference, however, for by this time these fighters were all recruited from outside Italy. For a brief period, Balaeric slingers and Cretan archers served the Roman army. Though slings and bows had been employed in the service of Rome many times before, it is notable that they had little place in the fighting tradition of the citizen soldier as a heavily armoured infantryman. Underscoring the continuing emphasis on the primacy of the legionary foot soldier was the disappearance of the citizen cavalryman. Cavalry were now also recruited from outside Italy, from Numidia, Germany and Gaul. Cicero's concern when Mark Antony, one of Caesar's opponents, seized recruiting grounds in Gaul reflects the growing dependence of commanders on these auxiliary forces as they sought to put ever greater numbers of men into the field.

THE LORD OF WAR AND PEACE

The triumph of Gaius Octavius (Octavian, later known as Augustus), ushered in a new era. Though Augustan propaganda frequently represented this as a return to the ideals of the Republic, it has rightly been termed a revolution. Under Augustus's auspices, the army underwent a transformation no less significant than that of the rest of the state; it had to, if it was to avoid a repetition of the problems that had pulled down the Republic. There was, of course, a cost to all this. Now all army commands, and indeed the very power to make war, fell into the hands of one man, Augustus, whom the writer Strabo aptly described as 'the lord of war and peace'.

A potentially destabilising legacy of the Civil Wars was the large number of men under arms. Augustus tackled this problem by retaining many of the new legions created during the wars, concluding that the Empire now needed a larger force than the traditional ten to fourteen legions. Regiments became permanent and rates of pay were standardised. Changes in 13 BC also involved extending the term of service from six years to sixteen, with an extra four years in reserve. Honourable discharge after this period was rewarded with a grant of land or cash, or both. In many respects Augustus could claim to be following Republican precedents with these rules, but the result was that more men served for longer – making the army one of the most experienced, man for man, of the ancient world. In time it became common practice for soldiers to serve twenty-five years before they were offered honourable discharge. Augustus followed his predecessors in rewarding time-expired veterans through the foundation of new colonies, many of them outside Italy. A land settlement was agreed in 30 BC to address the needs of the many veterans of the Civil Wars who anxiously awaited discharge. Other conditions for common soldiers were probably also introduced by Augustus at the same time, in particular the law that they could not marry. The Roman soldier was now truly a professional, set apart from civilian society.

The Augustan reforms were not simply concerned with the legions, but also with the *auxilia*. These units were originally intended as non-citizen regiments, but citizens are attested in their ranks from the reign of Augustus, and are found in larger numbers thereafter. Three new types of auxiliary unit created at this time – infantry cohorts, part-mounted cohorts (a mixture of cavalry and infantry) and cavalry *alae* – remained essential elements of the Roman army for over three centuries. Unlike the 5–6,000-strong legions, however, these were at this date all small formations of no more than five hundred men. Only in the second half of the first century AD do auxiliary regiments of eight hundred to one thousand men emerge. Nevertheless, the

Augustus's *imperium*

I undertook many civil and foreign wars by land and sea throughout the world, and as victor I spared the lives of all citizens who asked for mercy. When foreign peoples could safely be pardoned I preferred to preserve rather than exterminate them. The Roman citizens who took the soldier's oath of obedience to me numbered about 500,000. I settled rather more than 300,000 of these in colonies or sent them back to their home towns after their period of service; to all these I assigned lands or gave money as rewards for their military service. I captured six hundred ships not counting ships smaller than triremes.

The Achievements of the Divine Augustus *3, 1–4* (translated by P. A. Brunt and J. M. Moore)

auxilia as a whole amounted to as many men under arms as the legions. It was therefore a vital part of Rome's military strength. In theory, these auxiliary units were raised from specific tribes and regions, and at least initially several retained the fighting traditions of their home regions. Auxiliaries were usually distinguished from their legionary counterparts by their dress. The legions retained the *scutum* and weighted javelin (*pilum*) while the auxiliary equipment commonly included a flat shield (*clipeus*) and spear (*hasta*). This distinction owes something to an early Roman view that auxiliaries should act as skirmishers on the battlefield, it is clear that they were often used in similar ways to the legionary troops in major battles.

Augustus was also responsible for the creation of Rome's first permanent fleets. As the Empire expanded, new fleets were added to those on the Italian coast. Thus, for example, there were fleets responsible for the Danube, the Rhine and for Britain. Though the number of sailors, mostly non-citizens, grew to about 30,000 we hear remarkably little about them in our sources. Great sea battles, of the type that might catch the attention of contemporary writers, were rare in the centuries following Actium. The fleets therefore seem to have concentrated on roles in support of the army and perhaps on low-level anti-piracy patrols.

Senior command structures also underwent some important changes during this period. Individual senators were now placed in command of legions for several years at a time. Furthermore, though the organisation of senior officers for the *auxilia* was not formalised, with centurions and jointly appointed senators commanding individual units, there was a growing move towards an association of such command positions with membership of the equestrian class. This association was to become common by the end of the Julio-Claudian period; indeed, a command in the *auxilia* came to be recognised as a step in the normal career of an *eques*.

More important than any of these changes, however, was the identification of the army now with the person of Augustus, and in consequence with subsequent emperors. Allegiance to campaigning generals was to be, in theory at least, a thing of the past. The army looked upon the emperor for largess, and he in turn looked to it for his very survival. Augustus was the first of many emperors, therefore, whose bond with his soldiers was emphasised not only through pay and patronage, but also – on the part of the soldiers – through oath-taking, religious observance and due observation of the ceremonies of the imperial cult.

In addition to field armies and fleets, Augustus formed the Praetorian Guard, an elite force of bodyguards paid at three times the rate of ordinary soldiers, responsible for his personal security. Though occasionally embroiled in the more scandalous elements of imperial power, periodically disbanded and subsequently counter-balanced with other guard units drawn from the *auxilia*, the Praetorian Guard survived as the reigning emperor's own force right through to the fourth century AD.

The end result of Augustus's military reforms was a powerful force, eminently capable of tackling the emperor's enemies at home and abroad. Reflecting on its unprecedented size and professionalism, it is easy to see how Virgil, poet and propagandist, could see in contemporary history testimony that Rome enjoyed a divinely ordained right to *imperium sine fine*, power without limits.

Yet the forces of Rome were not to have it all their own way. In AD 9, in a disastrous campaign deep in Germany, Publius Quinctilius Varus led three legions and their associated auxiliaries to destruction in an ambush deep in the Teutoberger Forest. The architect of their slaughter, a German leader named Arminius, was himself a former Roman auxiliary. Shaken to the core by the disaster, the emperor responsible for the most rapid enlargement of the Empire advised his successor Tiberius to keep the Empire within its present boundaries. Though this may indicate a pragmatic acceptance of the limitations of imperial power, it is clearly did not mark the end of Roman expansion.

Officers and troops of the Praetorian Guard, seen in a relief from the second century AD. A powerful corps of imperial bodyguards, the Praetorians came to play an important political role in Rome despite the efforts of successive emperors to control them.

MAKING ROMAN PEACE

The pursuit of Roman peace should not be confused with our modern notions of peace-keeping. In times of conflict, Rome backed the strongest side that would support Roman interests, seldom hesitating to apply force when the need arose. The *pax Romana* was therefore an unequal peace, one that required violent and perpetual reassertion in many parts of the Roman world. The period prior to Hadrian's reign saw major developments that determined the form of this new peace, and who was to gain from it and who was to lose.

Almost from the moment of Augustus's death the dangers inherent in his new-style army were made painfully apparent. Mutiny broke out among the legions on the Rhine and in Pannonia. Tacitus's account of the mutineers paints them in a pathetic, almost theatrical light; we hear of toothless veterans lamenting their lot. Some of the luckless soldiers had allegedly served forty years. Pay, land grants to discharged men and the brutality of their centurions also ranked high amongst the mutineers' complaints. One centurion, nicknamed 'Bring me Another' from his habit of calling for his vine cane to be replaced after he had broken it in punishment beatings, was among those murdered by the unruly soldiery. It took the intercession of members of the imperial family, promises (later broken) and a burst of intense campaigning to bring the legions to order again.

Those communities from whom Rome drew auxiliaries also had cause to rue the cost of Roman peace. In one illuminating episode in the reign of Tiberius, Thracian tribes revolted in response to a levy (*dilectus*) of their community. Their concern – that their contingents would be mixed up with other peoples and sent to distant lands – proved justified. Few of those subsequently conscripted probably ever saw their homes again. Recruitment into the *auxilia* could constitute a form of exile, and indeed in some cases was used as a device to aid the pacification of a troubled territory. In typical Roman fashion, a local king, his irregulars and other auxiliary units (in this case recruited from the Rhineland) aided in the suppression of this revolt. Thereafter Rome continued to draw soldiers from Thrace for centuries. In the third century, one such recruit, Maximinus, was to become emperor.

It is possible that uprisings such as the Thracian revolt ultimately led to further improvement in auxiliary service conditions. Although Roman citizenship had long been awarded to loyal allies in the Republic, it was not until the first century AD that Rome began systematically to reward time-served auxiliaries in this way. Claudius rewarded all auxiliary soldiers who served for at least twenty-five years with a grant of citizenship and *conubium*, the legitimisation of any children they had had. Bronze certificates (diplomas) recording the names and details of both the grant and grantee have been discovered at sites across the Empire. These provide important information about recruitment, military deployment and veteran settlement. The earliest known example dates to AD 52.

Roman notions of peacemaking and imperial security were to confront their greatest test in the AD 60s and 70s, in a variety of challenges. The first, the revolt of the Iceni under Boudicca in AD 60–1 graphically illustrates the way in which abuse of peacemaking strategy could incite devastating rebellion. On the death of Boudicca's husband, the pro-Roman client ruler Prasutagus, the local Roman authorities chose to treat the Icenian kingdom as conquered territory. Bent on exploiting and expropriating tribal properties, the soldiers abused the queen and raped her daughters. Retribution was swift and terrifying. Joined by neighbouring tribes who had come to resent the arrogant behaviour of colonists at Camulodunum (Colchester), the Iceni swept through southern England, destroying first the colony and then the Roman settlements at Verulamium (St Albans) and London before their final defeat by the hastily summoned legions from the north and west of Britain. Rather than an advertisement for the Roman way of life as imperial theorists advocated, the colony had proved a source of resentment.

A different set of circumstances, no less illuminating, inspired local revolt on the Lower Rhine in AD 69. This was the infamous year of the Four Emperors, when once again Roman armies, now developing distinct characters and allegiances, espoused political loyalties and marched to put their competing candidates on the imperial throne. Seizing the moment, Julius Civilis, commander of an auxiliary cohort, called upon his Batavian tribesmen and their neighbours to revolt. It was to be the last major challenge by any provincial population to the *dilectus*. The motivations and ambitions of the rebels were mixed. Tacitus cites resentment at the crude and exploitative handling of a levy of Batavians, demands by the auxiliaries for higher wages and Civilis's own political ambitions as factors. In the fierce fighting that followed, auxiliary soldiers frequently bested their legionary opponents, giving the lie to any claims of martial superiority by the citizen soldiers. Ultimately, a settlement with the Batavian nobles was reached that enabled them to retain their traditional martial privileges in Roman service – something that the handling of the levy may have suggested was under threat. Certainly the traditional symbols of power among the peoples elsewhere in northern Europe, weapons and raids, were undermined by the Roman state's monopoly of military force. By no means all members of the native elite approved (or survived) the transformation to Latin-speaking, bath-taking and toga-wearing that constituted status markers under the new regime.

On the other side of the Roman world, AD 66 saw the outbreak of the Jewish War, discussed in more detail below. Recent scholarship emphasises how difficult it was for the Jewish elite to advance within the Roman system while retaining their religious identity. The failure of the state to incorporate this community more fully undoubtedly contributed to the outbreak of hostilities.

Pacification did not stop with the suppression of these conflicts, and on several fronts the Roman army continued to campaign with vigour. In Britain, the Romans recovered the initiative after Boudicca's revolt, but Tacitus paints a mixed picture of the consequences of Britain's incorporation into the Empire. Celebrating the success of Agricola, governor of Britain in the AD 80s, he notes how the latter managed to encourage the indigenous population to abandon lives accustomed to war and to compete for Roman honour by investing in such trappings as temples and town houses. Yet, in what is clearly part of a complex contemporary debate on the character of Roman authority, he also has a British leader lament that the Romans 'create a desolation and call it peace'.

THE LIMITS OF EMPIRE

Roman expansion did not cease in the late first century AD – indeed, in the early second century the warrior emperor Trajan was to undertake spectacular campaigns to the north in Dacia and less successfully for Rome to the east in Parthia – but the late first century does see the emergence of a new phenomenon: running frontier lines on the borders of the Empire. With the succession of Hadrian, the extent of Roman territory becomes still more clearly defined, with the unprecedented abandonment of territory and the establishment, in some areas, of frontier walls. Hadrian's Wall in northern Britain seems a very long way from Virgil's notion of *imperium sine fine*.

Appearances can deceive, however. The very solidity of monuments such as Hadrian's Wall suggests permanence, but within a few decades of its creation it had been abandoned, albeit temporarily, for a similar system further north, the Antonine Wall. Recent work on both Hadrian's Wall and the Antonine Wall show that these were no mere customs barriers, but that they were constructed in the very real expectation of major attacks. Elaborate pit traps and entanglements stood in front of the lines, while towers were added, out of sequence, to observe folds in the ground that might otherwise permit infiltration. Linear frontiers are also known from other parts of Europe – along the Rhine, for example. Yet even the best-established walls did not truly mark the limits of Roman hegemony. Imperial officials could and did police people beyond the walls, while imperial campaigns attest the freedom with which Rome's rulers projected power with fire and sword far beyond the frontiers.

Furthermore, the frontiers of the Empire were not everywhere defined by the same continuous walls, for the simple reason that the peoples the Romans faced were not everywhere the same. Large linear barriers on the North African frontier, for example, leave major gaps kilometres wide. They form part of a system designed not to preclude movement, but to regulate the passage of seasonal migrants by securing watering points in an arid landscape. This and the use of long-distance patrols far beyond the walls indicates that Rome continued to claim dominion over those outside the Empire, even if they did not always seek to occupy their territories.

Significantly, the Romans referred to their frontiers as *limes*, the same term they used for roads. This is an important testimony both to the evolution of the frontier systems of the Empire and to the way in which boundaries were understood. Roads played an important role in Rome's capacity to project military power, but they also served a crucial and related function: that of expediting communication across Roman territory. A recently-discovered report from Egypt records a raid on a Roman garrison post. After a hard-fought engagement, the raiders rode off, taking civilian captives with them. The Romans launched a follow-up patrol, finding the body of one of the captives. At the bottom of the report, instructions in another hand order that the text be copied to other installations in the region. Systematic communication between military posts was clearly routine. It is scarcely surprising to find therefore, that many parts of the frontier were marked not by linear barriers, but by watchtowers associated with trackways and road systems. Systems of signals allowed these small and otherwise vulnerable Roman outposts to transmit information rapidly to larger formations of troops.

The most dramatic stretch of Hadrian's Wall across northern Britain, seen in winter. The natural escarpment followed by the Wall is clear in this view eastwards over Cuddy's Crags, near Housesteads Fort. The Wall was a complex military structure, with regularly spaced forts, milecastles and turrets, a military road and, in some sections, a defensive ditch as well.

n many cases, these troops were located in forts astride the frontier line. Hadrian's Wall, the Antonine Wall and the Rhine frontier eloquently testify to this pattern of deployment and to a large extent have formed our understanding of the deployment of Roman troops. As a rule, auxiliary units, now 500 or 1,000 men strong, including new irregular formations simply entitled *numeri* (units), were stationed in forts and fortlets on the fringes of the Empire, while the legions remained in their huge fortresses dominating strategic locations in the hinterland. But the pattern of deployment may actually have been a great deal more complicated. Not only do Roman military bases in the eastern provinces generally take a very different form from those in the western part of the Empire, but across the Empire as a whole bases hosted soldiers from several different regiments at the same time. On almost any given day every unit in the Empire would have had soldiers on detachment – accompanying tax collectors, conveying messages, buying provisions or perhaps serving in the governor's bodyguard.

Perhaps the biggest departure from the fort-regiment-frontier model of deployment traditionally postulated by historians is the growing evidence that many soldiers were stationed at locations far behind the frontier. Recent discoveries have revealed how contingents of special duties troops (*beneficiarii*) were deployed at key points on the road network and at major mining complexes to ensure that the state's interests were served. Military equipment finds from a large number of settlements well behind the frontiers also suggest that soldiers were stationed wherever it was necessary for them to protect and run the army's own communications routes and sources of supply. This was the case regardless of the site's location within the larger provincial landscape.

Nevertheless, viewed on an imperial scale, it is clear that Roman military might was concentrated in the frontier provinces by Hadrian's reign. Over time, this pattern served to reinforce the local element in Roman armies. This may be seen in various ways. Soldiers tended to be recruited from the nearest convenient source. Sometimes, even during the more stable periods of the second century, that source was still quite a long way from a regiment's headquarters, perhaps even another province – but most often it was the province in which the unit was stationed. The *vici* and *canabae*, civilian settlements attached to auxiliary forts and legionary fortresses respectively, were clearly sources of recruits for their associated garrisons. By the middle of the second century AD it would have been hard to find Italians within the ranks of the legions. Rome's armies may have contained an increasing number of Roman citizens, but the people of Rome would have found them more alien and threatening by far than the Republican militias who had carved out the Empire.

A further feature of the evolving frontier systems was the increasing permanence of many military bases. Though large campaigns continued to be fought, many units appear to have remained at the same location for decades, even centuries. Indeed, from the second century AD onwards we see an increasing preference among military commanders for the use of detachments, rather than entire regiments, to build campaign armies. Continuity of station inevitably had consequences for soldier/civilian interaction, but these are not always clear. On the one hand, the *vici* and *canabae*, some of which achieved self-governing status, frequently had a strongly military flavour. We have clear evidence that several such settlements folded when the local garrison marched away. But the relationship between soldiers and civilians outside such settlements is far harder to gauge.

Many soldiers had parents and siblings living great distances from the camp walls, and we learn something of their private lives through surviving correspondence – but for a great many civilians contact with the army would have been less intimate and mostly very unwelcome. Apuleius's second-century AD tale *The Golden Ass* presents a plausible picture of a vicious soldiery. A luckless farmer is unable to comprehend the Latin instructions of a legionary soldier determined to appropriate his ass. The legionary then strikes the farmer and the farmer fights back, overpowering the soldier, seizing his sword and escaping. It is then, however, that the farmer's problems really begin, because the consequences of striking a soldier are dire. The soldiers' colleagues search for the farmer to mete out further punishment. Provincials had little realistic hope of justice when confronted by the violence and extortion of the military.

A surviving part of the approach road to the fort of Vindolanda, near Hadrian's Wall. As the Wall developed, settlements (*vici*) grew up around the associated forts, and became centres for the local population and the local economy. Their auxiliary garrisons originally drawn from diverse provinces, were increasingly recruited locally.

ROME ON THE FRONTIER

Excavations at Housesteads fort on Hadrian's Wall have revealed much about life in and around Roman military installations. Though forts varied in form across the Empire as a whole, those discovered to date in the western provinces share certain features. This is as true of the major legionary fortresses as it is of smaller bases like Housesteads, which held up to 1,000 men. One reason for this similarity is the common origin of all such forts in Republican campaign camps. These were themselves products of Roman ideas about the proper organisation of living space and society.

At the heart of Housesteads, as at most other Roman camps, lay the *Principia* or headquarters building. This consisted of a small open square and a hall. Its resemblance, albeit on a smaller scale, to the forum and town hall ensemble familiar in provincial towns is not coincidental. It was here that Roman soldiers, like their civilian counterparts, gathered for news, instruction and the judgement of the authorities. Also housed within the

Principia was the regimental shrine, home to the unit's standards and, judiciously co-located with it, the regimental pay chests. Nearby was the *Praetorium*, the commanding officer's house. Even in Britain, this retained the form of a Mediterranean town house, with an open courtyard. This was not just a place for the commanding officer's family, however, but a place where, as in Roman tradition, dignitaries could be met and official business conducted.

Substantial granaries, which are easily distinguishable archaeologically by their raised floors, were a key part of every fort. Environmental evidence from other sites, and writing tablets recovered at the neighbouring fort of Vindolanda, suggest that much of the grain that filled these would have come from long distances.

Long barracks, each capable of taking a century of soldiers, filled much of the rest of the fort's interior. At the end of each block lived the centurion. On the analogy of the tented camps of the Republic, historians suggest that two rooms in each block were allocated to each eight-man *contubernium* within a century, one for equipment and the other for sleeping, but the archaeology does not allow us to be certain of this.

Soldiers' lives did not stop at the fort walls. Beyond lay a bathhouse, a crucial feature of civilised Roman life, and several temples. Some soldiers worshipped Mithras, the Persian sun-god, while others venerated their native deities. There were also the buildings of the *vicus*, some of which served as taverns and shops for the soldiery, while others housed their families. Under the floor of one of these, archaeologists found the remains of a murdered man and woman – life could be rough on the frontier.

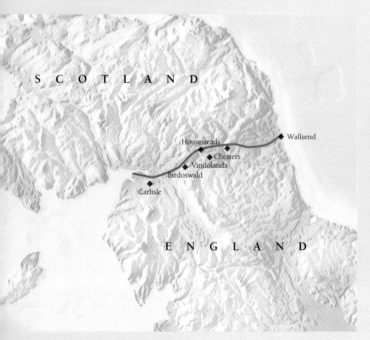

SCOTLAND

Housesteads
Chesters   Wallsend
Vindolanda
Birdoswald
Carlisle

ENGLAND

Hadrian's Wall was constructed to mark the northern limit of Hadrian's Roman Empire, and, it is assumed, to provide a means of exercising control over the frontier region of the north of England. Commencing in about AD 122, it ran over 73 miles and was on average about 7.5 feet thick.

An aerial view of Housesteads fort (*Vercovicium*). The fort was built in the AD 120s. with its northern side forming part of the structure of Hadrian's Wall itself. It is the best-known Roman fort in Britain, with evidence for many internal buildings.

ENRICH THE SOLDIERS, SCORN THE REST!

Septimius Severus's deathbed advice to his sons, 'stick together, enrich the soldiers and scorn the rest', echoes the same truth at an imperial scale. The winning and losing of imperial power depended on military support, not on the civilian population. This stark equation was amply proven by Severus's own career: he had himself come to power in AD 193 in a civil war between rival army commanders. When Severus emerged victorious, he revealed that he had learnt his lessons well. His reforms of the army, perceived by critical contemporaries as inimical to good military discipline, included pay increases and new marriage rights for soldiers. He also disbanded the Praetorian Guard, who had murdered his predecessor, and replaced them with a new guard recruited from his own loyal Danube legions.

When it came to the army, Severus's son Caracalla took at least some of his father's advice on board. He too sought to associate himself with the troops, living as an ordinary soldier and allegedly grinding his own ration of grain on campaign. His most famous action, however, in an edict of AD 212, was to extend the Roman citizenship to most of the Empire's freeborn population. What this meant in practice is still unclear, but at least in theory it demolished the principal division between the legions as citizen troops on the one hand and the *alae* and *cohortes* as non-citizen formations on the other. Probably this distinction had already been eroded, for by the mid-third century we see legionary soldiers simply transferring into auxiliary cohorts with no hint of demotion or punishment. Interestingly the *alae* and *cohortes* did not cease to exist after the edict, but remained an establishment for years to come.

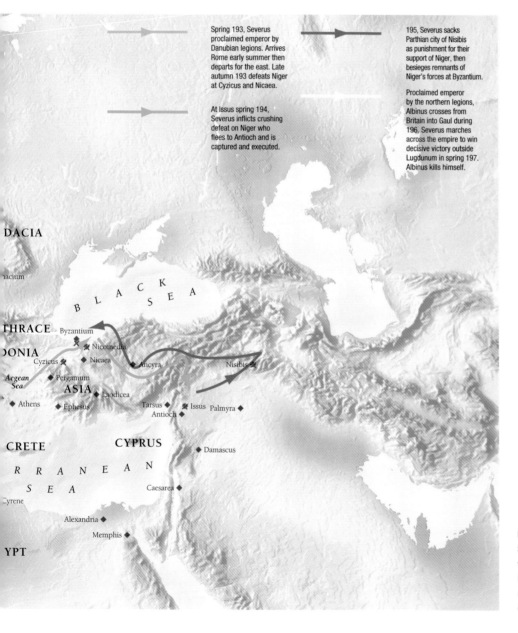

Spring 193, Severus proclaimed emperor by Danubian legions. Arrives Rome early summer then departs for the east. Late autumn 193 defeats Niger at Cyzicus and Nicaea.

At Issus spring 194, Severus inflicts crushing defeat on Niger who flees to Antioch and is captured and executed.

195, Severus sacks Parthian city of Nisibis as punishment for their support of Niger, then besieges remnants of Niger's forces at Byzantium.

Proclaimed emperor by the northern legions, Albinus crosses from Britain into Gaul during 196. Severus marches across the empire to win decisive victory outside Lugdunum in spring 197. Albinus kills himself.

In AD 193, the Danubian legions proclaimed Septimius Severus (the eventual victor), while the eastern legions backed Pescennius Niger. After Niger's death, the northern legions pressed the case of their own candidate, Clodius Albinus.

With elite interests under attack, it is hardly surprising that Severus's innovations subsequently provoked criticism from conservatives, but again the brutal pragmatism of military force worked. Even when the Severan dynasty ended, it collapsed largely because the then emperor, Severus Alexander, had proven unable command and reward his soldiers effectively. Furthermore, his murderer and successor, Maximinus Thrax (reigned AD 235–8) revealed a shrewd knowledge of how to win and maintain the army's allegiance. Maximinus was a soldier's emperor, a man who truly embodied the fellow-soldier (*commilito*) persona that Roman rulers had manipulated on and off from the time of Julius Caesar. He was the first emperor to actually fight in the battle line, and an almost hagiographical account of his life acclaims his humble origins – a cavalryman on the Danubian frontier, he would perspire so much that he could fill several cups with his sweat a day. In the Roman world, real soldiers sweated and were proud to do so.

It is common to speak of the period that followed Maximinus's rise to the imperial purple as a time of crisis. Emperors came and went with astonishing rapidity up to AD 284 and the ascension of Diocletian. Roman armies confronted Roman armies repeatedly on far-flung battlefields. Furthermore, Roman territory suffered attacks on various fronts and was actually lost in Dacia and Mesopotamia. The emperor Decius was killed in AD 251 when his army was defeated by the Goths, while the emperor Valerian surrendered to the Persians together with his army in AD 260. Yet the system did not collapse – indeed, in some respects it hung together well. Furthermore, signs of the crisis prove relatively scarce in the archaeological record; life in much of the Empire seems to have continued without grave interruption.

In many respects it was the Senatorial class that lost most from this period of crisis. In the tumultuous decades of the mid-third century, they provided the Empire with a series of ineffectual emperors and disloyal military commanders. Gallienus (AD 253–68) reacted to this by appointing increasing numbers of equestrians to the posts once reserved for senators. This rapidly became the normal practice for his successors. Furthermore, the cumulative impact of the change was still more significant. With equestrians now forming a more experienced body of military commanders, they became altogether better candidates for posts as provincial governors and campaign leaders. In particular, the appointment of equestrians to the post of *dux*, an office created in the mid-third century, represented a major challenge to the ancient pattern of senatorial dominance. At first the *dux* served as the leader of large military formations, but over time his post came to encompass wide geographical jurisdictions, many of them spanning existing provincial boundaries. The resultant evolution of a cadre of experienced senior officers represents a revolution in the balance of power within the Roman state.

A further significant feature of this difficult time was the rise of the Illyrians. Over the centuries, Rome's armies had come to draw unevenly on provincial manpower. In the first centuries BC and AD, Gaul was widely recognised as a major source of troops; in the second and third centuries, the Balkans – always an important source – took on still greater significance. In army commands, the third century saw the increasing influence of a relatively small group of Illyrian officers. Several became emperors, and one of these, Diocletian, went on to transform both Empire and army. His role in establishing the Tetrarchy is discussed elsewhere in this book, but it is important to emphasise here that the formalised separation of military and civil service that took place at this time had profound implications. Hitherto, the army had provided many of the state's lower-level administrators. The new arrangement thus undermined an important aspect of the army's power in provincial society. Under Diocletian too the distinction between frontier troops (*limitanei*) and the field army (*comitatus* or *comitatenses*) became pronounced, though it may not have reached its full, official form until Constantine. The *limitanei* operated from a range of strongpoints, many set back from the frontier line to provide defence in depth, though they were still able to participate in offensive operations. The field army, due in Rome's later armies to acquire senior status, served as a core of loyal troops on which the ruler felt he could rely and thus as the mainstay of his campaigning forces.

The army now looked quite different from the Roman armies of popular imagination. Though ancient regimental titles survived, new units with new titles, such as the cavalry *vexillationes*, emerged. Units were smaller on average too; the sixty or so legions of the later army each consisted of about 1,000 men, a fraction of the size of the legions of old. Oval shields now largely replaced the rectangular *scutum* that once distinguished the legions, so legionaries no longer appeared very different from their counterparts in the cohorts. Finally, there were changes in recruitment. These should perhaps be seen as changes more of degree than kind, as many are foreshadowed in the army of the Principate. Yet, our written sources for recruitment practices at this date stress themes very different to the ideals of the young Republic. Where once it was the citizens' privilege and duty to fight, just as it was to serve in public office, now we hear not simply of conscription and desertion (familiar features of earlier times), but of a growing number of men from beyond the Empire enlisting in the ranks. Becoming a Roman soldier no longer meant what it once had.

The emperor Gallienus (ruled 253–68) was unable to halt the Empire's slide into crisis in the mid-third century. His reforms were aimed at reducing the infuence of the Senatorial class, particularly in the army. He defeated the Goths but was unable to halt Persian advances in the East or rebellion in Gaul, Britain and Spain.

THE RECKONING

Assessments of the Roman army, agent of Roman war and peace, are commonly positive. It was an extraordinarily effective instrument of state. But this impression owes much to the glowing reports of Rome's own historians. Seldom if ever do we hear the voices of those who faced the army's brutality on the streets, or its ruthless efficiency on the battlefield. Such voices should form part of our reckoning. We find them in the New Testament, the *Histories* of Josephus and, for later years, the Talmud. Our picture of Judaea and – exceptional though that territory was in many ways – the whole Empire is the richer for their perspectives.

A relief from the Arch of Titus, built in the Forum in Rome in AD 81, shows Roman soldiers carrying in triumph the treasures of Jerusalem after the sack of the city in AD 70. The seven-branched candlestick (menorah) that stood in the Temple is clearly shown. The brutal Roman sack of the rebel city was recounted by the historian Josephus.

In the New Testament, soldiers appear as part of the landscape. We learn that an officer, the 'good' centurion of Capernaum, was responsible for building a synagogue. When soldiers seek advice from John the Baptist, he does not advise them to abandon the profession of arms, but rather exhorts them, 'Do not extort money and do not accuse people falsely – be content with your pay'. This is not an image of fire and slaughter, though it does reflect the routine misery that grasping soldiers can cause. Yet within the New Testament, too, there is a brooding sense of the potential for far greater Roman violence. In keeping with the prevailing morality of the *pax Romana*, the governor Pilate hands Christ over for crucifixion, even though he finds that Christ did no wrong. It is more important to keep order than to back the weak against the strong. In visions of the Temple of Jerusalem's destruction too, we catch a glimpse of the devastation that Roman armies will cause.

Josephus, eyewitness to the Jewish Revolt of AD 66–74, recounts the prelude to this awful event and its terrifying consequences. When revolt broke out, the governor hastily sent an army against Jerusalem, but the force was defeated. Four years of hard fighting followed, and a vigorous siege culminated in the burning of the Temple. The soldier policemen, taxman's lackeys and extortionists were now a unified force of implacable discipline. In AD 73, in follow-up operations, a group of rebels watched in horror as Roman troops built a huge siege ramp up to their apparently impregnable Herodian fortress of Masada. Archaeology shows how, as the ramp advanced, Roman soldiers built a wall around the entire circumference of the besieged area. No hilltop was too precarious or remote to be incorporated. The wall conveyed a clear message – there was no escape from Rome. Josephus records how, as Masada fell, the besieged killed their own families and themselves so that none should fall alive to the avenging hands of the Roman soldiers.

The brutal reality of both Roman peace and Roman war are exemplified in the way Vespasian marked the conclusion of the Jewish War. He ploughed some of his profits from the conflict into a fine temple-forum in the heart of Rome and displayed within it treasures captured from the Temple of Jerusalem. He dedicated it to Peace.

An aerial view from the north-west of the remains of the great Herodian fortress of Masada, on a steep rock plateau above the Dead Sea. Masada was the scene of the last stand of the Jewish rebels against Rome. The huge Roman siege ramp was built against the wall near the Western Palace, in the centre of the wall nearest the camera in this view.

FURTHER
READING

CHRONOLOGY

753 BC • Traditional date for the founding of Rome by Romulus.

616 BC • Rome comes under Etruscan rule.

507 BC • Republic begins after Romans overthrow the Tarquin dynasty of Etruscan kings.

496 BC • Romans narrowly defeat Latins at Lake Regillus

494 BC • First Secession of the Plebians. As a result, the plebians win for themselves a measure of political representation.

450 BC • First Roman law code, the Twelve Tables, is published.

396 BC • Romans capture the Etruscan city of Veii.

387 BC • Gauls sack Rome.

366 BC • Following a change in law, the first plebian consul is elected. From 342 BC the law required one consul to be plebian at all times.

343–341 BC • First Samnite War. Intermittent fighting against he Samnites of central-southern Italy would continue for almost 150 years.

340 BC • End of Latin War leaves Rome in control of Latium and Campania.

326–304 BC • Second Samnite War.

312 BC • Work on the Via Appia, the first Roman road, begins.

295 BC • In the Third Samnite War, the Romans are victorious against the Samnites and Gauls at Sentinum, winning dominance of the Italian peninsula.

287 BC • The formal utterances of the plebeian assembly gain the force of law.

280–275 BC • Pyrrhic Wars, in which Epirus supported Tarentum, a Greek colony in South Italy. The Romans are eventually victorious.

264–241 BC • First Punic War, between Rome and Carthage. This was the first war that Rome fought at sea.

241 BC • Sicily becomes the first province of the Roman Empire.

237 BC • Rome occupies Carthaginian Corsica and Sardinia.

225 BC • Roman army defeats invading Celts at Battle of Telemon.

218–201 BC • Second Punic War, in which Rome confronted the might of Carthaginian general Hannibal. After a massive Roman defeat at Cannae, (216 BC), the balance shifted in Rome's favour. The war ended with Scipio's defeat of Hannibal at Zama (203 BC)

211–205 BC • First Macedonian War, between the Macedonians and the Romans, angered by Macedon's alliance with Carthage.

200–196 BC • Second Macedonian War, in which Macedonian control of Greece is lost to Rome

171–168 BC • Third Macedonian War, waged by Rome to limit resurgent Macedonian power.

149–148 BC • Fourth Macedonian War, ending with Macedon becoming a province of Rome.

146 BC • Rome razes Carthage and Corinth, demonstrating its domination of the Mediterranean.

136 BC • Slave uprising in Sicily.

133–132 BC • Tribunate of Tiberius Gracchus, a supporter of land reform, ends with his murder at the hands of a mob of senators.

129 BC • The kingdom of Pergamum is annexed and becomes the Roman province of Asia.

121 BC • Romans conquer southern Gaul, which becomes the province of Gallia Narbonensis.

123–122 BC • Gaius Gracchus becomes tribune. Proposals for land and taxation reform won him popular support but the enmity of the Senate.

111–105 BC • War against Jugurtha of Numidia. Roman general Marius becomes consul in 107 BC and wins five more consulships, holding power until 100 BC.

91–88 BC • The Social War between Rome and the allied communities of Italy. At the end, Rome offers citizenship to all the communities of Italy.

88 BC • Sulla stages a coup, exiling Marius and taking control of the army

87 BC • Marius returns from exile and stages a coup with Cinna. Marius dies in 86 BC, leaving Cinna in control.

82 BC • Sulla returns to power, and as dictator, enlarges and strengthens the senate, reforms the courts, and limits the power of the tribunes.

80 BC • After abandoning his dictatorship in 81 BC, Sulla voluntarily retires from politics and public life.

73–71 BC • Slave uprising led by Spartacus brutally defeated by Roman forces, ending a decade of rural turmoil. Noted general Gnaeus Pompeius (Pompey) claims credit for Rome's ultimate victory.

67 BC • In one season, Pompey clears the Mediterranean of the pirates who had been disrupting trade for decades.

66–63 BC • BC Pompey extends Roman domination over Asia Minor.

64 BC • Cicero, famed for his oratory, becomes consul.

60 BC • Caesar, Pompey and Crassus form an alliance to limit the power of the Younger Cato.

59 BC • Caesar becomes consul.

58–51 BC • Caesar's Gallic War ends in victory for the Roman forces. An attempted invasion of Britain fails (55–54 BC).

53 BC • At Carrhae in Syria, the Parthians inflict a humiliating defeat on Crassus, who is killed.

52 BC • The senate appoints Pompey sole consul.

46 BC • Caesar is appointed dictator for 10 years.

49 BC • Caesar returns to Rome, crossing the Rubicon with his army, to seize power from Pompey, leading to civil war. He defeats Pompey at Pharsalus in 48 BC and Pompey is murdered after fleeing to Egypt.

44 BC • Caesar is assassinated on 15 March (the ides of March) by a large conspiracy that included Brutus and Cassius as well as many senators. He is succeeded as consul by Marcus Antonius (Mark Antony), chosen over Caesar's nephew Octavian.

43 BC • Octavian, Mark Antony and Lepidus form an alliance, ruling Rome as triumvirs. In practice, Octavian rules in the west and Mark Antony in the east.

42 BC • Mark Antony and Octavian defeat opposition forces at Philippi in Macedonia. Brutus and Cassius commit suicide following this defeat.

37–34 BC • Reign of Herod the Great in Judaea.

36 BC • Lepidus is forced to retire. Tensions between Mark Antony and Octavian increase.

31 BC • Octavian defeats the combined forces of Mark Antony and Cleopatra at the Battle of Actium. Mark Antony and Cleopatra commit suicide and Egypt becomes a Roman province.

27 BC • Octavian becomes the first Roman emperor, by decision of the Senate, and he is granted the name Augustus, meaning 'associated with the gods'. His reign was one of unprecedented peace and prosperity.

19 BC • Death of the poet Virgil.

12–9 BC • Balkan tribes pacified. Dalmatia and Pannonia established as Roman provinces.

8 BC • Death of the poet Horace.

AD 9 • German tribes led by Arminius massacre three Roman legions in Teutoberg Forest.

AD 14 • Death of Augustus (Octavian). He was succeeded by his stepson, Tiberius.

AD 41 • Assassination of Gaius Caligula, the successor of Tiberius, by officers of the Praetorian Guard.

AD 43 • Claudius conquers Britain. Despite this military success, he was unpopular with the Senate and the people and died by poisoning.

AD 59 • Nero, the successor of Claudius, orders the murder of his mother, Agrippina, and later the execution of his wife, Octavia.

AD 60 • Boudicca leads a revolt against the Romans in Britain.

AD 64 • Great fire in Rome destroys much of the city. It was rumoured that Nero himself started the fire to clear an area for a grand palace he wished to build.

AD 66–73 • The people of Judea revolt against Roman rule.

AD 68 • Following a revolt of the army, Nero commits suicide. He had survived an assassination attempt in 65.

AD 69 • With the support of the army Vespasian seizes power, ending a year of political turmoil and civil war. His reign introduced a 100-year long period of peace and prosperity for Rome.

AD 79 • The eruption of Vesuvius destroys Pompeii and Herculaneum.

AD 80 • Colosseum is completed during the reign of Titus.

AD 96 • Emperor Domitian (Vespasian's younger son) is assassinated; the senate appoints Nerva to succeed him.

AD 100–109 • Trajan extends the empire to the northeast, conquering Dacia. The

erection of his Column, in the Forum in Rome, commemorated this achievement. With his conquest of Armenia and Mesopotamia in 117 the empire reaches its largest extent.

AD 122–127 • Hadrian's Wall is built in Britain.

AD 132–135 • The people of Judea again rebel against Roman rule, and the revolt is harshly suppressed.

AD 168–175 • Protracted campaigning on the Danube frontier by Marcus Aurelius defeats a Germanic invasion.

AD 177 • Marcus Aurelius confirms the death penalty for intransigent Christians.

AD 193 • Commodus' corrupt rule is ended with his assassination, introducing a period of civil war. Supported by the army, Septimus Severus emerges as the next emperor.

AD 212 • Marcus Aurelius Antoninus (Caracalla) extends citizenship to include all free men of the empire, abolishing differences in status between Italy and the provinces.

AD 226 • The Sasanians replace the Parthians as rulers of the former Persian Empire.

AD 235–284 • Following the murder of Alexander Severus, a leadership vacuum leads to anarchy: more than 50 men rule consecutively as emperor, all with the sponsorship of the army, but all were ousted rapidly. There were 17 assassinations in 50 years.

AD 251 • Emperor Decius is killed in battle against the Goths.

AD 259 • The Sasanians capture, humiliate, and eventually kill the emperor Valerian.

AD 260 • Taking advantage of eastern distractions, Posthumus establishes an 'independent' Gallic empire in the west.

AD 267 • Athens is sacked by Germanic pirates operating from the Black Sea.

AD 268 • From Palmyra, in the east, the growing power of Zenobia begins to threaten Rome.

AD 273 • Aurelian abandons Dacia, but restores Roman rule in Gaul and destroys the power of Palmyra. He builds a great wall around the city of Rome.

AD 284 • Diocletian divides the empire, retaining control of the West and appointing Maximian as joint emperor for the East.

AD 301 • Diocletian attempts to stem disastrous inflation in the Empire with his Edict on Prices.

AD 312 • Constantine defeats Maxentius at the battle of Milvian Bridge and becomes sole emperor.

AD 312 • Constantine defeats Maxentius at the battle of Milvian Bridge and becomes undisputed emperor in the west.

AD 324 • Constantine becomes sole emperor.

AD 325 • Constantine presides over the Council of Nicaea, the first council of the Christian church.

AD 330 • Constantine moves the capital to Byzantium, renamed Constantinople.

AD 337–351 • Constantine's sons rule as joint emperors.

AD 361 • Julian the Apostate becomes emperor and attempts to restore the worship of traditional pagan gods.

AD 378 • Emperor Valens is killed in battle against the Goths at Adrianople.

AD 382 • Emperor Theodosius I gives the Goths legal status within the Empire.

AD 383 • The Roman army begins to withdraw from Britain.

AD 388 • Theodosius I temporarily reunites the Empire under his sole rule.

AD 395 • The split in the empire becomes permanent on the death of Theodosius. Honorius rules the western Roman Empire, and Arcadius rules the eastern Roman Empire.

AD 402 • Honorius makes Ravenna the capital of the western Empire.

AD 410 • The Goths, under Alaric, sack Rome. Meanwhile, Roman forces complete their withdrawal from Britain and Gaul.

AD 451 • With the help of the Franks, the Romans repulse the forces of Attila the Hun.

AD 455 • Invading from Africa, the Vandals sack Rome, led by Gaeseric

AD 476 • Odoacer, a German king, displaces Romulus Augustulus and declares himself king of Italy. While the Empire of the West is no more, the East continues to thrive as the Byzantine Empire.

GLOSSARY OF TERMS

AEDILE • the *aediles* were Roman civic officials or magistrates responsible in general for the care of the urban fabric and various aspects of urban life, such as the food and water supply, the markets and the public games; some of their responsibilities were transferred to other officials under the Principate.

'AGRARIAN LAWS' • occasional endeavours by politicians to effect the distribution of areas of public land (*ager publicus*) among groups of ordinary citizens, including former soldiers; they were a cause of social strife during the Late Republic in particular.

AMPHITHEATRE • arena for gladiatorial contests, built in elliptical shape and on various levels; one of the earliest stone amphitheatres is in Pompeii, and the most famous is the Colosseum in Rome.

AMPHORA • two-handled ceramic coarseware jar used for transporting a range of goods, such as olive oil, wine and fish sauce; they were particularly used in long-distance transport by sea and river.

ARIES • the battering ram, a vast beam tipped with iron and in later centuries suspended within a wooden frame (sometimes with wheels) under a protective canopy.

ARMILLA • bracelet used by the army as an equivalent of a medal, bestowed by generals.

AS • bronze coin, originally weighing a pound (*libra*); 1 denarius was originally worth 10 *asses*, but later 16 *asses*.

ATRIUM • a 'hall' both in a private house and in a temple or other building where used for business.

AUGURES 'AUGURS' • college of priests responsible largely for the observation and application of the auspices.

AUSPICIUM 'AUSPICE' • a sign, often from birds, through which the gods were believed to express their approval or disapproval of an action either contemplated or in progress.

BALISTA • stone-throwing military engine.

BALNEUM • bath, later a private household bath as opposed to *thermae* 'public baths'.

BASILICA • large, multi-purpose public hall, regularly accompanying the *forum* in the western half of the Empire, with a rectangular plan and roof supported by an internal colonnade; used as the basis for the early churches at Rome and elsewhere.

BIBLIOTHECA • public library; one of the grandest in Rome was the Bibliotheca Ulpiana established by Trajan; libraries included in some of the great imperial baths complexes.

CADUCEUS • staff carried by Roman heralds and ambassadors as a token of peace.

CAESAR • name assumed by Julius Caesar's adopted heir Octavian/Augustus and thereafter by all Roman emperors as a title of supreme rank and authority (abbreviated on coins and in inscriptions to CAES or C).

CALIGA • a soldier's boot (covering at least the foot and often the ankle and lower shin too); diminutive – *caligula*.

CAMPUS MARTIUS 'THE FIELD OF MARS' • open space for army musters and exercises (hence 'of Mars') that remained outside the city walls to the north-west of Rome until enclosed within them during the 3rd century AD, by which time many public buildings had been constructed on and around it.

CAPITOLIUM 'THE CAPITOL' • smallest of the hills of Rome forming both a citadel and a religious centre; site of the temple dedicated to Jupiter Optimus Maximus, Juno and Minerva, which was originally dedicated in 509 BC but burned down and rebuilt several times; it was the place where the consuls sacrificed at the beginning of the year, where the Sibylline books were kept, and where victorious generals processed in triumph in order to make sacrifice; copied in many other cities throughout the Empire.

CASTRA • military camp of standardised square or oblong design, protected by a ditch and rampart, and with at least four gates.

CATAPULTA • dart-firing military engine.

CENSOR • one of a pair of senior Roman magistrates responsible for conducting the census and for general supervision of the morals of the community – they could deprive individuals of voting rights or status if they deemed their conduct reprehensible; they also dealt with public contracts and the leasing of public property; elections to the office ceased after 22 BC.

CENSUS • national register of Roman citizens (and their families) and their property, normally compiled at Rome every five years by the censors during the Republic, but very irregularly thereafter; it formed the basis for determining voting rights and liability for military service and taxation; from Augustus' reign provincial censuses were organised.

CENTURIO 'CENTURION' • leader of an infantry company (of 50 to 100 legionaries); two centurions to a maniple, one senior in rank (prior) to the other (posterior); 30 maniples to the legion.

CIRCUS MAXIMUS • largest stadium for chariot-racing in Rome substantially modified or rebuilt under Julius Caesar and Trajan, which could accommodate 200,000 seated spectators.

COHORS 'COHORT' • army combat unit of three manipuli thus comprising 600 men commanded by six centuriones, together amounting to one-tenth of a legion.

COLONIA • colony of settlers in either of two classes, Roman or Latin, the settlers of the first of which had full Roman citizenship.

COMITIA • an assembly of the Roman people summoned by a magistrate with the right to do so, of which there were three types: *comitia curiata, comitia centuriata* and *comitia tributa*; their functions included the enactment of laws and the election of magistrates.

CONSUL • title of the chief annual civil and military magistracies in Rome during the Republic, of which two were elected annually in most years; under the Empire the position continued to confer honour, but its powers were held independently of the office by the emperors.

CURIA • originally a religious hall presided over by a curio ('master of ceremonies'), but later the term for the assembly-hall of the Senate.

DENARIUS • main Roman silver coin minted from the end of the 3rd century BC to the 3rd century AD and worth 10 *asses* (hence the name), although in about 141 BC it was retariffed as the equivalent of 16 *asses*.

DICTATOR • an extraordinary supreme magistrate elected for a maximum of six months to preside over military or domestic emergencies; the title was bestowed on Sulla and Julius Caesar, in the latter case for life.

DIES 'THE DAY' • 24 'hours' (formally 12 hours of daytime [dies] and 12 hours of night-time [nox]), although the 'hours' varied in length according to season.

EQUITES 'KNIGHTS' • patricians (traditionally descendants of the 300 knights established by Romulus) horsed at the expense of the state and forming the state's cavalry – although in time a class of *equites* maintaining its own horses was added; eventually an equestrian order developed which was second only to the senators in

social status and membership of which was determined by wealth; its members fulfilled various civil and military functions, especially under the Empire.

FASCES • symbolic bundle of elm or birch rods, bound round with a red strap and carried by the lictors on their left shoulder; outside Rome the *fasces* enclosed an axe symbolizing the state's absolute power to inflict the death penalty without appeal; in Rome there was such an appeal, and so there was no axe in the *fasces* (except under the rule of a dictator).

FETIALES • college of priests in Rome responsible for international state relations and for the formal (and ritual) declaring of war when necessary.

FORUM • open square or market-place forming the focal point of a Roman town, surrounded by various public buildings such as temples and basilicas, and adorned with honorific statues and other monuments; in Rome there were, in addition to the original forum, two fora for the sale of cattle and vegetables and a number of imperial fora, which were much more monumental complexes.

FRATRES ARVALES • college of 12 priests responsible for the festival of the goddess Dea Dia, held in May and connected to agricultural prosperity; also for rituals connected with the imperial house.

GLADIATORES 'GLADIATORS' • originating in Etruria, they were introduced to Rome in 264 BC, originally in the context of funeral games; there were four types: the heavily-armed *murmillones* (wearing a fish-crested helmet) and Samnites, the *retiarius* (lightly clad, fighting with net and trident) and the Thracian (with round shield and curved scimitar); although they were often prisoners of war or condemned criminals, there were professionals, whether slave or free.

IANITOR • slave (often a eunuch) kept on a chain at a wealthy household's main entrance and accompanied by a dog also on a chain, whose duty it was to receive and announce callers and turn away beggars; a *ianitor* guarded the *ianua* 'portal'.

IDES 'THE IDES' • ninth day after the Nones (Nonae) of the month, thus day 15 of March, May, Quinctilis (July) and October, day 13 of the other months.

IMPERATOR • general title for Roman commanders which became a special title of honour and was adopted as the first name and later the title of the emperors (abbreviated to IMP on coins).

IMPERIUM • supreme power, involving military command and the interpretation and execution of the law, including the infliction of the death penalty; it was attached to various magistracies and later to the emperors, but in different degrees.

IUGERUM • standard rectangular unit of square measure, twice as long in one direction as it was in the other and approximating in total to two-thirds of an acre (0.25 hectare); 2 *iugera* equalled 1 *heredium*.

KALENDAE 'CALENDS' • first day of the month, on which the proclamation was made concerning all the other special dates and festivals of the month, and interest on debts became due.

LEGATUS 'LEGATE' • ambassador dealing particularly with legal affairs of citizens abroad – today's 'consul'; also a deputy of the emperor, especially one appointed to govern one of the provinces allocated to him by the Senate, and, under the Empire, the commander of a legion.

LEGIO 'LEGION' • the largest unit of the Roman army, comprising between 4,200 and 6,000 infantry, together with a small force of cavalry.

LIBRA • a 'pound' weight, comprising 12 *unciae* 'Roman ounces', about 11? of today's ounces (327.5 grams); originally the weight of the coin called the *as* as weighed on the scales (*libra*).

LICTORS • attendants who accompanied and carried the *fasces* for magistrates with *imperium*, whose number varied according to the magistrate's rank.

LUDI • (public) games, staged in the circus, the theatre or the amphitheatre, usually in the context of religious festivals, thanksgivings for military victories, or funerary commemorations; they could comprise chariot-racing, fights involving gladiators and wild animals, and performances of plays, mime and pantomime.

LUPERCALIA • annual festival conducted on 15 February by the association of Luperci; it involved the sacrifice of goats and a dog at the Lupercal, a cave at the foot of the Palatine where Romulus and Remus were reared by a she-wolf; then the Luperci ran almost naked through the streets striking passers-by, especially women, with goatskin thongs; the rite combined purification and fertility magic.

MAGISTRATUS 'MAGISTRATE' • a civic official at Rome, whether regularly elected, e.g. consul, praetor, or occasionally appointed or elected, e.g. dictator; some possessed *imperium* but the rest did not; they were almost all elected, temporary (usually one year), unpaid, and organised in colleges.

MANIPULUS, MANIPLUS 'MANIPLE' • a unit of infantry in the Roman army comprising two centuries, thus up to 200 men (although the word literally means 'handful'); there were three maniples to a cohort and 30 to the legion.

MANUMISSIO 'MANUMISSION' • the formal release of a slave from slavery; there were three methods: by a fictitious claim before a magistrate with *imperium* that he/she was free (*vindicta*), by registering the slave as a citizen at a census (*censu*), or by the owner's will (*testamento*); a slave freed by a citizen normally achieved full citizenship, but not straightaway.

MILLE PASSUS 'THE (ROMAN) MILE' • 1,000 double-paces or 5,000 'feet' (today generally reckoned as about 1,618 yards or 1,480 metres).

NONAE 'NONES' • the ninth day before the Ides and hence day 7 of March, May, Quinctilis (July) and October, day 5 of the other months.

PATRICII 'PATRICIANS' • a privileged class of Roman citizens forming an aristocracy of birth under the Republic, although it may have originated under the kings; their monopoly of all the important priesthoods and of political office was eroded as a result of the 'Conflict of the Orders' with the *plebs*, although they continued to possess religious privileges; their numbers had declined substantially by the end of the Republic, but the emperors used their censorial powers to confer hereditary patrician status on favoured individuals.

PES 'A (ROMAN) FOOT' • of 12 unciae 'inches' – 11.65 modern inches (29.6 centimetres).

PLEBS • the name given to the mass of Roman citizens, as distinct from the privileged patricians; although the precise origin of the distinction is obscure, plebeians were subject during the Early Republic to legal, religious and civic discrimination (intermarriage with the patricians was barred); as a result of the 'Conflict of the Orders' the plebeians succeeded in gaining a large measure of political equality with the patricians, and their officers, the *tribuni plebis* and aediles, became magistrates of the Roman people.

PONTIFEX • member of the most illustrious priestly college, whose wide-ranging duties included oversight of state sacrifices, games and festivals and advising magistrates in particular on the sacred law; the position of its leading member, the *pontifex maximus*, was held by the emperors after Augustus (abbreviated on coins and in inscriptions to PM) and came to resemble a 'High Priest'.

PRAEFECTUS PRAETORIO 'PREFECT OF THE PRAETORIAN GUARD' • two equestrian posts created in 2 BC; their holders could gain considerable power through their influence over the emperor, e.g. L. Aelius Seianus under Tiberius; after Diocletian their regular duties were increasingly concentrated on civil rather than military administration and associated with specific areas of the Empire.

PRAEFECTUS URBI 'THE CITY PREFECT' • during the Republic, the deputy of the absent king or consuls; during the Empire, the magistrate ultimately responsible for maintaining order in Rome, always a senator and usually a senior ex-consul.

PRAETOR • originally the title bestowed on the two republican magistrates chosen annually as eponymous heads of state, after 367 BC it related to a new magistracy possessing lesser *imperium* than that of the two newly-designated 'consuls'; the number of posts increased throughout the Republic and was eventually fixed at 12 by Augustus; under the Republic it had both military and juridical duties, but only the latter continued under the Empire; it was a precondition for attaining the consulship, and its holders usually went out to govern a province or command a legion after their year of office.

PRAETORIANI 'THE PRAETORIAN GUARD' • emperor's permanent bodyguard established by Augustus in 27 BC and comprising originally nine cohorts, each of 500 (or possibly 1000) men, but from the reign of Domitian ten cohorts, each of 1000 men; from AD 23 was stationed in one permanent camp in the eastern suburbs of Rome; enjoying service conditions superior to ordinary legionaries, it quickly attained considerable influence over the imperial succession but was formally abolished by Constantine in AD 312.

PROCONSUL • a magistrate operating in place of a consul outside Rome and outside the regular annual magistracy; he could be an ex-consul undertaking or continuing in a military command after his consular year, or the governor of a province, whether as an ex-consul or an ex-praetor.

PROCURATOR • administrative official appointed by the emperor usually to oversee his properties or to supervise the collection of taxes in those provinces assigned to him by the senate; normally of equestrian status.

PUBLICANI • private individuals usually organised in companies who bid for public contracts to collect public revenue or engage in public works, supplies and services, reimbursing themselves with what profit they could; those engaged in tax-collection under the Late Republic became extremely wealthy and influential, but their political influence diminished considerably under the Empire.

QUAESTOR • the lowest of the regular magistracies with mainly financial, but also some judicial and military, duties exercised in most cases in the provinces; after Sulla all ex-quaestors automatically gained membership of the senate.

SATURNALIA • joyful midwinter festival beginning on 17 December during which the social order was inverted, gifts were exchanged and there was much feasting and playing.

SENATUS 'THE SENATE' • council of state (originally of elders – senes) which usually had 300 members under the Republic and 600 from the reign of Augustus; under the Republic it oversaw all matters of domestic and foreign policy, finance and religion, and retained important corporate functions under the Empire; membership was a precondition for holding key political and administrative roles, including the senior regular magistracies; Augustus tried to introduce a strong hereditary element and raised the minimum property qualification to 1 million sesterces; under the Later Empire the number of senators expanded dramatically and the position conferred social status rather than any political power.

SERVUS 'SLAVE' • slavery was common in Roman history and there may have been 2 million in Italy at the end of the Republic; slaveowning was widespread throughout society, although dominated by the wealthy (L. Pedanius Secundus possessed 400 in his house at Rome alone); slaves were obtained as captives in war, through piracy, through natural reproduction, and through trade, and the numbers available increased substantially as a result of the growth of the Roman Empire in the 2nd and 1st centuries BC; they performed almost every type of work, particularly domestic labour, manufacturing, mining and agriculture – estates relying heavily on slave-labour are particularly attested from Late Republican Italy; occasionally resistance led to the outbreak of full-scale revolts, such as that led by Spartacus in the late 70s BC; slaves were quite often set free by their owners by the process of manumission.

SESTERTIUS (OR SESTERCIUS) • coin worth a quarter of a denarius and thus 2.5 asses (later 4 asses) (hence the name, an abbreviated form of 'half less than three' in Latin).

SIBYLLINI LIBRI 'THE SIBYLLINE BOOKS' • mystic and oracular writings sold according to legend by the Cumaean Sibyl (woman with prophetic powers) to the king Tarquinius Priscus and thereafter preserved in the Temple of Capitoline Jupiter; they were destroyed in the burning of the Capitol in 83 BC and a new collection of mystic writings was later compiled under the same name (until that too was destroyed in AD 405).

SPQR • abbreviation standing for senatus populusque Romanus 'the senate and the people of Rome'.

TESTUDO • a 'tortoise' shell of interwoven shields held as protection above an advancing column of troops in an attack on town walls.

TRIBUNUS 'TRIBUNE' • two main types: tribuni militum, who were military officers allocated six to each legion, and tribuni plebis, civic officials empowered to act in the interests of the plebs 'common people', which included possessing the right to veto the actions of another magistrate, elections, laws and decrees of the senate; the office's revolutionary potential was exploited during the Late Republic; from Augustus on, the emperors arrogated its powers (tribunicia potestas) to themselves.

VESTALES 'THE VESTAL VIRGINS' • the six priestesses of the goddess Vesta, who were required to maintain strict sexual purity during their minimum of 30 years' service; Vesta was the goddess of the hearth-fire of the whole community that was the 'family' of Rome; a perpetual fire was accordingly kept burning in her shrine, with dire consequences for any priestess who allowed it to go out; the religious superior of the priestesses was the pontifex maximus – during the Empire, the emperor.

VIA • public road, constructed in standard dimensions in layers between ditches, mostly for military and official purposes and therefore as straight as practicable.

WHO'S WHO

AGRIPPINA (IULIA AGRIPPINA) (AD 15–59)

The mother of Nero and the wife of Claudius, Agrippina was born into a life of politics and intrigue. Her father was Germanicus, the adopted son of Tiberius, and her mother, Vipsania Agrippina, was the granddaughter of Augustus and foe of Tiberius. Her brother was the emperor Gaius (Caligula). During Gaius' reign, she was banished for her involvement in the conspiracy of Gaetulicus of 39, but in 49 her uncle and Gaius' successor, Claudius, recalled her to Rome to take her as his fourth wife. She influenced Claudius to adopt Nero (her son from her first marriage), who therefore gained precedence over his own (younger) son, Britannicus. Claudius died in 54 – it was alleged that Agrippina poisoned him – and Nero, aged only sixteen, succeeded him. Initially, Agrippina held a great deal of power, in practice acting almost as co-regent. But as he matured, Nero came to resent his mother's domination, particularly when she interfered in his love affairs. His first attempt on her life, by sending her out to sea in a boat designed to sink, failed when she managed to swim ashore, but he was more successful with his second attempt, when he ordered her to be murdered at her country house.

AUGUSTUS (63 BC–AD 14)

Born Gaius Octavius into a prosperous family from Velitrae in central Italy, Octavian (as he was known) was taken under the wing of his uncle, Julius Caesar, as a boy. It was on his uncle's assassination in 44 BC that he learned that he had been adopted by Caesar and named his heir. Although he was only eighteen, and against the advice of his family, he went to Rome and proved politically astute enough to win the support of both the senate and the people. At first, from 43 BC, he ruled jointly as triumvir with Mark Antony and Lepidus; Lepidus was ousted in 36 BC, and Octavian routed Mark Antony at the Battle of Actium in 31 BC. In 27 BC, recognising his supreme authority in the state, the Senate granted him the title 'Augustus', a term previously used only in a religious context, which was then to pass on to all subsequent Roman emperors. His reign saw the massive expansion of the Roman Empire, but the general maintenance of peace within it. Augustus reformed society at every level, from the role and structure of the government, taxation and coinage, through to civil institutions, such as marriage. He was educated and intelligent, a friend and sponsor of writers and artists. A major programme of public building saw the creation of many architectural masterpieces, both within and outside Rome. He was succeeded by Tiberius, the son of his faithful wife, Livia, by a previous marriage.

BRUTUS, MARCUS IUNIUS (c. 85–42 BC)

One of the leaders of the conspiracy against Julius Caesar, Brutus was an ambitious politician who ardently supported Republican ideals. He joined Pompey's forces in the civil war against Caesar, and was one of the beneficiaries of Caesar's amnesties following his victory. Not only was Brutus pardoned for his participation in Pompey's army, but he was also granted several political appointments. Nonetheless, Caesar's appointment as dictator for life led him to play a key role in his assassination plot. Brutus was later forced out of Rome to Greece by Mark Antony, where he raised an army in opposition. Following the defeat of his forces by Mark Antony and Octavian (Augustus) at the second Battle of Philippi, Brutus committed suicide.

JULIUS CAESAR, GAIUS (100–44 BC)

As astute a tactician politically as he was militarily, Julius Caesar has gone down in history as one of the most effective Roman rulers, even though his actual reign, as dictator, was less than a year long. His political genius was evidenced by the creation of the 'First Triumvirate' in 60, in which he formed an alliance with Pompey and Crassus, uniting these two sworn enemies and winning himself the consulship of 59 as a result. His leadership of the Roman army in Gaul (58-51) greatly extended Roman territory as far as the English Channel; his impressively written accounts of his Gallic campaigns, *De bello Gallico*, are among his few extant writings. After the senate, and Pompey, turned against him, Caesar returned to Italy with his army, famously crossing the Rubicon in 49. He was successful in this civil war, subduing yet ultimately reprieving his enemies and in 44 becoming dictator for life. His reform programme was cut short by his assassination the following month by a group of senators. Caesar's legacy is still apparent today in our calendar, which is based on his reformed, 'Julian' calendar of 45.

CALIGULA (GAIUS IULIUS CAESAR GERMANICUS) (AD 12–41)

The son of Germanicus (himself the adopted son of Tiberius) and Vipsania Agrippina, Gaius received his nickname, Caligula, meaning 'little boots', when as an infant he accompanied his father during his Rhine campaigns of 14–16. Gaius was adopted by Tiberius as joint heir with his son Gemellus, but became sole emperor in 37 with the help of Macro, prefect of the Praetorian Guard, although he had received very little training for public life. Only seven months after being proclaimed emperor, he fell seriously ill, and it has been suggested that this illness may have led to the mental instability which he later demonstrated. As emperor he was erratic and often extremely cruel, spending extravagantly on himself, extorting money from wealthy Romans, and casually putting to death his opponents. Caligula was assassinated in 41 by members of the Praetorian Guard and was succeeded by Claudius, his uncle.

CLAUDIUS (TIBERIUS CLAUDIUS NERO GERMANICUS) (10 BC–AD 54)

Discovered hiding behind a curtain in the palace by a member of the Praetorian Guard after Caligula's assassination, Claudius was proclaimed emperor by the army, without the senate's approval and despite the fact that he had little experience of public life. Part lame and suffering from a stutter, he was an unimpressive figure and a poor public speaker, in a culture that respected rhetorical genius. Throughout his reign he favoured the army and was responsible for extending the Empire into Britain in AD 43. His relations with the senate tended to be poor, but he took a keen interest in

government and introduced important new social legislation as well as effecting some sensible administrative reforms. However, he was easily influenced by his wealthy freedmen and by his third and fourth wives, Valeria Messalina and Iulia Agrippina. He died allegedly by poisoning at the hands of the latter, who had persuaded him to adopt her son, Nero, and prefer him over his natural son, Britannicus.

CONSTANTINE (FLAVIUS VALERIUS CONSTANTINUS) (c. AD 272/3–337)

Often known as Constantine the Great, he was the last emperor to rule over a united Eastern and Western empire, and also the first Christian emperor. He attributed his success in defeating his rival for the Western Empire, the usurper Maxentius, at the Milvian Bridge, to the hand of the Christian God. In 324 he forced the abdication of his rival in the East, Licinius, by virtue of his military prowess. At the helm of a united empire, Constantine proved to be a skilful administrator, building on the progress made by Diocletian. Among his successes were the reform of military organisation and of government, as well as the establishment of a new coin, the *solidus*, of which there were 72 to the pound. He also established a permanent imperial residence in his new foundation of Constantinople (formerly Byzantium), in order to be closer to the Danubian and Eastern frontiers. His greatest achievement, however, lay in recognising and strengthening the position of Christianity, with the Edict of Milan (313), which restored Christian property and gave privileges and benefactions to the Church. He openly rejected paganism but took an active part in attempts to seek doctrinal unity, such as the

First Ecumenical Council of Nicaea (325). Baptised on his deathbed, he left his empire to his three sons and two nephews.

CRASSUS, MARCUS LICINIUS (c.112–53 BC)

A skilful general and a shrewd politician and financier, Crassus was an early supporter of Sulla's successful claim to leadership and made a fortune in his proscriptions. Although Crassus suppressed the slave uprising led by Spartacus, the credit was claimed by Pompey, leading to a rift developing between them. Nonetheless, they were formally reconciled and served as consuls together in 70, following a mutual agenda to undo Sulla's constitution. They again came together, on Julius Caesar's instigation, in the 'First Triumvirate' in 60, although relations between them were always strained. After the renewal of this alliance in 56, Crassus was awarded a major military commission in Syria and was killed in 53 at the Battle of Carrhae. His death helped to bring Caesar and Pompey into civil war with each other.

DIOCLETIAN (GAIUS AURELIUS VALERIUS DIOCLETIANUS) (c. AD 240s–c. 312)

After the anarchy of the 3rd century, Diocletian implemented the reforms essential for a new stability. His changes laid the foundations for the long-term strength of the Byzantine Empire in the East and the survival of the Western Empire for as long as it did. From an undistinguished family in Dalmatia, he rose through the military ranks and was proclaimed emperor by the army in 284. He immediately recognised that the Empire was too big to be governed by one man and so split its administration in two. Diocletian himself became Augustus of the East, and he appointed Maximian as Augustus of the West; he also appointed two deputies, known as Caesars, one, Galerius, to the East and one, Constantius, to the West. He undertook a major reorganisation of the provinces as well as of the army, and for financial stability he reformed the system of taxation and attempted to create a unified currency, although to little avail. The last major persecution of Christians took place during his reign during 303–304. After twenty years in power, Diocletian abdicated in 305, beset by ill health, and his death occurred, virtually unnoticed, some seven years later.

DOMITIAN (TITUS FLAVIOUS DOMITIANUS) (AD 51–96)

The second son of the emperor Vespasian, Domitian exercised no formal power during the reigns of his father and his elder brother, Titus, although he held seven consulships. When he came to power in 81, he was determined to rule absolutely. He was a reasonably effective administrator and succeeded militarily in strengthening Rome's extensive borders. However, these military campaigns, in addition to an extravagant program of public building, may have put a strain on the Empire's finances. His autocratic impulses led him to limit the power of the senate, earning its enmity. To quash any opposition, he vigorously persecuted his supposed enemies, banishing the philosophers twice (89 and 95) and putting his presumed opponents to death before confiscating their property for the state. In 96 he was assassinated by some court officials and two praetorian prefects, possibly supported by his wife, and his memory was condemned by the senate.

THE GRACCHI: TIBERIUS SEMPRONIUS GRACCHUS (c.169–133 BC), and GAIUS SEMPRONIUS GRACCHUS (c.160–121 BC)

Although born into an aristocratic family, the brothers Tiberius and Gaius Gracchus were committed to reforms that would deal with various economic and administrative problems and improve the lives of poorer Romans. Their championship of the poor over the rich won the enmity of many members of the senate and ultimately cost them their lives. The elder of the brothers, Tiberius, proposed a land reform bill that would confiscate areas of *ager publicus* held by wealthy landowners in excess of the legal limit of 500 *iugera* and reallocate it among poorer citizens. He worked vigorously to pass and implement this bill, exploiting loopholes in the law to force its passage, instigating a constitutional crisis and creating many enemies along the way. He was killed during a mob of senators and their clients led by the *pontifex maximus*, Scipio Nasica. His brother, Gaius, continued with the work of land reform but also pursued his own wider political agenda. Among his measures was a new system of subsidised corn distribution to citizens, a programme of colonisation, measures to limit judicial corruption and abuse of power, and the extension of the citizenship. With his legislation facing attack, he resorted to armed insurrection and was killed in the course of its suppression.

HADRIAN (PUBLIUS AELIUS HADRIANUS) (AD 76–38)

The ward of the emperor Trajan, Hadrian was destined for a political career. He rose quickly through the ranks, becoming consul by 108. He was appointed archon of Athens in 112 and in 117 at the latest became governor of Syria. When Trajan died in Cilicia in 117, Hadrian's adoption by him was announced the following day and, with the support of the army, he was proclaimed emperor. He faced some opposition and four ex-consuls were killed for plotting treason before his return to Rome in 118. Hadrian's rule was distinguished by his extensive travels. Throughout his reign he toured the Empire, in part to cement his authority but also to satisfy his endless curiosity and wanderlust. He sponsored major building works throughout the Empire, including the famed wall in Britain. With his artistic temperament, he took a personal interest in many of the designs for new monuments, and his own poetry was of a high standard. He died at Tivoli outside Rome, after a long illness, having ensured the succession of Marcus Aurelius.

JULIAN (FLAVIUS CLAUDIUS IULIANUS) (AD 331–363)

A nephew of Constantine the Great, Julian escaped the massacres that followed Constantine's death, which were intended to secure succession for the emperor's sons. As a boy he spent six years confined to an estate in Cappadocia where he devoted himself to his studies. As a young man, however, he was summoned by Constantius II to be married to his sister and in 355 was appointed Caesar in charge of Gaul and Britain. He proved to be a talented general during campaigns in the Rhineland and was proclaimed Augustus by his troops in 361. Civil was was averted by Constantius' death that same year and Julian became emperor unopposed. He dedicated most of his energy to restoring the worship of the pagan gods and for this he became known as Julian 'the Apostate'. One of his first edicts (361) mandated freedom of worship for all religions; his policies, however, actively discriminated against Christians. He died in battle against Persia, aged only 31 and having served as emperor for only 20 months.

LIVIA (DRUSILLA) (58 BC– AD 29)

The faithful wife of Augustus, Livia was intelligent and dignified but also desirous of power. Her conduct during her marriage to Augustus seems to have been above reproach. Augustus had forced her to divorce her first husband, the military commander Tiberius Claudius Nero, to marry him, and he always held her in high esteem, respecting her advice. Their marriage, however, was childless, and Livia was untiring in her efforts to encourage Augustus to choose her son, Tiberius, as his heir over his own blood relations. Her efforts to support his succession won her a few enemies and her continuing influence after Augustus' death caused discord between her and Tiberius. As emperor, Tiberius kept her under a tight rein, even refusing to honour the terms of her will after her death. She was deified by the emperor Claudius, her grandson.

MARK ANTONY (MARCUS ANTONIUS) (83–30 BC)

Handsome and charming, Mark Antony was ambitious but somewhat lacking in political skill. After an allegedly dissipated youth, he distinguished himself as a cavalry commander in Palestine and Egypt. From 54, he was on Caesar's staff, serving him both in Gaul and later in a series of political appointments back in Italy. After Caesar's death, Mark Antony successfully led the moves to turn public opinion against

Caesar's assassins, Brutus and Cassius, but was compelled to join forces with the young Octavian. In 43 they, together with Lepidus, formed the Second Triumvirate, which led to the proscription of their enemies and the defeat of Brutus and Cassius at the Battle of Philippi in 42. He was then granted the Eastern provinces and in 40 took Octavia, Octavian's sister, as his wife. He first met Cleopatra, queen of Egypt, in Tarsus in 41 but did not settle with her until 37. Antony's abandonment of Octavia, combined with his political favours to Egypt and Cleopatra, aroused the anger of Octavian, who pursued him militarily, defeating the couple's forces decisively at the Battle of Actium (31). The two lovers fled to Egypt, where they were pursued by Octavian, and they died by their own hands a year later.

MARIUS, GAIUS (C.157–86 BC)

Born into a family without any history of membership of the senate, Marius succeeded in serving an unprecedented seven terms as consul (107, 104-100, 86). He succeeded politically because he won popular support, in part because of his reputation as a military leader and in part because he came from a non-noble background. He rose to prominence during the Numantine War in Spain (134), which led to his first political positions. Winning his initial consulship in 107, he used his position to oust his rival, Metellus, as general against Jugurtha (although he had earlier received political assistance from his family, the Metelli). The strength of the army was the backbone of Marius' electoral success throughout his political career, and he implemented numerous reforms of the military that enhanced its performance as well as abolishing the property qualification

for service. From 90, his rivalry with Sulla came to a head and was a cause for civil war in 88, when they were both competing for the command in the war against Mithridates in the East. Marius' last consulship, in 86, was a disaster, and he ordered the massacre of many prominent opponents. Embarking upon a reign of terror, he died within days, saving Rome from even more strife.

NERO (NERO CLAUDIUS CAESAR) (AD 37–68)

Succeeding as emperor in 54 to his adoptive father, Claudius, because of the machinations of his ambitious mother, Agrippina, Nero was totally unsuited to the job. His passions were for music, art, chariot-racing and Greek athletics, and his tastes were flamboyant. Only 16 when he became emperor, his mother at first wielded real power, but, angered by her interference in his love life and resentful of her ambition, Nero banished her from the palace. According to the ancient tradition, he at first ruled moderately and fairly, under the influence of the philosopher, Seneca, and Burrus, the prefect of the Praetorian Guard. Yet he soon started to show an irrational and despotic side. In 59 he had his mother murdered, followed shortly by his wife Octavia. His unsound fiscal policies, combined with public displays of vanity, earned him the disapproval and eventually the hatred of the upper classes. Rumours spread that Nero ordered the fire in 64 that destroyed Rome, and he further undermined his position by immediately beginning construction of his Golden Palace on scorched land near the Forum. As opposition grew and armies in the provinces rose up against him in 68, Nero committed suicide as he fled Rome.

NERVA, MARCUS COCCEIUS (c. AD35–98)

Born into an aristocratic family, Nerva had carved out a respectable political career, twice serving as consul, when he was chosen by the senate to succeed Domitian as emperor. Already an elderly man, he seemed a safe, traditional candidate, unlikely to do any harm to an already shaken state. During his short reign, he repealed many of Domitian's harsh measures and implemented numerous reforms. However, he never won the support of the army and in 97, exhausted and under threat, he passed power on to his adopted successor, Trajan. Although his rule was of a short duration, it was later represented as having begun the transition away from autocratic rule, and Nerva became known as the first of the 'Five Good Emperors'.

POMPEY (GNAEUS POMPEIUS MAGNUS) (106–48 BC)

Born into an aristocratic family from Picenum, Pompey achieved prominence as a military commander under Sulla, employing a private army of his father's veterans and clients. His military success then and during the decade after Sulla's death led to his achieving the consulship of 70, despite his youth and having never held any previous magistracies. He later won lucrative and high-profile military commands first against the pirates in the Mediterranean and then against Mithradates in the East. Achieving a rapid victory against Mithradates (66), Pompey annexed Syria as a province and laid the foundations of the subsequent Roman organisation of the East. Returning to Rome in 62, in 60 he entered into the 'First Triumvirate', with Caesar and Crassus,

because he could not succeed in securing land for his veterans and the ratification of his Eastern arrangements by any other means. In 52, disorder in Rome created an opportunity for Pompey to be appointed sole consul. His relationship with Caesar had deteriorated especially since the death of Crassus in 53 and he took command of the Republic's forces when Caesar crossed into Italy with his army. However, Pompey was defeated at the Battle of Pharsalus in 48 and, having fled to Egypt, was stabbed to death as he landed.

SCIPIO AFRICANUS, PUBLIUS CORNELIUS (236–183 BC)

The son of an aristocratic military general, Scipio followed in his father's footsteps from a young age. It is said that first demonstrated his heroic spirit when he saved his father's life during the Battle of Ticinus (218). He was granted his first command in 210, to go to Spain, where his father had been killed in battle. There he took the fight to the Carthaginian enemy, capturing their headquarters and applying new tactics, and he won Spain for Rome within four years. In 204 he went to Africa and in 202 his forces ultimately defeated Hannibal at the Battle of Zama, as a result of which peace was concluded on Rome's terms; Scipio was granted the surname Africanus in celebration of his great victory. He returned to Rome to take up a political career from 199, which lasted for fifteen years. However, accusations by his opponents of embezzlement and bribery drove him into retirement and voluntary exile from Rome, where he died the following year.

SULLA (LUCIUS CORNELIUS SULLA FELIX) (138–78 BC)

Although his rivalry with Marius was a cause of civil war (88-82), Sulla was an able ruler who attempted to strengthen the Republic with his constitutional reforms. Serving under Marius in the war against Numidia, Sulla succeeded in winning the credit for capturing Jugurtha, the enemy general. This was the root of the discord between the two men that was to have such dire consequences for the state. Success in the Social War won Sulla the consulship in 88, but, when he was preparing to wage war against Mithradates, Marius acquiesced in the transfer of the command to himself. Marching on Rome, Sulla won notable victories, with the battle at the Colline Gate the turning point (82). He was appointed dictator and used his position to implement many reforms aimed at increasing the power of the senate. He was known for treating his enemies harshly, confiscating their lands in order to settle his own veterans, and his rule became notorious for its conservatism and cruelty. He eventually retired voluntarily in 79, dying quietly the following year. Although his constitutional reforms were overturned by Crassus and Pompey in 70, his administrative reforms survived end of the Republic.

THEODOSIUS I (c. AD 346–395)

Son of a renowned general, Theodosius learned military strategy as he served alongside his father. After his father's sudden disgrace and execution in 376, however, Theodosius withdrew from public life, but Gratian recalled him to imperial service in 378 and in 379 proclaimed him Augustus of the Eastern parts, including Dacia and Macedonia. By agreeing to a ground-breaking treaty with the Goths, which allowed them to live on Roman soil while maintaining their autonomy, Theodosius was able to secure his territory against enemy incursions, and also won for himself firm allies. He increased his power in the West after he routed and killed the usurper Magnus Maximus, who had expelled Valentinian II from Italy in 387. In 394 he defeated the usurper Eugenius, who had displaced Valentinian in Gaul. He was a pious Christian adhering to the Catholic faith proclaimed in the Nicene Creed, and in 391 abruptly closed all temples and banned all forms of pagan cult. After his death, the Empire was formally divided into eastern and western parts.

TIBERIUS (TIBERIUS IULIUS CAESAR AUGUSTUS) (42 BC–AD 37)

Livia's elder son, Tiberius was brought up in Augustus' court and had an early entry into political life, becoming quaestor when he was only eighteen years old, followed by a highly successful military career spanning three decades. Nonetheless he was not favoured as successor by Augustus, who preferred his grandsons, Gaius and Lucius, whom he adopted as his sons. In 6 BC, Tiberius retired from private life, moving to Rhodes, and Augustus, insulted by this, refused to allow him back to Rome until AD 2. Augustus' adopted sons having both died, Tiberius was adopted in AD 4 and given extensive governmental powers, effectively making him co-*princeps* from AD 13. When Augustus died in AD 14, therefore, the succession was not in doubt. Tiberius respected the memory and policies of his predecessor, in particular in his dealings with peoples and kingdoms on the frontiers. However, problems at home and

abroad and his notorious frugality led to his becoming unpopular. From around AD 23 he came under the influence of Sejanus, then prefect of the Praetorian Guard. Sejanus become closely involved in the succession question following the deaths of Tiberius' adopted son, Germanicus, in AD 19 and his own son, Drusus, in AD 23, and organised a campaign of persecution against Germanicus' widow and children. Tiberius, however, withdrew in AD 25 to Campania and then Capri, leaving many matters of state in Sejanus' hands. In AD 31 Tiberius was given evidence of Sejanus' machinations, and in a letter to the senate had him and his allies arrested and put to death. For the remaining six years of his reign until his death Tiberius lived on Capri. His reign is particularly noted for the number of 'treason'-trials held before the senate, particularly in the wake of Sejanus' downfall.

TRAJAN (MARCUS ULPIUS TRAIANUS) (C. AD 53–117)

From Baetica, in southern Spain, Trajan was the first emperor to be born outside Rome. His father, however, was a distinguished ex-consul, and Trajan was raised largely in Rome. Consul under both Domitian and Nerva, he assumed the throne on Nerva's death. He reasserted imperial control over the army, treating it fairly although not liberally. He was generous to the Roman people and continued a scheme, probably established by Nerva, to provide for poor children in Italian communities. He also implemented an extensive program of public works throughout the empire, while in Rome he created public baths and an impressive new forum and basilica. His greatest claim to fame, however, was the expansion of the Empire for the first time

since Augustus. He continued Domitian's campaign against the Dacians, capturing their territory north of the Danube (101–106) – this victory is commemorated on Trajan's Column, still standing in his Forum. He also annexed Arabia and conquered Parthia, briefly extending the Empire as far as the Persian Gulf.

VESPASIAN (TITUS FLAVIUS VESPASIANUS) (AD 9–79)

Born into a family of the equestrian rank, Vespasian followed his brother into the senate, and the first part of his political career followed a normal but undistinguished pattern of advancement. However, with the accession of Claudius, Vespasian's rise quickened – he proved to be a sound military leader in Britain and became consul in 51. He continued to serve under Nero and was given a special command in the east in 66 to subdue the revolt in Judea. Still in the east at the time of Nero's suicide, Vespasian survived over a year of chaos before leading a revolt with the backing of the legions stationed in the Eastern provinces. He became emperor in 69 and quickly restored peace to the Empire. Raising provincial and other taxes, he funded the rebuilding of Rome – the Colosseum was begun in this period, but he also organised public works throughout the Empire. Reestablishing discipline in the army, he expanded the Empire further into Germany and Britain and shored up the frontiers. He also conferred rights on communities abroad, especially in Spain, and recruited many new Italian and provincial members to the senate. He died peacefully, having secured succession for his son, Titus.

NOTABLE ARCHAEOLOGICAL SITES AND MUSEUM COLLECTIONS

CHERCHEL (CAESAREA)
Algeria (95km/59mi west of Algiers)
ruined city: forum, baths, theatre, basilica, circus museum

DJEMILA (CUICUL)
Algeria (180km/114mi east of Algiers)
ruined city: forums, theatre, temples, stepped markets, houses, columns museum containing mosaics

TEBESSA (THEVESTE)
Algeria (near border with Tunisia)
ruined city: triumphal arch, temple with mosaics, basilica, large circus, aqueduct

TIMGAD (THAMUGADI)
Algeria (320km/200mi south-east of Algiers)
ruined city: forum, baths, capitolium, theatre, triumphal arch, mosaics

TIPAZA (TIPASA)
Algeria (mid-north coast)
ruined city: forum, baths, amphitheatre, basilica, temples, villa, mausoleum, road museum containing mosaics

TONGEREN
Belgium (90km/55mi south-east of Brussels)
ruins: city walls, open-air museum

PLOVDIV (PHILIPPOPOLIS, TRIMONTIUM)
Bulgaria (140km/87mi south-east of Sofia)
ruined city: mosaics, reliefs, pavements, restored theatre

SOFIA (SERDICA)
Bulgaria (capital)
ruins visible under modern buildings: baths, basilicas, house with mosaics, museums

VARNA (ODESSUS)
Bulgaria (Black Sea coast)
ruins: well-preserved baths

SPLIT (SPALATO)
Croatia (170km/106mi south-west of Sarajevo)
ruined and adapted city: temples, walls, mausoleum, catacombs, museum

PAPHOS
Cyprus (south-west coast)
ruined city: theatre, house with mosaics, sea walls

ALEXANDRIA
Egypt (210km/130mi north-west of Cairo)
traces of ruined city: baths, marble theatre with mosaics, houses, arched walls, harbour, catacombs, The Graeco-Roman Museum

BATH (AQUAE SULIS)
England (130km/80m west of London)
traces of ruined city: well-preserved baths, temple, mosaics, museum

CHESTER (DEVA)
England (95km/60mi south-west of Manchester)
ruins: amphitheatre, walls, fragments visible around and under modern buildings, Grosvenor Museum, Deva Roman Experience

CIRENCESTER (CORINIUM)
England (123km/80mi northwest of London)
traces of ruined city, museum

COLCHESTER (CAMULODUNUM)
England (80km/50mi north-east of London)
surviving Roman wall, museum

COVENTRY (LUNT ROMAN FORT)
England (Jordan Well, Coventry, West Midlands)
reconstructed Roman earth and timber fort

HADRIAN'S WALL
England (near border with Scotland)
remains of forts and watchtowers, stretches and fragments of wall across countryside museums at/between Carlisle and Newcastle (including Vindolanda)

LONDON (LONDINIUM)
England (capital)
traces of ruined city: temples, walls, wharves, Museum of London, British Museum

RICHBOROUGH (RUTUPIAE)
England (95km/60mi south-east of London)
ruined port: fortifications, walls, huge arch support

ST ALBANS (VERULAMIUM)
England (65km/40mi north of London)
ruined city: small amphitheatre, basilica, villas, shops, hypocaust, walls, museum containing mosaics

SILCHESTER (CALLEVA ATREBATUM)
England (65km/40mi west of London)
ruined city: amphitheatre, walls, Reading Museum, Silchester Gallery

SOUTH SHIELDS (ARBEIA)
England (8km/5mi east of Newcastle upon Tyne)
ruined fort with defensive walls and gateway, museum

WROXETER (VIROCONIUM)
England (40km/25mi north-east of Birmingham)
ruined city mostly still under turf: baths, walls, museum

YORK (EBORACUM)

England (170km/105mi northwest of London)

traces of ruined city: walls, houses, museums

AIX-EN-PROVENCE (AQUAE SEXTIAE)

France (32km/19mi north of Marseilles)

traces of ruined city: two aqueducts, museum

ARLES (ARELATE)

France (90km/55mi north-west of Marseilles)

ruined city: forum, baths, well-preserved amphitheatre, theatre, cemetery, museums

FREJUS (FORUM JULII)

France (20km/13mi south-west of Cannes)

ruined garrison town: amphitheatre, baths, large aqueduct, museums

LYON (LUGDUNUM)

France

traces of ruined city: two theatres, museum

MARSEILLES (MARSILIA)

France

ruined port; fragments of houses, shops, roads (laid out in parkland), museum

NICE (NICAEA)

France (20km/13mi north-east of Cannes)

ruined city: amphitheatre, baths, Christian baptistery, museum

NÎMES (NEMAUSUS)

France (190km/120mi north-west of Marseilles)

ruined city: amphitheatre, well-preserved temple, houses, (at some distance) aqueduct (Pont du Gard), museums

ORANGE (ARAUSIO)

France (22km/14mi north of Avignon)

ruined city: large theatre, triumphal arch

ST-RÉMY-EN-PROVENCE (GLANUM)

France (60km/38mi north-west of Marseilles)

ruined city: forum, basilica, baths, triumphal arch, mausoleum, museum

VAISON-LA-ROMAINE (VASIO VOCONTIORUM)

France (47km/33mi northeast of Avignon)

ruined city: theatre, baths, houses, shops, roads, ancient bridge, museum

COLOGNE (KÖLN; COLONIA AGRIPPINENSIS)

Germany (26km/16mi north of Bonn)

ruins: city wall with tower and gate, praetorium, mosaics, catacombs, Romano-Germanic Museum

NEUSS (NOVAESIUM)

Germany (7km/4mi west of Düsseldorf)

ruined fort and fortifications

TRIER (AUGUSTA TREVERORUM)

Germany (close to Luxembourg border)

ruined city: baths, amphitheatre, basilica, fortified city gate, ancient bridge supports, museum

NIJMEGEN (CASTRA OPPIDUM BATAVORUM)

Holland (120km/73mi east of Rotterdam)

ruins: traces of fortress and surrounding settlement, museum

OBUDA (AQUINCUM)

Hungary (5km/3mi north of Buda[pest])

ruined city: fragments, baths with statuary, roads, aqueduct

CAESAREA

Israel (Mediterranean coast)

ruined city: restored theatre, amphitheatre, hippodrome, harbour, aqueduct, columns, museum

JERUSALEM

Israel (capital)

traces of ruined city: Antonia fortress, (north) city gate, museums

TSIPPORI (SEPPHORIS)

Israel (west of Nazareth)

ruins: theatre, reconstructed villa, mosaics

ALBE (ALBA FUCENS)

Italy (80km/50mi east of Rome)

ruined city: forum, baths, amphitheatre, theatre, basilica, temples, houses, shops, walls with gateways

ANZIO (ANTIUM)

Italy (50km/31mi south of Rome)

ruined imperial resort: reconstructed villa with mosaics, fragmentary theatre, villa, harbour, museum

BENEVENTO (BENEVENTUM)

Italy (50km/31mi north-east of Naples)

ruined city: forum, theatre, temples, ornate arch, ancient bridge, obelisk, museum

FIESOLE (FAESULAE)

Italy (8km/5m north of Florence)

ruined city: baths, theatre, gymnasium, columns, museum

HERCULANEUM

Italy (32km/20mi south-east of Naples)

well-preserved ruined city: forum baths, various other baths, temples, houses, shops

OSTIA

Italy (25km/15mi west of Rome)

well-preserved ruined city: forum, Capitolium, baths, theatre, temples, houses, shops, granaries, roads, mosaics, walls with gateways, tombs, museum

PIAZZA ARMERINI

Italy (Sicily)

ruins: imperial villa with painted walls, baths, hypocaust, mosaics

POMPEII

Italy (32km/20mi south-east of Naples)

well-preserved ruined city: forum (with pavement), baths, theatre, temples, basilica, houses, shops and bars, barracks, tombs, columns, mosaics and paintings, city gates, roads

ROME (ROMA)

Italy (capital)

vast amount of remains in all states of preservation from complete and/or restored to fragmentary: forums, baths, amphitheatres (notably the Colosseum), theatres, basilicas, many temples, many arches, curia, shops, villas and houses, mausoleums, many columns, mosaics, walls, catacombs, several museums

SYRACUSE

Italy (Sicily)

ruins within an older Greek environment: amphitheatre, temple, houses, shops, columns, catacombs, museums

TRIESTE (TERGESTE)

Italy (close to border with Slovenia)

ruins: theatre, triumphal arch, museum

VERONA

Italy (100km/60mi west of Venice)

ruins: large amphitheatre, theatre, gateway, reconstructed arch, museum

JERASH (JARASH)

Jordan (38km/24mi north of Amman)

ruined city: baths, theatres, temples, other public buildings, hippodrome, triumphal arch, paved roads, columns, museum

BAALBEK

Lebanon (64km/40mi northeast of Beirut)

ruined city: well-preserved temples (notably the Temple of Jupiter), shops, houses, columns

TYRE (SOUR)

Lebanon (65km/40mi south of Beirut)

ruins: baths, theatre, arch, circus, necropolis, aqueduct, museums

LEPTIS MAGNA (LEPCIS)

Libya (123km/76mi east of Tripoli)

ruined city: forums, baths, impressive theatre, arches, temples, walls

SABRATA (SABRATHA)

Libya (70km/40mi west of Tripoli)

ruins: forum, baths, temple, shops and houses, basilica, mosaics

VOLUBILIS

Morocco (145km/90mi east of Rabat)

ruined city: forum, Capitolium, baths, basilica triumphal arch, houses (some with mosaics), shops, city walls

BEJA (PISÕES; PAX JULIA)

Portugal (155km/95mi south of Lisbon)

ruins: walls with gateways, Queen Leonor Museum

CHAVES (AQUAE FLAVIAE)

Portugal (120km/75mi north-east of Oporto)

ruins: ancient bridge, fragments, columns, museum

CONDEIXA (CONIMBRIGA)

Portugal (122km/77mi south of Oporto)

ruins: walls, mosaics and paintings, cemetery, museum

ÉVORA

Portugal (110km/70mi east of Lisbon)

traces of ruined city: temple, aqueduct, museums

SANTIAGO DO CACÉM (MIROBRIGA)

Portugal (90km/55mi south-east of Lisbon)

ruined city: forum, well-preserved baths, acropolis, hippodrome, houses with wall paintings

CONSTANTA (TOMI/CONSTANTIANA)

Romania (Black Sea coast)

ruined city: forum, houses, fragments, mosaics, walls, museum containing mosaics and statuary

DOBRETA-TURNU SEVERIN

Romania (295km/184mi west of Bucharest)

ruined garrison town: ancient bridge, fortifications, exercise ground

HALMYRIS

Romania (southern Danube delta, Black Sea coast)

ruins: baths, walled fort with gateways, Christian basilica, harbour, tombs

SARMIZEGETUSA (ULPIA TRAIANA)

Romania (310km/190mi north-west of Bucharest)

ruins of (Dacian) settlement, museum

containing artefacts from mausoleum

BELGRADE (BEOGRAD)

Serbia (capital)

ruins: fortified encampment, museum

MEDIANA

Serbia (200km/125mi south-east of Belgrade in the vicinity of Nis)

ruins: houses, walls, mosaics, museum

ALCUDIA (POLLENTIA)

Spain (Majorca)

ruined city: amphitheatre, houses, museum

EMPÚRIES (AMPURIAS; EMPORION)

Spain (Catalan coast)

ruined fort/city: forum, amphitheatre, shops, houses, mosaics, museum

ITALICA

Spain (9km/5mi north of Seville)

ruined city: amphitheatre, shops, houses, roads, Museo Arqueologico, Seville

MÉRIDA

Spain (265km/180mi south-west of Madrid)

ruined city: amphitheatre, temple, circus, aqueduct, ancient bridge, Museo Nacional de Arte Romano

TARRAGONA (TARRACO)

Spain (60mi south-west of Barcelona)

ruined city: amphitheatre, circus, walls museums

AUGST (AUGUSTA RAURICA)

Switzerland (10km/6mi east of Basle)

ruined city: theatre, reconstructed Roman villa, museum

AVENCHES (AVENTICUM)

Switzerland (32km/20mi south-west of Bern)

ruined city: baths, temples, (restored) amphitheatre, theatre, houses, columns, extensive walls, Musée Romain, containing mosaics

PALMYRA (TADMOR)

Syria (215km/134mi north-east of Damascus)

ruined fortress-city: temple, restored theatre, buildings, colonnades, monuments

CARTHAGE

Tunisia (on the outskirts of capital, Tunis)

scant remains: baths, harbour, museum

DOUGGA (THUGGA)

Tunisia (110km/70mi south-west of Tunis)

well-preserved ruined city: forum, baths, capitolium, theatre, triumphal arches, temples, villas; further remains scattered around nearby countryside

EL JEM (AL-DJEM; THYSDRUS)

Tunisia (130km/80mi south-east of Tunis)

ruins: large, well-preserved amphitheatre

SBEITLA (SUFETULA)

Tunisia (near El Douleb oilfield)

ruined city: forum, baths, triumphal arch, temples

SOUSSE

Tunisia (100km/65mi south-east of Tunis)

catacombs, museum containing fine mosaics

TUNIS

Tunisia (capital city, 5km/3mi north)

Bardo Museum, containing fine mosaics and other works of art

UTICA

Tunisia (40km/25mi north-west of Tunis)

ruins: baths, museum containing fine mosaics

ANTAKYA (ANTIOCH)

Turkey (on the border with Syria)

Hatay museum containing superb mosaics

BERGAMA (PERGAMUM)

Turkey (250km/150mi south-west of Istanbul)

ruined city: Romano-Greek shrines/temples, theatre, gymnasium

EFES (EPHESUS)

Turkey (350km/220mi south of Istanbul)

restored ruined city: amphitheatre, baths, temples, library, public buildings, houses with superb decorations

CAERLEON (CAERLEON-ON-USK; ISCA)

Wales (3km/2m north of Newport, Monmouth)

ruins: amphitheatre, fragments of baths, temples, shops, houses, Roman Legionary Museum

NOTABLE COLLECTIONS

AUSTRALIA

John Elliot Classics Museum, Hobart University, Tasmania

AUSTRIA

Regional Museum of Carinthia, Klagenfurt

BELGIUM

Musée de Louvain-la-Neuve, Ottignies-Louvain-la-Neuve

CANADA

Royal Ontario Museum, Toronto

ENGLAND

Ashmolean Museum of Art and Archaeology, Oxford University

British Museum, London

Museum of Antiquities, University of Newcastle upon Tyne

Museum of Classical Archaeology, University of Cambridge

Shefton Museum, University of Newcastle upon Tyne

Victoria and Albert Museum, London

Vindolanda and the Roman Army Museum, Bardon Mill, Hexham, Northumberland

FRANCE

Louvre, Paris

Musée d'Archéologie Méditerranéenne, Marseilles

Musée de la Civilisation Gallo-Romaine, Lyon

GERMANY

Limesmuseum Aalen

[Latin limes 'border', 'boundary']

Römisches Stadtmuseum Rottenburg

GREECE

National Archaeological Museum of Athens

HOLLAND

Allard Pierson Museum, Amsterdam

Rijksmuseum van Oudheden (National Museum of Antiquities), Leiden

Israel

Reuben and Edith Hecht Museum, University of Haifa

ITALY

Barracco Museum, Rome

Capitoline Museums, Rome

Museo Archeologico Nazionale di Cagliari

Museo Archeologico Nazionale, Napoli (Naples)

National Museum of Rome

NEW ZEALAND

Otago Museum, University of Otago

PORTUGAL

Museu Calouste Gulbenkian, Lisbon

SLOVENIA

National Museum of Slovenia, Ljubljana

SPAIN

Museo Arqueologico Municipal de Jerez

Museo de Arqueologia de Alava

Museu Nacional Arqeologic de Tarragona

SWITZERLAND

Basel Museum of Ancient Art, and the Ludwig Collection, Basel

USA

Ambrose Collection, University of Vermont

Arthur M. Sackler Museum, Harvard University

J. Paul Getty Museum, Los Angeles

Kelsey Museum of Archeology, University of Michigan

Lowe Art Museum, University of Miami

Michael C. Carlos Museum, Emory University, Atlanta

Museum of Art, Providence, Rhode Island

Museum of Fine Arts, Boston

San Antonio Museum of Art, San Antonio, Texas

Tampa Museum of Art, Tampa, Florida

University of Mississippi Museums, David M. Robinson Collection, University of Mississippi

WALES

Wellcome Museum, University of Wales, Swansea

LATIN AND GREEK AUTHORS

Accius [Lucius Accius] (170–c.86 BC) composer of over 40 tragedies, many concerning the Trojan cycle of legends, and a work in prose and verse dealing among other things with the history of both the Athenian and the Roman theatre.

Appian of Alexandria (end of 1st century–mid-2nd century AD) became a Roman citizen and eventually attained the rank of *procurator* under Antoninus Pius; wrote a history of Rome in Greek from the beginnings to his own times organised according to the individual peoples whom Rome conquered.

Apuleius (b. c. AD 125) North African public speaker and author of the only Latin novel to survive complete, the *Metamorphoses* (sometimes called *The Golden Ass*).

Ausonius [Decimus Magnus Ausonius] (4th century AD) teacher of grammar and rhetoric from Bordeaux who achieved a political ascendancy under the Emperor Gratian; author of a number of poems, the most famous being the lively and colourful *Moselle*.

Catullus [Gaius Valerius Catullus] (c.84–c.54 BC) born in Verona, he became one of the young 'neoteric' poets at Rome strongly influenced by Hellenistic Greek culture; his extremely varied but slim corpus of poems displays considerable elegance and facility with language, and includes the lyrical poems dealing with his love for the aristocratic 'Lesbia'.

Cicero [Marcus Tullius Cicero] (106–43 BC) leading politician and orator during the last decades of the Republic, who also composed rhetorical treatises, poems and works on philosophy in which he created philosophical vocabulary in Latin; he also left a very large and invaluable collection of correspondence.

Cinna [Gaius Helvius Cinna] (d. 44 BC) particularly learned and allusive poet friendly with Catullus and known for his miniature epic *Zmyrna*; lynched by mistake at Julius Caesar's funeral after being mistaken for one of his opponents.

Cornelius Nepos (c.110–24 BC) the earliest extant biographer in Latin, whose *On Famous Men* included perhaps 400 lives, as well as the author of a universal history in three books and a work on geography.

Cyprian [Thascius Caecilius Cyprianus] (c. AD 200–258) Christian convert who became bishop of his native Carthage and produced important letters and tracts dealing mainly with the difficulties within the Christian community resulting from the Emperor Decius' persecution of 248.

Dio Cassius [Cassius Dio 'Cocceianus'] (c. AD 164–after 229) successful Roman senator and high-ranking magistrate from Bithynia, who wrote a substantial history of Rome in Greek from the beginnings to his own times.

Diodorus Siculus (1st century BC) Sicilian Greek author of a universal history whose section on the later Roman period makes great use of the work of Polybius and Posidonius.

Ennius [Quintus Ennius] (239–169 BC) poet living in Rome from 204 whose work includes numerous tragedies, many based on models by Euripides, and the long narrative poem, the *Annales*, which deals with the history of the Roman people from the loss of Troy to his own day and which was influential on later writers such as Lucretius and Virgil; he created the Latin dactylic hexameter.

Eusebius of Caesarea (c. AD 260–339) bishop of Caesarea from c. 313 whose work included biblical commentaries, the *Chronicle*, synthesising Old Testament, Near Eastern and Graeco-Roman history, a history of the Church down to 324 and the controversial *Life of Constantine*.

Galen (AD 129–?199/216) Greek physician from Pergamum who settled in Rome as court physician to the Emperor Marcus Aurelius in 162; he was the author of numerous treatises on philosophy, especially logic, and all aspects of medicine, especially anatomy and physiology.

Horace [Quintus Horatius Flaccus] (65–8 BC) poet from Venusia in Apulia who joined the literary circle of Maecenas and later was on close terms with Augustus; his work displays a combination of sophistication and a pleasantly personal style; his most famous poems are the *Odes* (lyric poems) and the *Satires*.

Josephus [Flavius Iosephus] (b. AD 37/8) Jewish priest and political leader who changed sides during the Jewish Revolt of AD 66–70 and served Titus until the siege of Jerusalem, he was given Roman citizenship and an imperial house in Rome and wrote a history of the Jewish War, and another long work about the history of the Jews from the Creation to just before the outbreak of the revolt.

Julius Caesar [Gaius Iulius Caesar] (c.100–44 BC) politician and general who became dictator and was assassinated in a conspiracy; his surviving writings are an account of his conquest of Gaul (58–51 BC) and of the Civil War which he precipitated in 49 BC, both works being highly self-serving.

Juvenal [Decimus Iunius Iuvenalis] (*fl.* AD 110–130) composer of highly rhetorical satires in the 'grand style' appropriated from epic whose object of attack is apparently the Rome of his day.

Lactantius [Lucius Caelius Firmianus Lactantius] (c. AD 240–c.320) North-African-born Roman rhetorician who converted to Christianity and became a leading apologist, writing in the style of Cicero.

Livius Andronicus [Lucius Livius Andronicus] (3rd century BC) freedman who composed both tragedies and comedies as well as a translation of Homer's *Odyssey*.

Livy [Titus Livius] (59 BC–AD 17) Roman historian from Padua who composed a history of Rome from its origins to 9 BC in 142 books (*Ab urbe condita libri*); he was on good personal terms with Augustus and encouraged the young Claudius to write history.

Lucan [Marcus Annaeus Lucanus] (AD 39–65) poet famous for his epic *De bello civili* (often called *Pharsalia*) which presents a bleak and remorseless vision of the Civil War between Caesar and Pompey and is constructed as an antidote to Virgil's *Aeneid*; forced to commit suicide after involvement in a failed conspiracy against Nero.

Lucian of Samosata (b. c. AD 120) prolific writer in Greek notable for his literary dialogues, essays and parodic masterpiece, the *True Histories*.

Lucilius [Gaius Lucilius] (c.180–102/1 BC) personal poet from Campania credited as the pioneer of contemporary political and social satire in his 30 books of verses.

Lucretius [Titus Lucretius Carus] (c.94–55 or 51 BC) poet of the Greek Epicurean philosophical school (which argued for the atomic composition of the universe and of the human soul) and author of *De rerum natura* ('On the Nature of Things') outlining its physical theories in Latin hexameter verse, but with a strong ethical purpose.

Marcus Aurelius (AD 121–180, emperor from 161) famous as author of the *Meditations* – personal notes to himself (in Greek) recording his own reflections on human life and the ways of the gods and strongly influenced by Stoicism.

Martial [Marcus Valerius Martialis] (b. AD 38–41; d. AD 101–104) Latin poet from Spain famous for his epigrams, which typically offer a lively and merciless picture of Roman society full of wit and humour.

Meleager of Gadara (*fl.* 100 BC) composer of lost Menippean satires espousing Cynic philosophy in a medley of prose and verse, and collector and composer of epigrams.

Naevius [Gnaeus Naevius] (3rd century BC) writer of comedies and tragedies, mostly on Attic Greek models, and composer of a poem on the First Punic War, in which he served.

Origen [Origenes Adamantius] (c. AD 184 or 185–c.254 or 254) Egyptian-born Greek-writing commentator on Old and New Testament scripture and Christian doctrine (his *De Principiis* was intended as a formal statement of Christian beliefs).

Ovid [Publius Ovidius Naso] (43 BC–AD 17) poet best known for his erotic verse, especially the didactic poem *Ars amatoria* ('Art of Love') and epic, *The Metamorphoses*, which retells myths involving a supernatural change of shape; banished by Augustus to Tomis on the Black Sea in AD 8 allegedly as a result of the *Ars amatoria* and a mysterious indiscretion.

Pacuvius [Marcus Pacuvius] (220–c.130 BC) south Italian writer of tragedies, many of which were translations from or elaborations of Attic Greek originals.

Pausanias (*fl.* c. AD 150) Greek travel writer known for his *Description of Greece*, which describes the monuments (especially sculpture and painting) of the Archaic and Classical periods to be found in the province of Achaea, along with their historical and sacred contexts.

Persius [Aules Persius Flaccus] (AD 34–62) composer of six satires aspiring to uncompromising Stoicism and noted for their dense imagery and tortuous language.

Petronius Arbiter (d. AD 66?) author of the *Satyrica*, a satirical novel with a strong emphasis on the sexual adventures of its heroes and on literary and cultural criticism; the most famous extant episode is the *Cena Trimalchionis* ('Dinner-Party of Trimalchio').

Philo Judaeus (early 1st century AD) Jewish philosopher, writer and political leader in Alexandria; prolific commentator (in Greek) on Jewish scripture and heavily influenced by the Greek philosophical tradition, especially Platonism.

Plautus [Titus Maccius Plautus] (*fl.* c.205–184 BC) writer of at least 21 Latin comedies adapted from Greek originals; they are full of stock characters and verbal wit, and boast a significantly expanded musical element.

Pliny the Elder [Gaius Plinius Secundus] (AD 23/4–79) Roman lawyer and administrator whose most famous work is the *Natural History*, a 37-book encyclopaedia of all contemporary knowledge; died during the eruption of Mount Vesuvius.

Pliny the Younger [Gaius Plinius Caecilius Secundus] (c. AD 61–c.112) Roman lawyer and administrator known for his collection of literary letters which well illustrate his and his circle's daily activities and concerns; a tenth book contains his correspondence with the Emperor Trajan while governor of Bithynia-Pontus.

Plotinus (AD 205–269/70) Greek-writing Neoplatonist philosopher whose metaphysical ideas strongly influenced early Christian thinkers.

Plutarch of Chaeronea [Lucius(?) Mestrius Plutarchus] (b. before AD 50; d. after AD 120) Greek writer and Roman citizen, prolific essayist and author of *The Parallel Lives*, which aim to exemplify individual virtue (and vice) in the careers of great men in the history of Greece and Rome.

Pollio [Gaius Asinius Pollio] (76 BC–AD 4) supporter of Caesar and then Antony, who became consul in 40 BC and built the first public library in Rome; wrote poetry, tragedy, oratory and a history of the last two decades of the Republic.

Polybius (c.200–c.118 BC) Achaean Greek political hero who spent two decades as a captive in Rome and joined the circle of Scipio Aemilianus; author of a substantially surviving and methodologically rigorous history of Rome's rise to world dominion.

Propertius [Sextus Propertius] (b. 54–47 BC; d. before 2 BC) elegiac poet from Assisi whose love poetry celebrates his devotion to a mistress called Cynthia and whose work was strongly inspired by the Hellenistic Greek poet, Callimachus.

Ptolemy [Claudius Ptolemaeus] (*fl.* AD 146–c.170) Greek-writing mathematician, geographer and astronomer based at Alexandria; his major work was the *Almagest*, a complete textbook of astronomy which dominated the subject for 1300 years in Europe and the Islamic world.

Quintilian [Marcus Fabius Quintilianus] (c. AD 35–90s) Spanish-born Roman teacher of oratory whose literary masterpiece deals with the education of an orator from babyhood to the peak of his career.

Sallust [Gaius Sallustius Crispus] (probably 86–35 BC) politician and historian concerned with moral decline at Rome; author of monographs on the conspiracy of Catiline and the Jugurthan War as well as annalistic *Histories*.

Seneca [Lucius Annaeus Seneca, 'Seneca the Younger'] (b. 4 BC–AD 1; d. AD 65) Spanish-born orator who became tutor and later political adviser and minister to Nero; author of ethical and scientific works in prose and of nine extant tragedies inspired by the whole corpus of Greek tragedy, especially Euripides, and by Roman poets such as Virgil and Ovid.

Statius [Publius Papinius Statius] (b. AD 45–early 50s; d. before AD 96) composer of encomiastic poetry under Domitian (the *Silvae*) and of the highly self-conscious epic, the *Thebaid*.

Strabo of Amaseia (b. c.64 BC; d. after AD 14) widely travelled Greek geographer and historian based for some years in Rome.

Suetonius [Gaius Suetonius Tranquillus] (b. c. AD 70; d. c. AD 130) imperial administrator best known for his *Lives of the Caesars* and other biographical studies, although he also wrote odd pieces on various cultural topics.

Tacitus [Publius(?) Cornelius Tacitus] (b. c. AD 56; d. after AD 118) politician, orator and historian, noted for the *Histories* and the *Annals*; his works display pessimism about political life under the emperors and use innuendo to suggest a darker underlying reality, and his style is correspondingly dense and complex.

Terence [Publius Terentius Afer] (d. c.159 BC) Carthaginian-born writer of six Latin comedies which are reasonably faithful adaptations of Greek originals and written in a naturalistic style.

Tibullus [Albius Tibullus] (b. 55–48 BC; d. 19 BC) elegiac poet whose poems mostly deal with his love for mistresses called Delia and Nemesis and aspire to a country life.

Virgil [Publius Vergilius Maro] (70–19 BC) poet from Mantua who belonged to the literary circle of Maecenas and was therefore close to Octavian/Augustus; his works are the pastoral *Eclogues*, the *Georgics*, a didactic poem on farming, and the epic masterpiece, the *Aeneid*, which deals with Aeneas' mission to leave Troy and found a new home in Italy, the origin of Rome and became an instant classic of Latin literature.

BIBLIOGRAPHY

CHAPTER ONE

M. Beard and M.H. Crawford, *Rome in the Late Republic*, New York, Cornell University Press, 1985

E. Fantham, *Roman Literary Culture from Cicero to Apuleius*, Baltimore, John Hopkins University Press, 1994

E. Guren, *Culture and National Identity in Republican Rome,* New York, Cornell University Press, 1992

S. Hinds, *Allusion and Intertext. Dynamics of appropriation in Roman poetry,* Cambridge and New York, Cambridge University Press, 1998

J. Huskinson, (ed.) *Experiencing Rome. Culture, Identity and Power in the Roman Empire*, London and New York, Routledge, 2000

E. Rawson, *Intellectual Life in the Late Roman Republic*, Baltimore, John Hopkins University Press, 1985

CHAPTER TWO

T.J. Cornell, *The Beginnings of Rome, Italy and Rome from the Bronze Age to the Punic Wars (c.1000–264 BC),* London and New York, Routledge,1995

J.A. Crook, A Lintott, E. Rawson, (eds.) *Cambridge Ancient History, vol. 9., 3rd ed. The Last Age of the Roman Republic, 146–43 BC*, Cambridge and New York, Cambridge University Press, 1994

H.H. Scullard, *A History of the Roman World, 753–146 BC, 4th ed.* London and New York, Methuen, 1980

H.H. Scullard, *From the Gracchi to Nero: A History of Rome from 133 BC to AD 68, 5th ed.*, London and New York, Methuen, 1982

F.W. Walbank, A.E. Astin, M.W. Frederiksen, (eds.) *Cambridge Ancient History, vol. 7 pt. 2, 2nd ed. The Rise of Rome to 220 BC*, Cambridge and New York, Cambridge University Press, 1989

F.W. Walbank, A.E. Astin, M.W. Frederiksen, (eds.) *Cambridge Ancient History, vol. 8, 2nd ed. Rome and the Mediterranean to 133 B.C.*, Cambridge and New York, Cambridge University Press, 1989

CHAPTER THREE

J. Bennett, *Trajan: Optimus Princeps* (2nd ed.), London, Routledge, 2001

A.R. Birley, *Hadrian: The Restless Emperor*, London, Routledge, 1997

M.T. Boatwright, *Hadrian and the Cities of the Roman Empire*, Princeton and Oxford, Princeton University Press, 2000

A. Cameron, *The Later Roman Empire, AD 284–430*, London, Fontana, 1993

J.B. Campbell, *The Emperor and the Roman Army, 31 BC–AD 235,* Oxford, Oxford University Press, 1984

i. Corcoran, *The Empire of the Tetrarchs: Imperial Pronouncements and Government AD 284–324*, Oxford, Clarendon Press, rev. ed. 2000

A. Garzetti, *From Tiberius to the Antonines: A History of the Roman Empire, AD 14–192*, London, Methuen, 1974

M. Goodman, *The Roman World 44 BC–AD 180*, London, Routledge, 1997

I. Gradel, *Emperor Worship and Roman Religion*, Oxford, Clarendon Press, 2002

A.H.M. Jones, *Augustus (Ancient Culture and Society)*, London, Chatto & Windus, 1975

B. Levick, *Claudius*, London, Batsford, 1993

B. Levick, *Tiberius the Politician* (rev. ed.), London, Routledge, 1999

B. Levick, *Vespasian*, London, Routledge, 1999

S.R.F. Price, *Rituals and Power: The Roman Imperial Cult in Asia Minor*, Cambridge, Cambridge University Press, 1984

R.J.A. Talbert, *The Senate of Imperial Rome*, Princeton, Princeton University Press, 1984

A. Wallace-Hadrill, *Suetonius: The Scholar and his Caesars* (Classical Life and Letters), London, Yale University Press, 1983

P.R.C. Weaver, *Familia Caesaris: A Social Study of the Emperor's Freedmen and Slaves*, Cambridge, Cambridge University Press, 1972

C. Wells, *The Roman Empire*, London, Fontana, 1984

CHAPTER FOUR

K. Bradley, *Slavery and Society at Rome,* Cambridge and New York, Cambridge University Press,1994

P.A. Brunt, *Roman Imperial Themes*, Oxford, Clarendon Press, 1990

J. Gardner, *Being a Roman Citizen*, London and New York, Routledge, 1993

J. Gardner, *Family and* Familia *in Roman Law and Life*, Oxford, Clarendon Press, 1990

A.W. Lintott, *Imperium Romanum: Politics and Administration*, London and New York, Routledge, 1993

F.G.B. Millar, *The Emperor in the Roman World, 31 BC–AD 337,* New York, Cornell University Press, 1977

B. Rawson (ed.) *The Family in Ancient Rome,* New York, Cornell University Press, 1986

G.D. Woolf, *Becoming Roman, The Origins of Provincial Civilization in Gaul,* Cambridge and New York, Cambridge University Press, 1994

CHAPTER FIVE

S.E. Alcock, *Graecia Capta, The Landscapes of Roman Greece*, Cambridge and New York, Cambridge University Press, 1993

C. Edwards, *The Politics of Immorality in Ancient Rome*, Cambridge and New York, Cambridge University Press, 1993

S. Goldhill (ed.) *Being Greek under Rome – Cultural Identity, the Second Sophistic and the Development of Empire*, Cambridge and New York, Cambridge University Press, 2001

A.H.M. Jones, *The Greek City from Alexander to Justinian*, 1940

F.G.B. Millar, *The Roman Near East, 31 BC–AD 337*, Cambridge, Harvard University Press, 1993

S.C.R. Swain, *Hellenism and Empire, Language, Classicism and Power in the Greek World, AD 50–250*, Oxford, Clarendon Press, 2001

T. Whitmarsh, *Greek Literature and the Roman Empire. The Politics of Imitation*, Oxford, Oxford University Press, 2001

CHAPTER SIX

K. Bradley, *Slavery and Rebellion in the Roman World, 140 BC–70 BC*, Bloomington, Indiana University Press, 1989

T. Cornell, 'The Conquest of Italy', in CAH VII, 2 (2nd ed.) 1989

M. Crawford, 'Origini e sviluppi del sistema provinciale romano', in *Storia di Roma II: L'impero mediterraneo I: La repubblica imperiale* (Turin, 1990) 91–121.

The Roman Republic (2nd ed.), Cambridge, Harvard University Press, 1991

G. De Ste. Croix, *The Class Struggle in the Ancient Greek World from the Archaic Age to the Arab Conquests*, New York, Cornell University Press, 1981

W. Fitzgerald, *Slavery and the Roman Literary Imagination*, Cambridge, Cambridge University Press, 2000

P. Garnsey (ed.) *Non-Slave Labour in the Ancient World*, Cambridge, Cambridge University Press, 1980

P. Garnsey, *Ideas of Slavery from Aristotle to Augustine*, Cambridge, Cambridge University Press, 1996

A. Giardina (ed.) *The Romans*, Chicago, University of Chicago Press, tr. 1993, especially the essays by J. Andreau, J. Kolendo, C.R. Whittaker

A. Hands, *Charities and Social Aid in Greece and Rome*, London, Thames and Hudson, 1968

K. Hopkins, *Conquerors and Slaves*, Cambridge, Cambridge University Press, 1978

S. Joshel, *Work, Identity, and Legal Status at Rome*, Oklahoma, University of Oklahoma Press, 1992)

R. Kallet-Marx, *Hegemony to Empire: the Development of the Roman Imperium in the East from 148 to 62 BC*, Berkeley, University of California Press, 1995

CHAPTER SEVEN

P. J. Aicher, *Guide to the Aqueducts of Ancient Rome*, Illinois, Bolchazy-Carducci Publishers, 1995

M. Boatwright, *Hadrian and the City of Rome*, Princeton, Princeton University Press, 1987

A. Claridge, *Rome, Oxford Archaeological Guides*, Oxford, Oxford University Press, 1998

P. Connolly and H. Dodge, *The Ancient City*, Oxford, Oxford University Press, 1998

J. Coulston and H. Dodge, (eds.) *Ancient Rome: the Archaeology of the Eternal City*, Oxford, Oxford University School of Archaeology Monograph 54, 2000

J. Curran, *Pagan City and Christian Capital: Rome in the Fourth Century*, Oxford, Clarendon Press, 2000

D. Dudley, *Urbs Roma: A Source Book of Classical Texts on the City of Rome and Its Monuments*, Aberdeen, PUBLISHER?, 1967

C. Edwards and G. Woolf (eds.), *Rome the Cosmopolis*, New York, Cambridge University Press, 2003

D. Favro, *The Urban Image of Augustus*, Cambridge, PUBLISHER?, 1996

E. Nash, *A Pictorial Dictionary of Ancient Rome*, New York, Hacker Art Books, 1981

O. Robinson, *Ancient Rome: City Planning and Administration*, London, Routledge, 1992

J. E. Stambaugh, *The Ancient Roman City*, Baltimore, Johns Hopkins University Press, 1988

M. Steinby, *Lexicon Topographicum Urbis Romae I–V*, Rome, PUBLISHER?, 1993–9

CHAPTER EIGHT

G. B. Conte, *Latin Literature. A History*, PLACE, PUBLISHER?, 1994

A. Dihle, *Greek and Latin Literature of the Roman Empire*, London, Routledge, 1994

D. Fowler, *Roman Constructions. Readings in Postmodern Latin*, Oxford, Oxford University Press, 2000

E. J. Kenney, *Latin Literature (Cambridge History of Classical Literature* vol. 2), Cambridge, Cambridge University Press, 1982

S. Morton Braund, *Latin Literature*, 2002

O. Taplin, *Literature in the Roman World*, Oxford, Oxford University Press, 2001

M. von Albrecht, *A History of Roman Literature*, 2 vols, Leiden, 1997

CHAPTER NINE

A. and M. De Vos, *Ercolano, Stabia*, Rome, Guide archeologica Laterza, 1982

M.C. Holf and S. I. Rotroff, (eds.) *The Romanization of Athens: proceedings of an International Conference held at Lincoln, Nebraska* (April 1996), Oxford, Oxbow, 1997

S. Lancel, *Carthage: A History*, translated by Antonia Nevill, Oxford, Blackwell, 1995

P. MacKendrick, *The North African Stones Speak*, Chapel Hill, University of North Carolina Press, 1980

S. Nappo, *Pompeii: Guide to the Lost City*, London, Weidenfeld and Nicolson, 1998

E.J. Owens, *The City in the Greek and Roman World*, London and New York, Routledge, 1991

J.B. Rives, *Religion and Authority in Roman Carthage from Augustus to Constantine*, Oxford, Clarendon Press, 1995

J. Travlos, *A Pictorial Dictionary of Ancient Athens*, London, Thames and Hudson, 1971

J.B. Ward-Perkins, *Roman Imperial Architecture*, Harmondsworth, Penguin Books, 1981

E.M. Wightman, *Roman Trier and the Treveri*, London, Rupert Hart-Davis, 1970

CHAPTER TEN

T. Barton, *Ancient Astrology*, London, Routledge, 1994

M. Beagon, *Roman Nature: The Thought of Pliny the Elder*, Oxford, Clarendon Press, 1992

S. Cuomo, *Ancient Mathematics*, London, Routledge, 2001

O.A.W. Dilke, *Greek and Roman Maps*, London, Thames and Hudson, 1985

R. French, *Ancient Natural History: Histories of Nature*, London, Routledge, 1994

R. Jackson, *Doctors and Diseases in the Roman Empire*, London, British Museum Publications, 1988

J. G. Landels, *Engineering in the Ancient World*, London, Chatto & Windus, 1978

J. G. Landels, *Music in Ancient Greece and Rome*, London, Routledge, 1999

G.E.R. Lloyd, *Greek Science after Aristotle*, London, Chatto and Windus, 1973

E.W. Marsden, *Greek and Roman Artillery: historical development*, Oxford, Clarendon Press, 1969

E.W. Marsden, *Greek and Roman Artillery: Technical Treatises*, Oxford, Clarendon Press, 1971

O. Neugebauer, *The Exact Sciences in Antiquity*, Providence, Brown University Press, 1957

E. Rawson, *Intellectual Life in the Late Roman Republic*, London, Duckworth, 1985

C. Walker, (ed.) *Astronomy Before the Telescope*, London, British Museum Press, 1996

CHAPTER ELEVEN

M. Beard, J. North, S. Price, *Religions of Rome, Volume 1, History; Volume 2 , A Sourcebook*, Cambridge, Cambridge University Press, 1998

J. Ferguson, *The Religions of the Roman Empire*, Ithaca, NY, Cornell University Press, 1970

R. Lane Fox, *Pagans and Christians*, New York, Knopf, 1987

R. MacMullen, *Paganism in the Roman Empire*, New Haven, CN, Yale University Press, 1983

M.W. Meyer, (ed.) *The Ancient Mysteries: A Sourcebook: Sacred Texts of the Mystery Religions of the Ancient Mediterranean World*, Philadelphia, University of Pennsylvania Press, 1999

R.M. Ogilvie, *The Romans and Their Gods in the Age of Augustus*, New York, Norton, 1970

S.R.F. Price, *Rituals and Power: The Roman Imperial Cult in Asia Minor*, Cambridge, Cambridge University Press, 1984

H.H. Scullard, *Festivals and Ceremonies of the Roman Republic*, London, Thames and Hudson, 1981

R. Turcan, *The Cults of the Roman Empire*, translated by Antonia Neville, Oxford, Oxford University Press, 1996

R. Turcan, *The Gods of Ancient Rome: Religion in Everyday Life from Archaic to Imperial Times*, translated by Antonia Nevill, London, Routledge, 2001

R.E. Witt, *Isis in the Graeco-Roman World*, London, Thames and Hudson, 1971

CHAPTER TWELVE

J. Andreau, *Banking and Business in the Roman World*, Cambridge, Cambridge University Press, 1999

G. Barker and J. Lloyd, (eds.) *Roman Landscapes: archaeological survey in the Mediterranean region*, London, British School at Rome, 1991

P. Garnsey, *Famine and Food Supply in the Graeco-Roman World*, Cambridge, Cambridge University Press, 1988

P. Garnsey and R. Saller, *The Roman Empire: economy, society and culture*, London, Duckworth, 1987

P. Garnsey, K. Hopkins and C.R. Whittaker, (eds.) *Trade in the Ancient Economy* London, Chatto & Windus, 1983

K. Greene, *The Archaeology of the Roman Economy*. London, Batsford, 1986

P. Horden and N. Purcell, *The Corrupting Sea: a study of Mediterranean history*, Oxford, Blackwell, 2000

C.J. Howgego, *Ancient History from Coins*, London and New York, Routledge, 1995

D.J. Mattingly and J. Salmon, (eds.) *Economies Beyond Agriculture in the Classical World*, London and New York, Routledge, 2001

N. Morley, *Metropolis and Hinterland: the city of Rome and the Italian economy, 200 B.C.–A.D. 200*, Cambridge, Cambridge University Press, 1996

D.P.S. Peacock and D.F. Williams, *Amphorae and the Roman Economy: an introductory guide*, London, Longman, 1986

K.G. Persson, *Pre-Industrial Economic Growth: social organisation and technological progress in Europe*, Oxford, Blackwell, 1988

W. Scheidel and S. von Reden, (eds.) *The Ancient Economy*, Edinburgh, Edinburgh University Press, 2002

K.D. White, *Greek and Roman Technology*, Ithaca, NY, Cornell University Press, 1984

G. Woolf, *Becoming Roman: the origins of provincial civilization in Gaul*, Cambridge, Cambridge University Press, 1998

E.A. Wrigley, *Continuity, Chance and Change: the character of the industrial revolution in England*, Cambridge, Cambridge University Press, 1988

G.K. Young, *Rome's Eastern Trade: international commerce and imperial policy, 31 B.C.–A.D. 305*, London and New York, Routledge, 2001

CHAPTER THIRTEEN

B. Campbell, *Warfare and Society in Imperial Rome*, London, Routledge, 2002

A.K. Goldsworthy, *The Roman Army at War 100 BC–AD 200*, Oxford, Oxford University Press, 1996

A.K. Goldsworthy, *Roman Warfare*, London, Cassell, 2000

L. Keppie, *The Making of the Roman Army: From Republic to Empire*, London, Routledge, 1984

J. Rich and G. Shipley, *War and Society in the Roman World*, London, Routledge, 1993

G. Webster, *The Roman Imperial Army of the First and Second Centuries AD*, Totowa, 1985

INDEX

Page numbers in *italic* type refer to picture captions; *bold* numbers refer to main references.

CONTRIBUTORS

Penelope Allison has taught ancient history and archaeology at the University of Sydney, the Australian National University and the University of Sheffield. She has held research fellowships at the University of Sydney and in the Faculty of Classics, Cambridge, and is currently an Australian Research Council Queen Elizabeth II Fellow at the Australian National University. Her recent publications include: *The Archaeology of Household Activities* (Routledge, London and New York, 1999), *Casa della Caccia Antica, Häuser in Pompeji* vol 11 (Hirmer, Munich, 2002) *and Pompeian Households: an Analysis of the Material Culture* (The Cotsen Institute of Archaelolgy at UCLA, Los Angeles, 2003).

Jon Coulston is lecturer in Ancient History and Archaeology in the School of Classics at the University of St Andrews, Scotland. He has published widely on Roman archaeology, in particular in the fields of the Roman army, Roman military equipment, Roman sculpture and the city of Rome. He is joint editor with Dr Hazel Dodge of *Ancient Rome: the Archaeology of the Eternal City* (Oxford University Committee for Archaeology, Oxford, 2000) and is currently preparing a monograph on Trajan's Column.

Emma Dench has taught ancient history and classical culture at Birkbeck College, University of London since 1992. She studied at Oxford University, was a Rome Scholar at the British School at Rome, held a Hugh Last Fellowship also at the British School, and was most recently a Member in Historical Studies at the Institute for Advanced Study, Princeton. Her research centres on the cultural history of the Hellenistic and Roman worlds, especially on issues of identity and the ancient reception of the past. She is the author of *From Barbarians to New Men: Greek, Roman and Modern Perceptions of Peoples from the Central Apennines* (Clarendon Press, Oxford, 1995), and is just completing a new book on Roman identity.

Hazel Dodge is Louis Claude Purser Senior Lecturer in Classical Archaeology in the School of Classics, Trinity College Dublin. Her research and publications concern Roman architecture, ancient technology, building materials and techniques (particularly in the eastern Mediterrranean), and the city of Rome. She is currently working on a monograph on the quarrying, transport and use of decorative stones in the Roman world.

Rebecca Flemming is lecturer in ancient history at King's College London. Her research has focused on women and medicine in the ancient world, both separately and together. She is the author of *Medicine and the Making of Roman Women: Gender, Nature, and Authority from Celsus to Galen* (Oxford University Press, Oxford, 2000).

Ian Haynes teaches the archaeology of the Roman provinces at Birbeck College, University of London. He has undertaken fieldwork in Britain, Germany, the Czech Republic and Romania. He is currently serving as British Director of the Apulum Project, a tri-national investigation of the Sanctuary of Liber Pater at Alba Lulia, Romania. Ian is co-editor with Adrian Goldsworthy of *The Roman Army as a Community* (Journal of Roman Archaeology, 1999) and with W.S. Hanson of a forthcoming volume on the Roman province of Dacia. He was elected a fellow of the Society of Antiquaries in 2003.

Richard Lim has taught ancient history at the Department of History, Smith College, since 1990. Following his doctorate from Princeton University, he has held a Rome Prize Fellowship in Classical Studies at the American Academy in Rome, a National Endowment for the Humanities Fellowship and a Fellowship at the National Humanities Center. He is the author of *Public Disputations, Power, and Social Order in Late Antiquity* (University of California Press, Berkeley, 1995) and is writing a book on public spectacles and civic transformation in late antiquity.

Christopher S. Mackay received his doctorate in classical philology from Harvard University. After having taught at Harvard and at Brown University, he is now an associate professor at the University of Alberta. He has written numerous articles on all periods of Roman history, and is about to publish *A Concise History of Ancient Rome*, a text and translation of the witchhunting handbook entitled the Malleus Maleficarum, and a translation of the main contemporary source on the ill-fated Anabaptist kingdom of Münster (a Latin work composed in ca. 1565)

Neville Morley is Senior Lecturer in Ancient History at the University of Bristol. His research interests are in ancient economic history, historical theory and historiography, and the reception of antiquity in nineteenth-century economic and philosophical thought. His books include *Metropolis and Hinterland: the City of Rome and the Italian Economy* (Cambridge University Press, Cambridge, 1996) and *Writing Ancient History* (Cornell University Press, Cambridge,1999), along with articles on Roman demography, counter-factual approaches to ancient history and Karl Marx's views on antiquity.

David Potter is a professor of Classics and teaches Roman history, ancient sport, and Greek and Latin in his capacity as director of the Lloyd Hall Scholars program at the University of Michigan. He is the author of four books including *Literary Texts and the Roman Historian* (Routledge, London and New York, 1999) and *The Roman Empire at Bay* (180–395) (University of Michigan, 2004). He also co-edited *Life, Death and Entertainment in the Roman Empire* (University of Michigan, 1999)

Simon Swain is Professor of Classics and Head of Department at the University of Warwick and Fellow of All Souls College, Oxford. He has published extensively on the literature and history of the Roman Empire. His latest book is *Approaching Late Antiquity* and he is currently hard at work on the reception of Greek culture in Islam.

Greg Woolf has been Professor of Ancient History in the School of Classics of the University of St Andrews, Scotland since 1998. He was educated at the Universities of Oxford and Cambridge and had Fellowships in both before moving to Scotland. He is the author of Becoming Roman – The Origins of Provincial Civilization in Gaul (Cambridge University Press, Cambridge, 1998) and edited Literacy and power in the Ancient World (Cambridge University Press, Cambridge, 1994 with Alan Bowman) and Rome the Cosmopolis (Cambridge University Press, Cambridge, 2003 with Catharine Edwards). He has published on a wide range of subjects including iron-age prehistory, the Roman economy, Latin epigraphy and Roman religion. He is currently working on studies of Roman imperial culture and on religious creativity in the provinces.

PICTURE ACKNOWLEDGEMENTS

AKG/LONDON: pps.17 Vatican Museum, 33 Pirrozi/Museo Nationale Romano della Terme, 47 Walter Gallery, 112, 113, 327 A. Lorenzini/Museo della Civilta Romana, Rome

AKG, LONDON/ERIC LESSING: pps. 52 Kunsthistorisches Museum, Vienna, 55 Musée de Istoria, Romania, Bucarest, 56/57 Musée Louvre, 81 Bibliotheque Nationale, Paris, 84 Museo Archaeological Nazionale, Naples, 87 Kunsthistorisches Museum, Vienna, 90/91 Museo Archaeological Nazionale, Naples, 110, 132, Museo Nazionale, Naples, 133 Museum of Archaeology Nationale, Aquileia, 134, 135 Musée des Antiquities Nationales, St Germaine en Laye, 154, 163, 170/171 Rheinisches Landesmuseum, Trier, Germany, 195 Kunsthistorisches Museum, Vienna, 224 Istanbul Archaeological Musem, 236 Villa Romana del Casale, Italy, 252 Liebighaus Frankfurt am Main, 271 Bibliotheque Nationale, Paris, 280/281 286, 299 Museo Archaeological Nazionale, Naples, 304/305 Palazzo dei Conservatori, Rome, 316 Musée des Antiquities Nationales, St Germaine en Laye, 337 Louvre, Paris

AKG. LONDON: pps. Gilles Mermet : pps. 130, 190/191, 314 Musée du Bardo, Tunis

ART ARCHIVE /DAGLI ORTI: pps. 40, 115, 118 Museo della Civilta Romana, Rome, 296 Museo Capitolino, Rome, 323 Archaeological Museum Zara

BRIDGEMAN ART LIBRARY, LONDON: pps. 13T Giraudon, Bibliotheque Saint Genvieve, Paris, 19 Musée Conde, Chantilly, 20 Charmet Archives /Bibliotheque Nationale, Paris, 43 Lauros Giraudon, Louvre, Paris, 124 Giraudon, Musée D'Orsay, 124 Musée de Civilisation Gallo Romaine, Lyon, 128 Museo Archaeological Nazionale, Naples, 140, 173 Ashmolean Museum, 177, 192 Metropolitan Museum, New York, 245 Alinari, 292 Palazzo Vecchio, Florence

CAMERON COLLECTION: pps. 249, 250

CORBIS: pps. 241, 255 inset, 313

ARALDO DE LUCA: pps. 25, 30/31, 44, 48/49, 57, 71, 75, 88, 94, 95, 100, 122, 136, 153, 169, 183, 186, 198, 239, 241, 243T, 282, 287, 295, 306, 309, 349
ARCHIVO ICONOGRAFICO, S. A.: pps. 13b, 15, 21, 22, 68/69, 127, 172, 174, 210, 261, 300, 333,
YANN ARTUS-BERTRAND: p. 196
DAVE BARTRUFF: p. 350
BETTTMANN: pps. 64, 181
EDIFICE/PHILLIPPA LEWIS: p. 274
RICHARD HAMILTON SMITH: p. 161
JASON HAWKES: p. 345
JOHN HICKS: p. 77
JON COULSTON/HAZEL DODGE: pps. 145, 150, 154, 157, 164
ANGELO HORNAK: pps. 152, 158, 322
ROBBIE JACK: p. 188
MIMMO JODICE: pps. 10/11, 12, 89, 104, 114, 205, 207, 209, 212, 284/285
WOLFGANG KAEHLER: p. 216
DAVID LEES: p. 29
MCDONALD: p. 231
FRANCIS G. MAYER: pps. 58, 61

THE NATIONAL GALLERY, LONDON, BY KIND PERMISSION OF THE NATIONAL GALLERY: pps. 3, 103,
MICHAEL NICHOLSON: pps. 211b, 257
VOZ NOTICIAS: p. 254/255
MASSIMO LISTRI: p. 279
MICHAEL MASLAN HISTORICAL PHOTOGRAPHY: p. 141
VITTORIANO RASTELLI: p. 142/143, 320
JEFFREY L. ROTTMAN: p. 308
ROGER REES MEYER: p. 203
CARMEN REDONDO: p. 268
BILL ROSS: p. 184/185
SETBOUN: p. 272
STAPLETON COLLECTION: p. 178
TED SPIEGEL: p. 26/27
KAREN TWEEDY HOLMES: pps. 147
VANNI ARCHIVE: pps. 63, 167, 226, 229, 258, 264, 265
SANDRO VANNINI: pps. 217, 290/1, 343,
RUGGERO VANNINI: p. 228
FRANCESCO VENTURI: p. 351
ROGER WOOD: pps. 99, 106/107, 200/201, 267
ADAM WOOLFITT: 108/109, 341